Fighting for western land, life and liberty

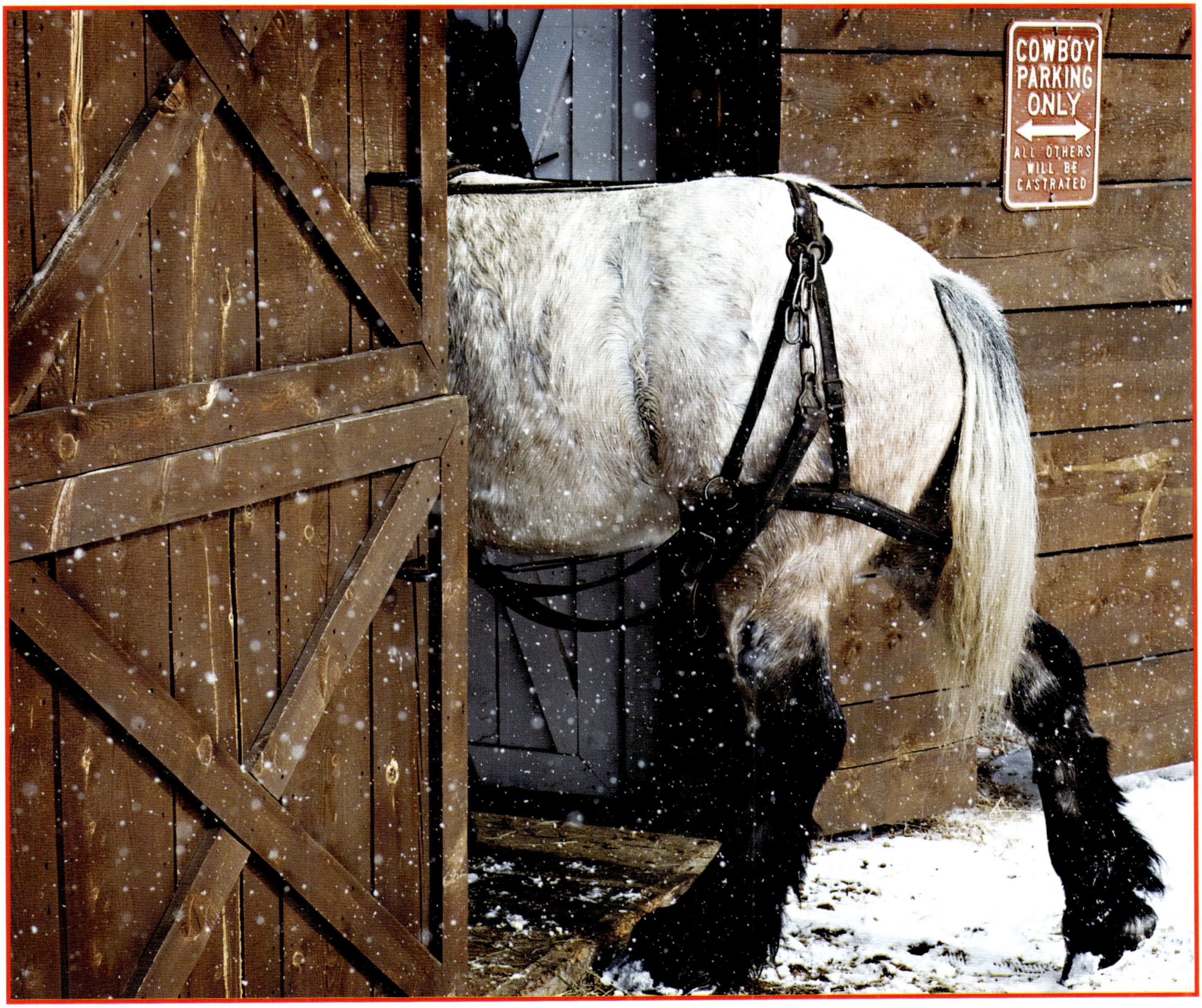

RANGE magazine's two decades of reporting from the front lines

COMPILED AND EDITED BY C.J. HADLEY

Published by Purple Coyote Corp. & RANGE magazine

with assistance from the Nevada Rangeland Resources Commission

Montana ranchers Casey and Rebecca Mott. Photo © Paul Mobley

"Conservation is the foresighted utilization, preservation and/or renewal of forests, waters, lands and minerals for the greatest good of the greatest number for the longest time."

GIFFORD PINCHOT, FIRST CHIEF OF THE U.S. FOREST SERVICE, 1905

Publication of this book was made possible by generous donations from people who care about the American West.

PUBLISHER / EDITOR: C.J. Hadley
EXECUTIVE EDITOR: Steve Thompson
SENIOR WRITER: Tim Findley
DESIGNER: John Bardwell
STAFF: Joey Hall, Joyce Smith, Denyse Pellettieri White

Library of Congress Cataloging-in-Publication Data
Hadley, C.J.
GRIT: Fighting for western land, life and liberty.
Caroline Joy Hadley
ISBN 978-0-9744563-6-2
LCCN 2009938181

Published by Purple Coyote Corp. & RANGE magazine
Carson City, Nevada, with assistance from the
Nevada Rangeland Resources Commission.

$40 U.S.A.
Printed in Hong Kong

RANGE
THE COWBOY SPIRIT ON AMERICA'S OUTBACK
Perseverance & Hope in New Mexico, Wyoming, Hawaii & California

RANGE
THE COWBOY SPIRIT ON AMERICA'S OUTBACK
THE WEST IS WILD, AND IT COMES ALIVE WITH A REBELLION.

RANGE
THE COWBOY SPIRIT ON AMERICA'S OUTBACK
Saddle sores & chardonnay. Great western vacations.
Bruce Babbitt's Abuse of Power.

RANGE
THE COWBOY SPIRIT ON AMERICA'S OUTBACK
MR. SPUD Idaho's inimitable billionaire, J. R. SIMPLOT
Pitchfork Ranch SURE AS THE WEST TEXAS WIND
PLUS
Life on the RAC
ECO-BUREAUCRATS
Photo Contest Winners

RANGE
THE COWBOY SPIRIT ON AMERICA'S OUTBACK
THIS LAND WAS YOUR LAND
A CRISIS IN ATTITUDE
WHERE IS AMERICA'S FARMLAND GOING?

RANGE
THE COWBOY SPIRIT ON AMERICA'S OUTBACK
PLAYING OUTSIDE THE RULES
GRIZZLY PICNIC
GRIT

RANGE
THE COWBOY SPIRIT ON AMERICA'S OUTBACK
PASSION & TERRORISM ON WESTERN LANDS
SELLING OUT TO STAY

RANGE
THE COWBOY SPIRIT ON AMERICA'S OUTBACK
COWBOYS & TREE-SQUEEZERS
CAN THE WEST FIND PEACE?
LYNX IN THE CROSSFIRE

RANGE
THE COWBOY SPIRIT ON AMERICA'S OUTBACK
WOLF at the DOOR
BIOLOGIST ALLAN SAVORY:
Saving The World or Frightening Scientists?

RANGE
THE COWBOY SPIRIT ON AMERICA'S OUTBACK
TED TURNER'S MURKY WATERS
Saving Texas Songbirds
Wild Cow Mary
FIRESTORM!
Dakota's Threatening Winds
Tom Lineberry: BOSS OF THE PLAINS

RANGE
THE COWBOY SPIRIT ON AMERICA'S OUTBACK
BUSTIN' OUTTA' THE RUTS!
Birds, Fish, & Buckaroos
PLUS A WILDERNESS TRAGEDY
SPECIAL REPORT
THE WEST 2000
Facts for the Future

RANGE
THE COWBOY SPIRIT ON AMERICA'S OUTBACK
Whiskey's for drinkin' Water's for fightin'
WHAT IF IT'S GORE?
PLUS: THE COST OF FREEDOM

RANGE
THE COWBOY SPIRIT ON AMERICA'S OUTBACK
SAD, MAD DAYS AT BLACK ROCK
The Greening of Planet Earth
RUNNING WITH WOLVES

RANGE
THE COWBOY SPIRIT ON AMERICA'S OUTBACK
Looking for LIBERTY
The Powerful Fist of Granny Cox
VOICE OF THE HEARTLAND
Happy Camp & the Eco-Pious
SPECIAL SECTION:
The Great American Land Grab, mapping what's left of the West

RANGE
THE COWBOY SPIRIT ON AMERICA'S OUTBACK
COWPUNCHERS and the Culture of Agriculture
BATTLE CRY!
Plight of a Ranch Girl in Urban L.A.
PROFILES IN PERSISTENCE
The Disappointment Bunch
PLUS: THE PERSECUTION OF AMISH "PLAIN FOLK"

RANGE
THE COWBOY SPIRIT ON AMERICA'S OUTBACK
Making Monuments
Taking Towns
ROCKY MOUNTAIN LAMBS
The Cowboy Days of Lewis & Clark
THOREAU & HIS BELOVED BOVINES
David vs. Goliath: The Wayne Hage Saga

RANGE
THE COWBOY SPIRIT ON AMERICA'S OUTBACK
WATER IN THE WEST
Betrayed by the Feds
Siege of the Tortoise in California's Mojave

RANGE
THE COWBOY SPIRIT ON AMERICA'S OUTBACK
The West: Holding on to Hope
KEEPING PACE WITH ENVIRONMENTAL HYPOCRISY
Unwilling Sellers
Wolf Attack!
1870: The Nuns' Harrowing Journey

RANGE
THE COWBOY SPIRIT ON AMERICA'S OUTBACK
WILDCATS IN THE WEST
Don't mess with TEXAS
TRASHING TEDDY ROOSEVELT'S LEGACY
The Grab for California's Gaviota Coast

RANGE
THE COWBOY SPIRIT ON AMERICA'S OUTBACK
COURAGE when it counts
100 YEARS OF CONSERVATION
Montana . Nebraska . Arizona
California . New Mexico . Nevada
Utah . Oregon . Wyoming

UP FRONT

Twenty years in the turbulence.
By C.J. Hadley

In the summer of 1989, a small group of ranchers and scientists decided to produce a brochure for members of Congress, to show them that ranchers and farmers are good guys, worthy of consideration. Based in Nevada, but with ties to California, Oregon, Montana, Idaho and New Mexico, the group concentrated on federal-lands' ranchers because there was a threat to charge the West the same price for renting the big, empty, high, dry lands of the western deserts as for knee-deep, fenced, watered and managed pastures in the East. There was no comparison and ranchers were scared.

Our intent was to share and celebrate a most important segment of society—food producers—whose passion, integrity, work ethic, understanding of and caring for nature is tough to even imagine. After that brochure was distributed, we heard groans from ranchers and complaints from environmental activists.

Ranchers said it's not the grazing-fee issue that's the problem, it's government regulation, wilderness designation, endangered species' listings—plus water and private-property takings, federal road closures, urban encroachment and environmental innocence.

Environmental activists thought livestock should be removed from the range completely, and they were encouraging conservation easements—which they said was a way to take private property without having to pay for it. They were also planning the most massive taking in world history, the Wildlands Project, taking *only 50 percent* of the country out of production (with most in the West), while destroying ranching, farming and logging. They desired empty country so that wolves, bears and mountain lions would not be bothered by humans from the Yucatán to the Yukon.

That was just the beginning, and that's why *RANGE* magazine was born.

The activists don't seem to care that, in the last few years, a wolf killed a student in Canada, mountain lions killed a California woman and a New Mexico man, and ripped the scalp off a small boy while he was hiking with his family on a marked trail on federal lands in the Southwest. They never worry about the thousands of cattle, sheep and wildlife that are killed or mutilated by lions, bears and wolves each month. They ignore the increasing predator threats to humans. And they know that the lack of federal management is often the result of their own environmental litigation.

All these issues were sneaking up on food and fiber producers. As America changed and resource providers diminished and lost representation, food, minerals and wood products poured in from abroad. But for too many in the cities and suburbs, American farmers and ranchers had become irrelevant to the future. What was relevant to the activists was the environment.

It mattered not that food handling and food processing in other countries were less stringently regulated than in ours. It mattered not that crops were grown using chemicals that had been banned in this country for decades. It mattered not that families and communities were being destroyed in the West. And, to most voters, it mattered not that a weakening United States has become a net food-importing nation.

With encouragement from the environmental activists, Congress passed protective acts like the Clean Water Act, the Clean Air Act, the Wilderness Act, the Endangered Species Act and more—which all sounded good but too often caused more damage than environmental or societal healing.

New money comes from real production. Tourist and service money changes hands and keeps people employed, but it doesn't replenish the Treasury. The benefits from real production—ranching, farming, logging and mining—would help repay our appalling national debt.

If we manage the resource sustainably, and selectively log our thick and dying forests, communities and families in the rural West will be invigorated. Good jobs will come back and the remaining trees will be healthier. If we use our own low-sulfur coal, natural gas and oil, and build more refineries, we will have less dependence on countries that would like to cause us grief. If we stop taking western land already damaged by overrest out of production, we will increase biodiversity and heal desertification. The land will be healthier and there will be even more jobs.

This book contains a taste of what *RANGE* has published over the past 20 years. It has taken much of that time for us to connect the dots. Each story includes the original date of publication, and a few have updates. But, sadly, most hold as true today as they did when they were written.

These are stories we wish we didn't have to tell. Some involve pain, oppression, greed, arrogance, bad management and bad manners. But there are also stories of good science and hope, of hard work, strong characters and success. It shows grit. And that—and perhaps a musket—is what will help to bring America back. ■

© SANDY OWENS

This Montana cow dog loves her work.

CONTENTS

Conservation

Water

Wildlife

Forestry

Takings

Enviros

Extras

On the Cover:
After some heavy labor, it's back to the barn in western Montana. Photo © Cynthia Baldauf

© JEFF ROSS

Tim Findley, formerly of Rolling Stone, San Francisco Chronicle and CBS, has changed as much as the country in the past two decades.

WATERMELONS, PARADIGMS AND CLASS WAR

By Tim Findley

It was a relatively small crowd for Berkeley, California, that gathered on a patch of lawn with a stage that had long ago been renamed Ho Chi Minh Park. It was 1973 and we were waiting for just the right moment in the nine-hour time difference when the Paris Peace Accords would be signed.

Checking his watch one more time, one of the radicals on the stage burst out with the chant of the day, "One, Two, Three, Four, the NLF has won the war!" Some in the crowd cringed at that. They might have opposed U.S. involvement in Vietnam, but they knew U.S. forces had never really lost a battle in those 10 years of fighting. They were glad the nightmarish mistake was finally over and oddly proud that the government had finally come to its senses.

Turning to see who else might be joining in the chant, I came almost face to face with a pretty graduate student barely five feet tall who I had come to know was at least a messenger for the Weather Underground and its bombing attacks on federal buildings. When she recognized me, I held up one hand with a two-finger "V" that had become a customary greeting for peace.

"Oh, no, no, no," she said, shooting up her rather tiny fist. "Class war. Class War!"

Somewhere, maybe in Chicago, the peace movement had turned a corner, leaving at least one wing out on a whole new rampage and looking for a fight. It would be nearly another 20 years before I realized how much they meant it, and how they would use their skills against some unlikely and completely surprised "enemies" in the rural West.

Perhaps it was just the first of what activists insisting on their own elitist use of language would come to call a "paradigm" moment, when something you have known for so long is suddenly put to a different purpose, forever.

The baby boomers who emerged after World War II as

the largest single generation in world history were not that different from generations of the past in their sense of rebellion against conformity and the call for their own social culture in music, the arts, and education. In the United States they were the wealthiest, best educated and, by their numbers and the astonishing new technology presented to them, possibly the most creative generation in history. They knew all that and used it like a badge to establish their place in the world.

Yet, those in the United States who marched in the civil rights and antiwar movements were not revolutionaries. Taking aside the rhetoric of some and the actions of a few, the causes of young people in the 1950s and '60s were to extend the same rights and privileges and opportunities as they enjoyed to everyone, just as they largely succeeded in doing by the Civil Rights Act. What they wanted in Vietnam were free elections, not victory. Most of them, in fact, considered themselves patriots, carrying out the ideals of the Founding Fathers and of John F. Kennedy's call to "Ask not what your country can do for you...." By the '70s they had more political awareness, but not enough among the movement to change the U.S. political system.

Earth Day was born as a headline running on the national wires, and quickly lit up as a trendy new message. On campuses all over the nation, planning for the event replaced the teach-ins on Vietnam.

But what on Gaylord Nelson's Great Green Earth did that have to do with class war against rural people in the West?

Nelson was a kindly senator from Wisconsin in the 1960s, a sort of liberal moderate as we might see him now. But he looked for issues and discovered that unrestrained air pollution, oil spills and general indifference to the environment was going on without much interest in Washington. He said he got his best idea in 1962, which was to sell President Kennedy on conservation as part of his next campaign. Nelson went to Attorney General Robert Kennedy who promoted the idea to his brother.

So, in September 1963, President Kennedy went on a five-day tour of 11 states urging more attention to conservation issues. Had he not been assassinated in November of that year, it is interesting to speculate on what the environmental movement might have become, as well as what might have happened in Vietnam.

In a sense, they became each other. It was six years later that Nelson recognized the possibilities in what he saw as the then flailing but growing aimless antiwar movement. Such youthful energy on behalf of a national cause needed new focus, and what could be more clear than his own crusade of saving the planet from human abuse?

At a conference in Seattle in 1969, he took a political gamble and announced to the news media that the following spring there would be a nationwide demonstration on behalf of the environment. He called it Earth Day, and invited everyone to attend.

Nelson would later say it was purely a grassroots movement that surprised him with the response, but the senator had perfect pitch with the press. Earth Day was born as a headline running on the national wires, and quickly lit up as a trendy new message. On campuses all over the nation, planning for the event replaced the teach-ins on Vietnam.

The potential Nelson had foreseen was astonishing, even to him. On the first April 22 Earth Day in 1970, an estimated 20 million people showed up in gatherings all over the nation. The senator set the wheels in motion and others—like Stewart Brand with his *Whole Earth Catalog* and Rachel Carson with her book, "Silent Spring"—provided part of the engine, but there would have been no such spontaneity, as was reported, without the media itself.

With the end of Vietnam, the new cause, rich in political potential, was ready and waiting. And even my small-fisted friend from the Weather Underground seemed a little right. Every cause must face an opponent to survive. Class war was coming, first against the indifferent corporations and their acid rain, later against the innocent, living as they had for too long in the way and by the old way.

For the most part, the rural West slumbered through the beginning of the new movement, unaware of the clouds of crisis building in their direction. American agriculture in general was continuing its long self-contradictory decline begun with the end of World War II. In 1965, farmers comprised 6.4 percent of the workforce, down by half from 12.2 percent in 1950. By 1970 the figure of farmers was 4.6 percent of the labor force and still shrinking month by month. Yet, while there were fewer numbers of farmers, the average acreage of farms had increased from 300 acres in the 1960s to nearly 400 acres by the '70s. Earned income against expense for family farmers steadily declined.

For those who watched, one important message found in the numbers was in the decrease of political influence among family farmers and the relentless, land-absorbing reach of corporate agriculture and new-housing development. It was an economic trend certain to wind up in somebody's political agenda.

In the 1980s, the Bureau of the Census said it would no longer count farming as an occupation since so many farmers admitted to having another job to provide their essential income. People wanted to stay on their land, their farms and their ranches, and were willing even to make them their "second job" as part of their livelihood. The corporations might have taken over the distribution of food in America, but it was still family pride that actually grew it.

Nelson's environmental movement grew like a sidewalk barbecue for newsmen. It was a public-relations dream. What kind of human could look in the eyes of a helpless white-furred baby harp seal and then bash it to death with a club or fire harpoons into the backs of gentle-giant whales? What happened to the dodo in Mauritius? What about the bison on the American plains? Why were people killing our national symbol, the bald eagle?

But they were not prepared for what was coming because, for all the public support generated by the newly captured word "ecology," there was recognition among political carnivores that it could also provide power and more wealth.

An active and profitable trade arose in photos, film, and videotape of creatures at risk from human behavior. Saving them, or saving the lands they lived on, had to be part of every politician's portfolio. Even most farmers and ranchers shared the belief in preserving wild critters wherever they could. It had been part of their culture for generations.

But they were not prepared for what was coming, because for all the public support generated by the newly captured word "ecology," there was recognition among political carnivores that it could also provide power and more wealth.

Among the first to recognize political currency in the environment was President Richard M. Nixon. Nixon was a conservative who lost in his first try for the presidency to John Kennedy, a mild irony to what Gaylord Nelson had planned. But rattled by protests to the war and in need of some unifying issue, Nixon signed a series of laws directed at ending pollution and protecting species, the most significant of them a third revision of the Endangered Species Act, extending its authority offshore and expanding the protection of species to include their habitats. Whether Nixon had carefully read or considered the ESA for what it might imply is not known, but San Francisco librarian Kevin Starr nailed it, saying, "The Endangered Species Act is the Magna Carta of the environmental movement." Another paradigm.

The established and longest-standing environmental groups such as John Muir's Sierra Club and the self-proclaimed savior of "best places," The Nature Conservancy (TNC), recognized that they had just been delivered a cash cow with a volunteer army behind it. TNC, run mostly in secret by a board composed of Wall Street financiers, was amassing a tax-exempt fortune of more than $5 billion, most of it financed by corporate contributions and the federal government itself, which enabled the world's richest nonprofit corporation to own 17 million acres in the United States and more than 117 million acres worldwide with almost no scrutiny. Even the Sierra Club was surprised at its success in nearly crippling the logging industry in the Northwest with the use of the tiny spotted owl as endangered by timber harvests in old-growth forests. "We have to thank Bambi for this," said one Sierra Club leader. "Without that owl to gain sympathy, we could never have done it."

Surrogate birds, fish, amphibians and bugs were just a few of the limitless numbers of unseen nature that could be used in arguments for the protection of habitat by reduction of agriculture. Wolves and grizzly bears were reintroduced in the Rockies, and the ranchers were warned. There was outrage at such actions as stopping construction of a hospital in the name of a fly, or preventing removal of fire-prone scrub to protect a jumping mouse that wasn't even there.

Internationally, Mikhail Gorbachev tore down the wall in Berlin, starting the domino collapse of the Soviet Union and bringing a cautious end to the Cold War. Perhaps, now, it would be possible to create a lasting world peace.

The United Nations, considered by many to be a virtual welfare case for the United States, saw its own opportunity and called for its first environmental conference in Stockholm in 1972. The international meeting raised questions about Third World poverty and excessive consumption in the West, but the world leaders invited to that first one were really just feeling their way into a new world. Twenty years later, in 1992, the United Nations hosted a follow-up conference in Rio de Janeiro that seemed poised to run away on its own under indigenous leadership ready to change the world from the bottom up.

Officially, 108 national invited heads of state attended, but nearly 2,500 representatives of nongovernment organizations made their presence known at the sessions, with close to 20,000 NGO "consultants" attending forums on the issues. The conference was clearly conducted by environmental activists and exploiters like TNC which were not elected by any national constituency and were not even known to most people in the world. It was a powerful display of what Earth Day's grassroots organization had become, and it implied unprecedented authority to dozens of organizations begun, like TNC, at a library meeting in the 1950s.

The conference in Rio produced its most important document, Agenda 21, virtually instructing nations to reorganize their societies in more "sustainable" communities that would direct their efforts, especially in the United States, to reducing the consumption of natural resources. Five years later, in 1997, at Kyoto, Japan, the United Nations followed up with a meeting demanding that nations implement important aspects of Agenda 21 or face worldwide disaster by 2050.

For the most part, the rural West slumbered through the beginning of the new movement, unaware of the clouds of crisis building in their direction. American agriculture in general was continuing its long self-contradictory decline begun with the end of World War II.

You didn't have to accept that, and you wouldn't get to vote on it anyway. You could disagree with the near screaming warnings of global disaster by election-bitter former Vice President Al Gore, but it told most Americans little more than where to buy their light bulbs.

The ESA was simply the law of the land, signed by a notorious Republican. A few politicians exploited it, such as Sen. Harry Reid of Nevada with his Las Vegas land schemes, and former Arizona Gov. Bruce Babbitt who swung it like a club to threaten grazing and property rights over his new empire as secretary of the Interior. No politician would dare challenge it. The only one who did, California Rep. Richard Pombo, was trounced in his next campaign by huge contributions of money and hundreds of volunteers shipped into his district by the Sierra Club to oppose him.

Lawyers lined up to find judges willing to issue federal orders and to file land and water-claiming lawsuits that seldom failed. It was almost never that a corporate agribusiness was targeted by the legal action, but smaller ranchers, farmers, and isolated rural residents found themselves deluged with suits demanding that they sell their land and livestock or that they cease their use of water administered by federal authorities. Even some of those bureaucrats who sympathized with their friends and families in agriculture gave up rather than face demotion and other penalties for resisting orders from Washington, D.C. Common sense did not seem to matter as hundreds of families and thousands of people were driven off land where they had lived and worked for generations.

In a couple of isolated situations, such as the denial of agricultural water to the Klamath Basin in Oregon and California, local citizens joined their farming neighbors to protest and bring about negotiations to save the farms that have already lasted for years.

My young Weather Underground friend in Berkeley had called it class war. She will be 40 years older now, and I suppose she may have children, even grandchildren whom she may tell about the great success of the civil rights movement in bringing new freedom, but I don't think that even then she meant class war in America. Nor would she want to see the sort of prejudice and bigotry some young people have today toward rural people, who they seem to regard as less intelligent than themselves. For their part, as manipulators of the environmental movement have been able to portray ranchers and farmers as obsolete and ignorant, I know people on the land who can only think of environmentalists as arrogant demagogues hiding on campus until they can take power.

And the biggest losers may be all of us who consume less and less food produced by oppressed American agriculture. In 2008, the United States became for the first time a net food-importing nation. And just as this book goes to press, on the west side of the Central Valley in California, available water remains denied to farmers in order to protect a small minnow, unproven to be endangered. In that valley which only two years ago produced up to one-fifth of all the truck crops like carrots and beans grown in the West, the people put out of work have begun to grow hungry. Federal authorities have opened warehouses of donated food to feed them.

The carrots come from China.

Paradigm? Or class war? ■

CONSERVATION

GRIZZLY BEAR HUNTING FOR SALMON IN THE WILDS OF ALASKA © DAVE WATTS/TOM STACK & ASSOCIATES

SPRING 1991

THEN & NOW

The western range used to be a free-for-all, settled by the tough. By J. Wayne Burkhardt, Ph.D.

For centuries, the ranges of the American West have been through many natural cycles. Before European settlement, they were overgrazed, undergrazed, dried out, flooded and burned. And even though flora and fauna can flourish together in natural grazing systems, Mother Nature's balance is not always harmonious.

The history of grazing throughout the world has been one of extremes. Fauna populations built up when ranges had a surplus of feed and the slowly increasing flocks or herds would overgraze until all forage was depleted. Then they would starve to death and the process would start all over again. The plant community and soils would begin to recover, sometimes with different flora, which would encourage a different grazing species. Antelope prefer grassy meadows, mule deer like to browse, while sheep like forbs or broadleaf plants in the high country.

When this country was settled, the whole operating philosophy was to multiply and subdue and conquer the West. It was a free-for-all, settled by the tough. There was no system to secure the use of public domain, so timid souls lost out while the aggressive and ruthless survived.

Significant rangeland grazing started about 1860 with the advent of the transcontinental railroad, the containment of buffalo, and treaties with Native Americans. By the mid-1880s the western range was filled with livestock and even though some brutal winters and agonizing droughts caused massive die-offs, there is little doubt that by the early part of the 20th century the range was overstocked and overgrazed.

In 1905, Teddy Roosevelt created the Forest Reserves (later to become the U.S. Forest Service), which offered protection for higher elevations. Then, in 1934, Congress passed the Taylor Grazing Act (later to become the Bureau of Land Management), creating a service agency to deal with the remaining public domain and establishing a permit system for allocating, securing and regulating grazing use on the public lands. Soon after that, grazing pressure was reduced by more than 50 percent. (Grazing pressure is measured in terms of an "Animal Unit Month." One 800-1,000-pound cow counts as one AUM; five deer would equal one range cow or one AUM. There were 50 million AUMs in 1900, about 20 million today.)

PHOTOS COURTESY WAYNE BURKHARDT

Trigarro Dip Springs, Elko County, Nevada, 1981. Inset: 1919.

Grazing of rangelands is a natural process, fundamentally, ecologically and biologically sound. It is at the base of the world's food chain, and probably the only natural food-production technology in this country. All the rest are intensive, artificial, buoyed up by fossil energy, fertilizer, pesticides and fuel. Grazing is extensive, low-fossil-energy consumptive, a natural process with renewable grass and forage being eaten by animals to produce protein that becomes food for something else.

The western range is a herding system. Horses, camels, giant bison, and antelope-like grazers and browsers roamed the continent prior to becoming extinct. They were followed by buffalo, elk, deer, antelope, wild sheep and goats, which, several hundred years ago, were joined by livestock.

In earlier times, grazing had no seasons; it was continuous. Today livestock use, because of better land-management practices, generally occurs under some form of rotation system with shorter grazing seasons and periodic intervals of rest. The effects of these changes are positive and apparent.

In the 1980s, environmentalists, citing land degradation and lack of significant contribution to society, launched a serious political campaign against livestock grazing on public lands which put it at the center of a major

Willis Creek near Mountain City, Nevada, 1982. INSET: *1911.*

land-use struggle. Sadly, their propaganda does not include many facts and is much at odds with documentation showing stable and improving range conditions.

Evidence of improvement comes from the land itself. Photographic records from the turn of the century compared to photos of current situations show tremendous improvement in the health and condition of grazed public lands in the West. Near-barren range landscapes and gutted stream courses of the early 1900s are today proven and productive stable rangelands. The desirable native species of grasses, forbs and shrubs which occupy these rangelands today are many times more productive of wildlife habitat, soil stability and livestock forage than conditions shown in the earlier pictures. And the records are by no means isolated occurrences.

These photographs deal far more directly with conditions on the land than do the numerical assessments and opinion questionnaires that are the basis for General Accounting Office reports to Congress. Equally compelling evidence of the improving health of the public rangelands comes from population trends of native wildlife. Huge increases this century are not the product of declining conditions on public lands, degraded riparian areas and bungled management but of substantial improvement. And these changes occurred in the presence of livestock grazing and despite increasing human population in the West.

Why the disparity between actual conditions on public rangelands and the negative depictions in many government reports? Subjectivity versus objectivity.

Agency assessments are often driven by political and funding considerations. These agencies, much like special-interest groups, owe much of their existence to the perpetuation of problems rather than to their solutions. Range-condition methodologies are at best crude approximations; there is lack of consistency between agencies; reports are often colored by personal philosophy regarding grazing on public lands; and young professional resource managers are notoriously impatient and lacking in historical perspective. Often information bases are questionable abstractions far removed from the land and resources.

Admittedly, there is much work yet to be done, but another seldom-mentioned fact remains: grazing is low-impact, low-input, natural food production. Ranchers are producing food for people. They take care of their livestock and the land, whether private or public, because they care, but also because it is in their best interest. Natural grazing damages little and is based on a renewable natural resource that can be harvested in no other way.

Professional critics earn their living, and boost their egos and political power, based on a crisis. They can walk into the halls of Congress and be listened to even though reality is seldom discussed. Never mentioned is the fact that plants grow and produce tissue in excess of their own needs and this surplus organic material has to be periodically removed. If it is not, two things occur: nutrients that need to go back into the soil are tied up in litter and accumulation; and plants stagnate, grass is not healthy, and they cannot thrive.

Doesn't a lawn look better if it's mowed? Grazing is a way of periodically removing the excess tissue. Fire is another. And fire, from the sagebrush up to the highest forest, has always been an important part of the natural system. Periodic burning stimulates, rejuvenates and controls balance between woody and nonwoody plants. The nonwoody plants are not killed by burning but the woody ones are set back temporarily, which gives grasses and forbs an advantage, at least for a while.

It is ecologically and biologically proper that this country's rangelands be used by livestock. Grazing takes very little from the public lands and when properly managed is good for plants, good for wildlife, and good for public range. ■

KEEPING IT ALL TOGETHER

The story of cattle and sheep grazing on these vast federal lands is an important part of the nation's heritage. Today, more than 100 years after the cattle and sheep drives and range wars figured so prominently in the settling of the West, livestock grazing continues as a valid, authorized use on public range. Livestock grazing produces food and fiber, along with many other environmental, economic, and social benefits. To achieve range management objectives, federal-land managers and ranchers are working as partners on range allotments all across the West, using livestock grazing as a vital tool to improve riparian areas, associated uplands and entire watersheds.

FEDERAL ROLE

In the West, the early settlers generally homesteaded the lands with the most water and forage, while vast areas of often remote, desolate, and arid lands remained in public ownership. As a result, the federal government still owns 724 million acres, almost one-third of the nation's land. Because of homesteading laws, railroad grants, and other factors, federal, state and private lands are now often intermingled, and cooperation among landowners is vital.

Over the years, Congress has passed a number of laws directing the Forest Service (U.S. Department of Agricul-

PHOTOS COURTESY WAYNE BURKHARDT

Martin Creek, Santa Rosas, 1982. Inset: 1920.

ture) and the Bureau of Land Management (U.S. Department of the Interior) to administer federal lands under a multiple-use concept for a variety of uses. The two agencies manage about 341 million acres of public range. Multiple-use values on these lands include range vegetation, soil, water, timber, minerals, wildlife habitat, recreation, historic and prehistoric resources, wilderness, scenery, open space, and a rural way of life. The management of livestock grazing and all other uses of federal lands is governed by comprehensive land-use plans, prepared by resource specialists, with public review and comment.

PERMITTEE PARTNERSHIPS

There are approximately 31,000 grazing permittees working with the BLM and Forest Service in managing cattle, sheep, horses and goats on federal lands in 35 states. Most run family-owned farms or ranches. All operate according to federal leases or permits that control the number of livestock and duration of grazing. About 13 percent of these permittees use both Forest Service and BLM lands. Allotment management plans are worked out with permittees to make the best use of forage and maintain soil, water, and vegetation while meeting public demands for other multiple-use values. These plans can be complex, and their success relies heavily on cooperation between permittees, federal managers, and others.

LIVESTOCK GRAZING FOR FOOD AND FIBER

Livestock grazing provides beef, lamb, leather, wool and other products that are important to local, regional, and national economies. Fully 50 percent of the nation's marketable lambs and 20 percent of the calves going to feedlots are raised in the western public-land states.

A big share of the livestock raised in the western states grazes at least part of the year on federal land. For example, 88 percent of the cattle produced in Idaho, 64 percent in Wyoming and 63 percent in Arizona graze on public range at some time. Overall, federal lands produce approximately 13 percent of the grazing forage in the United States.

VEGETATION

Grazing is used to maintain or restore plant communities. It also promotes the diversity of plant life. For range grasses to thrive, they must be cropped to promote vigor. Often, the lack of grazing results in unhealthy, less-dense stands that overwhelm good grasses, wildflowers, and other plants. Livestock and other animals fertilize and break up the soil crust, increasing rainwater penetration and scattering and trampling seed into the earth.

Unendangered species in Western U.S.

(Schmidt & Gilbert, 1978)

	1900	TODAY
Mule deer	500,000	3,000,000
Elk	41,000	1,000,000
Antelope	12,000	1,000,000
Bighorns	2,000	45,000

SOIL AND WATER

Water is precious, especially in the West. Proper watershed management aims to capture, store, and safely release water. By managing the timing and duration of livestock use, grazing helps improve grass and crop production, control erosion, recharge aquifers, enhance riparian conditions, and provide water for recreational, agricultural, and other needs.

WILDLIFE HABITAT

Range improvements for livestock grazing can increase wildlife numbers and improve habitat, especially in areas with little rainfall or running water. Over the years, federal agencies and livestock operators have built thousands of stock ponds and water holes, which benefit both livestock and wildlife. Salt distribution, brush control, grass seedings, and predator control also benefit wildlife species. Big game numbers are generally increasing as a result of these and other improvements. Intermingled private ranch and farmlands, which contain open spaces and often boast rich riparian habitat, also provide critical food, water, shelter, and protection for wildlife.

COMMUNITY STABILITY

Livestock production is a major industry in the West, providing jobs and income for rural communities and generating millions of dollars for regional economies. The social and economic existence of many of the small towns that dot the West depends in part on livestock producers who operate on federal lands. Public land permittees are an important part of their local tax base, providing employment and patronizing businesses in town for feed, equipment, gasoline, and supplies. In addition, ranchers on public range pay fees to the federal government, which are shared with local counties for roads and schools, go to the U.S. Treasury, or are used for range betterment projects.

Excerpted with permission from Program Aid Number 1439, USDA Forest Service, September 1989. Produced in partnership by: the Forest Service, Bureau of Land Management and Public Lands Council.

SPRING 1994

ENVIRONMENTALIST OF THE YEAR

Date Creek has experienced a rebirth under Phil Knight's unconventional stewardship.

By Dan Dagget

Whenever I visit Phil Knight, I can't help but think how much he reminds me of Mr. Green Jeans. That amiable character, some of you will remember, was the farmer sidekick of '60s kid-show host Captain Kangaroo. Tall and lanky in his bib overalls, Mr. Green Jeans brought goats and calves, corn plants and honeybees onto the show every morning and was the only evidence many urban kids ever had that all rural people weren't dumb rubes.

Phil Knight does his part to smash that caricature, too. Not only has he been selected 1993 Environmentalist of the Year by the Arizona Game and Fish Department ("Environmentalist rancher, isn't that an oxymoron?" he asks.), but he runs a pick-your-own organic peach and apple orchard that attracts people to Date Creek from as far away as Phoenix. They make the one-hour drive as much to enjoy Knight's country hospitality as to pick the peaches.

Those with families bring their kids (if they're young enough not to have been struck numb by neighborhood gangs and TV violence). They play on the rusty old farm machinery and fall in love with the animals that Knight leaves in the orchard to turn it into an impromptu petting zoo.

"There are geese and turkeys in there and an old mare who wouldn't hurt a fly. Usually, I've got a couple of calves on the mend too," says Knight, who not only acts the part of Green Jeans, but looks it. When he's serving as a host and not cowboying on his 38,000-acre Date Creek Ranch, Knight wears deck shoes and a plantation hat. The outfit graces his lean six-foot frame and ready smile in a way any ambassador of goodwill would envy.

Knight's ranch is west of Wickenburg, Arizona, a mining town turned tourist trap, in the Sonoran desert northwest of Phoenix. When he bought the place in 1966, it was against his father's advice.

© GLENN SHORT

Phil Knight shares his management style with nationally known ecologists, environmental leaders, and politicians.

"I was trained as a geological engineer," Knight says. "My father thought he got the country out of the family's blood when he moved to the city from an Indiana farm and got a job with a utility company. I guess he was wrong."

When Knight took over the ranch, Date Creek was little more than a trickle of water wandering down a hundred-foot wide bed of cow-dung spattered gravel. Twenty-five years later, the environmentalist rancher takes congressmen, environmental leaders and nationally known ecologists on tours of the showplace riparian zone that has experienced a rebirth under his thoughtful and unconventional stewardship.

So how'd he do it? He fenced the cows out, right? Or he cut their numbers drastically? That's what the conventional wisdom dictates for riparian areas. But Knight busts conventions; he doesn't accept them. "Everyone knows that cattle grazing destroys riparian areas, right? But suppose grazing can improve riparian areas. What then?" he asks, taking a good-natured jab. "Can environmentalists take it?"

The creek that Phil Knight has adopted as a lifetime project is a medium-sized desert stream, ephemeral through some of its reaches and perennial along others. It flows from the Date Creek Mountains, located northwest of Wickenburg, to Alamo Lake where it joins the Bill Williams River, a tributary of the lower Colorado. Along its course, Date Creek passes through a unique biome where the Sonoran and Mojave deserts mix. Beyond the cottonwoods and willows that line its banks, Joshua trees and giant saguaros stand shoulder to shoulder.

For roughly 25 years, Knight has been grazing more than 400 head of cattle on a two-mile stretch of the Date Creek riparian area from November to March and resting it the remainder of the year. In spite of the fact that it is grazed so heavily, or as Knight would have you think, because of it, the stream has been described as one of the healthiest in the state. In the winter of 1993, the Game and Fish Department transplanted a beaver there to underscore its faith in the creek's recovery. Knight says he's eager to see what the natural dam builders can do to hold back water and expand the creek's riparian zone.

"It took me three years to get this beaver," he says. "I hope it doesn't take me three more years to get another one." ■

The difference between good management and no management. LEFT: Date Creek under Phil Knight's care and attention, where his cattle graze. "Everyone knows that cattle grazing destroys riparian areas, right?" he asks. "But suppose grazing can improve riparian areas. What then?" BELOW: The Verde River, where cattle grazing was halted to "protect" habitat.

PHOTOS © DAN DAGGET

FALL 1995

THE CIRCLE OF LIFE

It depends on the Law of the Minimum.

By Steven H. Rich

The animals lay on their sides, near death, their limbs twitching.

"It's rattlesnakes, Boss. Them cows is done for. There's nuthin' we can do," the young cowboy said.

"Well, let's see," said the older man, drawing a syringe full of solution containing magnesium, calmly injecting one cow after another. About the time the last cow got its shot, the first was on its feet.

"That's mighty powerful snake medicine," said the kid, shaking his head with wonder.

"It wasn't rattlers, Bill," the older man grinned, "it was grass tetany. Too much new green stuff, not enough old stems."

The statement put the youngster in a quandary. The boss was clearly pulling his leg. Whoever heard of a cow getting too much green grass? He grew up on a ranch and had a lot of ranching and cowboy skills. He had never heard of grass tetany. But you can't tell the boss he's full of it. The situation called for delicacy.

"Well," he grinned back, "keep that snake medicine handy in case this grass bites any more cows."

"I'll do that," said the boss, "and you men get those mineral boxes filled up TODAY, like I told you."

"Yessir."

Those cows needed magnesium, fast, and no amount of anything else would help at all. Nature, and some good teachers—like Allan Savory, Kirk Heaton and Steve Cassady of the Natural Resources Conservation Service, and Kim Leany and Bob Sandburg of the Bureau of Land Management—have taught me that living things are organized as wholes. If some small but necessary factor is missing, the creature can't live. The principle is called the Law of the Minimum.

Miles Keogh, of Grand Junction, Colorado, performs a valuable service for farmers, golf-course managers and others who often throw away thousands of dollars on nitrogen, potassium and phosphorus when what they really need is a few bucks worth per acre of some "lesser" nutrient, like iron or sulphur. Miles understands the Law of the Minimum.

On rangeland prior to the Taylor Grazing Act, the thing in shortest supply was protection from overgrazing. Most plants got chewed down to the ground and rebitten over and over, never getting a real chance to grow. There were

This spot is 100 yards away from photo below and once looked just as bad. It has the same soil and slope. Water now sinks in, held by grass and flowers. When we planted a seeding nearby, it and the trees attracted deer and cattle which caused this change. The site is now covered with seedlings and the droppings of many species.

Fifty years ungrazed sagebrush steppe, piñon/juniper woodland study plot. The whole ranch was in that shape when we got it. Presence of trees indicates sufficient rain. There are no tracks on the ground, no droppings, no seedlings. The cryptogamic crust has not been disturbed for years. It did not get this way from overgrazing. Appropriate disturbance by animals creates healthy land.

PHOTOS COURTESY STEVEN H. RICH

Grassland under piñon/juniper canopy on Kaibab Plateau. There are thousands of acres of the same there. Piñon/juniper woodland does not need to be barren. Animal impact can bring it to life.

Native western wheatgrass rhizomes with seedlings. The site is heavily used by livestock. The plant is responding by sending out hundreds of new stems.

floods and dust storms. The soil eroded terribly and right-thinking people set out to supply protection. They got good results.

Justus von Liebig, who first described the Law of the Minimum in terms of plant nutrition, said: "The growth of the organism is limited to the availability of the least-available-necessary nutrient. The Law of the Minimum does not apply only to plant and animal nutrition. It's universal to any organism, organization or structure, whether it is living, mechanical, chemical or a combination of the three."

It applies to rangeland and the creatures that live there most profoundly. If we are going to make any more progress, we must improve our awareness of Law of the Minimum issues on the land. Plants need protection from overgrazing. They also need appropriate disturbance, nutrients, water, sunlight and the right temperatures, specific soil conditions, soil aeration, pollination and some place to establish as seedlings.

In nature, these requirements are met by complex processes, often requiring animals. We all are familiar with the role of bees and other insects as pollinators. Many plants depend on one kind of insect to deliver pollen. No insect, no seeds, no more plants, no more whatever depends on that plant.

Because bees do not eat plants (only plant products), it is easy to perceive the symbiosis (the beneficial relationship). It is harder to see how beavers benefit willows when they cut them down and chew the bark. Nevertheless, beavers increased willow habitat by several thousand percent when they were running the riparian systems in the West, and the willows thrived, as did many other organisms dependent on habitat factors beavers created.

In the same way, it is harder still to see how grazing-animal populations were dependent on predators which individually killed them and tore them to pieces. Esthetic and emotional values block the ability of many people to perceive that symbiosis.

Regardless of these prejudices, much of the functioning of nature and the health and survival of both predators and prey depended, and often still depends, on the interplay of these animals. The reciprocal relationship between grazers and the plants they eat is also misunderstood. The grazers get all the obvious benefits. But the actions of grazers fill minimums in several natural processes on which many plants depend.

Overgrazing is still a danger. Plants need protection from the exhaustion of their energy reserves. This can happen if they are bitten repeatedly during their growing phase without being allowed time to replace those reserves. Time is the key factor, and the need for protected recovery time is highly variable. In the simplest terms, if a plant has plenty of food and water, proper temperatures, sunshine, and good, well-aerated soil, it can grow very quickly, and is soon hardy and strong without need of protection. (A lawn is like that.) If one of these factors is in short supply, dribbling in slowly or available intermittently, it can take much longer.

A grazer-desirable plant, therefore, is most resistant when surrounded by a whole cast of supporters: decay organisms converting dead roots and surface litter to

Let the cryptogam cult put up their best patch of crust against this spot—the tracked-up grassy place will absorb and retain water and sediment many times better. Cryptocrusts are notably bad at feeding wildlife and livestock also, and inhibit grass seed germination.

Seedlings started in cow tracks. Hoofprints collect good stuff: water, seeds, nutrients, litter and soil.

humus and nutrients, as well as fixing nitrogen and creating tunnels for aeration and water passage; fungi, which perform many symbiotic activities; other plants which spring up nearby in good years when niches open temporarily, and later add to soil cover and food supplies; and hoofed and other animals punch water-catching, seed-catching and crust-opening holes in the ground, provide dung and urine.

I know of grass plants near water holes that have been overgrazed by wildlife and livestock for at least 30 years, but just keep hanging in there. They make seed when they get a chance, have huge basal diameters, and don't need protection. I have seen others which, in less developed soils and much more alone in the world, die out very easily.

There is magic in filling minimums, and in recognizing them. The limiting factor is not usually water, as we so often suppose, but stabilizing organic matter in the soil and on the surface to hold it and nutrients in place.

The bottom photo on page 18 shows bare ground. The presence of trees shows it to have sufficient moisture. It doesn't need protection because it has had too much of that. There are no tracks on the ground. No droppings. The topsoil remains only in little circular islands around the sagebrush. Water flows off from every thundershower.

The soil is covered with a cryptogamic crust, unbroken for years. This year the site has had double the average rainfall, but no grass is growing; there are no seedlings, no sprouts. The barrenness is not caused by overgrazing; it is starving. Without the support organisms, scarcity has set in and there is a fierce competition for water and the meager nitrogen the cryptogams provide. The trees are winning.

Barren, lifeless sagebrush steppe or piñon/juniper country covers millions of acres in the West. This degraded condition is so common that most people believe nothing can grow under or near those trees. That is far from true. Land with heavy animal impact will always grow something.

The first photo on page 18 shows a basically identical site. It once looked much like the one below it (taken 200 yards away) but is now well on its way to health. Same ridge close by, same basic soil, but the difference is that it is near a seeding we planted several years ago. Cattle and deer, attracted to the nearby grass and flowers (and by small salt blocks in the sage), bedded under the trees. Birds, small animals, and insects also came. The ground is covered with droppings and hoofprints. There are burrows in the ground. There are several species of seedlings everywhere. Diverse soil life is developing.

In the second location, the bare soil gets very hot. Water evaporates quickly, and the soil dries out weeks sooner than on the other site. Deer don't go there to cycle nutrients (i.e., to use and excrete them) in the interspaces between the semitoxic trees and shrubs. Any competent organic gardener would prescribe organics and compacted microsites for seedling establishment for this perishing patient. On rangeland, that means dung, urine, and hoofprints. Animals would have to be attracted there by salt or hay. There is no reason in the world for them to go there now.

PHOTOS COURTESY STEVEN H. RICH

Healing wash. Banks were vertical and barren a few years ago. It was 18 inches deeper and it almost never runs water now. The land soaks it up.

An old corral and barnyard in Kanab, Utah. Rainfall: 12 inches. Soil: sandy and nutrient-poor, except where the organics from all those years of intense animal impact have developed over time into a site where no water runs away, the soil is always cool and nutrients cycle rapidly. The trees are locusts (eastern hardwoods) which grew "volunteer." The site is not irrigated. It looks more like Kentucky than hot, dry southern Utah, and is a demonstration of the potential of dry lands.

The key organisms in all this are hoofed grazers. They can do damage, but without them things start to separate and unravel.

The loss of native knowledge of plant/animal/recovery time relationships left vast areas of the West in a condition where decay barely functions, and grass seeds particularly could find nowhere to germinate and establish. The soil sealed, with a clay crust first, then with cryptogams. Soil aeration levels plummeted. All really active soil organisms are aerobic—they need air. Soil functioning falls, below ground, by 95 percent if the air is shut off. Roots of grasses shrink, not so much in length as in thickness and mass of root hairs. Most of the soil creatures that feed on those roots, adding to soil fertility, die out.

The soil doesn't hold water as well. Plant spacings widen. Soil temperatures rise. Evaporation rates soar, the land gets drier. Runoff increases. Soil organics and seeds are washed away with the water and dirt itself. Seed production and viability drops. Again plants are vulnerable to disease and insect attack, now because of poor nutrition, water scarcity and, in the case of grasses, decreased sunlight. They are shaded by years of old growth.

You can call that natural if you want to, but overgrazing was more common in pre-Columbian nature (as were the remedies and recovery processes). The starved, barren, choked, overrested conditions I see on millions of acres, and thousands still to be rescued on our ranch, are human caused.

With overrest—which is overprotection—birth, growth, reproduction and decay are all inhibited. Death glides on greased skids.

I've talked mostly about plants, because the animal issues are fairly obvious. To be healthy, to survive birth and infancy, to grow and reproduce, animal life needs diverse, high-quality food, water and cover. With overgrazing by livestock, food for wildlife is mostly just scarce, though often of low quality. With overrest it's first abundant but of crummy quality, then it's really scarce and/or semitoxic, like juniper.

The land has taught me this: We want stable, active, living topsoil, and lots of wildlife. We need skillfully managed livestock planting, pruning, fertilizing and cycling nutrients. Mineral supplements and feeds offered to livestock end up in the ecosystem, filling critical minimums throughout the web of life. Properly managed livestock can do miracles of healing on the land, by just doing what comes naturally. For instance, they can increase the protein content of forage. Even in places that look alive, many species can't make a living. Ten million pounds of food that is toxic or deficient in key minerals, and/or energy and/or protein is not enough if animals need the missing nutrients.

Animals will take terrible risks to get needed nutrients. They have to, or they'll get sick, become infertile, or die. Plants and animals live with minimums (scarcity), and maximums (toxicity). Their birth, growth, reproduction, death, and decay are not matters of opinion. They are matters of law and life. The Law of the Minimum. The Circle of Life. ■

SUMMER 1997

THE DARK SIDE

A corrupt system of preservation science muzzles the government's own honest scholars. By Alston Chase

Is there a Dark Side? You don't have to be Luke Skywalker to know the answer is "yes."

African Americans are often victims of the Dark Side—the stealth racism that pervades America. Loggers and ranchers encounter the Dark Side when they are driven off the land by the maneuvers of greens and their bureaucratic allies. Corporate and governmental whistle-blowers meet the Dark Side when they dare to expose their employers' follies.

The Dark Side is silent conspiracy, accomplished with nods, winks and confidential memos, that seeks to harm individuals whose actions are troublesome to the powerful. And it could not exist without the tacit acquiescence of the majority. When it strikes, most folks look the other way.

Many believe in a Dark Side, but selectively. Liberals see it only in big business, conservatives just in government. But some institutions remain above suspicion by nearly everyone. Such is the status of science, which enjoys such a lofty reputation that few challenge its authority.

But science has a Dark Side too, that lurks in the shadowy realm of environmental research. In this fecund habitat it thrives, shielded from exposure to the bright light of truth. But occasionally the covers are pulled back, revealing this netherworld of false scholarship.

Such was the experience of attentive observers at congressional oversight hearings on National Park Service science, held in February 1997. This event revealed that not only is the agency's poor research a national tragedy, but that this failed effort is corrupting the institution of scholarship itself.

The meeting began ordinarily enough. A gentleman from the General Accounting Office testified to what experienced observers already knew: that service science is grossly inadequate. This presentation was followed by the usual self-aggrandizing testimony of the feds' favored scientists who said, in effect, that if Congress would give them more money everything could be fixed. To this they added a now familiar twist: that parks should be maintained as laboratories for themselves, where they can satisfy their curiosity at taxpayers' expense.

Then the deliberations got interesting. Three scholars testified that the service was allowing overly abundant elk and deer to destroy biodiversity throughout the park system. One, Richard Keigley of the Biological Resources Division of the U.S. Geological Survey, then added a zinger: His work, he said, is being suppressed by Interior Department authorities.

Fearing elk are eliminating critical vegetation in Yellowstone National Park, Keigley sought to investigate whether this is so. But officials wouldn't let him. They even tried to prevent his testifying at this hearing.

Another witness, Charles Kay from Utah State University, had similar experiences. He told the congressmen how influential scholars, co-opted by Park Service monies, regularly suppress articles in supposedly "independent" journals that do not support federal management.

© TOM & THERISA STACK/TOM STACK & ASSOCIATES

Elk in Yellowstone National Park

This was shocking stuff. Yet many congressmen listening from the dais seemed unmoved. Aside from the few lawmakers hailing from states where the Interior Department is the big bully on the block, few showed real curiosity about the plight of Keigley and none for the experiences of Kay. Congressmen from eastern states, in particular, like monkeys who wanted to hear no evil, refused to believe that the Dark Side Keigley and Kay experienced could even exist.

But it does exist, within virtually every federal agency conducting conservation science. Keigley and Kay are merely the latest victims of the corrupt system of official science that muzzles its own honest scholars and even seeks to ruin the careers of independent professors who oppose it. Whistle-blowers are whistled right out of their agencies, and university professors who dare to question policy find their research funding and opportunities dry up and their own articles rejected by academic journals whose editors are on the government payroll.

Why is this happening? To prevent the public from learning this simple truth: U.S. preservation policies rest on a fraudulent, pseudo-scientific hypothesis, and, as a result, these policies are failing.

◆ ◆ ◆

The official policy is called "natural regulation" or "ecosystems management." It is based on the hypothesis that nature is composed of networks of interconnected parts which interact to keep everything in equilibrium. So long as these systems retain all their members (i.e., sustain their biological diversity), it is supposed, they'll remain healthy. But if

they lose enough parts (i.e., species), their capacity for self-regulation fails and they become unstable.

This hypothesis is popular because it seems to explain what has gone wrong with the environment and how to fix it: Environmental health requires ecosystems to remain in balance—or within "the historic range of variability"—which in turn demands that they retain their biodiversity. And the best way to ensure these conditions is to leave ecosystems alone. Achieving preservation, according to the official policy, is to restore its "missing parts" (i.e., "reintroducing" creatures such as wolves) then "let nature take its course."

Hence, the aim of federal preservation is to restore habitats that supposedly existed before "ecosystems" were "damaged" by humans. In the federal lexicon, this is called "recreating pre-settlement conditions"—a notion that is written into every federal law and into the gamut of "ecosystem management" schemes of the U.S. Fish & Wildlife Service, National Park Service, U.S. Forest Service, Bureau of Land Management and other land management agencies.

And while this may look scientific, it's actually based on myth. The concept of a stable, self-regulating ecosystem, scientists concede, is fundamentally flawed. There is no "balance of nature." Original conditions never existed. Rather, landscapes are continually changing, in response to the vagaries of weather (floods and hurricanes), volcanoes and human activities. Random disturbance, not permanence or order, governs nature. Left alone, biological communities do not tend toward equilibrium, but fluctuate dramatically.

As the prominent ecological historian, Donald Worster explained, "The ecosystem has receded in usefulness, and in their place we have the idea of the lowly 'patch.' Nature should be regarded as a landscape of patches, big and little...changing continually through time and space, responding to an unceasing barrage of perturbations."

◆ ◆ ◆

The official science not only ignores this consensus on the declining usefulness of the ecosystem, it also overlooks another critical fact well known to scholars: rather than a forested Garden of Eden untouched by man, the pre-settlement landscape of North America had been continually and radically altered by humans.

North America wasn't an "empty continent" when settlers arrived. It was populated by millions of aboriginal peoples who limited wildlife populations through hunting and modified vegetation with fire. As geographer William M. Denevan observed, "The Native American landscape of the early sixteenth century was a humanized landscape almost everywhere. Populations were large, forest composition had been modified, grasslands had been created, wildlife disrupted, and erosion was severe in places. Earthworks, roads, fields and settlements were ubiquitous."

"The Native American landscape of the early sixteenth century was a humanized landscape almost everywhere. Populations were large, forest composition had been modified, grasslands had been created, wildlife disrupted, and erosion was severe in places. Earthworks, roads, fields and settlements were ubiquitous."

And the post-settlement removal of the Indians is bringing about conditions that have not existed since the last ice age. If, therefore, we wish to preserve the landscapes settlers first saw, we must not delegate this management responsibility to nature alone. Instead, we must replicate Native American stewardship.

As the conservation biologist Jared Diamond explained: "The twin goals of non-interference with nature and of preserving pristine natural habitats are incompatible. Both wildlife managers and conservation biologists are being forced to acknowledge that nature reserves can't be left to nature alone to manage."

◆ ◆ ◆

Unfortunately, federal science ignores this scholarly consensus and instead remains wedded to "letting nature take its course." Consequently, it is accelerating extinctions rather than preventing them.

In several western national parks, including Yellowstone, Grand Teton, Rocky Mountain and Mount Rainier, overly abundant elk, no longer hunted by Indians, are destroying vegetation critical to a variety of species, including beaver, bighorn sheep, white-tail and mule deer and even grizzly bears. "Yellowstone," the prominent biologist Daniel Janzen wrote me a few years ago, "is dumfounding.... I have not seen worse overgrazing since the 1960s in Costa Rica.... Adding more land to Yellowstone would do absolutely nothing."

Likewise in Yellowstone, bison, no longer facing predation from wolves and Indians, are also eating themselves out of house and home—because rangers have refused to cull the herds. Having severely damaged their range, thousands are leaving the park, invading bordering ranch lands and creating a political circus. Since some of these animals carry brucellosis, a communicable disease causing domestic

FLORIDA PANTHER © TOM & THERISA STACK/TOM STACK & ASSOCIATES

One step of the "restoration" is the "reintroduction" of "ecosystem missing links" such as wolves. Under the auspices of the Endangered Species Act, millions are spent to plant gray wolves in Yellowstone National Park, even though the original species in this area, canis lupus irremotis, went extinct in the 1920s. Likewise, in the Southeastern United States, the U.S. Fish & Wildlife Service has expended $10 million planting so-called "red wolves," despite warnings by the nation's top geneticists that this creature is not a wolf at all but a coyote-wolf hybrid. Similarly, the Florida panther, above, being "reintroduced" to parts of the Southeast, is not a unique species, but in part a descendant of South American wildcats brought to the U.S. as pets.

cattle to abort calves, Montana stockmen are extremely concerned.

But not just western parks suffer from the official doctrine. Natural regulation is triggering ecological calamities across the continent. In many lands and parks, dense deer populations are eliminating countless important plants, including many on the endangered species list.

As a prestigious team of scientists wrote in the 1995 book, "Wildlife Policies in the U.S. National Parks," thanks to over-protection white-tailed deer numbers "have increased four- to 10-fold," leading to "resource imbalances." Moose browsing in Isle Royale National Park have reduced the abundance of mountain ash and balsam fir and brought the American yew to "near extinction." Other studies find that in Virginia deer have been decimating small mammals and migratory birds such as vireos, warblers and ovenbirds. On Wisconsin's Madeline Island—which University of Wisconsin researcher Don Waller told me is "crawling" with deer—"there is no woody plant regeneration at all. It looks like a clear-cut."

Meanwhile in many national parks, federal officials, in vain efforts to "restore pre-settlement conditions," are spending millions to eliminate so-called "exotics"—i.e., plants and animals introduced by humans. Thus, rangers in Grand Canyon National Park struggled for years to eradicate salt cedar (Tamarisk), even though this plant was critical habitat to a rare bird, the Bell's vireo. Yellowstone managers have poisoned brook and rainbow trout introduced into the park nearly a century ago. And the managers of Redwood National Park have tried to exterminate the Port Orford cedar they deem exotic—even though in national forests just outside that park authorities are seeking to "save" this plant species.

Another step of this "restoration" is the "reintroduction" of "ecosystem missing links" such as wolves. Under the auspices of the Endangered Species Act, millions are spent to plant gray wolves to Yellowstone National Park, even though the original species in this area, *canis lupus irremotis,* went extinct in the 1920s. Likewise, in the Southeastern United States, the U.S. Fish & Wildlife Service has expended $10 million planting so-called "red wolves," despite warnings by the nation's top geneticists that this creature is not a wolf at all but a coyote-wolf hybrid. Similarly the Florida panther, being "reintroduced" to parts of the Southeast, is not a unique species, but in part a descendant of South American wildcats brought to the U.S. as pets.

◆ ◆ ◆

These laws and policies, all devoted to the ideal of non-interference, also ignore a fundamental ecological fact: that many creatures need disturbance to survive.

Left alone, many wild areas eventually become mature

forests, which are poor habitat for a variety of species, including many wild flowers, songbirds and butterflies. Such creatures require landscapes that are kept open by fire, hurricanes and floods, as well as by human activities such as logging, plowing and road building. Consequently, too much protection spells doom for them. The heath hen—also known as the prairie chicken and a native of the Eastern states—went extinct in the 1920s when its environment, open grassland, was colonized by spreading forests. The endangered Kirtland's warbler needs young stands of jack pine. The Furbish lousewort, an endangered plant, prefers disturbed soils.

But federal preservation science, pursuing mythological ideals of "primeval forests" ignores the needs for these creatures. Rather than promoting open habitats they need, it is obsessed with "restoring" ancient forests that never existed. President Clinton's ecosystem plan for the west slope forests of the Pacific Northwest, for example, would "restore" old-growth forests until they cover 65 percent of the region, even though solid evidence suggests that these mature trees seldom or never comprised more than 45 percent of the forest cover during the last several thousand years.

◆ ◆ ◆

But even though ecosystems management is flawed science, it remains popular, especially within the environmental community and federal agencies. Greens like it because it perpetuates the myth of wilderness. Bureaucrats appreciate its capacity to obscure accountability: when things go wrong, they can blame "nature." And both greens and bureaucrats like the ecosystem concept because it provides a rationale for infinite expansion of wilderness areas. Whenever biota of a sanctuary fail to stabilize, this is taken as proof that to "protect the complete ecosystem" the preserve must be expanded.

◆ ◆ ◆

Why aren't scientists blowing the whistle on this fraud? How can they stand by silently and let bad scholarship undermine preservation? The answer is that government uses rewards and threats to discourage or squash criticism.

To be sure, federal preservation research was never very good. National Park Service efforts, for example, have been inadequate for decades. As long ago as 1963, a prestigious committee of the National Academy of Sciences lambasted the agency for lacking "competent research scientists." Yet by 1992, the National Research Council found there had been little improvement during the intervening 29 years. And this failure, the council said, "is rooted in the culture of the NPS."

But added to this anti-science tradition is the fact that many governmental and university researchers have been co-opted by perks and grants that public agencies lavish on loyal scholars. Call it hush money, where researchers receive research privileges in exchange for silence. This way, the science establishment has become just another interest group feeding at the public trough, where it exercises considerable influence over what academic papers get published. Professors who accommodate policy makers benefit handsomely from federal largesse and rise to prominent positions in their profession, where they sometimes suppress the views of scholars with whom they disagree. Empowered to help disburse federal millions, they are the gatekeepers of politically correct research.

Such discrimination is what Charles Kay experienced. As an independent scholar who speaks his mind, he's been blackballed from the U.S. preservation science club so works primarily as an ecological consultant to Parks Canada—an agency that, unlike its American counterparts, recognizes the importance of historical ecology.

◆ ◆ ◆

Ecosystems management, therefore, is both a license for neglecting and a motivation for hiding the truth about federal lands. And when co-optation fails to silence critics, authorities resort to coercion.

For example, in 1993 a member of the Interagency Grizzly Bear Study Team in Yellowstone (who requested anonymity) was severely reprimanded and punished for challenging the accuracy of official pronouncements claiming that the park's grizzly population was increasing, when data clearly showed it declining. Authorities, he told me, erased the hard disk of his computer, took his research data away and began opening his mail.

In my 1986 book, "Playing God in Yellowstone," I told the stories of many who suffered this way, including: Park Service Everglades scientists James Kushlan, who was not permitted to publish the results of his work showing some ways that hands-off management was failing in Everglades; the eminent Yellowstone grizzly bear scholars, John and Frank Craighead, whose study privileges in Yellowstone were abruptly terminated by the Park Service for objecting to its version of "natural regulation"; and U.S. Fish & Wildlife grizzly-bear expert Robert B. Finley, the Craigheads' successor who suffered a similar fate.

But as Keigley and Kay's testimony reveals, this coercion continues to be practiced by many federal agencies. Consider: When Douglas Larson, a U.S. Army Corps of Engineers hydrologist, discovered the leakage from a National Park Service waste treatment plant was contaminating Crater Lake—hitherto one of the purest bodies of water on Earth—he was branded a troublemaker and made unwelcome in the park. Officials, blaming the pollution on outside sources, urged the Corps to fire Larson. Nothing was done about the pollution for 20 years.

In 1992, National Park Service geologist James Quinlin, one of the world's leading experts on underground rivers and a resident scholar at Mammoth Cave, Kentucky, was forced to leave the agency. Quinlan refused a superintendent's order to "research" what he considered "fraudulent."

The same year, Ron Mastroguiseppe, chief naturalist and forest ecologist in Redwood National Park since 1968, was fired by the National Park Service for such transgressions as criticizing the park's expensive and misguided efforts to "restore" redwood forests in that park.

In 1940 when Joseph Stalin ruled the Soviet Union, he installed a loyal follower, Trofim Denisovich Lysenko, as director of the Institute of Genetics of the Academy of Sciences of the U.S.S.R. This in effect made Lysenko ruler of biological sciences for the entire country. The man was actually a quack who touted a spurious doctrine known as "Michurinism"—an hypothesis that denied the mountains of evidence supporting modern evolutionary theory. But since Lysenko had Stalin behind him, his pronouncements reigned supreme. Collective farms were ordered to use Michurian methods, which resulted in massive crop failures, leading to death by starvation of millions. But few dared challenge Lysenko, for those who did were often shipped to the Siberian gulags. Lysenko set back Soviet biology more than three decades.

But today in America, we are in danger of repeating Stalin's mistake. For here, too, we have an official science, called natural regulation or ecosystems management. Like Lysenko's ideas, it isn't science and it is failing. And although scholars who disagree with this spurious doctrine aren't sent to labor camps, they often find their reputations assaulted and careers disrupted.

Affronts to freedom and nature represent the Dark Side of environmental science. And like Lysenko's, it is inflicting grievous wounds on the integrity of science itself.

Such is what the lawmakers glimpsed that day—what is, perhaps, the greatest scientific fraud in American history. Let's hope that now this has been brought to light, Congress and the administration, after decades of indifference, will finally do something about it. ■

California giant sequoias flourished under Native American forest management.

UPDATE: "The Dark Side" was written in 1997, but remains up-to-date. As the French writer Alphonse Karr observed in 1849, "The more things change, the more they remain the same." Nothing proves this point more emphatically than the stubborn incompetence of federal environmental management. Take the Park Service: In 1933, a prestigious independent study found national parks to be ecological disaster areas and their science nonexistent. In 1963, the National Academy of Sciences reported that the agency lacked "competent research scientists." Yet, by 1992 the Academy could find little improvement and concluded that scientific ineptitude was "rooted in the culture of the NPS."

FALL 1999

THE WILD LIFE OF ALLAN SAVORY

This biologist has been spreading the gospel of holistic management to the masses on several continents. Is this extraordinary man a genius or simply a contradiction? Is he saving the world or frightening scientists?
By C.J. Hadley

Allan Savory is a botanist and zoologist with a history as varied as the flora and fauna of the country in which he was born. Rhodesia was a white-ruled British territory and when he was a member of the Rhodesia Party, Savory broke ranks, crossed the aisle and worked for the black vote. Soon after, he had to flee the country in fear of his life.

He landed in Texas in the early '70s, and now lives in New Mexico, but for most of his 63 years, this maverick has been wandering wild places trying to stop desertification, which is a symptom of a worldwide and deadly serious loss of biodiversity.

"As a youngster, my only aim in life was to live in the African bush forever." He had that opportunity but ended up "forsaking it in order to work toward saving the wildlife that was my reason for being in the bush. Even in the wildest areas, the land was deteriorating, in fact turning to desert, rendering it ever less able to support life of any kind. I was determined to find a way to reverse this process."

Savory worked as a biologist, soldier, public servant, member of parliament, president of a political party, farmer, rancher, consultant. "Throughout that," he says, "there was constantly just one theme—poor land means poor people, social upheaval, political unrest. We farmers and ranchers have destroyed more civilizations than armies have done. Armies change civilizations. We farmers and ranchers destroy them; they never rise again. And I've been obsessed with this problem of why this is happening, why it's happened for 10 to 15,000 years, and why we've never been able to stop it."

Biodiversity loss, caused by humans, is taking place at a faster rate than at any time in history. "Desertification is a symptom of the loss of biodiversity caused by overloading the air through the burning of fossil fuels, biomass burning, chemicals, fertilizer, agriculture, pollution, burning of national parks and forests," says Savory. "Scientists only have three tools—rest, technology and fire, so they try to justify fire when technology fails, but no fire lit by a human being is natural. Put those three together and they are now threatening not just trees and birds and fish. These are now threatening human survival."

Savory's quest took him on a surprising route. He was compelled to work with farmers and ranchers, whose management he believed was responsible for initiating the deterioration. He's on public record in Rhodesia (now Zimbabwe) saying, "Let's shoot every damn cow and any bloody rancher that stands in the way" because he could see no point of being in the army, and defending his nation, when ranchers were raping it behind him. "My feelings are very, very deep as an environmentalist and I don't particularly like cattle, but I ended up running them on my own ranches, which used to be just elephants and lions and buffalo." He did change his mind and many times has said, "The number one public enemy is the cow. But the number one tool that can save mankind is the cow. We need every cow we can get back out on the range. It is almost criminal to have them in feedlots which are inhumane, antisocial, and environmentally and economically unsound."

Constantly searching for new ideas that worked, he thought all that had to be done was to get ecologists into parliament to produce change. "Well, I couldn't produce a scrap of change even when I was president of a political party."

He discovered remorseless spread of deserts and the human impoverishment that always resulted was related to management, but more fundamentally to the way people were making management decisions, whether or not those people lived or worked on the land. "Though our fate as a civilization is tied to the land and its health, and though millions of ordinary people in making their living from the land control that fate to a large degree, unless these people have the support of the hundreds of millions of others who depend on their efforts, they cannot succeed."

He read voraciously. He admires Thomas Samuel Kuhn, who wrote "The Structure of Scientific Revolutions." In it Kuhn talks about science advancing through shifting paradigms. "What he discovered of our scientists, and I know it's true of me, is that we have these effects that flow from our deep beliefs and our training. The information which fits our beliefs we see very quickly and easily. The data which does not fit our beliefs is almost invisible to us. We just cannot see it."

It's a deeply held belief that removing cattle from the public lands will heal it. No proof is necessary because it fits the paradigm. It is a deeply held belief that trampling by cattle is destructive to plants and soils. Cattle have been blamed for destruction of water points and rivers for thousands of years—because it fits the paradigm.

"General Jan Christiaan Smuts, a botanist by love, a lawyer by training, a soldier and statesman by force of circumstance, a brilliant man, fought through the Boer War and two world wars. Although not an Englishman, he served in the British cabinet. When he was out of office as prime minister of South Africa he wrote a book called 'Holism and Evolution.' He studied the development of the human personality. It was an obsession and he studied how it developed from solid matter through life, mind, to human personality. He pointed out that in this entire development from solid matter there were no parts. He warned us that we would never understand the world until we studied wholes. The concept of a part is totally alien to the world. Now when you think of it, that was staring us in the face."

ALLAN SAVORY © C.J. HADLEY

Eroding soil is the biggest single export from the United States, billions of tons outweighing all grain, timber, military hardware and commercial products—even with the greatest know-how in the world. Where there used to be soil cover there is none and all soil cover comes from life. Once there are exposed soils there is erosion, noneffective water cycles, mud slides off California, ever-increasing floods in Texas and along the Mississippi. "These floods and this flood damage will just get worse and worse and worse and the deserts will just keep advancing, advancing, advancing until somebody, someday, finally understands what I'm saying."

Savory is handsome, serious, jaunty, often sporting khakis, a tweed cap and an impish smile. He can charm easily, but his barbed tongue is just as likely to devastate. He's been called "an abrasive personality," "brilliantly original," "an offshoot of the loony left." He is truly unique. But his tone does not denote his real personality, which is gentle, intellectual and kind. But after more than four decades of research and work, his deep frustrations show because he sees history repeating itself, again and again.

"We used to burn people at the stake for coming up with truly original work and, tragically, one way or another throughout my life, I've tended to think ahead and come up with stuff that to me seems common sense but to other people seems way out and threatening." When his book, "Holistic Resource Management" was first published in 1988, he couldn't even get it reviewed. But it, and an update, has been selling slowly and consistently since and now 17 universities are using the textbook.

Savory's first job in the United States was to convince government and academia that desertification was not due to overgrazing or overstocking, as was commonly thought, but due to bad decision making. "That was a red rag to the bull, to all academics, to all universities." His thought processes were contrary to the deeply held beliefs of ranchers, academics, scientists. "It's the opposite of what people believed so I was roundly condemned." The dean of agriculture at Montana State University once told Savory, "We have no argument with you. We've got to heed the new way, holistic thinking and what you're saying, but our problem is what do we teach? All the textbooks are written the old way."

For years there have been antidesertification conferences around the world, some sponsored by the United Nations. "The developed countries are spending billions to cut the effects of greenhouse gasses," said the executive secretary to the United Nations at the biggest environmental meeting ever held in Africa. "We must show them that desertification is a global environmental problem and if they don't do something they'll feel the consequences themselves." He also said desertification "arises from placing too much pressure on the land, often because of overgrazing."

Savory has heard all this before. "That's just like the Royal Navy," he says with a sigh. "Captain James Lancaster sold four ships to India in 1601. He gave the crew on one ship limes and they got no scurvy. The other three ships got no limes and 50 percent of the crew died. That was pretty convincing evidence but because the Royal Navy is a bureaucracy, led by brilliant officers, they discussed and argued about that for approximately 150 years at which point James Lind, a surgeon in the Navy repeated it, and got patients to recover. Then the Royal Navy argued another 49 years before they accepted it." It took the Merchant Marine 70 more years to follow suit.

Nothing has changed. "You are dealing with humans and bureaucracies. Every environmental organization is a bureaucracy. Every university is a bureaucracy. Every one of these international agencies is a bureaucracy. We've gone for nearly 50 years already since we knew that overgrazing was not due to too many animals, and we've probably got another 100 years to go before they will accept new scientific thinking."

Savory likes the saying, The whole is greater than the sum of its parts, "but," he says, "when you put brilliant individuals in a bureaucracy, it's one of the few exceptions where the whole is less than the sum of the parts."

Savory hates cows and yet he admits to damaging an African wildlife preserve irreparably because he insisted on removing domestic livestock.

There is some light. Hundreds of ranchers are working with the Center for Holistic Management (recently renamed the Allan Savory Center for Holistic Management in honor of the man behind the cause). Unfortunately, people in power are still not listening.

This is the age of specialists and one problem is, scientists who study a single topic all have very dogmatic opinions. "All of them are probably right, from their point of view, but none of them are seeing the whole. Now, when you see the whole, you might get a totally different opinion, but the universities haven't trained scientists to look at the whole. With our scientific ways, if we had a Ph.D. in hydrogen and a Ph.D. in oxygen, we could bring them together to manage water but how much would they know about water? Nothing. They wouldn't even know it existed. It's only now that a theory of chaos is coming into being—people are beginning to take the word holistic seriously."

Savory asks if I like watching the sun rise. When assured that I do, he says, "Well, it doesn't rise and it doesn't set, it stays absolutely still and we've known that for 300 years but you've not been able to change. Now that shift in paradigm from a mechanical, linear, mechanistic world of today's science, to a mind-boggling, complex, holistic world that only functions in wholes and patterns and energy—for that shift to take place is going to be an even bigger shift than the sun staying still. And we've got to make that shift if we're going to survive as a species."

His teachings are, indeed, a major shift. "Holistic management is a unique, goal-driven, decision-making process that integrates human values with economic and environmental concerns, resulting in management that is proactive and sound—socially, ecologically and economically. Practitioners have learned how to restore the land profitably through practices that mimic nature. Many others have merely sought a more rewarding personal or family life. It has worked in communities—with a common vision that reflects what the people there value and hope to accomplish."

Savory has worked for governments on several continents, including the World Bank in North Yemen. "They believe, as everybody does, that deserts have too much livestock and too many nomads abusing them. I showed them evidence that desertification was human, man-made through inadequate use. The man who headed the team, Wade Gregory, was intrigued because it made sense to him. Rain fell while we were there—an inch of rain—and I was able to take a picture of the flood and the next day was able to take a picture of bone-dry ground. Not a meter of that rain was effective and I explained how it was due to rest and not due to overgrazing and there's a consequence of that."

Because they couldn't understand Savory's report, they asked if he would show them examples, so he chartered three planes and flew a dozen people around some projects he was doing in the United States. "I showed them good and bad. We went to a Texas ranch in the middle of a drought. We had doubled the livestock, increased it by another 209 pairs, cut the supplementary feed in half. It was the only ranch to do it in the whole of Texas that I'm aware of and I showed them grass right up to the water points. They looked at it all and it absolutely blew up in my face. They wrote letters denouncing me and sent them all over the place."

A Frenchman who was there told him years later, "Allan, how naive you were. We had just spent $20 billion on antidesertification work around the world. Members of that group you brought together were our specialists and you took us in the middle of a drought and showed us that! You showed them how clever you were and how stupid they were. Did you expect us to applaud you?"

There have been so many similar ego-deflating success stories that the Center now, as a matter of policy, refuses to do any demonstrations. "We just won't do them because they are counterproductive. The more successful the demonstration, the greater the anger and hatred. And it's heartbreaking if you're trying to move humans into a more constructive course. Humans find it very hard to accept new thinking."

Holistic management decision making, among other things, has helped increase beef production; in four years grass types jumped from six to 23 on a single ranch in northeastern New Mexico, markedly improving biodiversity; riparian areas have improved along with the watersheds; and ground cover has increased. In Namibia, Savory was given some of the worst farms available, "so I couldn't wreck it. They were very frank about it. They said it was beyond reclamation." He took 4,000 acres and pushed his ideas to the breaking point. He tried to make it fail. "And in five years, we couldn't. It just got better and better, and we were producing five times as much meat per acre from what was bare ground where I would have given you $100 if you could find a single perennial grass plant. We produced solid perennial grassland with no reseeding, no capital, no anything, just changing the animal behavior and planning the grazing."

Highy trained scientists tried to manage world desertification. How much did they know about the whole? Nothing.

When he was exiled, he couldn't return to the test farm for four years and it collapsed. No animals left. Back to bare ground. "That was a very big lesson to me and the mistake was mine. All the years we ran it, I flew in frequently and told the managers what to do. Guided them…thought I was teaching them, but I wasn't."

He admits they had become consultant-dependent. They didn't understand why they were doing things. "They said the collapse was due to drought. I told them drought didn't overgraze plants. What did you do when I left? They said, 'Breathed a sigh of relief.' I asked, Why? And they said, 'Well, we didn't have to do all that paperwork and planning.' What else? 'We just kept on with the short-duration grazing rotation and moved the cattle every one to two days, watching the grass and the cattle.' Well that's enough to wreck anything. You can't do that."

If you read Savory's books, if you've listened to every talk he's ever given in the United States, he's always insisted, "Don't do that." But his teaching is complex, and, once again, it's new. And, he says for the zillionth time, "Holistic management is not a grazing system; it's a decision-making process. I have tried to show ranchers it was about decision making on whether to build fence, how to graze the animals, should you do management-intensive grazing, should you do planned grazing? There are a lot of decisions that have to be made. They just couldn't get it. They liked management-intensive grazing and did that. Fine. Someday you'll come unstuck. And if you are in a nonbrittle environment, it will be very forgiving, you'll get away with it probably for your life. You can rotate stock for years and years and not see a problem but, if you're in a brittle environment, you'll come unstuck rather quickly.… We spend too much time on grazing and fencing. We've got to start thinking in different terms. Something beyond production. It has to be about caring."

Savory is asked about collaboration and Coordinated Resource Management Plans. "It's nice to get together but the land isn't deteriorating because we weren't collaborating. And you can't manage holistically without collaborating so it is a first step, but planting willows and doing those things is fiddling while Rome burns. The land was deteriorating because of conventional decision making. Even after they plant willows, please believe me that the land will continue to deteriorate until they've removed the cause of the deterioration."

He insists that cattle are not the cause. "I am an environmentalist and I'm trained conventionally as a scientist so I grew up hating cows, believing all the conventional myths. But then, from my own work and the work of others, I found that we were wrong. So I changed. Now, until more people change, the land will keep deteriorating. They will publish photographs of improved riparian areas, claim successes, get awards, but let time pass and you will find that I am right."

In major cities in the West, Las Vegas, Nevada, and Albuquerque, New Mexico—and many others—flood control has cost millions of dollars even though there's hardly any rainfall. Albuquerque gets nine inches of rain annually but its flood-control ditches are enormous. Children have drowned in them. "The reason for the floods around here is because of rest, because the land isn't used. If the land wasn't deteriorating nobody would be getting violent, and the ranchers are causing that deterioration because they insist on continuing to overrest the land."

Savory went back to basics. He asked himself, what did the forefathers of modern science try to do? They were trying to understand the world. Nature. He was trying to get people to think holistically and it caused anger, especially with government and university people. He separated scientific specialties in terms of color. When red and blue and yellow and green were mixed together they became gray. What did any scientist know of gray? The answer was nothing.

He figured it was an organizational problem. They didn't even understand each other's jargon. Scientists pulled together, each with their own strength. They formed collaborating teams, all focusing on the natural world. When he wanted to know how much the scientists knew about gray, the whole, the answer was nothing. It was a revelation. Integrated resource management started to cross train different disciplines. Highly trained scientists tried to manage world desertification. How much did they know about the whole? Nothing.

"What did we do? We reversed the process. We started from the point of view of gray, that's the whole, your whole resource space, your company, your business. We formed a holistic goal meeting your deepest values to the land, to your resource, to your life. We looked at the experts' opinions, read papers, scientific journals, went back to old knowledge, went to new knowledge, asked the right questions and tested that knowledge to see if it fit the whole. We asked, 'Is this the correct way to do this?' That's what holistic management is about. That's what gave us the breakthrough and it's almost the opposite of all the conventional management in some ways and the beauty of it is that everything good in conventional management is embraced by holistic management. You don't reject anything."

He talks about resting land and nonbrittle environments where there's high humidity and high rainfall. "Rest is the most powerful tool known to science to restore biodiversity, so if you rested major fields in England or on the East Coast or West Coast, it would come back to high biodiversity. Now, if you go to the other extreme, the very brittle environments, particularly the low-rainfall ones, rest is probably the most destructive tool known to science. Now the Forest Service and The Nature Conservancy are coming in and saying 'Let's leave that to nature' and that, by definition, means resting it. Well, that's very destructive because it's no longer natural. They don't get it because they don't understand the role of animals in nature."

Rancher George Work attended Allan Savory's first classes in holistic management in 1986 and says now, "After 13 years, I can say it is still the hardest simple thing I have ever tried to do. The lack of success we have had in some areas has not been because holistic management doesn't work; it is because we haven't practiced it properly."

There are many symptoms of biodiversity loss that are handled as problems. That is wrong. "Noxious plant invasions—if you treat these as a problem you will fail. Leaders in Montana spent over $50 million trying to kill knapweed. They may as well proclaim it the state flower because there are now more than ever. That's because it never was a problem; it's only a symptom of the loss of biodiversity. Texans have spent over $200 million chaining, poisoning, rooting up mesquite, and there's now more than ever. It never was a problem; it is a symptom of the loss of biodiversity. Small insect, animal outbreaks, locusts, etc.; another symptom. Underground water dries up. Another symptom. A beautiful example of this is the southern part of Africa. Three hundred years ago there were millions and millions of springbok and wildebeest and buffalo and giraffe and all the big game of Africa. Nine inch rainfall. Today, you can travel hundreds of miles and see maybe 50 sheep, 10 head of cattle and it's overstocked, all dried up.

"Next is dying villages and towns. People settle with their families in an area with high biodiversity and they are prosperous in farming and ranching. They form towns, villages, businesses, churches, schools. Then biodiversity starts to go. A butterfly has gone. A bird has gone that used to be there. Old ladies in tennis shoes draw attention to it and we deride them; we are worried about jobs and our cattle and farms. As the biodiversity continues to be lost, so we start to lose farmers and ranchers and the people are not sympathetic. 'Joe was stupid, he was greedy, he overstocked.' As the biodiversity loss continues, the population isn't big enough to support the schools and churches. The villages and towns fold up. The people in cities are not sympathetic. It's more workers for the factory. And as the biodiversity loss continues, finally, the cities fall. Throughout history, that has always happened."

Public enemy number one in the West is cattle. They're blamed for the bulk of these ailments, for causing deserts. The environmental movement has been trying for years to get cattle off the public lands. "You can find this in ancient Hebrew texts 2,000 years ago, blaming the nomads and their animals for causing deserts. It's a human belief of a long period. They are putting methane into the air, which is changing global weather patterns now. The public perception is that they are dripping with fat and oozing chemicals. Even people I respect deeply say you only have to control the three C's—carbon, chainsaws and cattle. Now it's very serious when you are handling the number one public enemy with the greatest problem that humanity faces threatening our very survival and you are condemned by the top ecologists and scientists in the world."

Savory has taken photographs all around the arid West and the results are not detrimental to cattle. What he has found is a horrible and frightening similarity on private ranches, on Indian land and on public land.

"On one side of the fence we have community property. Nobody loves it, nobody cares for it. There is overstocking, overgrazing, ignorance, greed. Everything that is bad. On the other side of the fence we have the best management that the United States can provide. It's the National Park Service. There is no overstocking, there are no cattle, no sheep—haven't been for 50 years. There is no stupidity, no ignorance, no greed, no communal ownership and there is all the know-how of every university in the world. Vast sums of money have been spent on range management and land management. Now, after 50 years of totally different treatments—one condemned by every ecologist, environmentalist and rancher, and the other praised by scientists—unfortunately, you can't tell which is which on a photo of a fence line between these properties. The results are the same!"

There are hundreds of sites around the West showing similar lack of success with the greatest minds working on the problem. People are in court suing each other over it, lobbyists are fighting each other in the halls of Congress, "and nobody knows what the hell they are talking about. It's time to start pulling together. It's time to start collaborating and healing and overcoming this terrible worldwide ignorance of this problem. As soon as we can get cattle back on the land where they belong and where we desperately need them, the sooner we can start to heal the land, cultures, societies, villages, etcetera."

COURTESY ALLAN SAVORY

On one side, all the things are practiced to which range science academics attribute such desertification—overgrazing and overstocking by livestock, communal tenure of land so no one cares for it, etc. On the other side is the best that mainstream range science can do—no overgrazing, no livestock, hundreds of thousands of dollars spent on soil conservation/erosion control measures, etc. Both of these totally different treatments have been in place for more than 50 years and the land desertifies much the same. There is no improvement.

The cycles of life are birth, growth, death, and decay, commonly known as a carbon cycle. When biodiversity is lost, the cycle is broken. Overgrazing is due to the time of exposure of the plant to the animal and reexposure of the plant to the animal. When a plant is grazed, it is given a few more years of life. "Severe grazing," says Savory, "is absolutely essential to maintain biodiversity."

When scientists stopped the overgrazing of plants by fencing exclosures, the plants all grew, reports were produced, and government regulations and laws were written. Then the scientists went home. "Thank God the plots remained. If you study them today you will find enormous evidence that rest doesn't work in brittle environments. There is biodiversity loss, soil erosion. Births have stopped, the carbon cycle stopped, everything is going to hell. We've removed pack hunter and we've removed herding prey and the whole breaks up. It's a disaster."

Using cattle as a tool, Savory has produced solid perennial grassland on what had become bare ground without any reseeding. "We simulated the predator with livestock and the perennial grassland returned. Just put the whole back, and there it was. You'll find the scientific method never discovers anything. Observant, creative people make discoveries. But the scientific method protects us from cranks like me."

The Center for Holistic Management has shared tremendous success with abject failures. "We had success for 15 years, then total collapse. Something was still missing. What was missing was this concept of Smuts' 'whole'. We weren't looking at the family. We weren't looking at community. We weren't looking at people. We were looking at economics and land and cattle and wildlife and it wasn't working."

Holistic management works with the whole—the people, the family, the community, the water base, the wealth. "We have to form a goal, the values of the family, their culture, language, religion. What forms of production will sustain that family or community? Visualizing the future landscape that will sustain those forms of production becomes the goal against which we make decisions. We add two more tools—animal impact and grazing—without which you cannot reverse desertification. That's why cattle are so vital to our futures now."

Long ago, Savory struck incredible opposition when he came to America. "I was one lonely insignificant little scientist with some new thinking and just got this bombardment of antagonism and resistance and hammering and hatred. And you realize you have got to keep your sense of humor, not take yourself too seriously, have good innings, and only look for recognition in your own eyes because you are not going to get it from the outside. Just do the best you can and don't worry about the rest." ■

SPRING 2000

THE WEST 2000

Ranching ▪ Farming ▪ Logging ▪ Mining ▪ Recreation.

By Tim Findley

"...a wise and frugal Government, which shall restrain men from injuring one another, shall leave them otherwise free to regulate their own pursuits of industry and improvement, and shall not take from the mouth of labor the bread it has earned. This is the sum of good government..."

President Thomas Jefferson
first inaugural address, March 1, 1801

There has always been a west in America, always and still beyond the last reach of a highway or a house with no neighbors, there has been a west that warms and promises of wilderness and opportunity.

The "West" as our generation has come to know it is perhaps still defined as it was at the end of our nation's first century in 1876, when the vast majority of the population, with six or more people per square mile, could be counted east of the 18th parallel. Beyond where that imaginary line slices down through the Dakotas west of the Mississippi and out the horn of Texas through the final reaches of the Rio Grande was said then to be The West.

Some say now it doesn't begin until you cross the great divide of the Rockies. Some say it doesn't exist at all, except as an expanse of lesser-settled space between the coastal regions. The West is less a locale or a region in America today than it is an idea, an image coming to mind of somewhere still presiding over the natural heritage belonging to us all.

United States Public Lands

It is a surprisingly difficult figure on which to find general agreement, but the United States is vastly more "publicly" owned than most Americans realize. Even the noted liberal economist, John Kenneth Galbraith, was stunned to discover in the 1970s the extent of government ownership in the United States that he recognized as exceeding, "the combined areas of Germany, France, Italy, Belgium, Holland, Switzerland, Denmark and Albania.

"Where socialized ownership of land is concerned," Galbraith wrote prior to the collapse of the Soviet Union, "only the USSR and China can claim company with the United States."

The extent of federal ownership seems to vary by accounting methods used in different administrations, but it is generally agreed to extend over about one million square miles, nearly a third of the total U.S. land mass, with by far the largest federal holdings in the West. Together with state, county, and Indian trust lands it is estimated that 42 percent of all the land in the United States is owned and controlled by government.

Nowhere is that more evident than in the West where federal authority over lands is divided among four agencies (in rounded figures):

- The U.S. Bureau of Land Management (Department of Interior) with 268 million acres—an area larger than the original 13 colonies;
- The U.S. Forest Service (Department of Agriculture) with 191 million acres;
- The U.S. Park Service (Department of Interior) with 77 million acres;
- The U.S. Fish & Wildlife Service (Department of Interior) with 87 million acres.

That is more than 600 million acres in all, two-thirds of it in the West. In several western states, federal ownership amounts to the majority of the state land mass. Nevada is 87 percent federal land, for example. Alaska is more than 65 percent federally owned, and combined with state lands, 95 percent government-owned. By contrast, the states of New York, Massachusetts, Illinois, Kansas, and Texas each have less than two percent federal land.

Allowed uses of these lands held by the federal government vary among the agencies directed to oversee them, but unlike the development of private property in the East from sale and homesteading of the public domain, western lands following the Civil War proved to be too arid and infertile to provide sustenance for a family on a 640-acre homestead. Offering more land favored more trouble. In a compromise meant to bring more order to westward expansion there was established much larger communal pasture lands on which permits for use would be granted and managed by the federal government. The birth of federal authority over the West was intended as a democratic means of distributing its wealth.

Until 1976, with the passage of the Federal Lands Poli-

Thunderstorm over the western Great Plains along the outwash of the Arkansas River west of Cañon City, Colorado.

cy Management Act (FLPMA), it was understood that fees for use of these communal pasture lands would be only intended to cover costs of federal oversight. FLPMA demanded the fees be tied to "fair market value" of the land itself, and at the same time directed that the government not "devolve," or sell to private ownership any of these lands. In effect, private ownership of lands in the West has been restricted since the 1870s as a means of encouraging cooperative production, and now is all but prohibited on remaining public lands as a means of retaining federal control.

Federal ownership or expansion of authority over additional lands in the West has continued over the last decade at a rate of about one million acres a year. The Clinton administration proposed measures in the last year that would provide $900 million annually for government acquisition of more land from "willing sellers." Short of Congressional approval for that, administrative and executive authority continues to be used in the West to acquire more public land, sometimes in a guise of purchase by a group such as The Nature Conservancy, which then turns the land over to the government, usually at a profit to the "nonprofit" sponsor.

From such circumstances, then, it may be easier to perceive the differences of opinion toward federal management between those who live in the East and those who live in the West. And yet, even more dramatic distinctions have been established in the last 30 years since the passage in 1964 of the National Wilderness Act.

**"These wild things, I admit,
had little human value until mechanization
assured us of a good breakfast,
and until science disclosed the drama
of where they came from
and how they live."**

ALDO LEOPOLD
"A SAND COUNTY ALMANAC," 1948

In our times, Aldo Leopold and his "Almanac" is more frequently quoted by environmentalists than Henry David

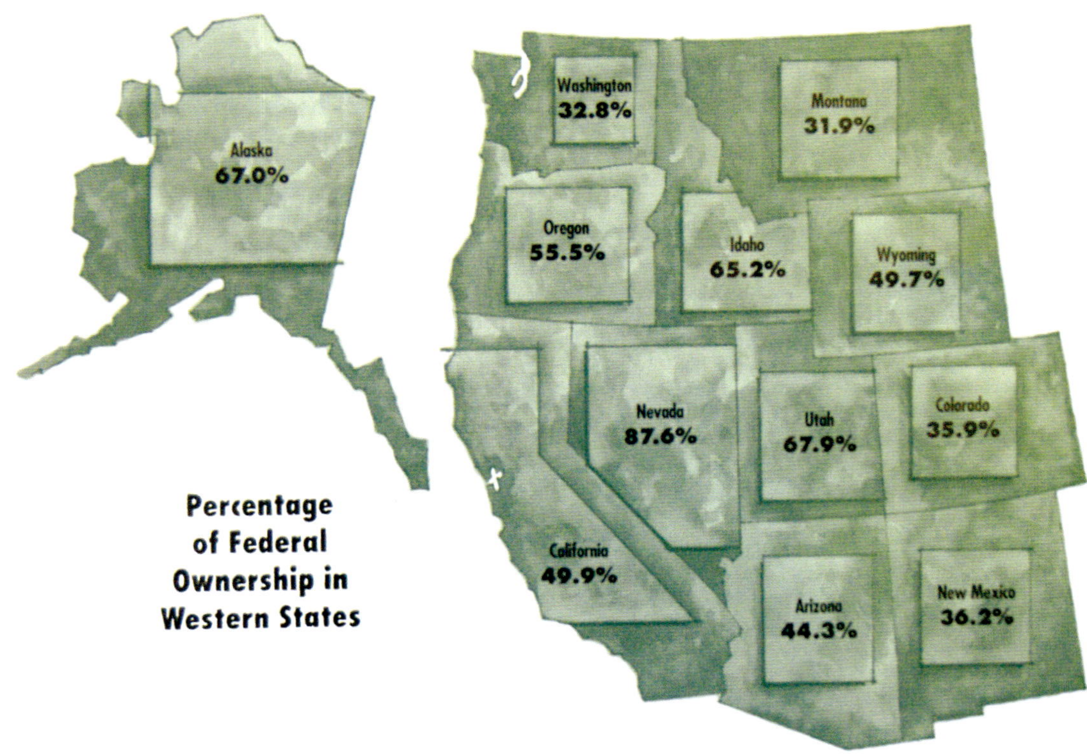

ILLUSTRATION © JOHN BARDWELL

Thoreau or even John Muir. Leopold had been both a farmer and a forest ranger. It was in large part through his efforts that portions of the Gila National Forest in New Mexico were designated as the nation's first wilderness area by administrative action of the U.S. Forest Service in 1924. There were similar administrative acts that would expand wilderness and primitive areas to about 15 million acres by the time the United States was entering its post World War II economic expansion. It was just about then, in 1948, and shortly after his death fighting a grass fire in Wisconsin, that Leopold's only published work was produced. The "Almanac" became an epistle for preservation that would inspire creation of the Wilderness Society and adherents to a belief in preserving the wild all over the world. Yet as much as he in his work blamed economic expansion and "Henry Ford" for destruction of the wild, Leopold and others of his time held no illusions about theirs being a spiritually inspiring, but little practiced, desire for a return to the primitive. Least of all did he expect the government to take on a task, "too large, too complex, or too widely dispersed" in dividing the land between its natural presence and its ultimate use.

AN EXPANDING WILDERNESS

Propelled in part by a nascent environmental movement that did not trust federal agencies to protect wildlands through administrative action, the U.S. Congress in 1964 passed the National Wilderness Act, establishing a National Wilderness Preservation System and reserving to Congress the authority to designate areas suggested for their wilderness potential. Fifty-four areas covering nine million acres of U.S. Forest Service land were immediately set aside.

By 1968, with the impetus of "legacy" lands deriving from political sponsorship, Congress began expanding the Wilderness System, bringing it to 631 areas covering nearly 144 million acres by 1994, more than 10 times the amount of designated wilderness known to Leopold in his time.

Current suggestions and proposals by federal agencies and special-interest groups propose expansion of the Wilderness System by at least another 90 million acres, thus incorporating more than 25 percent of all federal lands and nearly 10 percent of all land in the United States as wilderness.

Alaska would contain most of these proposed wilderness lands (up to 55 percent) and the greatest areas of wilderness would be in the western states, but only the states of Connecticut, Iowa, Kansas and Rhode Island have no lands designated or recommended as wilderness.

From the beginning of discussions, the most difficult aspect has been in defining what constitutes "wilderness." Especially from 1970 when the Forest Service began its Roadless Area Review and Evaluation (RARE I), challenges were presented by the states and other interests. It was not until a compromise was reached in 1984 that Congress enacted new laws establishing wilderness covering nearly nine million acres in 21 states, that the Act really took hold.

Numerous exemptions for uses such as logging, grazing and mining were provided and implemented in the 88 separate wilderness laws enacted by Congress up to 1994, leaving the conclusion that wilderness is defined as whatever Congress says it is. Nevertheless, the standard definition held by environmentalist groups is that of "areas where the earth is untrammeled by man, where man himself is a visitor who does not remain."

The most radical proposal of The Wildlands Project put forward in 1992 by David Foreman of Earth First! and others suggests that up to 50 percent of the continental United States (all of it in the West) should be restored to a condition dominated by predators and replicating the Pleistocene era, more than 12,000 years ago. Although seeming incredible in its suggestions to limit human habitation to permitted zones within and around the wilderness, the Wildlands Project is reported to have found favorable support among the Clinton administration.

Since reaching a peak soon after the establishment of Wilderness Areas with limited access, recorded visitor use has remained stable or shown a decline in every year, even taking into account additional designated areas. The reintroduction of predators, including wolves, grizzly bears and other carnivores has increased.

TSADO/NASA/TOM STACK & ASSOCIATES

Alaska from space. More than half the proposed wilderness acreage is in Alaska.

"Burn down your cities and leave our farms, and your cities will spring up again as if by magic, but destroy our farms and the grass will grow in every city in the country."

William Jennings Bryan, 1896

As a demographic region of the United States, the West continues to grow at a rate faster than the East, and has certainly established a population base deserving at least of equal consideration to the traditionally held political authority of the original colonies. But population alone is a deceiving figure. Even though the concentration of people on the coasts shows signs today of shifting into less populated areas, the limitation of available private land in the West creates zones of urbanized development in concentrated

© PAUL MOBLEY

The Aldrich family produces row crops in Excelsior Springs, Missouri. FROM LEFT: *Pam, Bethany, Lane and Darrell. The vast majority of farms in the United States—86 percent—remain family farms.*

pockets such as Las Vegas, Nevada. There is, in short, a bigger difference than ever today in the westerner who is "all hat, and no cows."

Those who still gain their livelihood from rural areas, whether they be farmer, rancher, hardware salesman or barber, recognize the change being brought upon them by technology and spendable wealth. The cultural significance of agrarian America, especially in the West, and not for the first time, is at a crossroad.

◆ ◆ ◆

Of the more than 268 million Americans alive today, it is no surprise that fewer than four million, or 1.6 percent, live on rural farms. Not all of them are farmers. Nevertheless, federal census figures indicate that nearly 25 percent of the population lives in rural areas with fewer than 2,500 residents. Compare that to 1940, when the U.S. had less than half its present population, but 43 percent of Americans were considered to live in rural areas and nearly 23 percent of them on rural farms.

That fewer actual farmers must be producing more to feed a growing nation is one conclusion to be drawn. Another is that steadily more non-farmers dominate rural social and economic foundations. "Rural," in fact, is not officially rural at all any more, but referred in government terms as "nonmetro," meaning that the region is unattached to a city of 50,000 or more.

It is in that vague idea of our rural regions that population is reported to have grown between 1990 and 1996 at a pace double that of the entire 1980s. In part, this is due to increasing life expectancy among the "baby boom" generation born during and after World War II and leading now to more older citizens "retiring" to the countryside. This has resulted in an increase in the number of elderly in "nonmetro" or rural areas. Today, children under the age of 10 outnumber preteens and teenagers in metropolitan areas. This is not the case in rural areas, where the school population tends to be older.

A conclusion from such statistics is that the American agriculturalist, or family reliant on farming, ranching, logging or mining, is part of an aging and dwindling class of society that retains land in amounts disproportionate to their population. They are being overtaken, in some views, by the "sprawl" of expanding urban wealth.

Even more evident, however, is the steadily rising cost of real estate in favored coastal areas especially, causing expansion into more affordable regions that were once rural. Two-acre "farms" and "view" ranches are replacing marginally productive agricultural operations.

Astonishingly, one researcher at the University of California at Davis, Steven C. Blank, produced a paper ("The End of the American Farm?") in 1999 suggesting that, "The U.S. economy no longer needs agriculture and is rapidly outgrowing it." In general, more Americans with more options provided by technology and transportation are choosing to make their homes in rural regions, and in most cases without intending to do so, are altering the economic and social description of rural America. Not that they aren't welcome, but because so many misunderstand, vital elements of our future are being put at risk by casting aside what has been learned from the past.

"The best business you can go into you will find on your father's farm or in his workshop. If you have no family or friends to aid you, and no prospect opened to you there, turn your face to the great West, and there build your home and fortune."

Horace Greeley, 1855

Not as pithy and memorable as "Go West, young man," but more accurate of Greeley's Advice to Aspiring Young Men, it was a suggestion followed by many who sought their fortunes in the West, as well as by others who remained "on the farm." But a century-and-a-half makes a big difference, both in farms and fortunes. On the website of the American Farmland Trust in 1999, there was a constantly changing figure on the amount of farmland in America being lost. It rolled on steadily at a rate of nearly an acre a minute, but it turned out it was going too slow. A report in December 1999 by the Department of Agriculture concluded that farmland was being lost to development at an ever faster rate in the 1990s—more than 16 million acres between 1992 and 1997, 3.2 million acres a year. Most of those losses were of the most productive prime farmland near urban centers. The losses continue at a rate of more than 50 acres an hour.

As an occupation in America, farming has been declining since the beginning of the 20th century. But if the American farmer is ever more rare, he or she is still ever more studied.

The federal government defines a farm as any establishment from which $1,000 or more in agricultural products would normally be sold in a year. Latest government reports indicate there are slightly fewer than two million farms in the U.S., covering about 968 million acres, a decline of about seven percent in numbers of farms since 1987 and about 3.1 percent in land use. The average size of a farm increased over that period from 451 acres in 1987 to 471 acres in 1997. Even so, the vast majority of farms in the United States, 86 percent, remain "family" farms. Three-quarters of those farms are regarded by government statistics as "non-commercial," or "hobby" farms with gross sales under $50,000 a year, requiring some form of non-farm income to support the family.

Production of farms, however, has increased at a rate of two percent a year since 1948, according to federal statistics, due to the use of fertilizers and improved technologies. But such production statistics may be misleading. U.S. agricultural output did show remarkable gains after World War II, reaching a growth in essential grain production alone in the 1970s of 2.3 percent, but the rate of growth since then has been declining to only 0.5 percent in the 1990s, leading some analysts to conclude that U.S. agricultural production is near its limit from existing farmlands.

Given anticipated global population and income growth, food demand is expected to increase by at least 64 percent over the next 25 years.

In its most dire prediction, the American Farmland Trust forecasts that if the rate of farmland being lost continues, the United States would be forced to go from a food exporting nation to a food importing nation by the middle of this century.

THE FARMERS

Fewer than 10 percent of American farm operators are under the age of 35. About half the farm operators are under 55, but the number of operators 65 or older exceeds that of the 35 or younger population by three to one. (Although those oldest farm operators control about the same share of farmland, they average less than half the sales and income per farm than younger operators. They also reported less than one third of lender debt than the youngest operators.)

On farms where the operators reported farming as their major job, occupying more than half their working hours, average gross income was $132,550 a year. However, less than half the farmers surveyed by USDA reported farming to be their major occupation. Others reported a gross income averaging less than $16,000 a year.

Farms with full-time operators control more than 70 percent of farmland acreage and 79 percent of farm income, but the disparities are sometimes enormous: out of two million farms, only about 123,000, or less than seven percent, receive the majority of farm receipts. This sometimes leads to the false conclusions that the larger farms produce most of the nation's food supply (they do not) or that large-scale operations are more efficient, when in fact studies have shown that mega-farms produce a "dis-economy of scale," both in production and general values of farm economies.

Nearly 80 percent of all farmers have at least a high school education, and half of those attended college. Those with the highest education reported on average the highest gross income.

So it appears that if it's not quite "grandpa's" farm any more, family farming remains the most vital element of American agriculture, despite the fact that grandsons and granddaughters seem less and less interested. Those farming the most land, and apparently making the most money,

This is Jules Marchesseault from Dillon, Montana. He has been cattle ranching and farming since 1960. If it's not quite "grandpa's" farm any more, family farming remains the most vital element of American agriculture.

are full-time farmers between the ages of 44 and 54.

"Corporate" farms, or those with gross receipts over $250,000 a year, amount to about six percent of total farms but account for nearly 60 percent of total farm income.

"Family" farms are difficult to define, since many families have incorporated their interests, and since the averaging in of all family farms distorts the statistics. However, family-owned farm operations in the United States earning less than a gross of $250,000 a year still account for about 94 percent of total farms.

Their value cannot be defined in farm receipts alone, since the value of family farms in rural areas is reflected in goods and services produced and farm contributions to community wealth including schools and infrastructure, as well as stewardship of the land.

One index of what has occurred in the United States, however, is the steady shift in profit from food production to processors and packagers. Between 1910 and 1990, the share of agricultural profit to the farmer has been reduced from 21 percent to five percent.

"To waste, to destroy, our natural resources, to skin and exhaust the land instead of using it to increase its usefulness, will result in undermining in the days of our children the very prosperity which we ought by right to hand down to them amplified and developed."

President Theodore Roosevelt
addressing Congress in 1907

They were the words of a conservationist who in his administration withdrew more than 200 million acres of public domain from sale to private interests. Yet they were also the words of a rancher, "old four eyes" as he was once called, who credited his own spirit to his time on the range. The heart of the controversy over rangeland today is contained in that seeming contradiction, for while a large portion of the public is being led to believe that grazing is incompatible with the preservation of western public lands, it is the rancher who has conserved those lands for generations foreseen by Roosevelt.

The beef cattle herd in the United States today stands at about 98.5 million head, a relatively stable figure over the century's last decade, but representative of some increases in the East along with similar declines in herds west of the Rockies. Of that total, fewer than 25 percent of ranchers in the 11 western states utilize grazing permits on federal land to provide about a quarter of their total forage. Yet because federal ownership so dominates western land, an estimated 60 percent of cattle brought to market from the West can be traced to some grazing on "public" lands.

In many western states, there has been an alarming decline in the use of private lands for agricultural and livestock-raising purposes. The state of Montana, for example, experienced the loss of 1,000 cattle-producing operations a year between 1995 and 1998. Most of those losses were to nonagricultural purposes.

Grazing fees for use of public land were first imposed with the suggestions and help of ranchers themselves on Forest Service lands in 1905 to aid in administrative costs for maintaining those lands and protecting the rights of permit holders. In 1936, two years after passage of the Taylor Grazing Act, which also had the support of ranchers, fees were imposed on lands generally in the public domain and now administered by the Bureau of Land Management. Those earliest fees amounted to five cents per Animal Unit Month—or the amount of time a cow and calf were permitted to graze. Payments to the government for AUMs amounted to more than $10 million in 1998.

At the heart of arguments about grazing on public lands is the question of a "subsidy" provided to federal permit holders who, in theory, would have to pay more to graze on private lands.

The federal government has attempted to address that question in numerous actions, beginning with the Independent Offices Appropriation Act of 1952, which required fair market value for federal lands leased or sold, and culminating most recently in the Department of Interior's Rangeland Reform of 1994, which attempted to tie grazing costs to supposed environmental damage.

However, two laws are the key to federal grazing fees: the Federal Land Policy Management Act of 1976, and the Public Rangelands Improvement Act of 1978, both of which attempted to tie fees to the value of the land and the value of what it annually produces.

Under PRIA in 1980, grazing fees reached their highest point in history of $2.36 per AUM on BLM land and $2.41 on Forest Service land. The fees proved to be unrealistically high for production and gradually fell back to $1.35 per AUM on all public land, where they stood in 1999, while legal challenges continue over Rangeland Reform.

IS IT A SUBSIDY?

In a variety of ways, from irrigation to price supports, the federal government is said to subsidize much of American agriculture. Government subsidies in one form or another, in fact, are common in most agriculturally producing nations, and encouraged by international trade agreements. Farm "subsidies" are undeniably essential in the fundamental economic value of the cost of food, which in the United States is the lowest of all industrialized nations.

One argument over public grazing is that artificially low grazing fees amount to a net loss for the government and benefit only a small number of permit holders, some of whom represent wealthy corporations in their own right. Combined losses of the BLM and Forest Service on revenues versus costs of public grazing were reported from 1994 to 1996 to have been $66 million. In the same period, the government reported losses of $355 million on recreation and $290 million on timber.

	PUBLIC LAND COSTS PER AUM*	PRIVATE LAND COSTS PER AUM
Grazing fee or rental	$1.35	7.77
Turn out	.19	.69
Gather	3.26	.97
Routine management	4.08	3.73
Maintenance	2.23	1.55
Salting & vet services	.16	.22
Meetings	.80	.01
Death loss	3.13	.37
Misc.	.17	0
Total cost per AUM	$16.17	15.31

One reason may be found in the fact that the federal agencies are overweight in administration, requiring 78 employees per million AUMs, compared to 20 employees per million AUMs on state grazing land.

Interior Secretary Bruce Babbitt has led environmental arguments that grazing permits benefit fewer than 27,000 ranchers and less than five percent of national beef production. This may be more true as a result of continued federal pressure on small operators, but even so, 80 percent of

Tim White is parting pairs at Muddy Meadows on the Dry Ranch, 40 miles south of Jordan Valley, Oregon.

ranchers using federal lands make a net income of less than $30,000 a year, and the BLM itself estimates that 20 percent of calves shipped to feeder lots come off the public range.

The relatively small number of ranchers benefitting from grazing permits is indicative of the historic nature of the cattle industry in the West especially, in which relatively few major producers control large herds. One of the nation's largest federal grazing permits in Rock Springs, Wyo., is held by the Rock Springs Grazing Association, which actually represents nearly 50 individual ranchers.

As a result not only of stagnant cattle prices, but increasing regulations, the number of active permits on public land has declined since 1988 by about 20 percent. Reduction in allowed AUMs on some permits have declined in this decade by as much as 50 percent. That the total number of cattle remains roughly the same reflects the pressure on smaller operators, not the larger ones.

Historically, the purpose of permits on public land was to aid in organized development of the West and its settlements, something that was accomplished. Permit holders were expected to operate from their own deeded land near to the permitted range. This is still true.

Improvements on grazing permits, including fences, water and spring improvements and protection of riparian areas are the responsibility of the livestock operator and done at substantial cost to the permittee.

Fair market value for grazing fees on private lands has been estimated to be from nearly $6 per AUM to more than $17, with an average estimate of $9.80 per AUM in 17 western states. However, unlike federal leases, a private owner, not the lease holder, is responsible for all improvements and care of the cattle as well as the range.

Almost by definition, public grazing lands in the West are not as productive of forage as are private pastures and thus require more restrictive care by the permit holder. Taking into account the total costs to the permit holder, independent academic research has concluded that the total cost to ranchers grazing on public lands is about $16.17 per AUM (including the federal grazing fee), compared to an average total cost of $15.31 on private land. The fact is that it would be cheaper for the rancher to graze his cattle on private land in the West—if that land were available.

According to industry reports, since 1989 about 50

percent of federal jobs in direct land-management staff, including range conservation officers, have been eliminated. This has compressed federal management of public lands into an increasingly administrative capacity without direct involvement on the range except to impose new regulations. At the same time, the value to rural communities in employment, services and goods from permittee ranchers commonly accounts for the most stable and significant share of the local economy in ranching areas.

In a 1996 survey that asked ranchers what they would do if grazing were prohibited on public land, 21 percent said they would retire, 16 percent said they would find a new occupation, 21 percent said they would sell their private land for development. The majority, 57 percent, said they would reduce the size of their operation.

THE RANCHERS

Much as is the case in all American agriculture, cattle-raisers tend to be middleaged or older, with ranchers under the age of 35 representing the least percentage with the heaviest debt. Of ranchers surveyed, most said that between 25 and 50 percent of family income is produced from an off-ranch source.

Like farmers, independent ranchers in America today find it difficult, but not impossible, to make a living from the ranch alone. The tendency to larger corporate operations in ranching is nothing new in the West, but the cost of doing business has risen significantly in legal fees and the requirements to meet new regulations.

As with farmers, sharp disparities are evident in production and profit: A medium-sized feedlot generally east of the Rockies, for example, averages about 10,000 head of cattle, while the average cow-calf operation is 49 head. In the West, where there are fewer feedlots, a viable cow-calf operation is considered to be around 300 head.

Although herds are clearly larger in the West, smaller operations are more jeopardized by flat prices and additional regulations. Calf production in the 1990s reached its lowest point since 1952. The result has been that while ranching remains an alluring occupation for many, economic and regulatory pressures have forced others to sell their deeded land, thus contributing to urbanized development and the concentration of production into fewer large operations.

While the federal agencies acknowledge they have an "inadequate database" in public lands grazing, several western states have begun analyzing effects of recent federal policy on local economies.

In Nevada, the most heavily federalized state, a study of six counties documented a loss of public grazing by over 340,000 AUMs since 1980. The annual monetary loss to local economies in this region was estimated by the University of Nevada, Reno, to be $12.3 million a year, and a one-time loss to the affected ranching operations of $12.8 million. At least 167 full time jobs were also eliminated.

The true value and cost of public grazing is thus left to be defined by government management in context with the effect on local cultural and economic values.

"This is the forest primeval. The murmuring pines and the hemlocks... stand like Druids of old."

Henry Wadsworth Longfellow, "Evangeline," 1847

Fewer Americans experience them today, except from the passing window of an airplane or a car, yet even after the century-and-a-half since Longfellow's poem, American forests still stand as vast as they did then. In fact, even with all the harvesting and their conversion in parts to millions of acres of farm land, and even with losses to natural causes, the nation's forest land is still about two-thirds the size it was before Pilgrims landed in 1620.

The heart of the bitter arguments today is in that romantic notion of a "primeval" old-growth forest untouched by man—something that probably didn't exist even in Longfellow's time. It is in the last century, and especially in the last decade, that federal policy has prohibited uses of the forest that were prevalent even among Native Americans five centuries ago, thus "preserving" a renewable resource that our government may end up destroying.

The problem, in fact, is not too few trees, but too many, something most Americans cannot grasp amid a pressure-laden campaign against the U.S. timber industry.

In 1900, forest growth and regeneration was a fraction of annual harvest. Today, however, growth exceeds harvest by more than 33 percent. This is not merely a factor of new policy. Net annual growth of the forest has increased 55 percent since 1952, and growth per acre has increased 62 percent, largely due to new technologies and management of the industry itself.

Nearly 60 percent of U.S. forest is still on private land. Harvesting on public land today is practically nil, but even at the beginning of the decade, when harvest from public land accounted for less than 10 percent of production, growth in National Forests exceeded harvest by more than 60 percent.

For every tree harvested, seven are planted. Of the 6.2 million acres of identified old-growth timber in national forests in Oregon and Washington, virtually all of it is now set aside in areas forbidden to harvest. Another one million acres is in National Parks where harvesting has always been prohibited.

Currently proposed roadless policies on public land would cut off access to between 40 and 60 million acres of forested land. The result is a staggering growth of fuel-loaded forests exceeding 30 million acres that even the U.S. Forest Service admits is at extreme danger to wildfires of previously unheard of proportions. At the same time, the Forest Service acknowledges that even domestic demand for wood fiber will increase by at least 50 percent in the next 20 years.

Wood consumption in the U.S., measured in tons, currently accounts for 47 percent of all primary industrial raw materials consumed, roughly equivilant in weight to all metals, plastics and cement combined.

Although the United States is the world's leader in importing other raw materials, most of the wood consumed in this nation is produced and manufactured here—so far.

USE IT OR LOSE IT?

Spanish explorers in the 16th century reported they were unable to approach the Pacific Coast of this continent at times because of the heavy smoke and ash blowing out to sea from huge forest fires probably set by native inhabitants as a regularly used method for clearing the forest.

It is only in the last quarter century that researchers have begun to appreciate the extent by which Indians all over the North American continent used fire in combination with other methods to harvest the forest resource. A "primeval" forest probably no longer existed after thousands of years of development of native civilizations prior to the arrival of Europeans. In fact, early settlers frequently commented on the "park-like" forests with open savannahs and easily traveled trails. Research indicates that overgrowth of these forests may have been due to the extraordinary loss of population among natives susceptible to diseases brought by early European explorers and settlers, and in even greater measure to federal reservation policies that removed tribes from their native lands.

In 1910, the condition of the largely untended forest of northern Idaho and western Montana that foresters called, "the high lonesome," was that of an old-growth forest unmanaged in any way. There was a drought, shattered in two terrible August nights when wind and lightning set off perhaps the largest fire ever known. It raged like an open blast furnace across three million acres, killing 86 people, and leading to the establishment of Forest Service policies on fire suppression. Recovery of the forest in "the high lonesome" was said to have required at least 40 years.

Under the Clinton administration, however, the Forest Service has presented an unclear policy largely favoring "natural" causes, including wildfires, to occur. Many former Forest Service employees say it is an invitation to disaster. Not surprisingly, the timber industry has recommended that harvesting of the forest for beneficial use would serve best for managing against such wildfires. Yet permits for salvaging even dead trees on Forest Service land have been steadily reduced during the Clinton administration and in some places in the Southwest eliminated altogether.

Under the Clinton administration, the Forest Service has presented an unclear policy largely favoring "natural" causes, including wildfires, to occur. Many former Forest Service employees say it is an invitation to disaster.

THE TIMBER PEOPLE

As with other forms of agriculture, the numbers of people directly involved in logging or harvesting of the forests are only representative of a larger industry that involves trucking, mills, finished production and innumerable services and goods provided by nearby communities.

No other industry has been more dramatically affected by federal policy changes. An estimated 132,000 jobs were lost or eliminated within five years of action, or inaction, taken by the Clinton administration after listing of the spotted owl as an endangered species in 1990. Standing economies in several northwestern towns collapsed and were not replaced by promises of tourism or technology training. In California, Oregon, Washington, Idaho, and Montana alone, 318 wood mills were closed between 1989 and the new century. Nearly all of them were in small towns dependent on the mills for their economy. The direct loss in jobs was over 35,000. The indirect losses to the local economies has not been calculated.

Perhaps most importantly, however, more than four billion board feet of a completely renewable resource was withheld from production, resulting in continued overgrowth, fuel loading and insect infestation in the forests, and indirectly leading to increased harvests in Third World nations where methods of reforestation are either not utilized or unknown. Unrenewable rainforests on far less stable ground are still being destroyed in response to global demand for wood and beef.

Because the loss of jobs in the timber industry had its greatest impact on skilled middle-aged workers, even a return to harvesting levels of 1990 would require a substantial period of retraining the work force.

An ecological disaster of world-wide proportions awaits in the meantime.

◆ ◆ ◆

What was raised from the land in the West frequently went to feed those who were extracting what was regarded as its greatest wealth. America found a vault of treasure waiting there as the industrial age began. Much more than most Americans realize is still there, and still being produced by an industry as essential to the next century as it was to the last.

Although the West today still lures prospectors, mining operations exist in all 50 states, producing materials from sand to exotic isotopes, so much in such variety that it is difficult to calculate.

© TOM STACK/TOM STACK & ASSOCIATES

Logging and harvesting of the forests are representative of a larger industry that involves trucking, mills, finished production and innumerable services and goods provided by nearby communities. No other industry has been more dramatically affected by federal policy changes. An estimated 132,000 jobs were lost or eliminated within five years of action, or inaction, taken by the Clinton administration after listing of the spotted owl as an endangered species in 1990.

The value of non-fuel mining in the United States in 1997 was estimated at $39.5 billion, with the highest value in products used for construction, agriculture and manufacturing totaling $27.1 billion.

Total production of metallic minerals such as gold, zinc, iron ore, and copper was valued at $12.4 billion in that year. Coal production was nearly $20 billion.

As with all production from natural resources, the actual values of mining are spread throughout the economy, producing about $525 billion a year according to the industry, or about seven percent of the nation's Gross Domestic Product (GDP).

So obvious that it is frequently ignored, mined products are essential to virtually every other part of the economy, from agriculture to cyber-space. Yet miners are today saddled with environmental and government suspicions of being looters of the public wealth.

There are nearly 40 separate laws and regulations governing federal control of mining.

THE MINERS

As of 1997, there were 355,000 Americans reported to be directly employed in mining. They were among the highest wage-earners in U.S. industry, averaging $44,000 a year. Industry estimates are that an additional five million Americans, including government employees, earn their income from mining production. The rate of occupational injury among miners is lower than that of employees in hospitals, hotels, or retail outlets.

Mining in America today is certainly no less beset with obstacles to individual enterprise than other industries, and in some ways the most threatened of them all. That is particularly true on public land, where the Mining Act of 1872 still offers the last remaining opportunity of converting federal property into private use.

Deep mounds of regulations and requirements piled up over years stand in the way of opening a new hole in the public earth today, but mining operators have found their way through most of them in the past 25 years to produce a record of regeneration and renewal of mining lands. Tens of millions more in dollars have been invested by the industry in voluntary restoration of abandoned mines.

© JOHN BARDWELL

Newmont Twin Creeks gold mine north of Winnemucca, Nevada. It is 1,200 feet deep and growing, thanks to about 600 well-paid employees who work 24/7. After all the ore is taken, this megapit will be reclaimed.

Unlike other resources on federal lands, mining actually produces a positive return to the government of $6 for every dollar budgeted for management. (Nine state governments, however, reported returns of $35 per dollar spent on state-managed mineral lands.)

Even so, newer environmental regulations, and even international concords, have been employed in the last decade to delay or halt new mining operations or explorations in the United States. One such administrative action recommended by the Department of the Interior would halt lead mining in southeast Missouri, effectively terminating 85 percent of lead production in the U.S.

Other Department of Interior actions, however, have concentrated on imposing restrictions to mining claims in the West and demanding higher royalties from existing mines. Both actions would override aspects of the 1872 Mining Law with executive authority not subject to Congressional approval. This is in contrast to actions taken by other nations, including emerging Third World countries, to eliminate barriers to exploration and production of their mineral resources. When the Grand Staircase Escalante region of Utah was declared a National Heritage Site in 1996 by President Clinton, access was prohibited to an estimated $2 billion in exceptionally high grade coal. The need for such coal required U.S. industry to begin importing it from Indonesia.

Even with the strictest environmental regulations and controls in the world, the United States is estimated to contain a large percent of the world's resources for mineral products, metallic minerals and fuel reserves. Coal reserves alone are estimated to contain 400 years of fuel energy.

By figures of the government itself, each American relies on 46,000 pounds of new mined materials, including 7,500 pounds of coal energy, each year.

◆ ◆ ◆

As a nature-loving club, long before it became a pressure group, John Muir's Sierra Club believed that the more Americans who could participate in the enjoyment of nature, the better the chances for preserving it from other uses. A Stanley Steamer made it into Yosemite Valley in 1900, the first of what has since become an overwhelming flood of motorized visitors to the park. In recent years, others have sought more solitary experiences with nature on roads and trails suitable to off highway vehicles (OHVs) and motorized bikes. They too have a club in the half-a-million-member Blue Ribbon Coalition, but theirs is so far a losing battle to federal actions that have literally dug tank-trap trenches through previously traveled forest roads, cutting off all wheeled access.

"President Clinton is acting more like King William, and it should send chills up the spines of everyone who uses public lands."

Senator Larry Craig (R-Idaho) in a 1999 statement on U.S. Forest Service road closures

John Muir would surely be appalled at how "loved" is his Yosemite Valley today. He might be alarmed by the disturbance of motorized vehicles finding their way deeper and deeper into the forests. But it's an open question about whether even Muir would favor "locking up" more than 40 million acres of public land in the West from use by any except those who come on foot, and then, only by permission.

Rafting on the Arkansas River, Colorado.

THE RECREATIONISTS

In a way, shutting off roads to vehicular use is another surrogate method like the spotted owl of preventing logging and, as is frequently argued, creating defacto wilderness without going to the trouble of Congressional approval.

Yet recreation groups like the Blue Ribbon Coalition have been willing to aid in road maintenance and improving trails and their numbers alone would indicate some possiblity for the Forest Service to address its budget problems in another way.

Unclear figures indicate that before major road closures, off highway vehicles accounted for more than 90 million visitor days a year in the National Forests, with the figure steadily growing. The numbers could present some possibility for opportunity or, as has actually happened, for confrontation.

With roads closed, the Forest Service now contends, OHV operators cut fences and make their own roads, thus leading to more damage in the forest and to inevitable confrontations with government agents. Yet associations and industry groups have repeatedly offered help and "adopt a trail" assistance to federal authorities and have stressed environmental concerns to their memberships.

The National Off Highway Vehicle Conservation Council organized in 1990 now has members in 40 states and conducted a survey of off-road users in 1998 that determined: the average age of OHV users is 39; nearly 60 percent are married with family; one-third are employed as professionals; and more than half have attended college. Average income was placed at $44,000 a year. Not only are they not likely to destroy existing roads and trails, polls among OHV users have indicated support for paying fees for use, so long as those fees were directed to actual maintenance.

As with other aspects in the issue of public lands, the argument over roads has simply been inflamed by what seem to be arbitrary actions of the federal administration on behalf of a single environmental agenda that favors nonmanagement of the forest and puts aside the investments of the past.

- The network of Forest Service roads represents a distance eight times longer than the interstate highway system.
- Many of the roads were built to accommodate heavy trucks and thus easily handle cars and recreation vehicles on weekends. Recreational use is estimated to account for 98 percent of traffic.
- The Forest Service reported average cost for one mile of such a road in 1997 as $64,000. (This is an extreme figure when compared, for example, to Montana's estimated cost of a state-built timber road of $5,000 a mile.)
- The maintenance backlog for road repair by the Forest Service is currently over $10 billion.
- Digging tank traps and closing access to up to 60 million acres of forest doesn't seem a likely solution, but it is so

far the policy of the Forest Service.

◆ ◆ ◆

Bruce Babbitt brought a pompous and argumentative attitude with him when he moved from the League of Conservation Voters (LCV) into the top job at the Department of Interior. The former Arizona governor had aspired to be President of the United States, and short of that to become a Justice of the U.S. Supreme Court, but when Bill Clinton named him as Secretary of the Interior, it was with the urging of politically powerful environmental interests. From the beginning, Babbitt did not disappoint them, naming no less than 20 executives from their own nonprofit ranks to key posts in the nation's land-managing agency.

Interior had long been regarded as the most thankless Cabinet post, and the least likely to promote a future career. It carried the baggage of inevitable controversies over management of the nation's enormous public lands, and of wrenching decisions to be made between competing interests. Despite his well-known arrogance, Babbitt regarded himself as a peacemaker. He has presided over the last eight years in perhaps the most contentious period in the history of the department.

WHAT ARE WE FIGHTING OVER?

Americans are not at war with each other. More than ever today, we are more alike than we are apart in our beliefs, ambitions, and ideology. Clearly the most powerful and richest nation on the planet, we are at once its greatest consumers and its most ardent protectors, a seeming contradiction of ourselves.

Most Americans today say they regard themselves as "environmentalist," because to say otherwise would deny some of the most evident truths about abuses caused by human behavior in the past. Still, saving the whales or protecting the rain forest or finding simple truth in the behavior of predators misleads many of us in an attempt to identify our adversaries. In order to secure the planet for future generations, we are told, we must overcome a vaguely-defined villain among ourselves, a force that, if left unchecked, will destroy the future.

"We have found the enemy," said Pogo, "and he is us."

The battleground may seem to be the environment, but the objective is really power.

CONDITIONS IN GENERAL

Much of what urban America imagines about the West in particular today is simply not true.

■ The forests have not been destroyed by loggers. If anything, forest lands as vast as any known by our ancestors are in far greater danger today from the absence of harvest and management.

■ The rangeland is not being grazed into desert. To the contrary, the public range in particular is today regarded to be in better condition than at any time in the last century, thanks mostly to agreements sought by ranchers themselves, but also to increasing knowledge on conservation provided by environmentally aware scientists. If the future of the range may be limited from what it once was, it is because ranchers themselves have more respect and understanding of its natural cycles than ever before.

■ We have not "mined out" our natural resources in fuel and minerals, and face no risk of doing so in the foreseeable future. What is at stake is our understanding of how to use the knowledge we have in making the best and least destructive use of the resources that exist.

■ Mankind alone is not responsible for all natural catastrophes. Humans have always had an effect on the environment, no less than buffalo or wolves or prairie dogs, but in many cases no more than other species. The obvious difference is in our understanding of how we affect the environ-

© JEAN LAUGHTON

Putting pairs out to pasture on the Old Double X Ranch south of Belvidere, South Dakota. Lyle O'Bryan rides Cody in the foreground. Casey Willard, Joe Stoddard, Rosen Hill and Baxter Badure are counting cows out the gate.

ment. The grasp we have of that comes from education and knowledge far more than from restrictive enforcement and threatened punishment.

We are, however, squandering our own natural wealth and the well-being of the planet itself in allowing the destruction of farms, managed forests, rangelands, and other means of natural, regenerative production in favor of what we are misguided to believe is an answer in global technology no longer reliant on natural resources.

Our need for food and for raw materials will not be served by the Internet alone, and cannot be met by a political policy that is short-sighted and guided by special interests. "Preservation" of productive and generally renewable resources in the United States in favor of importation of food and raw materials from emerging nations poses threats not only to national security, but to global survival. Such policy seems not only reckless, but totally unnecessary.

THE "SIDES"

The expansion of federal control and authority in the past 10 years especially is simply too obvious to be regarded as merely the evolving process of our government. Many in the West see what they suspect is a sinister move to socialism behind it all. Indeed, several of the key founders of what has become the environmentalist movement were in fact self-proclaimed socialists or acknowledged their interest in the theory. That includes Aldo Leopold and Bob Marshall, a socialist Democratic who instigated the formation of the Wilderness Society in 1935.

Yet for the most part, even though some point to the "Green Cross" role of former Soviet Premier Mikhail Gorbachev in the movement, environmentalists are not "communists" or even dogmatists. On their side, there is equally deep suspicion that those who use the land and its resources are directed by rich and greedy capitalists who would carelessly exploit all public wealth for themselves if left unchecked.

On the battleground for public opinion, those separate assumptions seem to underlie the contending messages between regulation and free enterprise. Attitudes and prejudice have been formed among the public in a way similar to political campaigns, and as is common to such campaigns,

opinions have been formed based less on truth than emotion.

It is a commonly held assumption, for example, that agriculture in general is represented by powerful political lobbyist groups and organizations which sometimes act against the public good in order to preserve their traditional advantages.

Such long-standing associations representing farmers, ranchers, loggers, miners and recreationists do exist in a complex, and sometimes conflicting, assortment of politically attentive offices. Yet there is also a body of equally complex environmental organizations with political bases in Washington, D.C., that certainly exert no less power and influence.

The difference for more than a quarter century has been that agricultural groups have found themselves disarrayed in actions commonly directed at a specific issue or region, while large environmental interest groups have employed huge sums of their nonprofit holdings in attempting to shape general public policy. No president or politician would ever say they are against farms, for example, yet it involves a more politically popular, and often more profitable, stance to declare themselves "pro-environment," even though that position may carry hidden baggage.

Some idea of what that's worth may be seen from the financial holdings of major nonprofit environmental organizations: The Nature Conservancy is the most outstanding example and reported nonprofit revenues of $1.6 billion in 1999. No other single environmental group can come close to TNC's holdings, which also include over a million acres of land, but recent practice has been for activist groups to form coalitions with shared funding targeted at a particular cause, such as halting logging in the Southwest, with financial coffers commonly totaling half a million dollars a year on each issue. It is spent on influence, both on politicians and in the public media.

By contrast, the total budget for lobbying activities of the National Cattle and Beef Association is about $2 million a year, including salaries and costs. Yet these funds, derived from a much smaller base of the population, must be devoted to a number of issues and even individual cases. Even if agricultural groups could combine their assets in the way that environmentalist groups do under shelter of foundations, the strain on a limited pool of rural contributors would itself threaten the continued existence of many of them. The bitter choice among those in agriculture is in whether they can afford to just stay even with a "movement" that enjoys enough funding to expend more and more in soliciting financial support from the cities and suburbs.

◆ ◆ ◆

The public popularity of "saving" the environment is by itself so potent that sometimes little special interest pressure at all is necessary to trigger administrative action that is not even offered for public debate. The outstanding example, though not the only one, was the 1996 campaign designation of the Grand Staircase Escalante in Utah as a National Heritage Site, surprising even the entire Utah Congressional delegation. Indeed, what has characterized the Clinton administration is evasion of public debate, even in Congress, by using administrative orders and regulations to carry out major policy changes on public lands.

Secretary Babbitt has frequently expressed his frustration with Congessional reluctance to approve his proposals. Not for the first time, Babbitt infuriated some in Congress recently by telling the *National Journal*: "We've switched the rules of the game. We're not going to do anything legislatively."

It's that kind of bluster, along with previous actions, that has helped stir opposition to the administration. Yet even mild political dissent to such authority has been branded as "anti-government" in the heated issue of public lands.

Opponents to environmental initiatives by the administration are frequently labeled as dupes or tools of powerful corporations such as oil companies. Ironically, however, a huge amount of wealth employed by the leading environmental organizations can be traced to grants from fortunes made in the 20th century from corporate exploitation of natural resources. This includes The Rockefeller Foundation (Standard Oil), The Pew Charitable Trusts (Sun Oil), The Ford Foundation, and a long list of other well-known corporate titles with charitable foundations that donate hundreds of millions of dollars a year to environmental groups. When it comes to funding, there is no doubt that the "big" money is in green hands.

◆ ◆ ◆

The idea persists among many westerners that it is some kind of international conspiracy involving a plan to turn over large parts of the United States to the United Nations. There are 47 Biosphere Reserves and 27 World Heritage sites in the United States covering as much as 70 percent of national parks and monuments which are in theory protected under international agreement with the United Nations.

That does not mean those lands are controlled by the U.N., but what is less understood is the power awarded in settling disputes over these lands to the influence of nationally and internationally recognized Non Government Organizations (NGOs) such as The Nature Conservancy.

Such politically weighted "international authority" has also been used by the Clinton administration to avoid a national debate (notably in blocking the New World Mine near the border of Yellowstone National Park).

Secretary Babbitt is certainly aware of the appearance of demagoguery in his administration and has initiated other measures such as Resource Advisory Councils to provide what some argue is only an appearance of democratic participation among ranchers, recreationists, academicians, environmental-

© JOE MCDONALD/TOM STACK & ASSOCIATES

Rocky Mountain grizzly. Interior secretary Babbitt initiated measures such as Resource Advisory Councils to provide what some argue is only an appearance of democratic participation among ranchers, recreationists, academicians, environmentalists and local government in deciding use of public lands.

ists and local government in deciding use of public lands.

In what they say is an attempt to reach consensus on such issues as multiple land use, federal authorities have established training programs for land management staff in "facilitated" meetings now commonly experienced by many westerners and recognizable in their signature direction by a "facilitator" writing the views of participants on easel-sized tablets of white butcher paper.

That the methodology is so common is no accident. Breaking participants into small groups generally unfamiliar with each other is intended not only to produce a variety of thought, but to discourage disagreement in a politely uncertain social setting. Translating their views into simple statements listed on the paper makes their differences seem even less significant. What comes of it, according to critics of this "Delphi" method, is the appearance of agreement on a preplanned solution. The critics say participants are simply manipulated into thinking they have found consensus. Whether or not the critics are right about that, such facilitated methods appear to be taking the place of social and scientific debate. Those with particular expertise and knowledge in the field, in fact, are characteristically excluded from the consensus process.

To say there is a conspiracy or some sort of grand plan for a socialist takeover of the West distorts the reality of a vastly more complex (not to mention more capitalist funded) environmental "movement" that has captured the enthusiasm of young people in particular through a public media campaign that presents an opportunity for redemption of some mutually held social guilt. If it distorts reality and ignores its own responsibility for the creation of social and even environmental crises, it has evolved less as a conspiracy than as a political agenda which yet requires an educated response.

SPECIES ENDANGERED: IS IT THE OWLS? OR IS IT US?

From the very beginning of their campaign in 1989, the Sierra Club made no secret of the fact that the spotted owl was virtually invented from questionable research as a "surrogate" useful to halting all old-growth forest harvesting in the Northwest.

Andy Stahl of the Sierra Club was delighted in comparing

Snow Geese (Chen caerulescens) on the Merced National Wildlife Refuge, Merced County, California.

the owl to "Bambi" as a symbol of the Club's intentions. It worked even beyond Sierra Club expectations and hopes, in a rapid few years shutting down virtually all logging on federal land. This even though the owl's supposed reliance on old-growth timber was put into serious question by hundreds of nests found in second-growth forests and one even discovered in a K-Mart sign.

There are 1,197 species of plants and animals in the United States listed as threatened or endangered. Since final passage of the Endangered Species Act in 1973, 11 species have been delisted as a result of their recovery; seven species have been declared extinct; and nine other species have been delisted after finding the original data was incorrect.

Of the 10 to 30 million species estimated to exist on the planet today, scientists estimate that 17,000 become extinct every year. That is not an alarming figure. Most of the species that ever existed are today extinct from natural processes.

Though science debates how much government actually had to do with it, the Endangered Species Act (ESA) can certainly claim its poster successes in the bald eagle or the peregrine falcon, even while ignoring that it was the elimination of pesticides such as DDT, and the private Peregrine Fund, that deserve the credit.

But the key to understanding the ESA today is in that "surrogate" issue. Most of the species listed are considered in danger because of loss of habitat, and the most frequently "lost" habitat involves fresh water. Which brings us to what has always been the bottom line in the West.

If the West had been blessed with nearly the same general distribution of rivers and waterways found east of the Mississippi, this would surely be a different nation, and no such disputes over "public land" could possibly have endured over more than a century. In the West, as Mark Twain observed, "Whiskey is for drinking. Water is for fighting."

Administration of the Endangered Species Act today is largely the responsibility of the U.S. Fish & Wildlife Service, headed by George Frampton. If water is what will unlock the door to species survival, Frampton holds the key. And, as in other parts of Interior Department policy, it is seldom a matter of representative debate about the outcome.

Water transformed the desert in some areas of the West, making it "bloom" as Theodore Roosevelt promised in new farms that were meant to feed industrial expansion to the coast. Such promises of water for irrigation brought people West at the beginning of the 20th century. Probably the most common issue at the heart of most disputes in the West today are over rights still held to that water. In an ever-growing West it is ever more the most valuable commodity. Water is power.

More than the land, the government wants the water.

That is the bottom line.

THERE WILL NEVER BE MORE, AND THERE IS NEVER ENOUGH

Never like the East, of course, water in the West has always been more scarce and more at issue over who should control its use.

Rainfall in the 17 western states is typically 30 to 50 percent of what it is in the East. In the East, general water doctrine is based on "riparian rights" of each landholder adjacent to a stream sharing equally in its "reasonable" use. In the West, water law follows a doctrine of "prior appropriation," allowing the first water user to take what is needed for "beneficial" use. In a drought, senior rights are met first, the basic rule being, "use it or lose it."

Agricultural users in the West have generally been losing it in the last 20 years due to new claims by federal authorities over what is "beneficial" use and "prior" rights.

Those priorities have changed since federal reclamation policy at the beginning of the 20th century encouraged families to settle in an arid West made to "bloom" from the creation of dams, reservoirs and irrigation systems.

Today, some 31 million people in the West rely in one way or another on the more than 300 dams and reservoirs built by the Bureau of Reclamation to provide water to more than nine million acres of farmland since 1902.

Despite promises made to those original settlers, however, increasing demand for water from growing urban areas and newly established wildlife habitats has resulted in major alterations in the policy and mission of federal agencies such as the Bureau of Reclamation. And although federal authority stems from the Reclamation Act of 1902, since then no less than 12 standing committees in Congress have jurisdiction over "federal" water, yet no comprehensive plan on federal water resources has been introduced since the 1965 Water Resources Planning Act generally provided for an assessment of the resource.

Since then, although states are acknowledged to generally have control over their own water resources, multiple federal agencies including the BLM, the Forest Service, U.S. Fish & Wildlife Service, the Bureau of Reclamation and the Environmental Protection Agency have claimed prior rights for the allocation of western water.

The complex issue of water rights is expected to be argued in one or more cases before the U.S. Supreme Court in this decade. In the meantime, however, losses of farmland due to elimination of irrigation or grazing rights by federal authorities amount to millions of acres and continue to be central to the issue in the West.

Brian Oneto family ranch in Amador County, California.

"Nature teaches more than she preaches. There are no sermons in stone. It is easier to get a spark out of a stone than a moral."

JOHN BURROUGHS, CA. 1900

More so than we would like, *RANGE* magazine is accused of "preaching to the choir" by reminding those in the rural West of what they already know. But neither we nor those readers closest to us want to be regarded as missionaries or adversaries in causes that need not divide the nation or the people of the

© JOHN BARDWELL

Fallon farm in Lahontan Valley, Nevada. This is part of the Newlands Project, one of Teddy Roosevelt's first "Let the desert bloom" reclamation projects in 1907.

West as much as they have in recent years. John Muir is a hero to us, too. Aldo Leopold could have written for *RANGE*. Contemporary environmentalists, even if their views are as radical as those of Dave Foreman and Reed Noss are part of our interest. But every trend deserves to be examined for its truth.

These things we think are true:

■ The honest production of food, fiber, and raw materials in the West is no less necessary today than ever.

■ If the numbers of farms and the viability of farming continues to decline in the United States, the least result will be a serious increase in the cost of food for all of us.

■ If the decline in legitimate livestock grazing continues at a rate of 20 percent each decade, the result will be not only higher costs for protein, but lower quality and even questionable supplies.

■ If timber production, reduced by 70 percent in the last decade, remains at such levels, consumer costs for an incredible variety of products will rise, while the forests will be in ever greater danger of catastrophic wildfires.

■ If the production of fuel and minerals in the United States is even more limited than it is today, this consuming nation will still acquire the necessary raw materials from imports, thus not only compromising national security, but contributing to environmental destruction in other countries.

■ If the national heritage contained in our public lands is set aside as a preservation of a mythical past, our future as a nation and as free people will be in dire doubt, and the balance of nature throughout the planet will be threatened.

■ If the trend of federal regulation and control continues, production of food, fiber and raw materials in the United States will be directed into the holdings of larger and more powerful corporate enterprises that will have influence over supply, demand and prices.

In calculating all of it in the last two decades, it is not the management of natural resources, but the attempt of management and control of human behavior and aspiration that is at the heart of the issues in the West. We believe, as people in the West have always believed, that we have a right to participate in shaping our own destiny. That is nothing more than what is promised to us all as free people. ■

SUMMER 2000

MONUMENTAL BETRAYAL

Babbitt told Clinton, "History is on our side."

By Tim Findley

By the time President Theodore Roosevelt made his first visit to the Grand Canyon in 1903, Benjamin Harrison had already invested more than a decade through his career in the Senate and part of his own presidency in an effort to set aside the magnificent canyon for the American people. History hardly notices Harrison's frustrated attempts and final modest success at creating at least a national forest on the site. It's Roosevelt and his "bully pulpit" style of using executive powers granted him under the Antiquities Act of 1906 who will always be remembered as the savior of the Grand Canyon.

Even then, though, the idea of creating a federal monument beyond local authority had its outspoken opponents. Among them was an ambitious rancher who had his eye on owning the Bright Angel Trail down to the bottom of the gorge and charging tourists for the mule-back trips. He was C.J. Babbitt, the patriarch of the Babbitt empire in northern Arizona, and the grandfather of U.S. Secretary of the Interior Bruce Babbitt.

As with other small contradictions in his family background, Bruce regards the matter with a sort of wryly amused arrogance. "In his mellow years," chortled the secretary, "my grandfather said he always was in favor of protecting the Grand Canyon. As I told the president, history is on our side."

It was just 11 days into the new century, a new era, and the pinnacle of what Babbitt immodestly refers to as "the Golden Age," of his administration in Interior. Only hours before, he and President Bill Clinton had indeed made history by declaring the sweep of high range and rust-red outcrops in Arizona west of the canyon park as the Parashant National Monument. Helicoptered back to Grand Junction, Colorado, Babbitt gloated and rocked on his heels like a pompous Mussolini agreeing to a timid few questions.

"Every member of [Arizona's] congressional delegation except one is opposed to this," began a reporter's query. "How do you account for that?"

AP PHOTO/MATT YORK

President Clinton listens as Secretary of Interior Bruce Babbitt speaks at Hopi Point in Grand Canyon, Arizona, on Tuesday, January 11, 2000. Clinton was visiting the Grand Canyon to dedicate three national monuments, the largest being a million-acre parcel of land along the North Rim of the Grand Canyon.

With a jowly imperial smirk, the secretary paused a beat before answering. "I read in the newspaper this morning that 78 percent of Arizonans support the pPresident's action."

"So you don't want to answer the question?" the reporter followed.

"What was the question?" Babbitt replied.

It's the one question that never really gets answered—who the hell does Bruce Babbitt think he is?

In Arizona, elected officials from Gov. Jane Dee Hull and Sen. John McCain on down fumed over the unexpected move by Clinton and Babbitt to grab the Parashant for their own glory, ignoring and effectively double-crossing the state's own elected leadership which was then backing a bill in Congress to declare virtually the same expanse of the Shivwitz Plateau a National Conservation Area.

It was the same move Clinton and Babbitt had put on Utah with Grand Staircase Escalante in 1996, and the same autocratic threat Babbitt held over half a dozen other western regions like some Nottingham sheriff controlling the lords and vassals of Prince John.

Only a few months before, at an October congressional hearing in Washington, Rep. John Shadegg (R-Arizona) had pressed Babbitt, asking that the Secretary provide Congress with a list of areas under consideration for arbitrary "monument" status. Babbitt replied with one word, "No." There was a stunned silence, not really the first of its kind in the many times Babbitt has expressed his defiance of congressional authority. "I don't mean to be disrespectful," the secretary added without apology.

By December, Babbitt sounded even more contemptuous of the House and Senate, saying, "We've switched the rules of the game. We're not doing anything legislatively." By then, Babbitt had been on another of his tours of the West, holding court and offering audiences in selected rural areas thinly veiled threats to local ranchers and minor officials about coming to agreement with him or facing the power of executive authority.

The Grand Canyon in Arizona took more than five million years to be created by the Colorado River. The canyon is 277 miles long, ranges in width from four to 18 miles, and attains a depth of over a mile. It is one of the first national parks in the United States.

But Arizona was not the only state in which local representation was unwilling to cave in to the despotic bullying of a cabinet secretary. Almost nowhere did Babbitt get the local rubber stamp agreement to a new "designation" for lands he wanted. Instead, representative groups including resource advisory councils, local and state government committees, and even congressional delegations agreed to hear out the concerns of people who earn their livelihood from the lands and tried to adjust new agreements that would assure them a future. It never came down to granting the additional federal authority Babbitt demanded.

The powerful secretary sulked at their disobedience from his richly paneled office above the Lincoln Memorial. It was only a short distance to the White House and to his old friend from the Wilderness Society, George Frampton, who is now acting chairman of the White House Council on Environmental Quality. Just a few words from the right people, and the president, as required by law, would come up with his "own" idea about what needed to be a national monument—for the good of future generations.

In Denver, a month after his grand grab of the Parashant, Babbitt bragged to students at the University of Denver Law School that he finally went to Clinton at the end of 1999 and told him it was time.

"'We've offered to engage the Congress, and what we got in return was a sham piece of legislation,'" Babbitt said he told the President. "That's the reason that President Clinton went to the Grand Canyon in January."

By then, the area Babbitt had demanded from local officials had doubled in size, from 250,000 to 500,000 acres, a region as large as Connecticut.

Now, with the Parashant hanging from his spear along with the figurative public heads of Arizonans who defied him, Babbitt could make his threats of the previous summer even more clear. "It would be great to get these protection issues resolved in the congressional, legislative process," he told the Denver students. "But if that's not possible, I'm prepared to go back to the president and not only ask, not only advise, but implore him to use his powers under the Antiquities Act and to say to him: 'Mr. President, if they don't and you do, you will be vindicated by history for generations to come.'"

Information provided to the press the day before made it clear Babbitt was talking about a long list, including the Anasazi region in Colorado, Steens Mountain in Oregon, Santa Rosa Mountain in California, and the Missouri Breaks in Montana as part of what he proclaimed to be a new "National Landscape Monument" system run by a revised Bureau of Land Management.

In each case, Babbitt was effectively sending a warning to elected representatives from each of those states who were already at work on agreements and legislation that would more fairly assure the future of those regions and the people reliant on them for their livelihood. Without any legal authority, he was telling them, do it his way, or he would do it himself.

ARIZONA

The matter of the Shivwitz Plateau and the largely wild region in what is called the "Arizona Strip" north and west of the Grand Canyon posed a problem almost akin to that of Babbitt's own family's control of northern Arizona at the turn of the century. Only this time, it wasn't Babbitt himself who owned the region, it was in large part the federal government and its administrative agency, the Bureau of Land Management, over which Secretary Babbitt had ultimate authority.

Blocked in by Native American reservations and set aside from main roads, the "strip" is a part of Arizona seldom seen even by adventuresome ecotourists. Most of it, however, had been utilized in peaceful production for generations by the stable Mormon families who had established their ranches there and willingly over the years agreed to the multiuse contracts with the government. As far as any of them could tell, there was no pressure from outside development, nor any outrage of environmental harm, nor even any tourist interest in the region they quietly continued to steward as generations before them had done.

Then, in 1998, as his place in Clinton's cabinet was nearing its close, Bruce Babbitt returned to what he called "home" on the south rim of the Grand Canyon. "This is a national shrine," he intoned, "...but there's something wrong here because the Grand Canyon National Park is not coextensive with the ecosystem of the Grand Canyon." Citing Roosevelt "and others," Babbitt looked 300 miles further down the Colorado River and said, "We've got to pick up where these people left off, because there's not a lot of time left."

Babbitt already had control of most of it anyway, with more than 390,000 acres in the region under management of the BLM. Grazing permits on that public land served as the essential link to the 8,000 acres of deeded homesteads and ranches. But no one could be sure of what Babbitt intended by his plan to extend the setaside status of the Grand Canyon into these remote regions.

The local ranchers and townsfolk appealed for help from their state legislature and got it in the form of resolutions opposing any new, restrictive designation for the federally owned territory, but state action was almost meaningless. In what the local people regarded as needless compromise, the Arizona congressional delegation sought to stave off Babbitt's arbitrary grab of Shivwitz as a monument by preparing a congressional bill to name it as a National Conservation Area that could include provisions for grazing and mining.

"Well, I kind of bought into that line in a moment of weakness and said, 'Okay, I'll stay my hand,'" Babbitt recalled to the Denver students. Actually, however, Babbitt was furious. He went to the president.

Betrayed after months of trying to bring local input to the issue, Arizona Cattle Growers President Jed Flake erupted in frustration. "This isn't about protecting land, it's about vying for political PR points with an uninformed suburban public," he said. "The land in question is already protected by the BLM and is depended upon by hundreds of ranch family members who, as stewards, protect the range and its sustainability. Most every important detail concerning [the Parashant Monument] creation proposed at public meetings or town halls has proven absolutely false."

COLORADO

Sen. Ben Nighthorse Campbell (R-Colorado) used to be a Democrat. Part of what pushed him over the edge into changing parties was an encounter with Babbitt's arrogance over Range Reform in 1992. Unable to convince western senators of his own plan, Babbitt accused Campbell and others of "torching their own ranchers just to prove their machismo." It was yet another outburst demonstrating Babbitt's contempt of any process that disagreed with him.

So when Babbitt went after the Anasazi region in the Four Corners area of southwest Colorado, Campbell and others were waiting for him. The secretary took note of the national parks already established around the pre-history ruins of Mesa Verde and other Anasazi sites and sneered at them as "little postage stamps on the landscape." He wanted at least a quarter million acres, incorporating the grazing land of the ranching families that had first discovered Mesa Verde and pressed for its preservation. Babbitt called his vision for a vast new monument part of "an anthropological ecosystem."

What shallow promises Babbitt made for continued multiple use didn't fool most people in Colorado. Just as in Arizona, his own annointed Resource Advisory Council (RAC) was not about to give him a rubber stamp for a new designation of the area. The working group stressed the years of success by community groups and multiple use while protecting their local treasure. They suggested that, with the aid of many willing volunteers, existing BLM management simply be improved.

"We must identify our enemies and drive them into oblivion."

BRUCE BABBITT IN HIS FIRST MESSAGE AS PRESIDENT OF THE LEAGUE OF CONSERVATION VOTERS, 1991

"The people in the group would have preferred no designation at all," said Mike Preston, co-chairman of the Anasazi committee, "but we trust a lot more in the legislative process to represent the interests of the people."

It wasn't enough for Babbitt, who wrote a rebuking letter to the cochairmen of the working group. He would talk to Colorado's congressional delegation, Babbitt said, but if they didn't do it his way, he would go to the White House.

Sen. Campbell knows well the arrogance of the Interior secretary. Campbell's own bill to protect 164,000 acres of the Four Corners region as a National Conservation Area took direct note of the public restrictions imposed by Clinton's 1996 Utah land grab and specifically provided for protection of multiple uses, including grazing and recreation.

"Now, the hour is late," Babbitt told the Denver students. "It's a presidential election year. Congress will recess 'early and often.' And we must bring this discussion to the kind of resolution that's important for the people of Colorado and the country." It was as clear a contemptuous threat as Babbitt could make it, but Campbell didn't blink.

"We'll see," said a spokesman for the senator. "The game won't be over this year."

OREGON

Len Shrewsbury had briefly walked out in a fury when the U.S. Forest Service "facilitator" defied the clear majority intent of the southern Oregon RAC and suggested they find a name for the new "designation" on Steens Mountain. Now, wintering with his ever-roaming RV in Arizona, Shrewsbury saw what he had expected from the Interior secretary. Despite all the public input and the clear position of not only the RAC, but a working committee of state officials that Steens should be left as it is, Babbitt had it on his list for a "landscape monument."

"I was told we would be used," said the 74-year-old Shrewsbury, "but I thought we could accomplish something in spite of it. It just makes you feel helpless."

Babbitt himself had warned them, just as he had warned their counterparts in Arizona and Colorado and elsewhere. "I'm here because I believe there's a window of opportunity and I intend to bring it to a conclusion on my watch," he said during a 24-hour visit in August.

The working partnership between landowners and federal authorities on the unfenced Steens Mountain was regarded as a model of successful stewardship. Even Babbitt called it, "the best in the West." But a radically determined group of environmentalists based in Portland and Bend had plans to use Steens as the anchor of a massive six-million-acre park and wilderness area. They were questionable even among more established environmental groups, but they had Babbitt's ear, and Babbitt now coveted the previously little-known mountain in a remote part of Oregon.

He regarded the region's RAC as stacked enough with interests beyond grazing to be easily led by the tediously tested method of a facilitator guiding them to the expected conclusion. But the public hearings on the issue, even loaded with bused-in enviros from Portland, heard ranchers, small businessmen, hikers and fishermen all saying the same thing—Steens works fine just as it is.

Drawing even more attention to it, as Babbitt was doing, could only cause problems. Giving it some new designation would virtually guarantee that fences would rise between public land and the two-thirds of the mountain that was in private hands. In their plan, the radical environmentalists had in mind to force those private owners out in a willing seller offer that would follow elimination of grazing rights. All that was obvious to the RAC, and certainly to Babbitt, but he left no doubt of what he expected in his "window of opportunity."

In a desert of sagebrush, coyotes and antelope, Steens Mountain is an alpine island rising above the Alvord Desert of southeastern Oregon. Stretching from Baker Pass in the north to Long Hollow in the south, The Steens are nearly 60 miles long and 18 miles across (from Frenchglen to Kigermann following the tilt direction of the fault block). The 9,000-foot crest alone runs over eight miles from north to south.

"I'm being ambiguous about that because the press is here," he said, but everyone knew that he wanted it his way, or he would do it the way he and Clinton had in Utah. Democratic Gov. John Kitzhaber was among those who understood it when Babbitt took him on a helicopter tour. But even Kitzhaber couldn't manage agreement to a new "designation" of Steens from a special committee set up to supercede the RAC.

"We feel victimized," said Stacy Davies of Roaring Springs Ranch, the 140,000-acre unfenced "model" of public-private stewardship on Steens. "The whole thing has destroyed the community atmosphere here; put neighbor against neighbor. This administration has no respect for that. It scares us to death."

MONTANA

The bicentennial of the Lewis and Clark expedition is approaching with widening public curiosity about how much the West has changed since President Thomas Jefferson sent the Corps of Discovery off to explore it in 1803. That's probably one reason why they see more and more "floaters" paddling and drifting along the Missouri River these days. That, and possibly the attention drawn by Babbitt to the badlands of the Missouri Breaks as a "landscape monument" he wants as part of Bill Clinton's legacy.

If anything, the Interior secretary was even less circumspect in sending out his message to the generational heirs of homesteaders and rugged small towners along the Missouri north of Great Falls, Montana. There seems little likelihood that this region of broken plateaus and deep coulees will be threatened by any sprawl of development. It is, in fact, little changed since Lewis and Clark camped there, except that where they might have seen buffalo, cattle now graze.

"They sent a guy from Babbitt's office here, and I just couldn't believe it," said Wilma Econom, a rancher's wife from Fort Benton. "He didn't really want to listen to anybody. It was more like just to threaten them."

The Missouri in this region is already designated as a wild and scenic river. Nobody has any real problem with that. But Babbitt's familiar proposal to throw a vast new federal cloak over the checkerboard of public and private lands in the "Breaks" made no more sense here than it had in Oregon. The same thing happened as it had elsewhere: local committees and the RAC Babbitt hoped would fall in line refused last year to set some new "designation" for the already-protected area.

Wolf-loving Bruce Babbitt was born in Los Angeles in 1939. His father brought him back to old C.J.'s ranch when Bruce was six, but Bruce, who grew up in Flagstaff, wasn't long welcome on the ranch. They say the self-absorbed boy liked to wander out on the range, and that was fine, but he never remembered to close a gate behind him.

"There was a charade of participation, but we knew they weren't listening," said Ron Poertner.

"It was just a veil in bringing it to the RAC," said Jim Petersen. "He was hell-bent to make the Missouri River a monument, and common sense didn't have any place in the process."

Matt Knox, another rancher in the Breaks, saw it as "needless, useless, and ultimately destructive" to what actually is still a living piece of developed history over the last 100 years of settlement and successful stewardship. "They'd eliminate that for the sake of their legacy," Knox said.

"They keep taking more and more. How do we stay?" said Wilma Econom. "You begin to think, is this really a government for the people, by the people?"

◆ ◆ ◆

In his press proclamation intended to attract the urban environmental support he always expects, Bruce Babbitt was not even above condemning his own loyal employees in order to take high stance in an imagined historic legacy.

"This nation's largest land management agency ought to be induced to have a sense of pride," Babbitt said, complaining that his own Bureau of Land Management has been too pro-logging and pro-mining and pro-grazing. He told reporters there will have to be changes in the BLM workings as a result of his new "system" created from some four million acres of the West on his list for national landscape monuments.

In every case where Babbitt has targeted a monument, from Arizona to Montana, a scratch below the surface finds honest BLM employees proud of what has been the relationship with local people, embarrassed by what Babbitt suggests it will be, but generally too afraid for their jobs to say more. Babbitt, they know, does not tolerate any disagreement. ■

The U.S. Antiquities Act of 1906

Section 2 of the Act says:

"The President of the United States is authorized, in his discretion, to declare by public proclamation historic landmarks, historic and prehistoric structures, and other objects of scientific interest that are situated upon the lands owned or controlled by the Government of the United States to be national monuments, and may reserve as part thereof parcels of land, the limits of which in all cases shall be confined to the smallest area compatible with the proper care and management of the objects to be protected."

The geologic curiosity of Devils Tower in Wyoming was first: only 1,153 acres. But by 1908, when Teddy Roosevelt employed the act to save more than 800,000 acres of the Grand Canyon, the idea of a "smallest area compatible" seemed to have been forgotten in the terms of the law. Although it has been challenged—and in the case of the Grand Tetons and Jackson Hole legislatively opposed all the way to a threatened veto by President Franklin Roosevelt—no use of the act by executive authority has ever been overturned. Although later adjusted into a broader terminology, President Jimmy Carter even used it to set aside more than 55 million acres of Alaska.

Next to Carter, President Bill Clinton stands to be the only president since Theodore Roosevelt to so actively employ his executive authority under the act. Presidents Nixon, Reagan and Bush never used it at all. ■

SUMMER 2002

BULLY!

What Theodore Roosevelt saw as conservation, modern politicians and enviros see as opportunity. By Tim Findley

Bully!" shouted President Theodore Roosevelt in his exuberance as a dead tree ignited by John Muir himself burst into a cackling blaze spitting fountains of bright orange sparks across Yosemite's black velvet sky. "Bully!" shouted the president.

They spent the night camped there together, and although they were surrounded at a distance by security officers and aides and the trailing press, none of them ever recorded or perhaps even overheard what talk there was between these two enormous personalities before the morning's light woke them to find a fresh covering of late spring snow. "Even bullier," Roosevelt is reported to have said. It was something of the equivalent to "far out," "awesome," or "cool," as some might say today, but no one could ever use a word like "bully" with better meaning than Roosevelt.

COURTESY THEODORE ROOSEVELT COLLECTION, HARVARD COLLEGE LIBRARY

Certainly not Muir, who at the urging of friends had only reluctantly canceled a planned visit to Asia to meet with the nation's chief executive in 1903 on the question of restoring federal authority over California's Yosemite Park.

Muir and Roosevelt were not nearly the kindred spirits popular history has led us to believe. Muir, the farmer, the naturalist, was awed by the architecture of nature's creation. Roosevelt, the rancher, the hunter, sensed the grandeur of life in a perfect setting. As Edmund Morris describes in his best-selling work "Theodore Rex":

"The president was disappointed to find that Muir had no ear for bird music. He was Wordsworthian rather than Keatsian, revering only 'rocks and stones and trees.' Garrulous, erudite, and walleyed, he talked a pure form of preservation that Roosevelt was not used to hearing."

What was formed between them would never be satisfying to Muir, who even after the establishment of Yosemite National Park would despair unto his death at Roosevelt's refusal to rescue the "sister" of Yosemite in the Hetch Hetchy Valley from a series of dams to create a water and power system for San Francisco.

The contradiction was always there between what Roosevelt understood as conservation and what Muir envisioned, with some sad results, as preservation. They were not quite kindred, not nearly perfect in their agreement. Yet with what seems some greater cosmic plan, they seemed purposefully matched for the times.

◆ ◆ ◆

In 1907, Oregon Republican Sen. Charles W. Fulton thought he had found a way to stymie the land-grabbing Roosevelt with an amendment to the Agricultural Appropriations Act that would specifically place more than 16 million acres of the West under the protection of Congress, shielded from the grasp of the president. "Hereafter no forest shall be created, nor shall any addition be made to one heretofore created, within the limits of the states of Oregon, Washington, Idaho, Montana, Colorado or Wyoming," declared the amendment passed by Congress and sent to Roosevelt's desk for his signature. Roosevelt let it lie there while, in astonishingly rapid order, proclaiming executive authority over 21 new forest reserves and enlarging his power over 11 more, all in the six states Fulton had specified to be protected. If Congress tried to stop him, Roosevelt let it be known he would simply veto their action. Not until that was done did Roosevelt sign the Agricultural Appropriations Act, still dragging the now-useless Fulton amendment.

It was that sort of arrogance in presiding from his "bully pulpit" over a currently roaring wealth in the national economy that was part of Roosevelt's enormous, and even disturbing, power.

Chief among them in developing Interior policy for Roosevelt was Gifford Pinchot, a slender, sharp blade of a man who was described by some as almost mystically driven by fierce ideals in his creation of the U.S. Forest Service as a hybrid agency between the Department of Interior and the Department of Agriculture. Pinchot was not a preservationist in the mode of John Muir. He saw a purpose and a need in the harvest of forests as a crop and in the controlled use of forest lands for livestock grazing. Even so, Pinchot, an academic elitist who studied at Exeter, Yale and the esteemed *École Nationale Forestière* in France, had no real trust in the crude agricultural apparatus of the West to determine their own fate. Between what he would propose to Roosevelt and what TR would translate as his favored means of executive authority was clearly meant as a means of controlling the cultural and economic development of the region—at times with the enthusiastic help of ranchers themselves.

PHOTO COURTESY THEODORE ROOSEVELT COLLECTION, HARVARD COLLEGE LIBRARY

Teddy Roosevelt (left) poses in Yosemite with nature writer John Muir.

Morris in his "Theodore Rex" reports Roosevelt as saying: "Pinchot truly believes that in case of certain conditions I am perfectly capable of killing either himself or me. If conditions were such that only one could live, he knows that I should possibly kill him as the weaker of the two, and he, therefore, worships this in me."

◆ ◆ ◆

If the 20th century history of the West might be said to have begun with the bonfire set by Muir himself on a Yosemite ridge, what lies ahead in the 21st century might still be found in that singular magnificent view. It is well to remember that on that chilly May night in 1903 when Muir and Roosevelt shared a shelter, it had been barely more than half a century since any but a handful of Europeans had even seen the great valley. To most it was still a place as remote and uncommon as the moon.

But now we think we know the moon and maybe even Mars, and from that ridge atop the valley at Yosemite on any day beyond the deepest of winter may be seen a slow-moving clog of visitors helplessly clawing their way among the crowd. John Muir should not be blamed, but it really is his fault, and that of the Sierra Club, more than it was that of Theodore Roosevelt. It was Muir and Sierra Club director William Colby who in 1905 presented the Club's hopes for the future of a federal park: "The result would be improvement of the valley and national park by the construction of the best roads, bridges and trails," their report reads. "Ample hotel accommodations of the best quality would be provided.... The toll road system would be abolished and in all probability a splendid boulevard constructed up the Merced Canyon, which would reduce the time and expense of travel one half and greatly increase the comfort...."

Muir wanted Yosemite to be seen, and yet remain untouched. As controversial in their time as their acts would be, the approach of Roosevelt and Pinchot to conservation was in part utilitarian, taking into account preservation, but also continued use of the resource.

In an Arbor Day message to school children in 1907 Roosevelt said, "We of an older generation can get along with what we have, though with growing hardship; but in your full manhood and womanhood you will want what nature once so bountifully supplied and man so thoughtlessly destroyed; and because of that want you will reproach us, not for what we have used, but for what we have wasted."

In a not-so-subtle line drawn between exploitative greed and meaningful use, the Roosevelt administration set its pattern for the seeming contradictions between the creation of historic reclamation projects reshaping western lands on the one hand and globally unprecedented acts to protect wild regions on the other. That was truly the marvel and legacy of a uniquely bold national leader. *National Geographic* years later took account and concluded that Roosevelt had placed under some form of federal authority approximately 230 million acres of the West, or an average of 84,000 acres a day for his seven-year term of office. Federal forest reserves alone increased by more than 400 percent to an area greater than all the Atlantic Coast states

Sawmill Geyser, Upper Geyser Basin, Yellowstone National Park.

from Maine to Virginia and larger than the nations of France, Belgium and the Netherlands combined.

It was astonishing, even epic in the creation of a federal empire worthy of comparison to European conquerors, yet few Americans absorbed in wrenching economic and social changes brought about by the Industrial Age and approaching world war even noticed. The West remained still something of an open frontier, presumed by most easterners to be "owned" in sprawling wild ranches and endless deserts and forests that surrounded the now-captive Indian tribes. That actual private property in much of the West was in fact a rarity did not seem to occur to the westerners themselves who took for granted the land-use rights established for them by Pinchot and others.

◆ ◆ ◆

In 1996, on his second visit to the Yellowstone region, President Clinton made no real pretenses about horses or hiking boots. He rode in a helicopter, gazing down from an altitude that had the effect of blending all the steep and sudden contrasts of the landscape. Some three miles northeast of the park itself, but separated by peaks as high as 11,000 feet, the helicopter circled over the site of the New World Gold Mine, about 90 percent of it on privately owned land spilling into a national forest, not the park itself. Ten minutes, perhaps 15 of flying time, was enough for Clinton to make his decision. Whatever it cost the federal government, there would be no working mine there, and the whole region would be included as part of a buffer zone to the "Endangered World Heritage Site" of Yellowstone Park. No longer just a national treasure, Yellowstone now enjoyed the full international protection of the United Nations World Heritage Committee.

Not quite noticed as such at the time, "Babe Ruth Babbitt" and his new team in the Department of Interior had just hit their first long one, and this time they were playing in the truly big leagues.

It had long been a dream among the generations of preservationists who learned from John Muir's mistake at Yosemite. More public participation wasn't an answer, it was part of the problem. People and private property needed to be restricted. The time of its formation in the 1930s was a period of political doubt all over the United States, and so it is not so revealing that many of those who formed the Wilderness Society in 1935 were avowed socialists intent on government control of resources. Forester Bob Marshall, considered to be the architect of the group, was even self-revealing in the title of his book, "The People's Forests." The 13 directors who formed the leadership of the Wilderness Society without any membership vote were almost exclusively well-educated and well-connected easterners. Something like Muir, they were weekend hikers but, unlike the Sierra Club, they dedicated their efforts less to the experience of wilderness than to the dogged political opposition of entrepreneurs and capitalists exploiting the resource. However subtly it might be disguised with grand views and inspiring wildlife, it was fundamental politics in a fight over whether social freedom included rights to private property.

"Our only rational options are to reject privatization and commercial exploitation of our precious public resources in favor of long-range planning, careful stewardship and protection. We must not squander our heritage or forsake our birthright," wrote Wilderness Society president George Frampton in 1988.

It was Frampton who coined the term "Our Babe Ruth" when President Clinton appointed Bruce Babbitt as his Secretary of the Interior. Babbitt would reward the Wilderness Society leader, Yale graduate and former Washington lawyer with the post of assistant secretary for Fish, Wildlife & Parks. Not surprisingly, it would be Frampton who invited members of the United Nations World Heritage Committee to tour Yellowstone in 1995 and find it endangered by the New World Gold Mine, thus circumventing regional and local hearings on the question.

"It's astonishing that a group of extreme environmentalists can invite a few folks from the United Nations to circumvent laws that Americans and Montanans have worked hard for and lent their voices to," said Sen. Conrad Burns (R-Montana) in futile protest. "We have an exhaustive procedure on the books in Montana to decide where mines can and cannot be sited. Why should we allow the United Nations to pick and choose when these laws and rules will be allowed to work?"

It seems unlikely that Clinton himself ever saw any of the 21 monuments he arbitrarily proclaimed between 1996 and virtually his last day in office, January 17, 2001. At least Roosevelt had been capable of writing his own speeches and saying what he thought without the help of spin doctors and propagandists. When he reached for the Grand Canyon in 1903, it was in his own words and from his own experience when he said, "Keep this great wonder of nature as it is.... You can not improve it. The ages have been at work on it, and man can only mar it."

But Roosevelt expected opposition, and in the case of the Grand Canyon he got it in sufficient strength to delay the great conservationist's attempts to make it a national

Young Theodore Roosevelt proudly commemorates climbing the Matterhorn on his wedding trip in 1881.

park, causing him instead to proclaim it a national monument in the first great stretch of Antiquities Act limitations. Among those protesting was the most powerful rancher and entrepreneur of the time on the rim of the canyon, C.J. Babbitt, grandfather of the as yet unborn man destined to be "Clinton's Pinchot."

By the beginning of Clinton's second term, Babbitt felt supremely confident in his ability to control the fate of the West without accountability to Congress and without any restraints from a president who appreciated the steady flow of contributions from nonprofit powerhouses and corporate shills paying off the environmentalist movement. From his own appointed bureaucracy, the Interior secretary could draw on research and data compiled by their former environmental organizations, many with wish lists of their own. The networking also provided Babbitt with a ready resource of "concerned" volunteers eager to serve on the stage-managed citizens' advisory councils he set up to legitimatize his grabs of "open" land.

This wasn't Pinchot, with his ideas of "utilitarian" conservation, or Roosevelt with his often-restated argument that "Conservation means development as much as it does protection." This was Babbitt as Dillinger or Capone, or maybe Stalin might have been, demanding that it be done his way or else. He had the power to sic wolves on their herds, and he did. He could bust dams that held their irrigation water, and he did. He could cripple their livelihood by reducing their stock permits. Again and again, he did.

"Either come up with something acceptable, or it's a short walk for me to the president's office," said Babbitt.

Yet even with the shills he planted on them, almost no local or regional body thus intimidated by the arrogant cabinet officer and his agents gave in to his demands. Some did try to produce local legislation modified to protect their needs at the same time that it recognized federal authority. Babbitt rejected them all, while at the same time managing a public relations campaign producing poll results from cities not even near the chosen areas. Consistently, the contrived propaganda showed more than 60 percent of "the people" eager for more protected lands and practically begging for Babbitt's help. One after another, President William Clinton kept discovering new places "humankind cannot improve upon," and finding exceptional reasons to declare them national monuments.

Talk of a "Clinton legacy" in this was short-sighted. The agenda and methodology of the Clinton-Gore administration was in no way intended to end with Bill Clinton's eighth year in office. It was assumed, and supported by polls and influence plugs, that the transition in 2001 would be to Al Gore, a second-rate student but son of political prominence, who had staked much of his own political ambition on his posture as an environmentalist. Gore's own staff had played active, sometimes intrepid roles in the development of Babbitt's personal tyranny. They were poised to take over for him in a Gore administration that could be expected to be even less reasonable and more ruthless in taking total control over the politically expendable West. How close that came is historic not only for the West, but perhaps for world freedom.

◆ ◆ ◆

As President George W. Bush settled somewhat uncomfortably into office, the land rights-protecting Mountain States Legal Foundation sued in federal court on behalf of the Blue Ribbon Coalition, an off-road vehicle group, claiming President Clinton had exceeded his constitutional and legal authority by assuming he had unlimited power to proclaim the monuments.

The Bush administration itself, still rife with bureaucratic holdovers from the Clinton years, moved to dismiss the case, and the federal district court agreed with their argument that the courts could not review whether the lands were "of scientific interest," "historic," or "of the smallest area," the ruling said. "It is not the court's role to plumb the record to see that there is substantial evidence [or] to hold a trial to determine what facts or factors [were involved] beyond what is in the proclamation."

Babbitt, his minions and his patron Clinton had used the right words, the ruling was saying, and it was beyond the capacity of the court to question their veracity or their motives.

Unless and until the issue is taken up by the U.S. Supreme Court, it means they got away with it, and, even more, it means the West is still up for grabs by those willing to "discard the concept of property." Hardly what Roosevelt might have meant by "Bully." ■

© TOM & THERISA STACK/TOM STACK & ASSOCIATES

This is Arapahoe National Forest in Colorado. Gifford Pinchot, Teddy Roosevelt's founding chief of the U.S. Forest Service, said, "Conservation is the foresighted utilization, preservation and/or renewal of forests, waters, lands and minerals for the greatest good of the greatest number for the longest time." Pinchot and Roosevelt wanted the forests to be used.

WINTER 2004

FOREVER and EVER, AMEN

Land trusts and the frightening thought of perpetuity.

By Tim Findley

In May 1999, EarthFirst! founder and environmental renegade Dave Foreman was promoting his almost unbelievable concept of a Wildlands Project to a New Mexico State University audience.

"Conservation easements are the key to the corridors," he told them. "Once the easements are legally in place, we can impose habitat restrictions for wildlife, thus ending grazing and other agricultural practices. If the landowner refuses, the easement management loophole will allow us to sue the landowner and impose those restrictions."

Well out of Foreman's grasp in the gorgeous blue-green meadows of the Upper Elk River near Steamboat Springs, Colorado, rancher Jay Fetcher could smile coolly at such wild threats. Fetcher donated 1,300 of his acres as a conservation easement in "perpetuity" to American Farmland Trust in 1994, and nearly 10 years later feels more secure than ever about his decision.

"It's still my and my family's land, and it will be for as long as I can imagine. If you're careful, if you deal with the right people and understand what you're doing, it will work," says Fetcher, whose Cattlemen's Agricultural Land Trust is now being copied by similar resource-producer organizations all over the West.

"The one thing I could not let happen was to be the one in my family who was forced to sell it all."

TIM KOOPMAN, CALIFORNIA RANCHER

© TIM FINDLEY

By accepting a conservation easement that limits the use of their property, the owners are juggling a sub-cold concept of perpetuity that doubters say may someday burn them, and that other critics regard as a dangerous trend in altering American concepts of private property and freedom.

"Nincompoops, shortsighted nincompoops!" snaps Carol W. LaGrasse of the trust-busting Property Rights Foundation of America based in Stony Creek, New York. "They're making themselves tenants on their own land."

"If they are forced to sell, then that's forever too," counters University of California scholar and associate dean of ecology studies Lynn Huntsinger. "An easement at least assures a future of stewardship instead of development."

Making the Diggery Do

Land trusts, with their implied superior social authority over property use, are not new. In Great Britain, for example, the National Trust has since 1895 expanded its preservation authority over more than 600,000 acres of English castles and estates, especially along the coastline.

Even before that, however, the concept of funded groups leveraging community standards over private property emerged in the United States soon after the Civil War. Much of it came from the concepts of a sad-eyed intellectual spinster with a whip-snapping wit and a busybody's attitude. She happened to be the prim New England daughter of America's classical frontier novelist, James Fenimore Cooper. Offspring and prodigal of the mind that created "The Last of the Mohicans," Susan Fenimore Cooper formed a fad of Village Improvement Societies and in 1869 published what amounts to a "McGuffy's Reader" on the subject of land trusts in *Putnam's Magazine*.

The erudite, if rather elitist, young woman seen posed in a lacy-necked collar was blunt in her contempt for French and English country towns. "In the days of Shakespeare, and Bacon, and Spenser, your Hobbinol and Lobbinol, and Diggery, your Mopsa and Dorcas, were all dull and loutish, scarcely knowing B from bullsfoot," she wrote. "All the difference of centuries lay between the burgher of the city and the boor of the village." What she meant by Hobbinol, Lobbinol, Diggery, etc., we could probably put in contemporary terms as "crackers," "rednecks," and "rubes." "Bullsfoot" has its own connotation.

But Susan had an oddly Yankee affection for the American village of her time, where new technologies such as steam engines, telegraph wires, and gaslights were bringing "every real advantage of modern life."

"In former centuries," she wrote, "he was a wise man who left the village for the city. Today, he is wise who goes to the city as to a market, but has a home in the country." All the country towns of her time really lacked, she said, were certain finishing touches which could be brought about, "requiring only a moderate fund placed in the hands of judicious persons—requiring, in short, a local Society for Village Improvement."

Well in advance of zoning laws and public parks, Ms. Cooper rallied her followers in New England to tap into public and private funds that would back their authority over improvement of private lands for the benefit of the community. She had no idea, of course, of 21st century

© CAROLYN FOX

Moving cattle passed the round stone corral at the Rosasco Ranch in the Sierra foothills of California.

technology reaching far beyond her suburban village into the Hobbinol and Diggery who labor still on her father's lost frontier, but her advice captured the interest of both the virtuous and villainous who followed it.

As recently as 1965, there were still fewer than 150 land-trust organizations in the United States, almost all in eastern regions, and most, like The Nature Conservancy (TNC), ostensibly dedicated to saving open lands. But scarcely 30 years later, as the Clinton and Babbitt administration welcomed a surge of environmentalism, there were more than 1,500 land trusts all over the nation, with what some said was a new trust formed almost every week to take advantage of government grants and what some called the "guilt money" of major corporate donors.

They are not like banks, or, legally at least, like federal agencies. State and federal laws, as well as their own nonprofit charters, generally restrain the trusts from going out looking for business among stressed and vulnerable landowners. But rules are often stretched, especially by the ubiquitous and corporate-operated TNC, which seemed in the '90s to be everywhere and frequently in close company of federal cohorts.

TNC and the other big trusts dealt strictly in willing sellers they claimed to be their partners, even though the sellers were most often made willing by pressure from the government or the conservation organization itself, and sometimes by a combination of both. The idea of easements allowing property owners to continue to work their land while relinquishing the right to develop it became popular only after TNC and other groups had gorged themselves on outright purchases of ranches, farmland and other property that were frequently flipped back or traded to the government for a windfall to the nonprofit trust.

By the mid-1980s it was becoming clear that just buying up land and trading it among themselves was a burden, both for the conservation trusts and for the government. Ideally, the concept of offering the owner a way to save his land, but limit its use and its value, could accomplish the same purpose without as much political or social liability. And, thanks to new environmental priorities, federal funds, as well as limitless private grants, were available to cover the cost.

What makes the difference now is not so much that sellers are really any more willing, but that the buyers are no longer just the government or TNC.

Willing Sellers

It was just that sort of dilemma that faced the half-dozen property owners near the Upper Elk River when they met on Jay Fetcher's deck in 1993. One of them, Steve Stranahan, ran a 500-acre dude ranch. Another, Mary Mosher, was a grandmother in her 80s who was considered the outspoken conscience of the entire Routt County valley. Others were like Fetcher, struggling to continue with the family ranch despite the relentless approach of more 30-acre vacation sites and one-horse, view ranchettes that moved closer every season.

In a way, it was Fetcher's own father's fault. He had been among the group in the 1960s which saw the future in selling the 10,000-foot slopes of Storm Mountain as a new,

Texas-developed ski resort. They did not anticipate the metamorphosis that resort-town growth would bring to the once-isolated mountain town of Steamboat Springs and in sprawling miles beyond it into the awesome stream-fed meadows that couched ranches much like their own.

From a character-laden mountain village that was a center for ranching and mining, Steamboat was transformed into a franchise-familiar international playground. Money was everywhere, but like the bubbling sulfur vent that gave the town its name, Steamboat Springs seemed gone and going worse.

Perhaps scenting blood, The Nature Conservancy had moved in soon after the developers, and acquired a working ranch along the highway south of town. As it did in every western state and almost anywhere willing sellers might be found, TNC established itself as a helpful presence in Steamboat and Routt County, always apparent at any community meeting.

"...when 10 years have passed, the ground will be yours."

SUSAN FENIMORE COOPER, 1813-1894

But Fetcher had by chance been given the opportunity to see the pitfalls of dealing with such wealthy trusts at a conference 10 years before that meeting on his deck. He suggested to the six neighbors that they form a compact of mutual interest in preserving the Elk River valley and its productive values, and that they first try for help from a group that at least made overtures to preserving working land. The agreement they worked out with American Farmland Trust in Washington, D.C., was the first of its kind.

Fetcher himself donated 1,300 acres of meadowland at the heart of the valley that when valued for the production of pasture and hay was worth around $500 an acre, but when appraised for development was worth at least $7,000 an acre. As an easement donation to the nonprofit American Farmland Trust, he was able to write part of it off his taxes, but he was also sacrificing its highest appraised value. You could say he lost millions in the promise never to sell it for any purpose other than agriculture or conservation. Or you could say that the legacy he plans to leave to his children is beyond appraisable value.

There are no restrictions on grazing, and Fetcher was allowed to set aside three homesites on which his family could build. Once a year, someone from the American Farmland Trust comes out to look it over. Fetcher drives him around, assuring him that it is still an intact unit of a healthy, working ranch. But Fetcher is reluctant even to tell the trust representative how many cattle he runs, because he doesn't have to. "It's ours," he says. "I don't feel like a tenant at all, and neither do my kids."

A Salamander's Tale

Stand beside California rancher Tim Koopman on a tawny slope of slippery late-summer grasses and watch his daughter, two more rolling hills in the distance, as she runs to the head-tossing roan that taunts her like a friend.

Below that view, deep in the valley, a busy ribbon of U.S. 680 hums with traffic between San Jose and Pleasanton. In their cars they watch forward, oblivious to the charming little drama of the teenager and her horse on the hills above them, and unaware that they are being seen without being noticed. Stand there and glance at the soft glow from a tough man's face as he watches his daughter with pride. There's something fragile there that knows about forever.

Koopman is counting on her and her older brother to carry on with this ranch that has been in the family for four generations, since Tim's great-grandparents came ashore at Half Moon Bay. Even where the freeway runs was once a part of it until Koopman's father sold the right-of-way under threat of condemnation. It is a clutch of cupcake canyons just one big commuter hill away from one of the world's most intensely developed regions around San Francisco Bay, and Koopman knows well what it is worth.

Koopman had learned a lesson when his grandfather died in 1968 leaving a simple will, but no estate plan. Officially, California has no death tax. In fact, the state's Williamson Act was intended to preserve agricultural land from development by assessing property taxes on production rather than speculative value. Nevertheless, the federal government established an inheritance tax liability on the ranch amounting to over $125,000. In part to help meet the crippling expenses that were soon compounded by drought, Koopman left the ranch, earned a degree, and began teaching vocational science. He was the first of his family to even temporarily leave the land, and it was nearly 10 years before he came back home to Sunol, far better educated and, so he thought, far better prepared to contend with the traps of property ownership.

But when his father died unexpectedly in 1991, followed by his mother only three years later, Koopman was confronted with federal and state tax audits demanding over half a million dollars in taxes on the increasingly valuable land. Even the family trust he had prepared fell short of estate planning capable of heading off the catastrophic tax bill.

"I was ready to do whatever I could," says Koopman, "but the one thing I could not let happen was to be the one in my family who was forced to sell it all."

At the same time, Koopman had become one of the leading voices in the California Cattlemen's Association and would later take a leading role in the California Rangeland Trust (CRT).

Koopman's grandfather once told him that the sinkhole just up from the old road had appeared there when the hillside sloughed off in the 1906 earthquake. Except for the driest of summers, it held a small amount of water year-round that Koopman used as a stock pond. It was also, as he discovered in his boyhood, the springtime home for black-and-gold-striped tiger salamanders. Just, in fact, like a swampy area standing in the way of another new upscale housing development elsewhere in the valley.

It became one of the first mitigation deals brokered by CRT. Koopman was paid to keep some 30 acres in perpetuity as salamander habitat, mitigating the loss to similar critters in the path of development. Happily, everybody agrees they get along just fine with grazing cattle around their water hole. The easement prevents those acres from ever being sold for development or for any reason other than conservation. As a result, the appraised value dropped—and so did Koopman's tax bill. Other than that, nothing really had changed. In effect, the ranch was saved, thanks to a salamander and the 1906 earthquake—as well as to developers themselves.

© JEREMY GREEN

"It's still my family's land, and it will be for as long as I can imagine."

JAY FETCHER, WITH WIFE GAEL, COLORADO RANCHERS

First the family, then the land

Devere Dressler is in a direct line of sons you might imagine as descendants of "Bonanza's" Ben Cartwright himself. The Dressler ranch, settled in 1862, is still in the right place, centered on the bright and beautifully maintained Victorian where Dressler and his family still live. You can imagine it as once the main house of a private domain, almost an empire that stretched from above and beyond the eastern toes of the Sierra near Carson City, Nevada, and south to the rich desert-to-alpine valleys of Bridgeport, California. Dressler's grandfather Fred was the classic American rancher businessman, a member of the Cowboy Hall of Fame who was both greatly respected and sometimes feared. He is still a legend in Nevada.

"Just the same," Devere Dressler recalls, "he told my dad and my aunt that he didn't want them to become ranchers and go through the same things he did."

The empire of thousands of acres, if that's what you could call it, has been peeled away in chunks beginning with Fred's decision in 1987 to sell most of the Sierra valleys to the Trust for Public Land, which in turn traded it to the California Department of Fish & Game and the U.S. Forest Service. Fred's intention was to preserve the land from development with enough money earned to balance out the liabilities of estate taxes on the remaining property he would pass on to his two kids. But not long after that, Dressler's aunt decided to divide it again with the sale of her share to private interests. Not because of that, and beyond the family's control, more and more 20- and 30-acre sites of what Dressler calls "weedettes" were moving in along the front range, driving higher land prices ahead of them. Dressler's own two sisters felt it was time to sell their interests.

If the Dressler ranch really could have been a "Bonanza" model of another time, the dramatic sequels in the contemporary story might be as a soap opera set in a real-estate office. Dressler, knowing his own family had divided interests about keeping the land in ranching, was, like his grandfather, determined to at least maintain the open-range integrity of the 6,300-acre Bridgeport Valley. It was an awesome prize forming a natural migration route into Yosemite itself, and perhaps the last pristine valley without development on the Sierra's eastern slopes. On TV, Ben and the boys might have gone guns blazing to save it. In reality, Dressler went to the new California Rangeland Trust to help solve his worries for land and for family.

Partnered for the purpose with the American Land Conservancy and using funds from the California Department of Fish & Game as well as the Wildlife Conservation Board and the Department of Transportation, the deal paid off his sisters and awarded two willing new ranchers with land that "in perpetuity" may never be sold for any other purpose.

"God only made so much land," says Dressler. "It makes me feel better knowing that at least some of it will never change." ■

FALL 2004

REFUTING THE MYTHS

It is time to expose anti-livestock bias in federal culture. The truth is, long-term livestock removal in the West is usually an environmental disaster. What else could you call something that wipes out most plants and most wildlife? By Steven H. Rich

Do cows really eat fish? Do they eat fish eggs? I have replied on behalf of clients to multiple Draft Biological Opinions regarding two national forests where U.S. Fish & Wildlife Service biologists made these claims. They claimed that cows destroyed the nests (redds) of fish species that don't build nests, stepped on fish, and muddied the water of fish that spawn only in muddy water. They also designated dry washes as critical habitat for endangered species of fish.

Anti-livestock claims just as imaginative and unsubstantiated as those are often found in government documents. This one was an obvious attempt to claim "direct take" of an endangered species and trigger draconian anti-livestock actions.

Such claims are justified in the minds of highly-imaginitive persons with apocalyptic visions of pillaging bovines raping every riparian system in the West. I have heard versions of this "cows (or sheep or goats) will destroy the world" rant from dozens of federal officials.

"There is an entrenched culture in federal land and resource management agencies based on sociopolitical philosophy rather than scientific inquiry," said biologist and attorney Dennis Parker, who loves wildlife and is a passionate advocate of good management. "For example, Region 3 of the Forest Service has created 'grazing guidance criteria' for endangered species consultations which are notorious among responsible scientists for institutionalizing speculation and assumption as if such were scientific fact, while ignoring excellent research by its own Rocky Mountain Research Station scientists, of which the agency was fully aware."

Outrageous claims are too often regarded as fact, even when proven false. Here are just a few:

The Infamous Desert Tortoise Scam

U.S. Fish & Wildlife Service biologists claimed widespread destruction of tortoises by livestock. They claimed cows stepped on tortoises and crushed their burrows. No cow has been documented to have stepped on a tortoise and only one accidentally trampled burrow has been found. They claimed cows also deprived tortoises of food. Any desert rancher, desert dweller or competent desert reptile biologist will know that tortoises cluster around corrals to get fresh cow dung to eat. They need it for moisture, B vitamins, and easy nutrition. Cow dung greatly increases their health, active periods and egg production. Also, the desert annuals and other herbaceous plants tortoises depend on greatly decrease when livestock removal stops nutrient cycling and soil disturbance. All this and more was raised in the Environmental Impact Statement but the bias won out. Locals report fewer tortoises; scientists report increases in tortoise diseases.

© LARRY ANGIER

Curious cattle in California.

The Infamous Southwestern Willow Flycatcher Scam

Beginning with biologist Dennis Parker, private, university and federal biologists have documented the largest by far (half of the subspecies) and most successful concentration of Southwest willow flycatchers on earth in New Mexico's Gila Cliff Valley. They are nesting in predominantly man-made second-growth box elder-dominated woodland (not willows because they avoid the willows) on irrigation ditches and returns. They eat bees, wasps, and yellow jackets by preference (not flies or mosquitoes). This population refuses to occupy gallery forests on streams lined by willows adjacent, upstream and downstream from the Gila Cliff Valley—the kind of habitat federal endangered species' documents insist they want.

The flycatchers on the ranches experience the lowest rate of cowbird parasitism of any population in the United States. Some of the highest cowbird parasitism rates are in

Grand Canyon National Park, where there are no cows. The Gila Cliff Valley has the highest concentration of livestock in southwestern New Mexico. Despite this and much more, thousands of cattle have been removed allegedly to protect flycatchers. Right now in Rock House, Arizona, the feds are building mosquito ponds lined with willows for flycatchers. This is a West Nile Virus hot spot. These birds don't like willows, don't like mosquitoes, and have no immunity.

© JEFF FOOTT/TOM STACK & ASSOCIATES

Desert tortoises like cows, but feds and enviros don't.

The Infamous Mexican Spotted Owl Scam

According to Bent's "Life History of North American Birds," there were none of these in the U.S. before 1929 or until large-scale logging began. These owls prefer steep, deep, dry, cool canyons. They dine by preference on wood rats (packrats) and other rodents. Most actual Mexican spotted owl habitat is inaccessible by livestock, but livestock are removed because they allegedly threaten the owls through exposing wood rats to avian predation. (Avian included owls last time I checked.)

The Infamous Lesser Long-Nosed Bat Scam

This organism has millions of acres of protected habitat on federal land. It has been used to reduce livestock numbers and de-stock ranges. In fact, its numbers are limited primarily by lack of roosting and nursery habitat in caves. The Forest Service has closed more than 200 abandoned mine entrances which could have served this need. More are being closed.

The Infamous Cactus Ferruginous Pygmy Owl Scam

Ranchers have been destocked by 90 percent over this bird, abundant in Mexico. Its listing as an endangered species was recently ruled by the Ninth Circuit Court in San Francisco as "arbitrary and capricious." Politics have prevented the lower court from ordering its delisting.

The Infamous Masked Bobwhite Quail Scam

Millions were spent buying Arizona land to "protect" these birds (whose core habitat is in Mexico). The Buenos Aires National Wildlife Refuge was created and the cattle were removed. The tame, pen-raised quail usually got eaten by coyotes and other predators within a week, so the escapees left and went to nearby ranches for protection. This is a very common outcome.

It's What They Know That Isn't So

These are just a few of a very big list of examples and anti-grazers passionately believe in the validity of all of them. Activists have even planted evidence (remember the bogus lynx hairs planted on a rubbing post by federal and state biologists in a Washington forest in 2001?). Tucson's *Daily Star* on May 16, 2004, published a similar story about a former U.S. Fish & Wildlife Service refuge manager planting Chiricahua leopard frogs, apparently to create continued justification for the Buenos Aires National Wildlife Refuge.

In Grand Staircase-Escalante National Monument, cows under federal grazing prescriptions have also been alleged to create "dung fire" risk to underground artifacts; rub petroglyphs off cliff walls; endanger a historic structure (a corral); endanger native grasses and forbs; endanger native wildlife; cause floods, erosion, water-quality degradation, widespread public outrage, lost tourism revenues and juniper invasions (all untrue); and destroy some recreationists' experience of the outdoors by their mere presence. All this was found, along with the flycatchers and the spotted owls, in one federal document.

Hundreds of conversations with anti-grazing activists inside the federal government have outlined their reasons and motives clearly. They see themselves as principled, heroic figures performing civil disobedience to save nature from industry. They hold fellow workers who defend scientific grazing in disdain as having "sold out to the Man." They know that ranchers experience their deliberate trouble-making as a form of domestic terrorism, but they feel that the end justifies the means.

Even though some activists act in full knowledge that they use falsehoods as weapons, even more pervasive, but just as damaging, are those who simply and uncritically believe the body of false information passed on to them from what they believe to be authoritative sources. This tragic multiplier of dangerous (to nature) beliefs operates in the media as well, which then spread bias to the public. It all speaks to the huge disconnect between urban people and the truth about nature. ■

WINTER 2005

ENDING the FREE RIDE for the GET'emoff GANG

Al Medina and the Drake Exclosure.
By Dan Dagget

The compact man in the Cowboys ball cap waved his arm at the bare dirt around him and asked, "How many times are we going to have to learn this lesson before we finally get it?"

The rest of us shifted from foot to foot. Not many seminars on rangeland health start with something so "in your face."

The occasion for this gathering was a rangeland health workshop organized by the Quivira Coalition, a Santa Fe, New Mexico-based environmental group, and EcoResults!, a Flagstaff, Arizona-based group I helped create. The speaker was Al Medina, a research ecologist with the U.S. Department of Agriculture Rocky Mountain Research Station in Flagstaff.

The setting was the Drake Exclosure, a 40-acre piece of rangeland in the Verde River watershed about 100 miles north of Phoenix. This area had become so devastated in the early 20th century that a portion of it was fenced to protect it from grazing and other human uses in 1946, so various ways to heal the land might be tried and studied. The area had come to its sorry state after more than a half century of grazing, woodcutting, burning and crop raising. In other words, it had been subjected to the same sort of uses and abuses as much of the rest of the West.

The means used to try to fix the area have become typical. Seeds of a variety of plants were sown, including exotics known to be able to survive and even prosper in the most devastated land. Juniper trees that had proliferated during the deterioration were removed on the theory that they had become so effective at capturing water that virtually nothing could compete with them. And, of course, a considerable portion of the exclosure was left untouched to see how effectively leaving the land "to nature" would heal it.

It was on one of those back-to-nature areas that Medina challenged us with his question. Some of the junipers here were as much as 40 feet apart. Separating these shrubby trees were large expanses of bare dirt where much of the soil had been eroded away in spite of the fact that the land was nearly flat and, therefore, an unlikely candidate for erosion. The surface that was left consisted largely of small rocks imbedded in a crust compacted by wind and raindrops and baked by the sun into something ecologists call "desert pavement." In other words, the left-alone area of the Drake, except for the intermittent trees, looks very much like a parking lot.

Many ungrazed public lands are becoming "desert pavement." Rest is the worst thing for this kind of arid country. It needs animal impact to rejuvenate.

Having gotten our attention, Al continued: "We've been putting fences around places like this so they aren't disturbed by human activity and watching what happens to them for a hundred years now. And when what we see here keeps happening, we don't say, 'All right, I get it. This doesn't work.' We say, 'We need another study.'"

Medina swept his hand from just above the bare ground to a series of finger punches aimed into the distance and the future. "Is this what we want the West to look like?" he challenged. "Because if this is what we want, we know how to get it. We know that if you fence five acres or five hundred or five million, much of it will end up looking like this."

There are thousands of exclosures like the Drake around the West, maybe hundreds of thousands if you count all the little bent-wire cages scattered around to protect a few square feet of rangeland. Some of them have been exclosed for more than a century. In fact, Medina was the chief scientist for more than six years on the Santa Rita Experimental Range, a series of study areas and exclosures near Tucson, Arizona, that were set aside in 1903.

Medina explains that not all these exclosures are in a condition as bad as the Drake, but the point is that a lot of them are. "All of them may not show the same degree of deterioration as the Drake," Medina offered, "but they all exhibit the same processes of deterioration." In fact, he says many of these same processes are common on public and private lands on areas that aren't being intentionally rested, but are being managed in such a way that the effect is the same.

Most important among these processes, according to Medina, is the loss of an area's ability to absorb water. Water runs off desert pavement almost as effectively as it runs off real pavement. In a study conducted by Texas A&M University, only a quarter of the water that fell on bare dirt was absorbed by it. Quite likely that means the bare dirt of the Drake only absorbs about three inches of the 12 inches of precipitation that fall on it in an average year.

Trees and the litter under them intercept rain too. The same study shows that on the average, 81 percent of the rain that falls on a tree reaches the soil surface under it. Since only 10 percent of the rested area of the Drake is canopied by trees, and 90 percent of it is bare dirt, the back-to-nature part of the Drake receives only an average of about 3.5 inches of moisture a year. That's not a lot. The Sahara Desert averages eight inches.

Grasslands, on the other hand, are relatively effective at absorbing water. According to the Texas A&M study, bunchgrass areas absorb three-fourths of the rain that fall on them. Sod grasses absorb more than half. Immediately outside the Drake Exclosure, the lands of the Bar Hart Ranch managed by Don and Anne Verner have a healthy component of bunchgrasses. That means they receive more water than the land inside the fence even though the same amount of rain falls on both sides. The hooves of the cattle on the Bar Hart that break up the desert pavement help out too. In fact, Dr. Jim Richardson of North Dakota State University has shown that livestock managed properly can increase the land's ability to absorb water as much as 600 percent.

Both sides of the Drake fence were identical at the time the fence was built. Both had the same elevation, same rainfall, same soil, same proportion of bare dirt to trees, same management. They still have the same everything, except that the land inside is now protected, and the land

PHOTOS © TOM BEAN

"Is this what we want the West to look like?" Al Medina, research ecologist with the U.S. Department of Agriculture, points out deteriorating soils where cattle have been excluded.

outside is used. Cattle graze on it; people cut trees for firewood and drive their trucks across it to pick up the wood.

Counter to what many of us would expect, the land that is used is home to more plants and more animals than the land that is protected. Since the only difference between the former and the latter is how those lands are managed, that must account for any difference in their condition. The land inside the fence must be more barren because it is protected.

Another process by which Medina says rest causes land to deteriorate is by increasing plant senescence and death. The Drake also provides a stark example of this. Most of the plants inside the Drake's "protective" fence show significant signs of senescence. Many are dead. Seedlings are rare to nonexistent. In fact, studies show that 90 percent of the plant species that were present when the Drake was exclosed are no longer present.

Medina pointed out that this is not due solely to the increased dryness of the area within the exclosure. Another factor is the skewed composition of the soil microbial community there. Tests show that the soil under the junipers in the exclosure is populated almost entirely by fungi. Areas of bare dirt out from under the trees are populated almost entirely by bacteria. One of the functions of soil fungi is to aid plants in seed germination and the absorption of moisture and nutrients via a web of wispy connectors called mycorrhizae. With less water available inside the exclosure due to the land's reduced ability to absorb water and the water-capturing effectiveness of the junipers, the lack of mycorrhizae raises the challenge plants face in order to survive there from difficult to nearly impossible.

The fact that plants are scarcer and less vital inside the exclosure impairs the ability of the plant community there to perform a couple of important ecosystem functions. The first—removing carbon from the atmosphere and releasing oxygen into it—is important to everything that breathes.

A rangeland health workshop studies the effect of "negative impact" (rest). An acre of healthy grassland is more effective at removing carbon from the air than an acre of rainforest. The land outside the rested exclosure is closer to being healthy grassland than the land left untouched for decades.

Pete Jackson, past president of the Society for Range Management, has said an acre of healthy grassland is more effective at removing carbon from the air than an acre of rainforest. The land outside the Drake is closer to being healthy grassland than the land inside.

Plants remove carbon from the atmosphere by capturing it through photosynthesis and transforming it into organic material (tissue, food, and waste). Because most of a grass plant is underground, much of that organic material ends up underground as well. There it serves to absorb and store moisture. Any gardener knows that soil with a significant organic content is better at storing water than soil with less organic material. The barren areas of the Drake include little to no organic material and therefore are extremely ineffective at storing water. The land outside the Drake, on the other hand, has more organic material above and below ground. It's greener and lusher, and, obviously, stores more water.

All this amounts to the fact that resting the land has a significant environmental impact on it. As I understand the National Environmental Policy Act in any situation where it applies, any means of managing the land that would cause a significant environmental impact must be studied to assess the extent of that impact, and where that impact would be unacceptable it must be mitigated.

During the field trip, I asked a couple of staffers of the Prescott National Forest whether they considered the negative impacts of rest, such as those Medina had just pointed out, and whether they required measures to mitigate those impacts when they made a decision about land use. They said they didn't because "rest isn't considered to have negative impacts, because it is assumed to be the absence of use and therefore the absence of activities that have negative impacts."

The lands of the Drake, and plenty of places like it around the West, contradict that assumption with plain and simple facts. Those facts show us that rest does have negative impacts—very significant ones. But don't look for the national environmental groups to wage a campaign to save the West from this environmental threat. With a few exceptions, such as the Quivira Coalition, the position of the environmental groups is the one from which that Forest Service assumption is derived—that use by humans is harmful and the only way to heal the land is to leave it alone.

As unlikely as it may sound, there is a way to deal with this that, in the end, will have positive effects for everyone, including the environment. All management plans and proposed actions that are subject to environmental review and don't address the impacts of rest and provide for its mitigation are subject to challenge. This includes all those instances in which environmental groups, or anyone else, buy federal grazing allotments or state grazing leases and retire them from grazing.

In order for these challenges to be successful, the issue of the negative impacts of rest must be raised in the information-gathering stage of the planning process. Help in gathering this information is available via a number of sources. The Center for Holistic Management in Albuquerque, New Mexico, and the Quivira Coalition in Santa Fe, New Mexico, have produced a number of publications describing the impacts of rest. Both also hold workshops on the subject. The Rocky Mountain Research Station of the U.S. Department of Agriculture is even available to provide scientific resources for the effort.

Once this information is collected and included in the planning process, it makes that document subject to appeal, or even a lawsuit, if the issue isn't adequately addressed. A few successful applications of this approach with the help of a lawyer who would like to gain a reputation for transforming national environmental law for the better, and those who buy federal grazing allotments or state grazing leases in order to retire them may soon find themselves required to bring in ranchers and their stock to mitigate the damage they do to the land. ■

WINTER 2005

ODE to the HUMBLE COW PIE

The Tao and ecology of poo and the key role of endangered feces. By Steven H. Rich

Ecologically, good, clean, high-quality organic cow dung is great stuff. When it's full of life (beetles, larvae, worms, bacteria, fungi), it's a thing of beauty. Birds love cow dung. They eat the seeds, bugs, larvae and worms in it, and some of the dung itself. Mice, voles and other rodents tear it apart just like the birds, looking for nutritious morsels. Reptiles stake out hunting territories around it. Reptile herbivores like desert tortoises eat the dung for easy calories and B vitamins. Curlews probe for vermiform and insect lunches under cow pies (or buffalo chips) with curved bills precisely adapted for that purpose.

Cow dung is a fountain of food—a banquet of delights. It provides moisture, sustenance and shelter for a long list of creatures that support another very long list of other creatures.

© C.J. HADLEY

Dung beetles are vital actors in the balance and harmony of nature.

Cow pies support the soil food web in many ways. As a response to rain and snowmelt, dried dung provides many batches of high-quality compost tea, carrying with it readily available nutrients and micro-organic inoculants. Fungi reach white mycelic tendrils out of the ground to suck enzyme-dissolved carbohydrates and other goodies into the soil.

Cow pies are nectar and ambrosia to dung beetles that hugely improve soils and do all that work for—dung! These beetles have exquisitely sensitive dung detectors. A fresh deposit leaves a spreading plume of delectable odors that the beetles can sense in tiny parts per billion.

These sturdy fliers rise into the softly scented air, vectoring on increasing concentration until they arrive (plop!) at the prize. There are three basic strategies for dung beetles originally adapted to bison droppings. Some species burrow right into the pie and build an elaborate tracery of tunnels. They lay eggs that quickly hatch into some of the larvae so prized as juicy delicacies by carnivorous species. Other dung beetles, sometimes called tumblebugs, grab a chunk which forms into a ball as they roll it away to an excavation where it is sealed in and adorned with eggs. The eggs hatch, feed on the dung, and soon mature to seek a pile of their own. The final strategy is to tunnel into soil under the protective cover of the pie, laying eggs to be nourished by plugs of poop deposited by hardworking parents who loosen, fertilize, and aerate soils in the process, as the tumblebugs do.

My friends Dr. Pat Richardson (the Dung Beetle Lady) and her husband Dr. Dick Richardson (both of the University of Texas at Austin, Department of Integrative Biology) made me a connoisseur of cow pies. I prod them, sniff them, turn them over, open and examine them. They speak volumes about the health of the land. I once counted 17 species of insects visiting an Idaho cow pie in a four- or five-minute period. There were butterflies, wasps, bees, beetles, moths, flies, hornets, dragonflies, lacewings and a mantis. Ecologically, dung is a big deal.

But it's also the number-one, anti-livestock issue. Why do some people hate it (except the traumatic-botched-potty-training-leading-to-anal-retentive-personalities theory)? Healthy landscapes have for centuries on end received the dung of many species, processed it, and given it back as new life. Cow pies can disappear into the soil in a single day where there are lots of dung beetles. Remember that the sacred Egyptian scarab, a symbol of rebirth, is a dung beetle.

Good cow pies have little odor. Feedlots and dairies have many times the odor of rangeland corrals because of the rich diets confined cattle get from feed troughs. Rangeland pastures smell like grass and flowers.

Unfortunately, some anal retentives in the federal government buy into the Eurocentric, anthropocentric, urban-elite-centered prejudice against manure. For example, page 25 of Environmental Assessment Number UT-030-02-001, prepared by Grand Staircase/Escalante National Monument staffers, recommends the complete de-stocking of an allotment, stating: "primary recreation activities would continue. However, as a result of removing cattle from the allotment, the quality of these experiences would improve."

Come on people, lighten up! Buffalo chips and cow pies are indispensable, integral parts of the West. Most people love to see cowboys and cows together. They stop and wave. They smile. They take pictures. They want to pose with them. The cows (and the pies) don't deter them at all.

When you see cow pies, pray they're full of life. An early British naturalist stated that God must be extraordinarily fond of beetles because he created zillions of varieties. And look what he gave so many species of them to eat. Learn to love and appreciate healthy, life-giving dung.

And as for that potty-training thing—get over it. ■

WINTER 2007

PLAYING WITH FIRE

With no scientific feedback process Forest Service firebugs in Grand Canyon country are stuck on stupid. By Steven H. Rich

Have they burned your forest yet? That's a fair question ever since the Clinton administration and trendy, activist academicians began packing the U.S. Forest Service with people who believe fire can do no harm. Please understand that they are planning hot-weather burns in your forest. The odds are that many of them will escape.

Huge destructive escaped hot-season "management" burns have gone on unchallenged for years. Federal agencies are now demonstrating a reckless disregard for biodiversity, endangered species, wildlife in general, soils, watersheds and everything else they're supposed to preserve. Their pro-fire, damn-the-consequences attitude shows utter contempt for the extreme sacrifices rural people expend in the cause of protecting nature and endangered species. They are casually consuming values that conscientious government and local people have worked generations to create. It's a blazing orgy of death and destruction, and they smugly call it "natural." The doctrinaire "green" agenda is really a smoking black one.

Now the North Kaibab is bleeding from deep burns. Black floods 150 feet wide rush through meadows and canyons as fire-crusted slopes shed desperately needed rains in torrential ash and soil-filled flows. Water holes fill with ash and a caustic solution of lye and water. Aquatic organisms cannot survive. Nothing can drink. The floods repeatedly roar 25 miles across bone-dry Houserock Valley into the Colorado River. The Colorado runs black for days after rains—from Marble Canyon through the Grand Canyon to Lake Mead. This inevitable post-fire disaster always continues for years.

Abnormal post-fire flood flows typically last seven to 14 years and more, according to scientists' fire research quoted in a Forest Service General Technical Report (RMRS-GTR-63-2000, Peter Robichaud, Jan Beyers and Dan Neary). Recovery, the report states, can take centuries and may never fully happen. It further states that Southwestern fires commonly increase peak storm flows 500 percent to 9,600 percent. Fire-caused floods 35,000 percent worse than pre-fire runoff have been measured. By contrast, the same Forest Service document says that even logging every tree in a clear cut—which activists revile as a fish-killing obscenity—temporarily increases peak flows

PHOTOS © STEVEN H. RICH

Current federal fire management doesn't work. OPPOSITE: *After a major fire, every tree in this photo is dead or dying. Washes up to 40 feet deep have been cut by flood waters roaring off this ruined watershed. In soil sterilized two to six inches deep by severe fire, most grass, flowers, endangered goshawks and other federally protected wildlife are dead. Forest Service has no money for rehabilitation.*

only a comparatively insignificant average of 25 percent to 100 percent over runoff from undisturbed woodland. The public is never told these facts.

On June 18, 2006, forest rangers found a lightning-strike fire about 30 inches across in the upper Warm Springs canyon area of the North Kaibab district. They could have put it out by stepping on it. Instead, they were ordered, under a delirious interpretation of "Wildland Fire-Use Policy," to let it burn. Drought maps showed the area in red—severe drought—a cross between a tinderbox and a sea of gasoline. The Forest Service had prohibited the public from using open flames in Kaibab National Forest.

John Chambers, for eight years the Forest Service national office chief of fire operations called the hot, dry-season, let-burn decision and the agency's refusal to manage forest fuels through harvesting and thinning "stupid." He wrote: "If the only fuel management tool you have is a match, sooner or later you'll be in deep sh**!"

The "management" fire showed high severity ground fire characteristics early on. Tons of heavy fallen logs per acre burned to ashes. Forest-floor organics burned so hot that the green pine needles boiled internally on thousands of tall (now dead) pines—which can then play host to lethal bark-beetle infestations. Grass root crowns were fatally incinerated on thousands of acres.

All this alarmed new fire-control officers not at all, despite the fact the blaze kept crossing "action lines" drawn to protect northern goshawks. They just made more lines. A bizarre double standard was officially revealed later when, according to Forest Service sources, a Native American forest ranger was expected to pay for a new Bobcat tractor that burned up. He parked it six miles from the fire area. His superiors said he should have known it was obviously unsafe.

Experienced locals—many of them trained fire fighters and/or former forest rangers—warned that the horribly dangerous fire should have been extinguished immediately. As they predicted, the fire boiled up into a desolating cataclysm. It formed a gigantic thundercloud made of water blasted from drought-stricken grass, flowers, trees, soils and the bodies of burned wildlife. The cloud collapsed in the early morning instantly spreading the fire for miles.

Above: Critical to wildlife, aspen groves average 2,000 pounds of grass and flowers per acre. Below: Severe ground fire has killed all the trees. Aspens resprout, but watershed stabilization and full use of wildlife takes from decades to centuries.

This burned area includes approximately 25 percent of the core habitat of the white-tailed Kaibab squirrel—found nowhere else on earth. The burning certainly consumed young flightless goshawks in their nests. Most young Kaibab squirrels and other newborn animals such as hawks, foxes, owls, rabbits, porcupines, coyotes, songbirds, bobcats, golden eagles, woodpeckers, deer, Arizona tiger salamanders, chipmunks and other federally protected species could not have escaped.

It burned rare Kaibab pediocacti (also found nowhere else), and potential Mexican spotted owl habitat. All wildlife were exposed to wildfire in a pincers movement. The "management phase" fire still burned on top of the mountain while the escaped wildfire phase roared up the forested east slopes—trapping and confusing even adults between the two blazes. Then it turned southwest into the

PHOTOS © STEVEN H. RICH

The Kaibab Plateau is famous as a mule deer haven. Mule deer are in decline around the West due to a loss of habitat to development (particularly winter range), tough weather, and competition from elk. BELOW: *The fate of this important deer habitat is uncertain. There are no plans to repair the watershed. Floods rip soils and even boulders off the mountain and blast them all the way to the Colorado River 25 miles away.*

mixed conifer high country—goshawk central.

The North Kaibab Plateau forms the North Rim of the Grand Canyon, known for its serene forested beauty surrounded by desert. It is also home to the densest breeding population of rare northern goshawks on earth. Their success is due to decades of careful, conscientious select-cut logging by Kaibab Industries in partnership with foresters and biologists from the pre-Clinton Forest Service. It opened biological deserts of over-dense trees into paradises of diversity.

In the adjacent unlogged Grand Canyon National Park far fewer goshawks dwell in narrow strips on points of the canyon's rim and forest edges. In the long-logged national forest the hawks penetrate every wooded habitat—even into piñon/juniper woodland treated with openings for wildlife and cattle.

The fire ruined tens of thousands of acres of excellent goshawk country. Researcher Richard Reynolds and others (U.S. Forest Service Rocky Mountain Research Station) have learned goshawks need multiage forest mosaics just like those created by select-cut bioplanned logging. They avoid even-age tree stands because they lack diverse prey species and starve the goshawks out. Only even-age stands of trees can grow back after stand-replacing fires.

Kaibab Industries was driven out of business because it had produced so many goshawks that logging operations were never out of sight or hearing of them. U.S. Fish & Wildlife Service officers insisted the birds could not bear sights, sounds and disturbances they had thrived with for years. Hundreds of families in job-starved northern Arizona and southern Utah lost their livelihoods.

The 58,000-acre fire came within a scant 14 miles of the Grand Canyon. More than a thousand travelers and staff were trapped by 100-foot flames across Highway 67—the only paved way out. They had to be evacuated on dirt back roads. Hundreds could have died if not for favorable winds and providential weeks-early rains.

The district fire management officer wondered on regional TV (KSL-Salt Lake City) what the big deal was.

"In two or three hundred years it will look just the same," he glibly opined. "A human lifetime's just a blip on the radar screen." He didn't mention endangering hundreds of such blips, including his own crews, the $8 million suppression cost, a similar cost for rehabilitation, the half-billion dollars in lumber or the dead wildlife and habitats.

Smelling cover-up, respected experts are challenging the agency spin. They scoff at claims that "65 percent burned at low severity." After viewing the ruin, a former highly placed Forest Service employee e-mailed:

"The folks I was with said they had never seen such devastation over such a large contiguous area—certainly I haven't.... If this had been a simple 'wildfire' and not a 'fire-use fire' gone bad, with the same results, the Forest Service would have been talking about the huge amounts of resource damage being done; esthetic values being lost on the way to the Canyon; wildlife losses on the [Grand Canyon National] Game Preserve; years to replace the lost resource, etc., to justify the huge suppression costs that were being incurred."

To locals it was arrogant cynicism when Forest Service P.R. people called this tragedy the "Warm Fire." They're contacting Congress. They wonder why locals can't even startle a goshawk in the process of vastly improving their habitat if the Forest Service can cook 'em in the process of destroying it. Locals could go to jail under Section 9 of the Endangered Species Act and be fined millions for a particle of the damage this fire caused. There are no consequences to those who let it happen.

Under any objective standard, either continual years with vast acreages burned by escaped hot-weather catastrophic fires are ecological disasters or the Endangered

Species Act, National Environmental Policy Act, Forest Service Organic Act (the one that says they're to preserve the forest) and the Administrative Procedures Act are just bitter, contemptuous jokes on the rural populace and a trusting American public. The consequences of these destructive hot-weather fires destroy protected species and their habitats as well as ecological conditions protected by these acts. The scale by which they violate the intent of those acts dwarfs any damage the very worst industrial activity creates. This unexamined "naturalness" fetish is running amok.

There are no words to express the biological weirdness of this "fire is always good" attitude. Burned soils form water-resistant crusts. They lose all surface organics and are sterilized to a depth of two inches—killing even the most fire-tolerant grasses. In firespeak, this is called a moderate event. Even high-severity fires which consume logs, form worse crusts, alter the soil's physical structure and sterilize them six inches deep and more are imagined to be natural, beneficial and even ecologically necessary.

Calling fires burning in 100-year-fire-suppression fuel-loads "natural" is crazy. In the words of playwright Christopher Marlowe: "Such reasons make noon night and dark night day." The previous big Kaibab fire—the Bridger Fire Complex left (after the flood phase) large areas treeless and covered with nonnative annual cheatgrass replacing dozens of native perennial plant species. Was that beneficial or natural?

The famous Yellowstone Fire—sold to the public as the best thing since bald eagles—left tens of thousands of acres in close-packed, stunted lodgepole pine monocultures with no grass, no flowers and no wildlife. Beneficial? Hardly. Natural? Not that either.

No amount of ideological naturalness can equal the lost value of vast areas of biodiverse, wildlife-filled, stable forest. Native Americans learned that ages ago. They used cool, wet-season prescribed fire to prevent catastrophic wildfire. Lightning strikes usually made little fires. The Forest Service used to follow their example. Now fire-happy federal officers believe a simplistic upside-down cascading academic fallacy that ignores Native American history and biological reality. They say: "Hot weather has highest fire danger so most fires happened then so that's natural/necessary." Necessary to what? There's nothing hot-weather fires can do that cool/wet-season fires or logging/fuel-wood harvest/biomass harvest/thinning followed by cool-season fire can't do 10 to 10,000 times better.

Folks in the small towns of Kanab and Fredonia and others around the West could do a much better job managing the Kaibab Plateau and other forests than the Forest Service can under lawsuit-skewed, politically correct pressures and policies. We and many others love the Kaibab Forest. We've cared for it; cherished it. Many of our best memories were in places the Warm Fire destroyed. We spent childhoods and lifetimes there and took our kids there to fill their lives with beauty. It's unspeakably painful to see the destruction. Don't tell us it will be okay in 300 years. ■

Even the heaviest rains normally create no runoff in this Kaibab Plateau meadow. Since the "Warm Fire," repeated floods have covered this valley with black water and ashes.

Crystal clear water at Lees' Ferry on the Colorado River. After the fire, boaters in the Grand Canyon awoke to find the Colorado River black with polluting flood waters pouring off devastated forest land. The black muck travels all the way to Lake Mead in Nevada.

SUMMER 2007

LAND IN CRISIS

Killer canines in Catron County, New Mexico.

By Mike Cade

The inhabitants of Catron County, New Mexico, have always been tough and resilient. They first began drifting into this vast and rugged land in the 1880s and, by the turn of the century, had carved out a vibrant economy based on mining, logging and ranching.

For 90 years the formula worked well. Any young man, with hard work and a banker's handshake, could raise a family, build a business and pass it on to his children.

With the passage of the Endangered Species Act in 1973, however, this rural economy began to decline. It seems all kinds of critters—the Southwestern willow flycatcher, the Cherokee crawler, the Chiricahua leopard frog, the loach minnow, to name a few—might suddenly be endangered after nearly a century of coexistence with lumberjacks and cowboys.

An adversarial relationship began to fester between the Forest Service and ranchers, who suffered grazing cuts and had to jump through all kinds of regulatory hoops to stay in business.

Then the logging industry suffered a fatal blow in 1992 with the listing of the Mexican spotted owl. As loggers began leaving the county in search of work, the forest canopy began to close. Less sunlight reaching the forest floor meant less feed for livestock, wildlife and spotted owls. At lower elevations juniper and other woody species also had been choking out grass, a consequence of Smokey the Bear's fire-suppression policy.

Even with sharp grazing cuts across the county, many ranchers hung on. But the advent of the Mexican Gray Wolf Recovery Program in 1998 was the final straw. "We're going to lose six ranchers this year and probably eight more next year," says Catron County Commissioner Ed Wehrheim.

COWS OR CONDOS

Joel Alderete of New Mexico Farm and Livestock Bureau recalls a Game & Fish Commission meeting in Reserve a couple of summers back in which the wolf recovery program was discussed.

"Don't you guys realize what's going to happen?" he asked. "The wolf is going to put these ranchers out of business and they're going to subdivide their land."

After the meeting, a gentleman from the Center for Biological Diversity pulled Alderete aside and asked: "What do you mean they're going to subdivide? That's all government land up there."

Alderete had to explain that every federal grazing permit is attached to private land, which ranges anywhere from 40 acres to many thousands of acres. "You should have seen the worried look in his eyes," says Alderete. "He just couldn't believe that anyone would do that."

Sewell Goodwin can believe it. Through the 1970s and mid-'80s, he was ranching the AD Bar and the XXX in the Blue Range of eastern Arizona, 160 square miles permitted for 500 cows. Then the Forest Service cut his permits to 170 cows. This prompted one of his sons to find work elsewhere. "It was no longer economically feasible to operate."

In his youth Goodwin had been offered a college education but chose a $60-a-month cowboy job instead. Since then he's owned eight ranches in seven Forest Service districts and figures he's well versed in the agency's ways. "They're destroying these family ranches," says Goodwin, who still believes that good range management isn't possible without grazing.

© JACKIE CADE

Sewell and Lois Goodwin, L Bar H Ranch on the San Francisco River north of Glenwood. The house was built by the McKeen family, who homesteaded here about 1885. Recently the Forest Service made some noise about cutting his cattle numbers. "That'll be fine," says Goodwin. "I'll just subdivide and you can have everybody's out-of-control four-wheelers, dogs, horses, goats, pigs and chickens out on the forest."

Goodwin finally sold the AD Bar and the XXX and through a trade involving some of the deeded land was able to move to Catron County, where he's making his stand on the L Bar H along the San Francisco River north of Glenwood. The ranch consists of nine homesteads scattered throughout 30 sections of the Gila National Forest. Recently the Forest Service made some noise about cutting his cattle numbers.

"That'll be fine," says Goodwin. "I'll just subdivide and you can have everybody's out-of-control four-wheelers, dogs, horses, goats, pigs and chickens out on the forest."

"It was unanimous," says large-predator expert Roy McBride. "They'd looked at all the ones in captivity and decided they weren't pure wolves. So they sent me to Mexico to catch some real ones."

Goodwin's cows are still there, but recently a pack of wolves was seen near the northwest corner of his allotment. They're busy eating a neighbor's cows on up the country, but he knows it's just a matter of time until they start on his.

"It's really pretty simple," says Goodwin. "The environmentalists have a choice. It's cows or condos."

GOV'MENT "WOLVES" OR FERAL DOGS?

According to popular mythology, the Mexican Gray Wolf Recovery Program began with the successful capture and breeding of a few remaining wild wolves in Mexico. But the real history of the program is one of skullduggery that began with hybrid genetics more than 20 years earlier.

In 1959 a Mexican cowboy caught a male wolf hybrid in Ramanote Canyon in the Tumacacori Mountains northwest of Nogales, Arizona. The animal ended up at the Arizona-Sonora Desert Museum outside of Tucson.

Three years later a couple of tourists on motorcycles rolled into the Desert Museum with a young female wolf that they claimed to have acquired in Mexico. Worried that the wolf wouldn't survive the rest of the trip, they donated her to the museum as well.

After siring a single litter of pups, the hybrid male escaped in 1964 and was killed before he could be recaptured. His skull was preserved at the museum. The female was then bred back to her sons from that litter and subsequent litters were sold to other zoos and museums as brother-sister pairs. This hybridized and highly inbred line of wolves became known as the Ghost Ranch lineage.

In 1979 the participants at a Mexican wolf workshop, organized by the U.S. Fish & Wildlife Service (FWS), concluded that the Ghost Ranch lineage wasn't fit for inclusion in the recovery program. Although the skull of the founding male of the line had inconveniently disappeared from the Desert Museum before it could be analyzed, the workshop participants concluded that many of the Ghost Ranch animals showed definite dog characteristics.

Jack B. Woody of FWS wrote about the workshop's recommendations in a 1986 status report on the recovery program: "Wanting to protect the genetic purity of the wolves used as founders for the Mexican Wolf Recovery Program, it was concluded that, for the time being, the

PHOTOS COURTESY LAURA SCHNEBERGER

Two wolf-like animals were shot north of Luna, New Mexico, in December 2006. A landowner saw three of them killing a yearling elk and since the FWS wouldn't investigate, the landowner took a chance and shot them. Due to the proximity to known Mexican wolves, it's believed they may be Mexican wolf hybrids. FWS is DNA testing these animals. The closeup is of a Mule Creek animal.

only wolves that can be accepted by the program are those that come from the wild range of the subspecies in Mexico."

Roy McBride, world-renowned large-predator expert from Alpine, Texas, recalls attending numerous wolf recovery meetings in which the question was asked: Can we use the Ghost Ranch or any other captive lineage in the recovery program?

"It was unanimous," says McBride. "They'd looked at all the ones in captivity and decided they weren't pure wolves. So they sent me to Mexico to catch some real ones."

McBride caught eight wolves for FWS, but only one female and three males survived their care in captivity to actually breed. Although based on a small number of founders, the McBride or "certified" line of Mexican wolves was at least genetically pure.

In 1997 McBride learned to his chagrin through another status report that FWS had added Ghost Ranch animals to the certified line they had established for captive-breeding purposes. Animals from the Aragon lineage, another captive population of uncertain ancestry, also had been added to the studbook.

"David Parsons promised everyone on the wolf recovery team that he would never do that," says McBride. In a letter to Parsons, then director of the program, McBride wrote: "You are threatening the validity of genetics of the entire wolf reintroduction program, both north and south."

McBride, in the earlier days of the program, also had examined some of the Ghost Ranch animals. "Some of their ears folded over; some had curls in their tails. While some showed wolf characteristics, they didn't resemble any wolves that I had ever caught in Mexico or anywhere else."

As for the agency's explanation that the Ghost Ranch animals don't look like wolves because of captivity and diet, McBride responded: "The real reason that many Ghost Ranch animals look like dogs is because that is what they are."

The high degree of inbreeding in the three lineages begged for the infusion of fresh genetics. But without pure genetics the planned reintroduction would have been illegal under the Endangered Species Act. FWS, therefore, commissioned and funded, in partnership with the Heritage Fund of Arizona, a study by Phil Hedrick of Arizona State University to determine the genetic status of its "wolves." The study examined blood samples and concluded that "they likely represent the descendants of pure Mexican wolves." This left many to wonder by what sort of alchemy animals that were dog hybrids (according to visual inspection) could be thus transformed.

"You may put dog blood in the wolves, but you will never take it out," wrote McBride in his letter to Parsons. "And you will forever cloud the issue of what it is you have released into the wild."

As for the concern of genetic variability, "Why not augment the Mexican wolf genes with those from Canada? Isn't that exactly what is going to happen in the wild when the reintroductions from Idaho and Wyoming meet the reintroductions from the Southwest?"

But with their genetic study in hand, the FWS mixed the three lineages and proceeded with the 1998 release of a "nonessential, experimental population" of wolves into the Blue Range Wolf Recovery Area of eastern Arizona and western New Mexico.

Two lawsuits, one led by New Mexico Cattle Growers in 1998 and another led by the Arizona/New Mexico Coalition of Counties in 2003, challenged the legality of the reintroduction program. In both suits the court deferred to FWS's "expertise."

Neither suit addressed the purity of the wolves' ancestry. "Skulls, hides and other genetic material had mysteriously disappeared," says Howard Hutchinson, executive director for the coalition. But the issue of hybridization wasn't going to go away, as the plaintiffs tried to demonstrate in their second suit.

About four years after the 1998 release the FWS discovered, quite by accident, a litter of hybrid pups while trying to capture and relocate the Pipestem pack, which had two confirmed strikes against it for livestock depredation. While six of the pups had typical Mexican wolf markings, one had a much lighter coat, almost white with speckles in it. Was this the first documented case of ancestral genetics coming home to roost?

According to blood tests, the pups were indeed hybrid but the alpha male wasn't the father. The real culprit was most likely a domestic dog or a wolf-dog hybrid, several of which are known to have been dumped in the area. It's not known how the alpha female managed to leave the alpha male long enough to have a tryst with a domestic dog, nor whether the alpha male was similarly engaged elsewhere.

About a year later the FWS found another litter of hybrid pups belonging to a female wolf on the White Mountain Apache Reservation in Arizona. Although field personnel had tried to hook her up with another male, it didn't work out and she also bred with a domestic dog.

John Oakleaf, field projects coordinator for the FWS, says the agency takes hybridization seriously. In his time with the program, Oakleaf has caught about 31 uncollared wolves born in the wild, about as many coyotes, and maybe 10 dogs, he says. "But there's no evidence of anything other than pure Mexican wolf genetics."

Laura Schneberger of the Gila Livestock Growers Association, however, isn't impressed with the agency's record and believes hybridization will continue to be a problem. She says at least 18 wolves have been reported in five different areas, to which the FWS has yet to respond. About a year ago a pack of wolves killed a puppy near Quemado, about 50 miles outside the recovery area. Although it was a confirmed wolf kill, the pack still hasn't been caught, collared or tested to see what they are.

According to the terms of the Environmental Impact Statement under which the recovery program operates, all wolves are to be collared and monitored. But whether due to lack of expertise, manpower, funding or willpower, Schneberger says the agency isn't fulfilling its obligation: "They refuse to investigate these different wolf reports." Furthermore, it isn't known how many hybrid litters have escaped detection, nor the number of their pups, as in the Pipestem litter, that are indistinguishable from pure wolves. Even if the question of ancestral genetics were settled, the area lends itself to hybridization, she says.

The Blue Range Wolf Recovery Area isn't true wilderness but is full of inholdings, home to hundreds of ranching families, subdivisions, small towns and communities and many, many dogs in close proximity to pen-raised, human-habituated wolves.

For a growing number of people in the wolf-recovery area, it's more than an abstract question about genetic purity. Is that animal that's out in the yard killing my chickens a wolf hybrid that I can legally shoot, or do I risk a $100,000 fine and/or a year in jail?

That is the very question that could land the hybrid issue once again in the courts. So far it's been taken for granted that the FWS's wolves are genetically pure. In a takings case the burden of proof would, or at least should, be held to a higher standard, as McBride suggested in his letter to Parsons.

"When the first Mexican wolf is killed by some rancher or trapper, and it enters the courts as a legal matter, you will never be able to convict anyone of killing a true wolf."

Meanwhile the Center for Biological Diversity has sued the FWS to implement new rules recommended by a "scientific panel" in 2001. If implemented, the rules would allow the agency to release captive wolves directly into the Gila, allow wolves to establish territories outside the recovery area, and redefine "problem wolves" so as to exempt those that kill livestock after having scavenged on carcasses. It's unclear whether wolves that kill emus, chickens, cats and horses also acquired their taste for such cuisine by first scavenging on carcasses.

Parsons, in a separate statement, also argues that these rule changes are necessary because overzealous control of depredating wolves threatens the viability of the recovery program. According to the FWS's numbers, only 59 wolves and seven packs have been successfully reintroduced, while the program's 1996 EIS called for 102 wolves and 13 packs by the end of 2006.

Parsons, now retired from the FWS, is a steering committee member of the Southern Rockies Wolf Restoration Project, a coalition of environmental organizations such as Forest Guardians, Defenders of Wildlife and the Wilderness Society, long known for their opposition to multiple use of federally administered lands.

CLOSE ENCOUNTERS

The popular perception of the wolf is that of a family oriented animal that plays with its cuddly pups, avoids humans and benefits wildlife by culling the sick and weak. But for a growing number of people at ground zero in the wolf-recovery area in eastern Arizona and western New Mexico, the reality gives new meaning to the ancient expression "wolves at the door."

For the Millers, owners of the Link at Diamond Creek and Mimbres Outfitters, it carries a terrible double meaning.

It was to be another day in the saddle following the hounds. Mark, Mary and another hunter had just collared and loaded their hounds when they sent their eight-year-old daughter Stacy to call in the horses. Kirby, a nine-year-old hound she had grown up with, went with her.

"We heard this god-awful screaming," says Mary. "Stacy was yelling, 'wolf, wolf,' and we heard sounds of a terrible fight. I didn't know at that point whether the wolf had Stacy or Kirby."

It was Kirby. The wolf had him by the throat and was shaking him violently. If not for the tracking collar and the quick action of the adults, Kirby would have been killed not 20 yards from Stacy. As it was he suffered a crushed windpipe and multiple chest injuries.

USDA's Wildlife Services listed it as a "probable" wolf attack. Two months later it was Six, the 13-year-old Scharbauer-bred horse from Texas that Stacy had been riding since she was big enough to sit in the saddle with her father. The Millers arrived home to find Six's carcass in the corral, where the wolves had chased him from the pasture and hemmed him up. Tracks showed where one wolf had peered through a back window of their house and another had defecated only feet from the front door.

A week prior, the U.S. Fish & Wildlife Service, when specifically asked, had assured the Millers that wolves don't attack horses and that theirs were safe. Wildlife Services confirmed that Six had been killed by wolves, but somehow the rumor got around that the horse might have died of colic.

Politics aside, all Stacy knows is that she lost a member of her family to a horrible death. "She can't sleep and is terrified that her horses or dogs are going to get eaten alive in the front yard," says Mark. "Until you experience a pack of wolves living around your house, constantly terrorizing you, holding you hostage, you have no idea what it's like."

When Jess Carey, Catron County wolf interaction investigator, started hearing complaints of insomnia, nightmares and bedwetting by constituents who had suffered similar encounters, commissioners authorized a psychological study. Preliminary results, taken from interviews with 35 people, found mild to moderately severe psychological stress and trauma resulting from encounters with wolves.

For the Millers, it's not just chronic fear for safety but sadness over the loss of a cherished way of life. Mark and Mary bought the Link for its remote location and abundant wildlife. They had plans to open a wilderness youth camp to provide kids the opportunity to learn about and experience wildlife in its natural environment. But using FWS's own conservative numbers about wolf predation on elk, they know that within three to five years the elk herd will be drastically reduced.

"What a tragedy to lose our game for the sake of hearing a wolf howl," says Mark. "It's a huge price to pay for a lot of people—ranchers, outfitters, hunters, or any outdoor enthusiast. It's all going to be a thing of the past. And then they have the gall to tell us we shouldn't live up here.

PHOTOS COURTESY MILLER FAMILY

Mark Miller and his eight-year-old daughter Stacy. "She can't sleep and is terrified that her horses or dogs are going to get eaten alive in the front yard," says Mark. "Until you experience a pack of wolves living around your house, constantly terrorizing you, holding you hostage, you have no idea what it's like." RIGHT: *Wolves injured the dog and later killed a prize horse within feet of the house. These are wolf tracks and the remains of the beloved equine named Six.*

Well why shouldn't we? This land was homesteaded before the forest was even formed."

The Link at Diamond Creek lies isolated, high in the Gila. But as ranchers give up and ship their cattle, and elk numbers decline, the government's wolves will still have to eat. As they move lower in search of food, the denizens of the urban fringes might also learn something of the terrible reality behind that ancient expression—wolves at the door.

HUMAN SAFETY

Jess Carey likes to say he came to Catron County from Arkansas by way of California. Born the son of "Arkies" who migrated to Bakersfield, California, to pick crops in the San Joaquin Valley, Carey graduated from high school, served in the Marines and worked his way into a good paying job with the city of Ventura. But when the California Legislature informed him that he'd no longer be able to run his coon dogs at night, Carey knew it was time to gather his traps.

Several months and odd jobs later, while gazing at the majestic, pine-covered hills that surround the tiny logging village of Reserve, New Mexico, Carey said to his wife Lynn: "Honey, if I can find a job, we're staying here."

© JACKIE CADE

Jim Blair (left), owner for 40 years of the O Bar O Ranch, and Jess Carey, Catron County wolf interaction investigator.

Since that day 30 years ago, Carey has served four years as undersheriff, two as sheriff and four as a criminal investigator. His forensic experience, along with a lifetime of trapping and running hounds, uniquely qualify him for his current job as Catron County wolf interaction investigator.

The county created the job when it realized that the federal government's incentive to document wolf predation didn't exactly coincide with that of ranchers. When Carey started working with USDA's Wildlife Services, the reports on verified kills doubled almost overnight.

But if livestock predation is a big concern, that of human safety is bigger. An increasing number of complaints involve human encounters with habituated wolves. In one chilling incident, 14-year-old J.C. Nelson was stalking elk in the forest when he found himself surrounded by wolves. He backed up against a tree and kept his rifle pointed at the wolf that stood facing him while the others circled around behind.

"I didn't want to shoot him because I was afraid they'd blame my father and take away his grazing permit or send him to jail," says Nelson. While the FWS gave Nelson credit for keeping a cool head, they otherwise dismissed the incident. Carey believes it was an example of wolves testing prey. The wolves walked away this time. The next person might not be so fortunate.

"It's like a kid with his hand in the cookie jar," says Carey. "These wolves, because of their protected status, aren't getting spanked. So they're getting bolder."

Current rules allow someone who feels threatened by a wolf to shoot if attacked. By then it could be too late. "If it was a dinosaur you'd go out and shoot it. That's for sure," says Catron County manager Bill Aymar. "What are we going to do? Wait until they kill a kid?"

That was the question on everybody's mind when county commissioners met in February before a standing-room-only crowd to pass an ordinance giving Carey authority to handle problem wolves. Under the carefully written ordinance, heavy on protocol, the county could issue a dispatch order authorizing Carey to permanently remove any habituated wolf in close proximity to humans if the feds fail to do so within 24 hours.

Michael Robinson of the Center for Biological Diversity told the *Albuquerque Journal* that "they are asserting county rights where they have no legal basis" and called on federal officials to "make sure that vigilante justice does not prevail."

But growing potential for vigilante justice is in part why the ordinance was put into place, says Aymar. "These aren't pretty little wolves. They're on private property killing people's animals. The pro-wolf people very handily discount the human-welfare concerns." FWS is evaluating the new ordinance and has yet to respond.

"I know one thing," says Carey. "This commission's got the resolve. They're not going to fold up. And we'd rather do it this way than to have somebody go off the deep end and start shooting people."

If worse comes to worse, Carey knows he might have to trap or even kill one of the government's wolves, and that could mean a trip to the jailhouse. "I figure it's worth the price in order to protect our children," says Carey, who lives in a rustic, two-room cabin. "Besides, I hear they've got color TV in those federal pens."

COMPENSATION, ECOTOURISM & OTHER MYTHS

Defenders of Wildlife, on its website, blames ranchers for the fact that the government's pen-raised "wolves" are eating their cows. If these "welfare ranchers" had been diligent in removing carcasses of dead cows from their rugged rangelands, DOW says, these wolves never would have learned to eat beef in the first place.

"That's how I learned to like beef," quips Joe Nelson, who ranches near Glenwood. "I'd cut a piece of rotten meat out of a carcass and waller that around until I finally acquired a taste for it."

In spite of the ranchers' sloth, Defenders, in its magnanimity, boasts that it pays 100 percent of the market value of each animal proven to have been killed by wolves. Of course, by their own admission, only one kill out of seven is confirmed. They also advise that compensation isn't guaranteed.

As cattlemen suffer the economic impacts of endangered species' regulations and now wolves, so does the county treasury. As hard as ranching has been hit, grazing still generates 48 percent of the county's revenues. As more ranches fold up, new sources of revenue will have to be found. Environmentalists suggest that rural areas, hard hit by their costly schemes, can make up for lost revenue through ecotourism.

Bill Aymar, Catron County manager, disagrees. "The average tourist comes down here from Santa Fe, drives around in the forest for a couple of hours, says, 'Oh, I think I heard a wolf,' and leaves," Aymar says. "He might buy a couple of candy bars and a Coke, but he contributes little to the economy. The tourism thing is a fallacy. This isn't Yellowstone."

Hunting, on the other hand, is big business in Catron County, long known for its trophy elk. Tom Klumker of San Francisco River Outfitters, who operates mostly in the Gila Wilderness, says wolves are beginning to affect the movement of the elk, making them harder to hunt and causing a decline in their conception rate. "The hunter's ox hasn't really been gored yet," says Klumker, "but it's fixing to be. We're seeing more and more wolves and we believe they're going to start doing us a lot of damage."

Jack Diamond of Beaverhead Outfitters agrees and mentions all the outfitters in Montana, Idaho and Wyoming who have gone out of business since reintroduction of the northern gray wolf. "It's really just started in the last six months," says Diamond. "I believe that in the next year or so Game & Fish is going to have to start managing these elk herds with the wolf in mind."

That would be the same state game commission appointed by Gov. Bill Richardson, who upon taking office fired the former director and seven commissioners, all adamantly opposed to wolf reintroduction.

A couple of years ago at a town meeting in Reserve, everyone but Richardson wanted to talk about wolves. Finally, toward the end of the meeting, he suggested forming a task force that could look at possible solutions—grazing buyouts, compensation…well, you get the picture.

AMERICAN DREAM DENIED

Like many ranch couples who work for wages, Jim and Sherri Haught dreamed someday of having their own spread. When the nearby Deadman allotment came up for sale, it seemed like the opportunity they'd been waiting for. "It was going to be our retirement," says Sherri. "It's a beautiful place where our kids could bring people as part of their youth and family ministries."

But in fall 2004 the Haughts started seeing wolf tracks, scat with cow hair in it, and tight-bagged cows missing their calves along the north fork of the Negrito. They soon learned that the San Francisco pack, which had been wreaking havoc on several neighbors, was camped on their ranch. To make matters worse, the Ring pack, which had been removed a year earlier because of two confirmed livestock kills, had been rereleased.

Jim recalls coming up on John Oakleaf of the U.S. Fish & Wildlife Service, who was tracking a collared wolf. "I asked him, 'What are you going to do with that wolf when you catch him?' He said, 'His collar's a little goofed up. I'm going to put a new collar on him and turn him loose.'"

Jim believes management of problem wolves should be left to those who are impacted by them. "I've worked a lot in rough country and when a bear or lion starts killing livestock we've always been able to catch it and survive," says Jim. "But here, they've put a new predator into the mix and told us we can't do anything about it."

© JACKIE CADE

"The wolves are going to starve us out," says Preston Bates of the N Bar Ranch.

The Deadman allotment historically has produced 85-percent calf crops. Jim and Sherri could survive on 75 percent. But with 30-percent and 50-percent calf crops the last two years, their dream is shattered and their ranch is for sale. "You see all these Disney films like 'The Lion King,' that talk about the 'Circle of Life,'" says Sherri. "Is there something missing here? What about livestock? What about us? Are we not a part of the Circle of Life?"

Preston Bates of the N Bar Ranch considers himself to be a conservationist. He even tried to coin the phrase "green rancher." Growing up around dairies and racetracks in Virginia, Bates dreamed of being a cowboy. Finally, at age 20, he came to New Mexico and started from scratch. He learned to cowboy and broke BLM horses to sell back East.

The owners of the N Bar believed in him and gave him the opportunity to lease and later to buy the sprawling, high-country ranch, which boasts as fine a stand of grama grasses as can be found anywhere. "I had the idea of starting a working guest ranch for horse owners back East to come out and learn how to cowboy," says Bates. "I went way into debt on this deal, but I knew it could work."

And so it did for several years. The cows paid the mortgage, while the guest business grew and prospered. Bates even married one of his guests, Margaret, who came with a friend from Dallas. At its peak the N Bar had five full-time employees and pumped at least $80,000 a year into the downtown Reserve businesses. "Live and let live," says Bates. "That's what I thought when I first heard about this wolf recovery program."

Jim and Sherri Haught. "I've worked a lot in rough country and when a bear or lion starts killing livestock we've always been able to catch it and survive," says Jim. "But here, they've put a new predator into the mix and told us we can't do anything about it."

That was until the Luna pack moved onto the N Bar, where it spends about 99 percent of its time. The Saddle pack leaves about half the time to feed on the neighbors' stock. "I tried to get people to take notice of what's happening and work with the FWS and Defenders of Wildlife," says Bates. "But I got no reciprocation."

Bates has watched his calf crop go from 79 percent to 49 percent. We met him coming over a snow-covered mountain pass on his way back from Phoenix, where he'd been trying to sell the last of his 60 top-of-the-line string of guest horses to pay the mortgage.

With only 11 horses left, he's out of the guest business. What's left of his cows are going next. He hopes to pasture yearlings and hang on for another year. Short of that the only thing left is to sell his private land for vacation homes.

"Your ranch is your 401-K," says Bates. "And I've been Enronned."

FIGHTING BACK

It's a paradox that while the children of rural families are fleeing economic malaise to find work in the cities, baby boomers are fleeing the social malaise of the cities to look for a piece of what America once was. In this sense Catron County, New Mexico, is a microcosm of what's happening all over the Mountain West as verdant valleys, once home to spacious farms, give way to vacation homes surrounded by once-productive national forests, now choked with overgrowth, often diseased and dying on the stump. In no small part, this is the product of a federal government that is bloated and arrogant on the one hand, negligent and incompetent on the other.

Dick Manning and Buddy Allred of Catron County and Art Lee of Apache County in Arizona recognized the trend years ago. Deciding to do something about it, they formed the Coalition of Arizona/New Mexico Counties. Often reviled by opponents as the "county sovereignty" movement that seeks to usurp federal authority, its true mission is simple—hold the federal government accountable for obeying its own laws

Howard Hutchinson, executive director, has been with the coalition almost from the beginning. "All of the ordinances and plans put forward by the member counties mirror the federal, statutory requirements," he says. "The counties have never initiated anything outside of existing federal law."

Catron County Commissioner Ed Wehrheim on private land along the banks of the Tularosa River, home to the loach minnow, near Reserve, New Mexico. The minnow was listed as threatened in 1986. A study by J.N. Rinne and D. Miller (1996-2000) concluded that the extirpation of the loach minnow in Arizona's Upper Verde River was due partly to removal of livestock, which caused stream bank vegetation to increase markedly and the channel to become deeper and narrower. Nevertheless, the Forest Service fenced off all federal land along the Tularosa, rendering six good ranches almost useless, because the Tularosa was their only dependable supply of water.

Since its humble beginning in 1990, the coalition has won nine of 12 suits filed against federal agencies—some of them even in the notorious 9th U.S. Circuit Court of Appeals—and its spirit has spawned a movement that has spread to other counties across America. But Catron County faces its biggest challenge now as it tries to save its culture and economy from the agents of a government that seems bent on policies of rural cleansing and the outsourcing of America's wealth.

"Basically, these are bullies who are taking advantage of people who don't really have the resources to fight," says Hutchinson. "But they do have the spirit."

Commissioner Wehrheim agrees. "The feds have had their way in a lot of places. But they know when they come to Catron County that they're going to get a fight." ■

WATER

ROCKY MOUNTAIN CREEK © THERISA STACK/TOM STACK & ASSOCIATES

FALL 2001

WATER IN THE WEST

Of the hundreds of legal cases and challenges filed over water in the last two decades, most, if not all, are still held in a gridlock of appeals and arguments to higher courts. No decisive case is considered as yet to have been put before the U.S. Supreme Court, although several involving land and water issues appear likely to reach that level. Congress, by several actions over the last century, has strongly affirmed the authority of the states over water within their boundaries, but newer key issues centering especially on the Endangered Species Act remain to be resolved. A decision this year by a federal claims court found that denying irrigation from Tule-lake, California, in order to save fish amounted to a "taking" of property prohibited by the Fifth Amendment. The ruling said the federal action had the effect of "complete extinction of all value" to water due farmers. Federal and environmental appeals on that case are considered by many to present the most significant possibilities of a landmark U.S. Supreme Court decision. By Tim Findley

Water is the essence of all life. It is also perhaps the most indestructible substance on our planet, for while it may be altered in form and mass and become the carrier of other elements, there is little if any difference in the amount of water on the planet today than there has been through the eons of time. Even with the infinite uses mankind makes of it, there exists enough freshwater alone to provide every human being with more than 40 million gallons—far more in constantly replenished form than could be consumed in any lifetime.

Of all the paradoxes of existence, this one is the true master of human behavior and social order—thirst on a planet virtually made of water. Famine and feast, war and peace, civilization and extinction all begin in what seems the whim of a winter cloud.

Water defines the continental expanse of the United States in a manner so dramatically obvious that it appears planned as a challenge to human ingenuity. Running in nearly perfect line along the 100th meridian north to south, the nation is cut in half between arid regions west of the Rockies and the humid green of the region from the Mississippi east. Even the transition zone of the Great Plains receives more annual rainfall than much of the West.

But the difference drawn by the mother of all American rivers is more complex. For while the East is a climate of showers and rain pumped through the spring and summer

TSADO/IMAGE SCIENCE & ANAYLSIS LAB/NASA/TOM STACK & ASSOCIATES

The All-American Canal, the largest irrigation canal in the world and a key landmark along the U.S.-Mexico border, shows up in this astronaut photograph. This image captures about 15 kilometers (9.3 miles) of the important infrastructure corridor just west of Yuma, Arizona. The prominent dark line crossing the image is the canal, which is crossed in this view by Interstate Highway 8. The canal carries 26,155 cubic feet of water per second westward from the Colorado River to support the intensive agriculture of California's Imperial Valley to the northwest and nine cities, including San Diego. The canal system is the Imperial Valley's only source of water, and it allows irrigation of more than 500,000 acres of agricultural fields. The Coachella Canal, one of four main branch canals, leads water north to Imperial Valley. This section of the canal requires constant maintenance. Approximately 68,000 acre-feet of water per year are lost by seepage from the All-American Canal, especially where the canal crosses the great Algodones Dune Field, a portion of which is visible extending from top to bottom in the center of the image.

Lower Klamath Wildlife Refuge. Trillions of birds on the Pacific Flyway glean the post-harvest stubble of irrigated fields in the shadow of Mount Shasta. Without the irrigated crops nearby, they will find very little winter feed.

by sturdy, short rivers, the West is winter-born with its greatest treasure locked sometimes for years on frozen peaks before it is released into its two greatest drainage systems—the Colorado and the Columbia rivers. There, in the mountains, is the eternal secret of western survival, still as coldly unpredictable as winter itself.

America as a nation has confronted this distinction for nearly half its two centuries of formation, yet it may be these early years of a new millennium that will define our greatest differences in the fundamental conflict—east to west.

Once again, as it has in some ways done continually, Congress is taking up the issue of western water resources this year [2001] in hearings before the subcommittee on Energy and Water Development. Implied by such interest are potentially far-reaching decisions to be made on not only the nature of the resource, but on its future use to provide power, domestic supplies and, ultimately, food. Overstated, perhaps, but still at the heart of what actions government can take, is a question not about water, but about social and cultural survival in the West. ■

Betrayed by the Feds

It is a drought decreed by lawsuit and being enforced, ironically, by the U.S. Bureau of Reclamation in Klamath Basin. Some estimates are that the result may be the death of farm-dependent communities like Merrill and Malin and Tulelake on the Oregon/California line, and varying degrees of economic disaster for as many as 25,000 residents of Klamath Basin, including the city of Klamath Falls itself. A rural economy productive of at least $300 million a year is on the verge of catastrophe. By Tim Findley

Even at 10 a.m., a light chill still drifted off Lake Ewauna and huddled in the deep willow shade of Veterans Park in Klamath Falls. It would melt away in record heat for the first Monday in May [2001] before the day ended, but as the crowd steadily filtered in that morning, many wore jackets or light sweaters. Most of them lugged signs and placards of their own making, stapled onto wooden staffs or draped around their necks like sandwich boards, and they milled about below the park's long slope of lawn like a grieving parade, a personal story behind virtually every painted message.

"Klamath Betrayed," said one. "Four Communities Destroyed," read another. "Dial 911," proclaimed the best, "some sucker stole my water."

The earliest arrivals had driven the half hour or less north from the "project" communities of Merrill or Tulelake or from the little gem of Czechoslovakian settlement in Malin where the kids dressed in brightly ornate ethnic costumes that made statements of their own. It presented a steadily growing splash of colorful reunion among country people and town neighbors, even among fishermen and farmers, brought together by the promise of a great river and a crisis threatening them all.

There is a drought in the Klamath Basin this spring. Early in April, when a huge dry windstorm blew down

© LARRY TURNER

John Bowen stands in his empty irrigation ditch. Because of the lack of water for crops many farmers in the area will not survive until next year.

inland from Alaska, it struck the lower Klamath Basin with swirling brown clouds of dust blown up from unplanted fields, presenting unmistakable silhouette images of the Depression-era "dust bowl" against empty sheds and vaguely struggling people and machines. The previous winter produced barely 30 percent of the average snowpack in the thickly wooded mountains soaring west to the vast shoulders of Mount Shasta in the distance. In April it seemed like Oklahoma, and the kids in Merrill High School were directed to read Steinbeck's "Grapes of Wrath" for explanation.

And yet, it was not the natural dry winter drought that left the fields of potatoes and onions and alfalfa choked in dust. Even in early May, the spring-fed upper lake that would normally provide water for early planting was still brim-full, slapping nearly over the boards that blocked irrigation supplies under court order and that will deny all irrigation to the Lower Basin for this entire season. Klamath Basin's rural economy is on the verge of catastrophe and this in order to serve the needs of an officially endangered sucker fish in the lake and a threatened species of salmon at least 60 miles downstream.

That was what brought them together around Lake Ewauna, itself a scenic symbolic portion of the river system, but still bank-full along the shores of a park dedicated to military service in an Oregon county that meaningfully proclaims in its road signs, "Klamath County Honors Veterans."

◆ ◆ ◆

In the sunny, pin-perfect living room of her farm home near Tulelake, 84-year-old Eleanor Bolesta busily shifted between sitting briefly in a firm rocker and getting up to answer the telephone or tend to some incidental chore. She has always been a strong woman, not inclined to let time be wasted. The little white Scottie dog constantly at her side seemed almost hard put to keep up.

"Betrayed, that's how I feel. Betrayed, like I'm in a bad dream," Bolesta said flatly, not looking for sympathy or even agreement. Among some 1,200 farmers, she is one of about 40 veterans of World Wars I and II still living on the project who were awarded their land of 110 acres or so as recognition and gratitude for their military service. Eleanor, a former Navy WAVE and aircraft machinist, was one of only two women to succeed in the lottery for a homestead here after World War II. Delighted with that, she ran the farm with her husband, a Marine veteran wounded on Guam, until they split up. Since then she has worked it alone with admiration and respect from her neighbors and irrigation officials.

"I just felt lucky," she recalled. "It was the greatest excitement in my life to have a farm."

Never before in the entire 94-year history of the Klamath Irrigation Project, not even in the severe fifth year of drought in 1992, have farmers been denied all water to their crops. The total loss of an entire season is incalculable to most of them, but the costs of maintaining equipment or merely paying bills looms today in potential bankruptcy for many.

◆ ◆ ◆

In the shady park dedicated to veterans, Ric Costales and his wife Judy moved continuously through the growing crowd, welcoming the latest arrivals, renewing old friendships and acquaintances. This was a triumph in the making

PHOTOS © LARRY TURNER

Due to federal decisions and environmental pressure, what was once a lush, green valley below Klamath Lake is drying up and blowing away with the wind. America's biggest export, ahead of all produce and goods, is eroded soil. INSET: Elizabeth Prates, one of the 20,000-plus participants in the Bucket Brigade. Their message is clear. The decision to save suckers over family farms is devastating not only to farmers but to all businesses and schools in the area.

for Costales, who represents People for the USA/Frontiers of Freedom in this region. The idea for a "bucket brigade" to symbolically restore water to the irrigators came to him from the success of the Jarbidge Shovel Brigade that reopened a Nevada road closed by actions of the U.S. Forest Service and U.S. Fish & Wildlife Service. He spent weeks organizing by Internet and through endless calls and meetings, piecing together support from often distrusting groups in the two-state irrigation project, and drawing backing for them from throughout the West.

Costales, bearded, broad chested and seeming ever to find delight in the energy of it all, is not a farmer. He is a tree faller, a lumberman, working when he can from the log house he and Judy built themselves in Scott Valley, 80 miles west as the crow flies across Mount Shasta from the Klamath Basin. At heart, however, Costales is a self-reliant free spirit from a time when "hippie" became an abused term to define a youthful quest into the counterculture of the Vietnam era. He found work in logging, but was disturbed by what he saw as abuses from Forest Service management. And what he saw of the then-emerging environmentalist movement troubled him even more. There was a difference he recognized between good stewardship and ideological arrogance.

"All of us, I guess, had the idea that common sense would somehow prevail," Costales said. "But it didn't. Now, we've found success in organizing people who've finally decided they've had a bellyful."

The Bucket Brigade was Costales' idea, but he would make only a small introductory speech that day, and his presence was otherwise never at the podium, but always among the crowd and their great dazzling clutter of signs and posters.

"Endangered Farmer, Will Work for Food" and "Fish Before Farms?" the signs read. And there was one more mean-spirited that required some intimate knowledge. "Felice Pace—Your Village Called. They're Missing Their Idiot."

Pace might be the most disliked, or at least the most misunderstood, man in all the border region of southern Oregon and northern California, but he still believes he can find peace and happiness among the rural people he has chosen to be his neighbors there. Some of them admit to hating him; many more think his antics on behalf of his Kla-

© LARRY TURNER

Tens of thousands of people gathered in parks and on the streets of Klamath Falls to support the farmers and the May 7 Bucket Brigade.

math Forest Alliance are the actions of a deranged environmental extremist determined to unreasonably ruin their lives. His Klamath Forest Alliance is one of many environmental fronts he has championed—some say shattered—over the last 25 years in causes ranging from saving the spotted owl and protecting riparian streams to halting irrigation this year in the Klamath Basin.

"This is happening all over the West," he said confidently. "We've been advocating for years the downsizing of farming in the Klamath Valley, but they've been stonewalling against change. So what happens is when change does come inevitably, it's a crisis."

His is one of the two names attached to the federal lawsuit brought before an Oakland, California, judge in April that resulted in an order to the U.S. Bureau of Reclamation to halt irrigation in the lower-basin project. Pace says it was necessary to save the short-nosed sucker fish in the upper lake during this drought year, but, he adds, the real objective is to balance the use of water on an "overallocated" system that he feels would be better managed by the Klamath Indian tribe, which sacrificed much of its land in a 1950s agreement to termination. Court rulings since then have restored hunting and fishing rights to the tribe. Though many from Etna and Scott Valley were there, Pace, of course, was not among those at Costales' Bucket Brigade demonstration.

Simple pride is part of what defines the Lower Basin. It's the kind of pride that comes from self-reliance and shows itself best in doors that have no locks or in pickups parked head-in along the old high curbs of Tulelake with the keys still dangling in the ignition. It's a sense of mutual pride expressed in casual trust that never needed to be mentioned. But by early June, even that would begin to crack in unpredictable patterns like the bottom of a dried-up ditch.

"We are obligated to carry out the law of the land," said Karl Wirkus, almost too obviously trying to portray the bureaucratic discipline he knew would be expected of him. Wirkus has been the Bureau of Reclamation manager on the Klamath Project for the last five years. Trimly fit and businesslike, he regards himself still as a scientist and engineer in a job intended for those skills, but he knows that by announcing the end of all irrigation on the project, he made political history.

"If the question is, 'If we had no constraints by the Endangered Species Act, would we have delivered water this year?' the answer is 'Absolutely,'" Wirkus said. "But that wasn't the case."

In the calendar celebrating a century of western reclamation, Wirkus has a favorite photo. It shows a family in front of their homestead near his own home region around Boise, Idaho. They have made a sign that says, "Thank God for the USA...and for the Bureau of Reclamation."

"We've been advocating for years the downsizing of farming in the Klamath Valley, but they've been stonewalling against change. So what happens is when change does come inevitably, it's a crisis." FELICE PACE

But there is another photo that at one time was so favored among Reclamation officials that it became their poster of success. It still hangs in the front reception area of the Klamath BOR office, showing a pretty young woman behind the wheel of a tractor, determination and country grit brightening her smile. It was taken of Eleanor Bolesta in 1952.

Although the decision to halt irrigation in the Lower Basin came in April like a sudden gut punch to many of the farmers, the plan had been laid years before, awaiting the right political moment—and the useful condition of drought. A few years ago, Andy Kerr, as usual full of himself and of his Oregon Natural Resources Council success over the timber industry, had bluntly warned the farmers in Tulelake that agriculture, like logging, would soon be "finished" in their region. And only a year ago, Interior Secretary Bruce Babbitt, riding the same arrogant high horse he used all over the West in the closing days of his administration, warned the farmers that if they thought decisions on the future of the basin would be made by "local input," they were sadly mistaken.

The threats were there since at least 1993 when U.S. Fish & Wildlife Service on behalf of the Bureau of Indian Affairs began studying the condition of the sucker fish. But the final step needed the help in 2000 of a scientific opinion, like that on the spotted owl, to seal the case.

At Utah State University, biologist Thomas Hardy is considered something of a scientist for hire in the battles over western environment. His contribution this time was a set of conclusions based on his study of Coho salmon in the Klamath at least 60 miles below the farming region. The so-called "Hardy Flows" report, Phases I and II, were the basis for National Marine Fisheries Service to join with Fish & Wildlife in the assault on the farmers.

PHOTOS © LARRY TURNER

No irrigation, no crops. In April it seemed like Oklahoma during the "Dust Bowl" and eroding soil from water-deprived farms blew across roads throughout Klamath Basin. The kids in Merrill High School were directed to read John Steinbeck's "Grapes of Wrath" for explanation. INSET: *Maxine Wirth's family began farming in 1885. She worries that their multi-generations of work have been for nothing.*

The farmers were not totally unprepared. For a decade, they had employed biologists and hydrologists of their own to study the condition of the threatened salmon. But their conclusions questioning the scientific validity of the Hardy report were not considered by the federal agencies in their rush to halt irrigation. In fact, biologist David Vogel, who has worked for the irrigation district for 10 years, was not even permitted to speak to Hardy or examine his methods before Hardy was accepted as gospel on the Klamath in Washington, D.C.

"Hardy was what they call a 'desktop' report that doesn't even require that anyone go out in the field," said Vogel. "It's based on records and conclusions and is the kind of thing that can be useful to people who know what they want."

Hardy's Phase II report has not even been produced, but will require scientific peer review. The "peers" are being selected by the U.S. Bureau of Indian Affairs. David Vogel's own findings weren't even considered by the government. Among those findings was that Coho losses are more jeopardized among adult fish taken "incidentally" offshore and young fry lost in tributaries downstream, not in the main stem of the Klamath.

"None of this really has to do with science," said Vogel, who formerly worked for both Fish & Wildlife and National Marine Fisheries. "It has to do with provisions in the Endangered Species Act that allow one individual to have final say-so on what he thinks is the best science. Often that simply fits an agenda."

Sen. Gordon Smith (R-Oregon) and Rep. Wally Herger (R-Oregon) repeated their oft-made promise to the Bucket Brigade crowd that they would work to amend, or even abolish, the Endangered Species Act, and they hinted that times had changed since the last election.

Even in May, four months into her administration, Secretary of Interior Gail Norton was still way behind in appointing deputies to carry out leadership of the complex and internally contentious divisions of Interior. No names had even been mentioned for congressional consideration to head the Bureau of Reclamation or, for that matter, the Bureau of Land Management and Fish & Wildlife. Norton, in fact, seemed to have only one secure aide in place, Deputy Chief of Staff Sue Ellen Woolridge. Vogel knew that Woolridge, admittedly new to the job, had reviewed the Hardy Flows' report, and even data contradicting its findings, and yet did nothing.

Buckets of water from Lake Ewauna were passed hand to hand for two miles through town to the A line irrigation canal. It was a gesture of defiance against the Bureau of Reclamation.

In the last weeks of April, as bitter and desperate last-minute legal moves failed to restore irrigation rights, Klamath Basin residents confronted Oregon Gov. John Kitzhaber in a meeting of some 6,000 people at the local fairground. Kitzhaber, a former emergency-room doctor who strikes a handsome mustachioed pose as a western governor, had ridden with Babbitt in his helicopter during the secretary's tours of intimidation the previous year. "If you're not going to help us, take off the proud rural symbol, those cowboy boots, because you don't deserve to wear them," taunted one woman in the April crowd. Kitzhaber fumbled and dodged, vaguely and clumsily, suggesting his own interest in somehow "modifying" the ESA.

Along with Felice Pace, the other petitioner in the federal suit to halt Klamath irrigation was Glen Spain, representing the Pacific Coast Federation of Fishermen. Spain, like Pace, came to the Klamath by way of San Francisco, though he counts his own family background as being in Arizona ranching and some California farming on his own. A little too slick and somehow too sinister to pretend it, Spain doesn't really claim to be a fisherman and, although he holds a law degree, he admits he hasn't practiced in quite some time. Spain, in his early 50s as well, works for Zeke Grader, a very well-known salmon party-boat operator out of San Francisco Bay.

Pace and Spain chose a California federal court in Oakland to make their case for fish. The judge, Saundra Brown Armstrong, was a late appointee of President George H.W. Bush. She had earned her reputation rising through law enforcement from the time during the Black Panther period of the 1970s when she became Oakland's first black-female police officer.

Lawyers for the irrigation district elected to appeal for an injunction in an Oregon federal court. There, in the college-centered city of Eugene before Judge Ann Aiken, they failed. "Given the high priority the law places on species threatened with extinction, I cannot find that the balance of hardship tips sharply in the plaintiff's favor," the judge wrote in her opinion.

At least 10,000 now strained the border of the park and clustered against each other along the shores of Lake Ewauna where buckets were waiting. The politicians had spoken and made their promises, although Kitzhaber and his mudless boots stayed home. The last few at the microphone told personal stories. Teenager Hollis Baley eloquently related one about her best friend, whose Hispanic family had already been driven to bankruptcy and forced to leave because of the lack of farmwork in the valley.

"Where is the justice when my friend's college dreams are shattered?" she asked. "When we are told our community has no value, where is the justice? Where is the honor in giving land to veterans and then turning around and taking it away?"

One by one, plastic buckets, each painted with the name of a state, began passing from hand to hand out of Lake Ewauna. Even that symbolic act was, under the court order, illegal, but watching police did nothing as the buckets made their steady way, fist by fist through two parallel lines out of the park and then, astonishingly, up the paved street to the waiting grip of thousands more in long ragged rails of people—men, women, and children—eager to pass the message all the way up Klamath Falls' Main Street. The parallel lines reached on at least two miles into and through the athletic fields of the high school and atop a concrete bridge crossing the "A" line irrigation canal. It took more than an hour for the first bucket to reach the canal, which was nearly empty except for leakage from a closed headgate. No single bucket need have been touched more than once by those in the long snaking line. It was easy to believe they now numbered 25,000 and represented perhaps the largest demonstration in Oregon history.

PHOTO COURTESY ELEANOR BOLESTA

© LARRY TURNER

LEFT: The pride of the Bureau of Reclamation is a poster of Eleanor Bolesta taken in 1952. ABOVE: The same Eleanor Bolesta, now 84, fought back tears when the irrigation water was cut off to the farm she was awarded as gratitude for her military service during World War II.

A helicopter clattered over their heads and many believed, or hoped, that it carried news media who would find an impressive picture. But it was a craft filled with federal and police agents. Looking for what? On the high roof of the county government building, two men peered over its peak with binoculars, like snipers. Looking for what?

South and east toward the towns of Merrill and Malin and Tulelake, the roadside messages mark the route as in the days of Burma Shave. "Federally Created Disaster Area." "Danger, Dust Storms Next 30 Miles Thanks to Fish & Wildlife." A light breeze blew up to greet the evening, not enough to raise the dust again, and maybe well water will at least provide ground cover for dry days ahead. But "For Sale" signs have appeared in the little towns where once they were unknown, and other signs "For Rent" remind the residents that the first to leave have been the workers from the fields and the packing sheds and the fertilizer barns, some of whom have themselves been here with their families for 20 years or more.

This, as Karl Wirkus pointed out, "is definitely a family farm community" three and four generations deep. "And I continue to be astonished at the way we [in the BOR] are treated in the basin as human beings, friends, neighbors. It's an incredibly civil community considering the pressure they're under."

Less than a month after the May demonstration, Wirkus was transferred to a new post with greater authority in the Midwest. He was replaced by a new manager whose background on the Columbia River was noted for his successful relationship with Native Americans.

Except for what can be produced from wells to hold the topsoil, most crops won't be grown in the Lower Basin this year. And the political vultures have already circled. The American Land Conservancy is offering as much as $4,000 an acre for the first "willing sellers" ready to give up, knowing those most willing will be those least able to stand the strain of the phony season. Others can be made more willing at lower prices as it goes on.

Without water on the fields to make crops, the geese so normally common in this center of the Pacific Flyway will find no stubble for forage. Ducks and other wildlife dependent on the water will, even by admission of environmentalists themselves, be stressed for survival. In the truly natural drought of 1992, a wave of botulism spread through the bird population, killing hundreds of waterfowl. Even the impressive population of 200 pairs of bald eagles in the nearby sanctuary may find their prey lacking this year.

Records of the U.S. Fish & Wildlife Service itself indicate that historically the greatest losses in numbers of supposedly endangered short-nosed sucker fish occurred when Klamath Lake was at its highest, as it is now, dammed from irrigation. And studies by biologists on the lower stem of the river have found that Coho salmon died in large numbers from previous late releases of water warmed by steady evaporation in shallow Klamath Lake.

At last, as even the relatively cool June dried the prized lawn of the Tulelake fairgrounds into a crumbling gray, farmer John Crawford offered at least a small part of what he had heard from Secretary Norton's aide. "She said not to offer these people false hope for the next year," Crawford recalled. "And I said what else can we offer them when you've taken everything?"

Fish, wildlife and farmers are suffering, and some are dying. The disaster ahead in this summer of political drought on the Klamath won't be to farmers alone. ■

WATER, WATER (almost) EVERYWHERE

West of the 100th meridian is a climate apart, and sometimes little understood, from the rest of the continental United States. It is a region that ranges from rain forests with more than 100 inches of precipitation a year to desert depths with less than two inches of rainfall a year.

More importantly, however, the West and its six major basins represent a multitude of mini-climates, where rainfall may vary by as much as a tenth of an inch within the space of a single campsite, and where the mountain effects of snowfall and "shadow" determine seasonal dryness or flood in sudden ways unknown in the East.

In each basin of the West, water is essential not just from its historic existence, but from its current beneficial use. United States law has always favored the states in the control of their own water in the West, but efforts over the last decade especially have been directed at taking federal control of those resources.

The Bureau of Land Management's claims alone to water include:

Arizona—The Gila River Basin and the Little Colorado River Basin (covering approximately two-thirds of the state).

California—Protected in some part by state law making an appropriated water right real property, the BLM nevertheless seeks rights in more than 70 wilderness areas and has utilized the Endangered Species Act and other federal laws to block transfers or other beneficial uses.

Colorado—State law opens sources to continuous new claims for beneficial use. The BLM applies for at least 25 new water rights in the state every year, with even more claims made for wildlife usage, resulting in almost continuous legal actions, hundreds of which remain unsettled.

Idaho—The Snake River Basin and the Bear River Basin. These two claims cover 38 of 43 Idaho counties and constitute the largest unsettled water adjudication in the United States.

Montana—Claims on "public" lands in 20 basins involving claims by the BLM of 22,000 water rights with 200 more submitted to state authorities each year.

Nevada—Virtually every river source flowing into the Great Basin or the Columbia Basin has claims by the BLM and other federal authorities, although unsettled state law regarding stock-watering rights questions many of them.

© TOM STACK/TOM STACK & ASSOCIATES

New Mexico—At least 17 rivers and tributaries of the Rio Grande are claimed or are being adjudicated as BLM claims for water rights. The total covers more than 1,500 water sources in the state.

Oregon—Primarily the Yakima and Klamath rivers, but particularly in conjunction with Native American tribes, the BLM files 20 new applications a year for state water appropriations.

Utah—The Jordan, the Price, the Colorado, the Virgin, and half a dozen more river systems in the state are claimed for priority rights by the BLM.

Wyoming—The Big Horn River, where Wyoming authorities continue to assert their position on state control despite numerous federal claims over 700 stock-watering wells and some 1,100 reservoirs.

The Bureau of Land Management has made no claims whatsoever to water resources east of the 100th meridian. ■

FALL 2001

DROUGHT

The disaster that disarms the farmers and ranchers in the endless fight for water rights. By Tim Findley

It is a naturally recurring event in the American West especially, and in these times that has proven not only costly, but politically useful. In some ways, it might be appropriate to compare drought in the West with floods in the Mississippi Basin. Both weather events, if not fully predictable, occur with some regularity. Like floods, droughts vary in their severity, sometimes lasting a season or less, and rarely going on into catastrophic years without adequate winter water supplies.

According to federal weather experts, the most expensive natural disaster in U.S. history was the three-year drought of 1987-1989. Actually, that drought, which at one point covered 36 percent of the United States from the West Coast to the northern Great Plains was not broken in parts of the Far West until the winter of 1992-93. By then, it had cost an estimated $39 billion in losses to agriculture, energy production, and environmental needs. Most people in the eastern United States are probably still unaware that it happened at all. It is, however, often cited by environmentalists as proof that western agriculture is unsustainable. Some of those in the "green" movement undeniably await another great drought as a means of proving their political priority.

That is just what happened this year in the Klamath Basin. An exceptionally low snowpack in the Cascades and the Siskiyous showed up as a sharply dropping spike on state precipitation charts. By April, it was nearing the lowest point ever recorded in 1977, causing environmentalists to declare this shortage of barely four-months duration to be the "second greatest drought" in state history. And yet, precisely as was intended by creation of federal reclamation

© TOM STACK/TOM STACK & ASSOCIATES

Land in need of moisture. Despite population growth, the 339 billion gallons of water per day withdrawn by homes, farms, and industries in the U.S. in 1990 was seven percent less than in 1980, and has continued to show a stabilizing downward trend largely due to conservation and new technology.

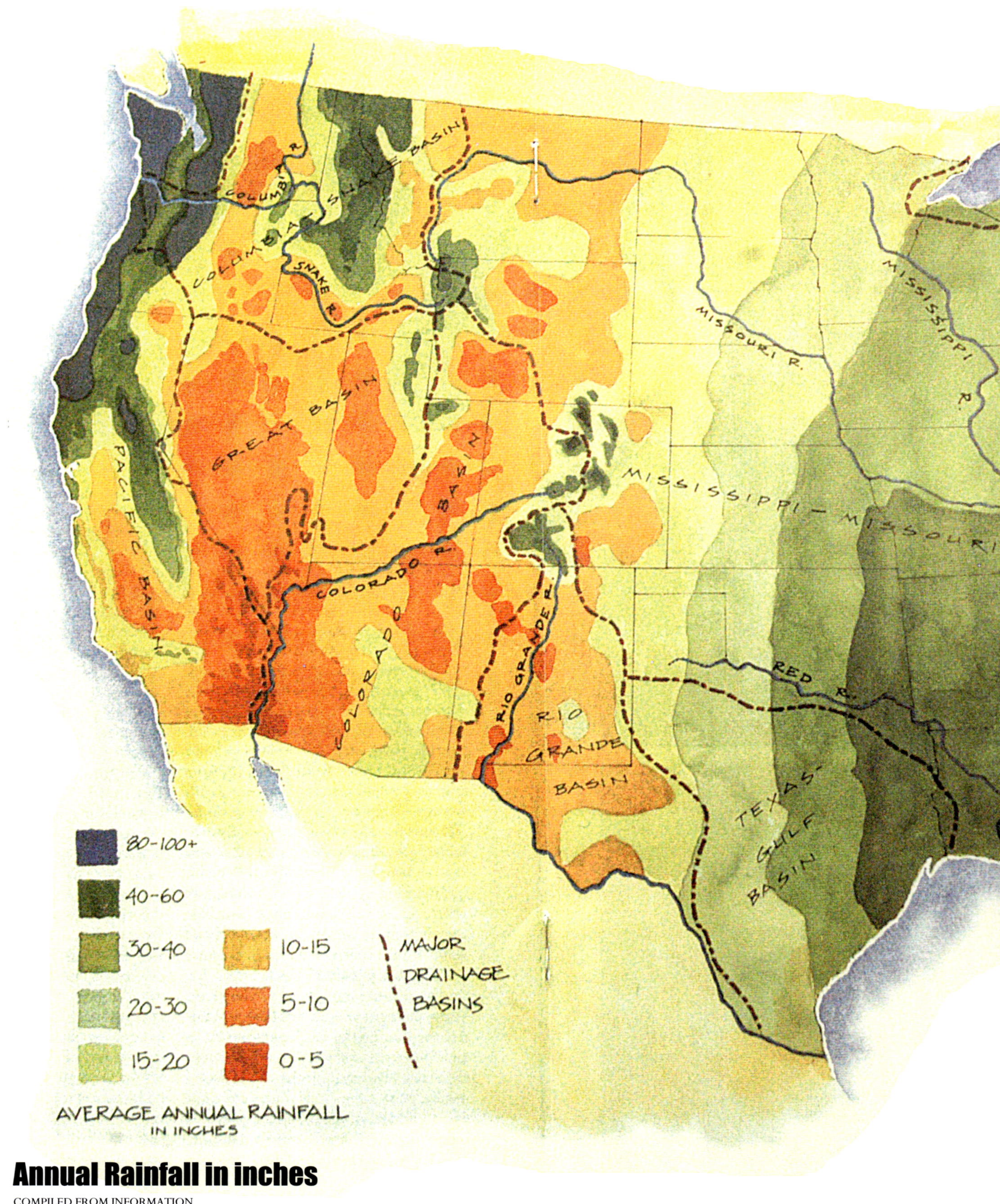

Annual Rainfall in inches

COMPILED FROM INFORMATION
FROM SPATIAL CLIMATE ANALYSIS,
OREGON STATE UNIVERSITY.

ILLUSTRATION BY JOHN BARDWELL

ILLUSTRATION BY JOHN BARDWELL, COMPILED FROM INFORMATION FROM SPATIAL CLIMATE ANALYSIS, OREGON STATE UNIVERSITY

"We must control the water," said former secretary of Interior Bruce Babbitt, "and then we will control the West."

services, the dam at Klamath Lake was brim-full. Despite that, drought was declared as one motivation for the Bureau of Reclamation to deny irrigation water to more than 170,000 acres of farmland.

Never before, not even at the end of the years-long drought in 1992, had the bureau taken such drastic action. Certainly it did not after that last suddenly dry winter of 1977. It may be instructive to note that the year preceding that dry plunge marks the highest precipitation ever recorded in the region, and the following year, 1978, resumed a normal pattern. Though not as extreme at either end, the graph for 2000 to 2001 suggests a similar cycle. Is this the "second greatest drought" or another anomaly in a 100-year record of precipitation? The call was made by U.S. Fish & Wildlife Service and the National Marine Fisheries Service, eager to use drought in an attempt to strangle farms. As phony a disaster as it may be, prevention of irrigation for a full season to the lower-basin farms is expected to drive many of them into bankruptcy. When this drought is over, even if it's this winter, it will be too late for many of them, and the cause for fish over farms will have at least made headway.

Such cynical use of natural phenomenon and even natural disaster is not uncommon in the politically charged battle over water for environmental purposes versus water for agriculture. Farmers and ranchers put at a sudden economic disadvantage, and deserted by the federal agencies originally designed to protect them, are thus disarmed in the fight. As always—in the Klamath Basin and everywhere else there emerge large and small water issues in the West—lurking predators from The Nature Conservancy and similar organizations stand ready with cash for the first farmers willing to give up.

It was drought, not mismanaged overgrowth, that the U.S. Forest Service preferred to blame last year when seven million acres of timberland, most of it in Idaho and Montana, were lost to wildfire. Still refusing to allow even the harvest of burned trees, let alone the thinning of admittedly overloaded forests, federal weather experts have warned this year that some 60 million acres and 23,000 communities are at "high risk" due to the low snowpack in the West. They point especially to Washington state, spared from much of the damage last year, but even more imperiled this summer.

Western drought, as common as floods, was part of the reason the federal government took on its epic period of building dams, reservoirs and irrigation facilities in the first half of the last century. Ironically it is that very same phenomenon of western weather that is today being used as an argument for dismantling it all. ■

WINTER 2002

HOPES & DREAMS

Shattered by a day that will live in infamy.

Fred and Velma Robison when they won the lottery, cheered on by a friend. BELOW: *Velma Robison shows her mother a chicken for the pot!*

"This is a good community and it saddens us all to envision what it might become without water. Where is liberty and justice for all? The day of April 6, 2001, was as infamous to the people of Tulelake as December 7, 1941, Pearl Harbor, was to the people of the United States. We were provided this wonderful gift of land and water by the Department of the Interior, Bureau of Reclamation. They were our friends and did much to help us get started. The kids all grew up with a love of the land and knowing the purpose of growing food on the land to feed others. Now these government agencies are taking from us what was awarded more than 50 years ago and destroying the livelihoods of many. We have been betrayed by our own government!"
—FRED AND VELMA ROBISON

Joe Victorine

"Joe and I both farmed all our lives. Our Social Security is so little we can't live on it, even owning our own home. We don't want charity. We just want water so we can farm! Joe says with a brave grimace, 'We can do either of two choices: rent a very small house and starve or live under a bridge and eat!' I, Mary, am not that brave. I just cry."—JOE AND MARY VICTORINE

"Bob Lillard was part of the force that landed on Utah Beach on D-Day. Homesteading was a challenging experience. We loved it and wouldn't have traded it for anything. Bob loved this land so much. This taking has been devastating, as my property can't be farmed."—KATHERINE LILLARD

The first homes were old Army barracks, with no running water or electricity.

PHOTOS COURTESY WORLD WAR II FAMILIES AND JACQUI KRIZO

"I participated in 23 missions in a night-fighter squadron in Italy, and the China-Burma-India theater. In 1946, a dream came true. Mine was one of 86 names drawn from a total of 1,305 for a farm near Tulelake, California. Barbara and I and our children Dorothy and David moved to the farm in April 1947. There were hard times and many problems, but neighbors shared irrigation water and we always got by. Now our children farm our land. The EPA is unfair. Please help us get our water back."
—PHILIP KRIZO

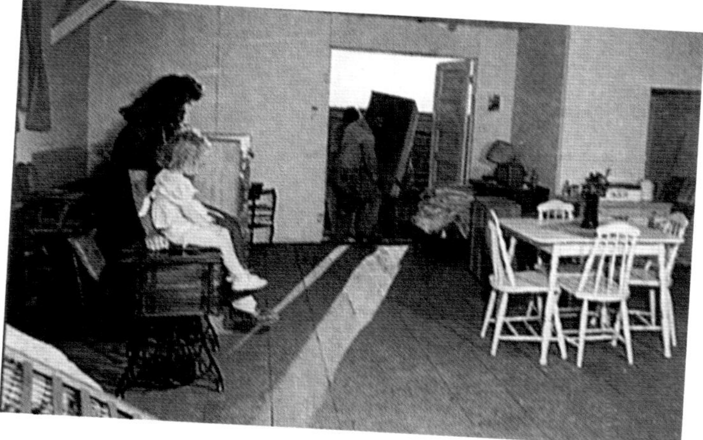

ABOVE: Philip and Barbara Krizo with children Dorothy and David.
LEFT: The Krizos' first home in Klamath Basin.

"Gerald's outfit had the honor to load the first and last bombs to go over Germany. Along with our fellow veterans, we set up housekeeping in Tulelake and farmed with our neighbors. We settled here in good faith, lived up to our commitments. I believe a promise by our government should be kept. If promises to a veteran can be broken, what is there for us to believe in?"
—GERALD AND FRANCES JOHNSON

Gerald and Frances Johnson

Doris and Carl Voorhees

"My husband Carl was a glider pilot in England and France, risking his life on each flight into enemy territory with a loaded glider. Our first home here was a tar paper-covered barracks with no water, no electricity and no plumbing—but we did have rattlesnakes. This is the most serious issue most of us have faced. Carl died in '93. We're not a group of people who can go out and do it all over again—our honeymoon is over."—DORIS VOORHEES

Laverne and Manuel Silva.

"I am a veteran of World War II. In 1948, I applied for and was awarded a homestead in the Klamath Oregon Project. I agreed 'to participate in the organization of an irrigation district at the earliest practicable date.' Payment was an annual charge, and payment has been completed. This implied a contract to supply irrigation water to my homestead. The final document was title to my homestead called a 'patent' which states: Congress 'Does give and grant to me, Manuel P. Silva, and to his assigns and heirs forever, land and water rights.' Why are we veterans being treated this way?"—MANUEL P. SILVA

"They gave returning veterans an opportunity to work to raise and support a family and contribute to our community. We had to level our homestead unit by moving 38,000 cubic yards of soil so we could flood irrigate. Now we learn that fish are more important than we who served our country in war, our country that we have loved and subsidized for years with cheap food. To have them do this to us—take our promised water—is very difficult to understand. Is this the appreciation we get for our years of hard labor to make our Basin productive?"—LEONARD I. WILL

Leonard Will (light shirt), with buddies.

John Terry

"I enlisted in 1941 and served the Air Force Military Police in the Southwest Pacific. I thought the Tulelake basin was the best place in the world to raise a family and farm. After 51 years, I wonder how much longer we can survive with no water for our alfalfa and cattle. Don't forget that our farmers feed the nation. Without us, you can't survive. Our pasture is dying and our cattle are starving."—JOHN AND ALINE TERRY

Paul Rogers remembers when President Truman extended to veterans "the heartfelt thanks of a grateful nation." Rogers didn't believe it when he won a homestead in the 1946 lottery for veterans. He thought they were kidding. He found the soil "as productive as the characters who homesteaded the basin. If you have water," he says, "you can grow just about anything." But farms without water? "Anytime a fish has precedence over a farmer, well somebody has a screw loose. It doesn't make sense."—PAUL AND MABEL ROGERS

Paul Rogers

"At the invitation of the U.S. government, John and I got a homestead in Tulelake. We left family and friends to come to a place that had nothing, no roads, and mostly dirt. In 50 years of farming, we have built a beautiful homestead. There was always enough water, even during drought years. If John were alive, he wouldn't believe that this could happen to a community that once started with nothing, where he worked so very hard to make a good life for his family. He would feel so betrayed and angry."—RUTH MASTERSON

John Masterson

Woodrow Chambers

"I am 84 years old, a 1949 homesteader. The Tulelake Irrigation System delivered water to my homestead for over 50 years. Just take a drive through the basin, most every other farm is overgrown in weeds. Dust has partially covered irrigation pipe left stacked due to no water. Soil is eroding in the wind. I am a born Democrat, but the last eight years of the Democratic administration have not been a government of 'for the people and by the people' but 'for the government and by the government.' If irrigation water is denied us, you will be walking on the graves of World War I homesteaders and digging graves for us World War II homesteaders."—WOODROW CHAMBERS

"My husband was an Air Force veteran. We won a homestead and moved to Tulelake—the end of the world for a city gal. We worked hard, helped build a community, a church, a school, raised our seven children. My first husband died at 55. I married another World War II veteran homesteader. I am 77. Two of my sons have a hardware store in Tulelake and are about to go broke after 20 years, because the farmers and workers have no income. Another has a bar in town and is in the same position. One of my sons served two years in Vietnam, another served in Korea—sure is a nice thanks to them!"
—KATHLEEN TODD ST. PETER

Kathleen and her first husband Clyde Todd.

WINTER 2008

KLAMATH REDUX

In the federally dominated West, water remains the essence of wealth and the currency of real political power. Take control of the water and you have control over everything and everyone. By Tim Findley

We sit in the farmer's pickup parked at the fence behind centerfield at Tule Lake High School's ball field. From there, he can just about keep an eye on his onion field out in the wetlands and still watch his son covering third base. A stack of half-opened mail is piled on the dashboard, like an extra chore for idle moments.

That's a lot of what it is, the pickups around the fence, the summer fading quietly with distant sounds of early arriving geese, the smiles from neighbors, the wave from a boy covering the same ground you did years before when you were known as Spuds.

He had played an important part in the crisis of 2001, and only narrowly averted an economic disaster to his family. He was working then for moments like this that can only be felt in such rural communities of family farms like the Lower Klamath Basin.

For 20 years, at least since passage of the 1988 Endangered Species Act (ESA) made it the law of the land, coalitions of outside "environmentalists" have prowled the Klamath like predators intent on removing the generations of agriculturalists they regard as threats to nature. They are not mere tree huggers who climb, childlike, into the branches. Many are agents of powerful and wealthy non-profit organizations with solid histories of their own and propaganda capabilities that disguise a ruthless political motive and an arrogant prejudice that often expresses itself as bigotry against those who work the land.

Echoes of Curses in the Klamath

To senses strained and wearied by the cacophony of years of name-calling and political posturing, the view across wetlands of the Lower Klamath Basin seems to sing in a quiet harmony of its own, like a patriotic hymn.

There is a gentle aroma from the dark green fields of mint and onions that reach to tawny acres of barley cut in alternating rows to preserve habitat and feed for migrating birds and, beyond that, tules shelter the edge of the shallow lake that forms a shimmering blue ribbon beneath the horizon where the magnificent monolith of 14,000-foot Mount Shasta bears its snow-draped dominion over all.

This is a picture of the success that followed the bitter attempt of politically driven bureaucrats to punish and even destroy the agrarian economy and culture of the entire Kla-

© LARRY TURNER

For almost a century the Klamath Basin has flourished through productive farms. Agriculture from the basin is responsible for $300 million per year sustaining a once-vigorous community.

math Basin in 2001. These carefully managed sections of land leased from the government represent what they call a "walking wetlands." Here on some of the most fertile ground in America, crops are periodically rotated with stretches of open water serving the needs of this vital link in the North American flyway.

Pelicans patrol offshore from standing wheat fields; geese feed on the stubble and standing crops of oats and barley; and mule deer clip across the levees and into the shade.

Farmers and federal agents of the U.S. Fish & Wildlife Service jointly created this innovative answer to part of the dilemma of claims on Oregon's richest waterway. They take joint pride in it and meet among it as they should, as friends. It is one answer, but not the solution in the vast puzzle of the Klamath Basin, reaching from Oregon into California like a jigsaw of pieces that don't fit together in the rubric of more than a score of interests. They have been working for years to resolve a century of conflicts and finally bring peace to a place so blessed. Yet now, when they are nearer solution than ever, the echoes of others who demand sacrifice and capitulation are heard again. The echoes, and the curses, mean to end it.

Tens of thousands of people from around the nation joined in support of Klamath farmers in the summer of 2001. Symbolically forming a Bucket Brigade and filling stadiums with rallies, the largest demonstration in Oregon history protested the "fish over farms" decision of the U.S. Bureau of Reclamation (BOR) to deny irrigation water to farmers for the first time in the federal project's 95-year history. For many of the 1,400 farmers—as well as for hundreds more employed in providing supplies, processing and transportation in the basin—the sudden action of the bureau portended economic disaster. Even many who survived it did so only with generous food given by the local supermarket and free medical care offered by the local clinic. It was still not enough to save some from the devastating loss of livelihood that the false drought created.

In the years that followed the 2001 debacle, George W. Bush would prove by his spending to be more of an environmentalist than Bill Clinton ever had been—at least in the Klamath. Farmers most affected benefited from a $20-million supplemental appropriation in the farm budget, but more than $500 million was poured into the Klamath Basin by the Bush administration for conservation solutions such as the walking wetlands, fish ladders, or aquatic studies on lands acquired by the ubiquitous Nature Conservancy.

Farmers like Steve Kandra, who had been president of the Klamath Irrigation District in 2001, were expected to match the federal investments with innovations of their own, and they did.

"I survived, but some of my neighbors didn't," says Kandra, who raises grain in the walking wetlands. "Since that time we've been battling back as best we can, and at

© TIM FINDLEY

Irrigation begins in early morning in the Lower Basin.

least we have had this administration's attention. We've access to resources that allow us to do water-conservation projects here like crazy, cooperative projects. But I'm concerned that once the money runs out, the regulations come back, and there are people who want to use those regulations to drive us off."

Kandra is concerned about the creatures getting lost in all this. "I spend thousands of dollars every year on critters—on ducks, geese and mule deer—and I'm glad I do. And yet, some folks want to kick me off this place. We farmers know from 90-years experience on this project that we can produce crops and protect wildlife with irrigat-

"I'm concerned about the critters getting lost in all this," says Klamath farmer Steve Kandra. "I spend thousands of dollars every year on critters—on ducks, geese and mule deer—and I'm glad I do. And yet, they want to kick me off this place. We farmers know from 90-years experience on this project that we can produce crops and protect wildlife with irrigated agriculture. We must do that. If you take the water from me, you only produce hunger for us all."

ed agriculture. We must do that. If you take the water from me, you only produce hunger for us all."

But while basin farmers looked for ways to bring peace to the numbing array of interests in the basin, other self-imposing environmentalists took it on themselves to rekindle the fight with lawsuits, if they could, and with other means, if necessary.

It was again a relatively dry but still-productive season in 2002. Despite warnings, endangered sucker fish had survived well and even increased their numbers in Klamath Lake. Another appeal in federal court to halt irrigation was rejected, and farms began to recover with the help of new wells and better rotation. Increased return flows from the fields even added to the generating power of the river by an estimated $18 million. Then, as the season ended, events of nature provided a new and still-mysterious twist.

For years, the run of salmon in from the ocean to spawning pools in the Klamath River had been less than was hoped for, even in years when water was plentiful. Runs up the Sacramento River to the south had reached record proportions only the year before, but nobody expected the overpowering flood of chinook and coho that raced up from the mouth of the Klamath in September 2002. Native American fishermen who once had to fight off sea lions for a day's catch at the mouth of the river now filled their nets in an abundance of fish that they were unable to sell to the glutted market. It was a bonanza of a few days that suddenly came to a tragic conclusion when huge numbers of fish—some say 70,000 or more—floated dead back down the river.

Indian tribal members and newly professed fish experts immediately blamed what they called "welfare farmers" in the Lower Basin, at least 150 miles upstream. The farmers were as shocked as the tribe, but could find no precedence that could explain such a die-off.

Scientists had no immediate answer. In fact, critics say they know of only one fish that was examined before hydrologists and biologists concluded that the combination of the warmth of the water in a hot, dry season combined with the overwhelming volume of fish in the run altered the oxygen supply of the river itself. The fish massed in great numbers offshore awaiting a pulse of cool water that could only have been brought by rain. Disease spread rapidly among the crowded over-stressed fish by the time they began the run, the scientists said. Nothing else, except poisoning the water, could account for such a catastrophe.

To politically obsessed environmentalists, however, the gasping fish were like a godsend.

In June 2008, *The Washington Post* began a series of articles slicing at the sturdy seat of Vice President Dick Cheney. A piece headlined "Leaving No Tracks" accused Cheney of intervening in a number of clean air and environmental issues inherited from the Clinton administration. Among them was the matter of 2001's last-minute irrigation releases on the Klamath, which Cheney was accused of directing despite scientific findings (the Hardy report) that the releases would imperil threatened fish.

Washington Democrats, seemingly obsessed to the point of irrational hatred of the Bush administration, called for congressional hearings to grill Cheney on the *Post's* "farmers over fish" accusations.

In Oregon and California, previously dormant radicals used the powerful Washington newspaper to propel themselves like locusts dropping into every available op-ed page, website, and blog to accuse Cheney of "political favoritism" on behalf of "powerful agribusiness interests."

The great Klamath scandal orchestrated into the pages of the *Post* in 2007 drew a long distance between reality and truth. If any undue political influence was exerted on the water gatekeepers of the BOR in 2001, it seemed clearly to have been from leftover bureaucrats in Fish & Wildlife.

The "Cheney did it! Cheney did it!" hysteria in the hearing conducted at the end of July this year was calmly confronted with testimony from the National Academy of Sciences Research Council on endangered and threatened fish in the Klamath River Basin—the same esteemed body that had conducted a peer review of the Hardy conclusions and found them to be lacking adequate research and possibly agenda-driven. The argument that a cool pulse of water that might have saved the fish was held back by management of Lower Basin irrigation was found to be "very unlikely" by the independent National Academy.

© TIM FINDLEY

Klamath Lake. Freezing the water for fish alone, cutting new swaths of wilderness to divide the continent, outsourcing the elements of our survival, seems like a generous strategy for national suicide.

The former chairman of the council, professor William M. Lewis, noted that, first of all, water from the irrigation project is not cool, but warm from being held in storage lakes behind downstream dams. In any case, Lewis told the committee that water from the project accounts for only 10 percent of the flow at the mouth of the river, which is mostly fed by large tributaries miles below the Klamath Basin.

In a reasonable world, that testimony might have stilled, or chilled, the swarming radicals from calling Cheney and the farmers "fish murderers" and "salmon killers." But by the time Lewis was allowed to present his evidence, most of them, along with most of the Democrats on the committee convened to "get" Cheney, were not there to hear it.

There remain strong hopes that the sincere representatives of 26 separate sides of interest in the Klamath resources will reach agreement before the end of this year. But the political drums and bongo beaters are gathering again on the horizon. "The administration and its agribusiness allies have hijacked closed-door talks over the removal of four Klamath River dams," railed Steve Pedery of Oregon Wild in a July opinion piece written for the Eugene *Register-Guard*.

Pedery, still preaching "scandal" wherever he can imagine it, insists that "phasing out commercial farming" in the Lower Basin, combined with removal of dams on the Klamath, is the only way to save the salmon. Dismissing the negotiations that reject him, he is waiting for a new administration in Washington that won't do favors for agribusiness.

But the shrill voices of the so-green like Pedery can also be deafening in understanding what may be the greatest problem for the Klamath negotiators—the four dams below the Lower Basin Irrigation Project. The dams have nothing really to do with water for irrigation, but they do supply the vital power to run irrigation pumps in the system. Two years ago, the dams were sold to the second richest man in the nation, Warren Buffett.

Buffett's dams, run by his subsidiary Pacificorp, were quickly blamed for producing a toxic algae that could result in fish kills. As the Federal Energy Regulatory Commission began considering the issue of a new 30- to 50-year license to the hydropower dams, the tribes and the environmentalists demanded they be torn down. Buffett, a man familiar with the bottom line, hinted he might be receptive to a request from the entire 26-member negotiating team. In the meantime, Pacificorp began a series of rate increases that could amount to a raise of more than 1,300 percent for irrigators. Losing the dams wouldn't bother them if another source of power production was identified. Coal- or oil-fired plants? Not likely, so long as environmentalists are armed with Al Gore's dire warnings of global warming.

Echoes and curses drift back across one of the West's most productive agricultural regions where fish and wildlife mingle with food grown to feed a nation.

Spuds watches the play at third with satisfaction, wanting not to be distracted by the question. "I don't want to fight it anymore," he says. "I mean, I just don't want to be up front." He sighs a little like he isn't sure it will be possible. "I just want to farm," he says simply.

Some mail on the dash remains unopened. It is all bills from the power company. The last one he reads and places on the top of the stack is from June. It totals $32,000. ■

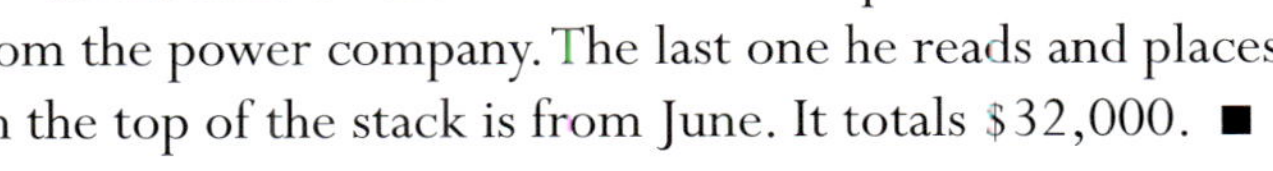

FALL 2009

Agriculture, Jobs, Towns, TERMINATED

Enviros get their way, but where will they get their food?

By Tim Findley

You couldn't see the irony any more than you could see the heat, but it was equally dominant as Gov. Arnold Schwarzenegger stood above the half-empty San Luis Reservoir and joined at least 10,000 farmworkers in their chant.

"We want water! We want water!" they called, Schwarzenegger's deep Bavarian accent heard above those around him. Mr. Universe; The Terminator; an odd Republican married into the Kennedy political dynasty; the desperation governor who took over from California's last failed executive. One of the best-known men on earth in a region that once claimed it could feed the world now joining in a futile cry of "We want water! We want water!"

Was he asking a deity to make it rain, thus ending a three-year period of less-than-normal precipitation? They call it a drought, but snowpack in the Sierra this year was at least 70 percent of normal and filled the rivers into the Central Valley with heavy runoff. He might have been appealing to Fresno Federal Judge Oliver Wanger, who ruled at the beginning of this growing season that the major portion of the valley would receive no federal irrigation supplies. But Wanger had already expressed his regret, and The Terminator just doesn't carry more weight than the Natural Resources Defense Council (NRDC). It brought suit on behalf of the Delta smelt, which, it argued, might go extinct without its full appropriation of water. Schwarzenegger couldn't really blame the smelt, which looks pretty much the same as every other minnow found in the region and may not have even been native to the Delta. The fish, scientists say, will survive or not, regardless of additional water. But the governor's cry on behalf of farmworkers would find deaf ears with the NRDC, which has the Endangered Species Act on its side and privately says it doesn't think the Westside or "Westland" region should be farmed anyway.

PHOTOS © MIKE HENRY

California's political minnow is made into a maneater by the Natural Resources Defense Council. With no irrigation water in the spring of 2009, crops and orchards died (inset). More than 25,000 people are without work and there is no guarantee that fish life has improved. AT TOP: Arnold Schwarzenegger had no power to help 10,000 marchers at San Luis Reservoir.

Interior Secretary Ken Salazar, who grew up in a near-replica irrigated valley in Colorado with even the same names such as San Luis, flew over the drought-shocked fields in a helicopter with Schwarzenegger and would later manage a meager 10 percent allocation for the farms, but he would do no more in convincing his own Bureau of Reclamation of the gravity of the problem.

So Schwarzenegger—much of the economy in his "Golden State" crumbling behind him—could do no more than repeat something that sounded a little like "I'll be back," except that the mantra was "We want water," and it was said without promise.

The governor might be unaware of one ultimate irony in the creation of this rich agricultural region by another immigrant who came here during the Gold Rush and built what was the mightiest cattle empire in the world. Henry Miller and his partner Charles Lux (a German immigrant) bought, traded and claimed more than half a million acres, most of it along the San Joaquin River, and when Miller needed to prove his fields were on navigable access for riparian rights, he loaded a rowboat on the back of his wagon and towed it around the whole valley.

"We want water. We want water!" The governor's cry on behalf of farmworkers would find deaf ears.

It was Miller, at his own expense of some $300,000, who first brought irrigation to the valley and made possible what was once the proud economic engine of California. It is only in the last two decades that computer-related production in California has exceeded agriculture as the state's most important product, and the Central Valley has always been the heart of California agriculture.

But don't bother arguing that with attorneys who have the Environmental Protection Agency (EPA) in their pocket and a stop-the-farmer attitude in their heads. Even the *Contra Costa Times*, based along the coast near San Francisco, put its editorial feet in the fray with a clear "sustainable" bias.

"In fact, the conflict, rather than a case of 'fish versus people,' is a clear case of people employed in the commercial fishing and recreational fishing industries throughout the state and on Delta farms and businesses versus subsidized agribusiness on the west side of the San Joaquin Valley. It is in reality a battle between sustainable fisheries and farms versus keeping in production drainage-impaired, selenium-laced soil in the Westlands Irrigation District, the 'Darth Vader' of California water politics," wrote *Times* reporter Dan Bacher.

Actually, the Westlands Irrigation District is the largest water district in the nation, generating over $12 billion in economic production. Its Darth Vader image stems from federal failure to provide promised drainage for the Kesterson Wildlife Refuge in the 1980s. Irrigated farms in the region are limited by law to 960 acres and cover some 600,000 acres.

There is an irony within the irony there in that the large Westlands' growers won't really be stopped or hurt nearly as much as the thousands of farmworkers put out of jobs. In all, the University of California at Davis has reported it expects 25,000 to be unemployed in the valley. Ironically, that is the same number the California Water Project was intended to put to work in the 1930s.

You can find them now in small towns like Firebaugh and Mendota where there is a village feel as close to Mexico and Latin America as this far north gets. In Mendota, near the high heat of the day, a group of men gather under the awninged shade of the Westside Grocery. It used to be a gas station, but now the covered pump bays serve with some cool relief for a couple of guitar players singing in Spanish. The place is owned and operated by Joseph Riofrio, who grew up here and is now in his sixth term on the Mendota City Council, including a term as mayor. He used to run the business as a small grocery and as a place for the workers, some undocumented, to cash their checks.

"Not many checks anymore," Riofrio says, sadly shaking his head. "People have nowhere to go, nothing to do. Now I rent videos more than I sell any food."

He is a young, strong man, with a no-nonsense approach to customers who he knows face the effects of hard times. The future is deeply troubling. "We have at least 40 percent unemployment now," he says, "and this is just the beginning of the season. The equipment operators, the restaurants, even the car dealer will all be affected as it gets deeper. There's no bailout for us." On a top shelf in his store is the poster he carried in the march to San Luis Reservoir. It says, "Water = Food."

There have been droughts in this region before. Miller and his irrigation canal from the San Joaquin as well as his generosity to new settlers is credited for holding off the crushing effects of one such dry spell at the end of the 19th century. But the most serious similar drought came in the 1930s, at the height of the Great Depression and, with yet more irony, it served to create the federal water system that now denies its water to crops in the Westlands. The governor in those days was Sunny Jim Rolph from San Francisco, who saw both the need and the advantage of saving agriculture in the valley. Over objection primarily by the power companies, Rolph issued bonds and accepted a

$49 million contribution of the federal government to build dams, canals and the pumps between the Sacramento and San Joaquin rivers in the Delta above where they enter the salt intrusion of San Francisco Bay. In the end, virtually all the $170 million project was covered by federally financed bonds. The pumping and canal system eventually sending water south down the length of the state would become one of the remarkable engineering achievements of that time when the way out of the Depression was to put people to work building.

Not this time. The 10 percent gesture Schwarzenegger secured from the feds would not arrive until the first crop should already have been in the ground. And out there, in the broken dry fields plowed but few planted, the results were already obvious in the irrigation pipes lying idle, the furrows and turnouts unconnected, and rows of almond groves struggling with mineral-laced well water, or simply standing dead, like squads of skeletons.

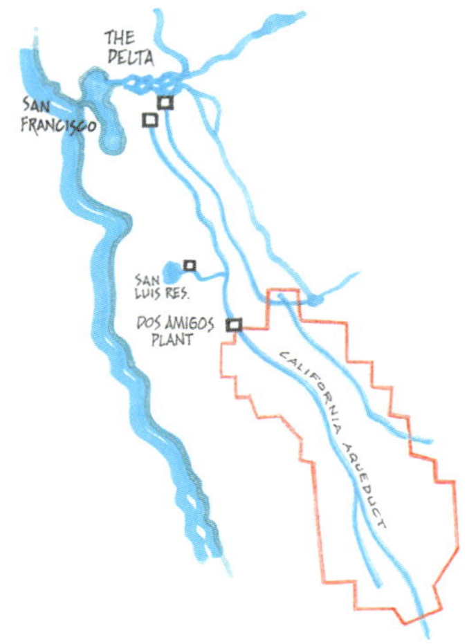

More than 300,000 acre-feet of water that was meant for these fields now pours into the Pacific to save a little fish that some scientists say won't be and can't be rescued by it. Many of the fish are still lost in the unfiltered pumps themselves, and others may be dying from pollution and sewage added to the water by upstream cities and towns in the Delta itself. The valley strangles while the freshwater mingles wastefully with the salt of the ocean.

The area framed in red used to be California's best food-producing region.

That was all said in April by the 10,000 marchers who began their 50-mile walk from Firebaugh. What they got back was the argument that it is a drought—yet in reality not quite the drought they claim. "The federal government created this drought," say the signposts flashing by as you drive up Interstate 5.

"It's a judicial drought," says Jose Ramirez, the city manager of Firebaugh. He looks younger than his 36 years, but even as a child, before he began his determined effort to secure a master's degree in public administration, Ramirez worked the fields with his family, all the way to Gilroy. He has never seen anything quite like this. "We faced a long dry spell in the 1970s," he says, "but we were able to get through it. Now, if there weren't [private] contract water out there for some growers, I'm not sure this city would be a city anymore."

As in Mendota, unemployment in Firebaugh is now at least 40 percent, and likely to get worse.

"People are not bitter. Not yet," says Councilman Riofrio, "but most of them know what happened in Klamath, and there's talk." In the Klamath Basin of Oregon, when environmental activists succeeded in cutting off irrigation water by a lawsuit claiming it threatened an endangered sucker fish, it was angry townspeople, really, who finally surrounded the pumping station demanding that the water be released.

"It's that kind of thing," Riofrio says. "Rural Americans are just not seen as an endangered portion of America. We have to defend ourselves or watch the destruction of rural America."

But it's not just rural America at stake. The attack on agriculture ripples quickly and deepens like a flood. At one of the most popular restaurants and fuel stops on I-5, the owner looks over empty tables where he used to see farmers and bankers, truckers and investors meeting at lunch. He asks that we not use his name or that of his restaurant, but he can't resist saying how he feels. "Last year, it was the price of fuel," he says. "This year, water costs more than gasoline." The water and power companies have won what Sunny Jim Rolph once denied them. Water is no longer served to the few customers unless they specifically ask for it.

Another march to the pumps can likely draw even more than the 10,000 who walked to the San Luis Reservoir, but it is those who will not march who are part of yet another irony. The United Farm Workers of the late Cesar Chavez refused to join the last march, saying it was payback for the more conservative farmworkers on the Westside not taking part in UFW work stoppages.

That division was formed in the 1960s when El Salvadoran immigrants, many without documents, refused to join the Mexican nationals who comprised most of the UFW. "Most of them are still here," Riofrio says grimly. "Still poor, but still here, and not expecting any help from the union." They say around Mendota that if you get close enough to watch a cow pie-tossing contest, the game is bound to get some on you.

And the pools of trickle-up poverty also reach higher, if more slowly, as people in California and all over the United States begin to feel the cost of choosing a dubiously endangered fish over irrigated fields that once claimed to produce 50 percent of the nation's food supply. Maybe the North American Free Trade Agreement can cover it from south of the border.

And there's another irony. ■

COURTESY NATIONAL ARCHIVES

Corn field on an Indian farm near Tuba City, Arizona, in rain, 1941. Photo by Ansel Adams.

SUMMER 1995
VOICES

Ansel Adams became famous as a black-and-white photographer who specialized in wild nature, unspoiled by man. Although often called an environmentalist, his photography was interpreted as political activism. In his own autobiography, he said, "People are surprised when I say that I never intentionally made a creative photograph that related directly to an environmental issue."

Wild animals never appear in his photographs, only domestic ones, even though he often photographed national parks. Famous for romantic "wilderness" vistas, he also photographed the West as it truly was, helping people to see beauty in reality instead of fantasy.

Like many others who appreciated the outdoors, Adams joined the Sierra Club when it was composed of fun-loving hikers and campers. Together they fought to protect beautiful camping places threatened by dam sites, development, or highway construction. But as the Sierra Club's focus gradually shifted toward radical preservation politics, Adams disagreed more and more with the club leaders, saying, "Unfortunately, power and success often breed ego and arrogance." The Sierra Club had become plagued, Adams felt, with "overzealous" crusaders.

After one serious quarrel over a power company, Adams said, "I am certainly biased to the nature scene, but I also recognized the need for electrical power. The problem as I saw it was to maintain a balance of use, thereby assuring that the truly important areas would stand a better chance of protection." He believed "too many of the club had grown unreasonable."

Adams continued to support environmental concerns of his own for the rest of his life, but resigned from the Sierra Club in 1971. ■

BIG BROTHER'S WATER

If you think the "Delta smelt" scandal smells, you ain't smelt nothin' yet. By Henry Lamb

Since the beginning of this nation, the federal government has regulated the use of navigable water under the authority of the U.S. Constitution, which says Congress has the power to: "Regulate Commerce with foreign Nations, and among the several States, and with the Indian Tribes."

This authority is pretty clear, straightforward, and reasonable. For commerce to flow through our ports and on our rivers, it makes perfectly good sense for the federal government, directed by Congress, to regulate the use of navigable water.

Wisconsin's Sen. Russ Feingold and 24 of his colleagues have introduced the Clean Water Restoration Act (S787) that will expand the power of Congress beyond the enumerated powers set forth in the Constitution, and authorize the regulation of virtually all water everywhere, as well as activities that may affect water wherever it may be.

Feingold's bill says: "The term 'waters of the United States' means all waters subject to the ebb and flow of the tide, the territorial seas, and all interstate and intrastate waters and their tributaries, including lakes, rivers, streams (including intermittent streams), mudflats, sand flats, wetlands, sloughs, prairie potholes, wet meadows, playa lakes, natural ponds, and all impoundments of the foregoing, to the fullest extent that these waters, or activities affecting these waters, are subject to the legislative power of Congress under the Constitution."

Read this definition very carefully: "activities affecting these waters are subject to the legislative power of Congress under the Constitution." We asked Sen. Feingold's office: "Where, exactly, is the constitutional authority to empower Congress to regulate wetlands, prairie potholes, intermittent streams, natural and man-made ponds, and all the other areas specified in the bill's definition that may be on private property?"

After an e-mail inquiry and several phone calls, Sen. Feingold's press spokesman, Zach Lowe, said...nothing. That's right, the senator's office flatly refused to answer the question and refused to provide a reason for not answering the question.

The purpose of Feingold's bill is to remove all doubt about who holds the authority to control water, as well as any and all activity that may affect water. This authority, should this bill become law, is the federal government. Until now, states have had the responsibility and authority to regulate nonnavigable waters within their borders. In recent years, however, federal law has incrementally usurped state authority to the extent that the state governments have become little more than administrative units of the federal government. Feingold's bill will make state employees involved with water regulation functionaries for the feds while remaining paid by the state.

This stream originates from a spring on private property and provides clear water, wildlife habitat, and great pleasure for the current owner. With the passage of S787, this becomes "waters of the United States" and gives the federal government authority to dictate any and all activity on the land the deed holder bought, and on which he is still required to pay taxes.

Perhaps more important is the phrase, "activity affecting these waters." This phrase would give the federal government the excuse to intervene in virtually any activity anywhere rain falls. The federal government extended its reach over private property when it claimed jurisdiction over nearly 200 million acres of wetlands on private property. Feingold's bill will extend federal government jurisdiction over virtually every square inch of land in the United States.

People who live in communist countries know full well what it feels like for government to have complete control over the use of land. Americans have been learning this lesson case by case. Ocie Mills, for example, who put 19 loads of building sand on his own land for a home foundation, was convicted of polluting the "waters of the United States." The feds didn't care that the state of Florida had approved the building site or that the county had issued a building permit. Both Ocie and his son spent nearly two years in a federal prison for putting clean sand on dry land which the feds arbitrarily defined to be "waters of the United States." Ocie is only one of thousands of people who have been prosecuted by the feds for the heinous crime of moving dirt around on their own private property.

PHOTOS © MARK LAMB

The water in this drainage ditch in the middle of a privately owned cornfield will become "waters of the United States," and by definition in the law, any activity on the adjacent land that affects the waters of the United States becomes subject to the control of the federal government. The entity that has legal control over the use of land is the effective "owner" of the land, while the person whose name appears on the deed must pay the taxes. Nothing in the bill acknowledges the Fifth Amendment's requirement that when private property is taken for public use, just compensation must be paid.

Michigan farmer John Rapanos also spent time in federal prison because he too moved some dirt on his own cornfield in preparation for building a home. But the Pacific Legal Foundation took John's case to the Supreme Court, and on June 19, 2006—after nearly 20 years of litigation—the Supreme Court ruled in his favor. The decision declared that the feds have to prove that land which they declare to be a wetland is, indeed, "navigable" waters as required by law. (*RANGE,* Winter 2005)

This decision infuriated the environmental community. Apparently, it also offended Russ Feingold and his 24 co-sponsors, because his bill makes the Rapanos decision and all previous wetland decisions irrelevant by defining everything that is wet—or that may get wet—to be within the regulatory jurisdiction of the federal government.

This bill puts farmers and ranchers in great jeopardy. Until now, it has been necessary to find some endangered critter to justify shutting off irrigation pumps. No more. If the water in the irrigation system is, by legal definition, the waters of the United States, the feds do not have to have a reason for denying farmers the use of it.

Until now, ranchers have had access to pasture by virtue of the beneficial use of water assigned under the doctrine of prior appropriation. This bill will assign the water to the United States and can leave ranchers without access to water or to pasture—at the whim of the federal government. While promoters of this bill may claim that the feds will not change the water-use policies, there is absolutely no reason to suspect the government will honor such claims. If the government claims effective "ownership" of the water by declaring all water to be the "waters of the United States," there is every reason to suspect that the government intends to regulate its use.

People who live in urban areas may welcome federal ownership of water—at first. Drought in the Southeast had Atlanta residents quite concerned last year. Local and state officials, who live in the area and were elected by local residents, developed the rules that governed water use. The Feingold bill would give federal agencies the authority to dictate the distribution of water and the regulations regarding water use, without regard to what the local officials or local people may want.

There is neither constitutional nor rational justification for this enormous power grab by the federal government. The feds should continue to regulate navigable or commercial waterways. But the federal government has no business interfering with state water regulations, nor does it have any business involving itself in how ranchers, farmers, and other private property owners use the water that nature provides to them. There are already a multitude of laws on the books to prevent and correct instances of water pollution. This bill has nothing to do with improving water quality. It has everything to do with a bald-faced expansion of Big Government. Water rights would become totally meaningless.

Resist! ■

WILD LIFE

MOUNTAIN LION © TOM STACK/TOM STACK & ASSOCIATES

FALL 1992/WINTER 1993

WILD HORSES

Unintended consequences. By C.J. Hadley

The Act

For decades, mustangers chased free-roaming horses, captured them and sold them for dog meat. They culled the bad ones and sold the good ones for saddle horses, using any method available to subdue.

It was Wild Horse Annie who decided the mustangs should be protected. This feisty Reno, Nevada, woman, whose real name was Velma Johnston, took it upon herself to change the West, to make sure the wild horse would not be used and abused.

Wild Horse Annie was right. She had seen firsthand that some of these symbols of the West were packed too tight into trucks, at times bleeding and broken. She knew that a few mustangers lassoed horses with ropes tied to heavy tires and let the horses drag the rubber until they were too winded to run any more. She set out to fix that situation.

In 1959, because of Wild Horse Annie's entreaties, Congress made capturing horses by aircraft and motorized vehicle illegal. She formed a nonprofit group called Wild Horse Organized Assistance (WHOA) and, in 1971, with emotion and sentiment on her side and no dissenting votes, the Wild, Free-Roaming Horse and Burro Act was signed into law.

"Congress finds and declares," the law read, "that wild free-roaming horses and burros are living symbols of the historic and pioneer spirit of the West; that they contribute to the diversity of life forms within the Nation and enrich the lives of the American people."

At the time, there were 9,000 horses in Nevada and the law insisted that they remain at the same level and in the same places that they were found when the law passed. But that law didn't pay any attention to fenceless range, amount of forage and water, horse reproduction rates and the unpredictability of nature.

The law passed so easily it even surprised Wild Horse annie. She was ready for battle, expected compromise, but got the works. It worried her some because she knew that the herds on the range could increase rapidly, so she suggested at a Nevada legislative meeting on the wild horse that some studs be sterilized. Chauvinistic and egotistical legislators laughed her right out of the room.

Within a decade there was no more laughing, because Wild Horse Annie had been right again. Control was necessary. The problem was, even though the Bureau of Land

There are 50,000 wild horses on the western range, 33,000 in Nevada. After seven years of drought and a population explosion, there are too many horses for the resource. The pressure is on for wildlife, livestock and mustangs. The federal agencies, particularly the BLM, are trying to play fair with what's out there. ABOVE: Pilot Jim Hicks gently pushes the mustangs toward the corrals. OPPOSITE: Mustangs usually travel in small bunches, controlled by a stud, led by a mare. More healthy bands, like this one in Wyoming, will thrive on the western range with better control.

Management (BLM) and the Forest Service (FS) were responsible for the horses, there was nothing in the law that allowed them to manage them properly. Every time the federal agencies made a move to try to improve the situation, to cut the herd numbers, their days were filled with complaints.

Velma Johnston died in 1977, and her work has been continued by Dawn Lappin, former secretary to WHOA. Lappin will accept no cruelty to animals or excessive removals and adoptions, and the folks at WHOA occasionally slap lawsuits on the BLM to make sure it is doing the job right. But Lappin, too, knows there must be control along with protection.

"Wild Horse Annie had a firm commitment to the animals and to the public lands," Lappin says. "She knew what she was talking about. She didn't try to pull the wool over other people's eyes and say they are all Black Beauty out there. But she did know they had to be managed."

The Passion

Ranchers have permitted rights to graze livestock on the open range. Wildlife is tended and encouraged by fish and game agencies. Miners dig for precious or semiprecious metals. And campers, fishermen, hikers, hunters, bikers, off-roaders, bird watchers, photographers and other recreationists share the same public land.

The law says that the federal agencies must manage these vast western lands for multiple use. Everyone has an opinion on the subject, and most believe wild horses have a place on the range. Passion for the horse became a problem with all the sentiment, pain and drama connected to the subject. Only equines—applauded and defended by people who would never see them—were unmanaged on the public domain and their numbers increased quickly.

"The real problem with the wild horse has nothing to do with numbers," says Nancy Whitaker, director of public-lands issues for Animal Protection Institute (API). "The issue is the administration's refusal to implement the law."

Whitaker says horses have to be managed as a part of the biological diversity of the land. They have to be part of the overall multiple grazing decisions under other laws like the Wilderness Act, the National Environmental Policy Act and the Federal Land Policy Management Act (which amended the 1971 act to bring back aircraft for use in horse and wildlife gathers and monitoring in the late '70s).

"These acts said vegetation on rangeland is more than forage or board feet of lumber," Whitaker says. "They provide habitat, watershed protection, soil stability and a diverse plant community. That is what the agencies are to manage for—a healthy ecosystem."

© C.J. HADLEY

Dave Catoor's portable corrals are set up carefully, to assure safe and humane treatment for the horses.

Some cattlemen differ with the API on a key point. They say the horses out on the range are not feral, or part of the natural ecosystem. They argue that fossil records show that the horse became extinct on the North American continent 10,000 years ago, to be reintroduced by the Spanish conquistadors in the 1500s. History shows that by the 17th century, some Indian tribes were using horses to ride. For the next 300 years, escaped or abandoned horses roamed free.

As settlement increased, habitat shrank. Herd size was controlled by ranchers and mustangers, who hunted the horses to use for work or gather for sale. And this healthy culling and cleansing continued until the 1960s. The protective law had altered the high-desert's balance—which for more than a century had been manipulated by people. Horses reproduced at a generous rate and what was supposed to be a wandering herd of a thousand on the military's Nellis Gunnery Range on the Nevada Test Site in southern Nevada increased 10-fold in little more than a decade. Ranchers' water improvements—they had cleaned pipes and troughs, dug wells, checked springs and small creeks—were now left to nature. And nature was cruel.

The BLM planned to remove several thousand stressed horses from Nellis in 1990 but Whitaker and API protested, filing an appeal with the Interior Board of Land Appeals. "It is a boundary issue," she told them. "Your resource management law is wrong, it is invalid, the alternatives that you list as the criteria are illegal. You cannot remove horses unless you can show that they need to be removed."

Fred Wyatt has a degree in animal husbandry and is chief of BLM's Wild Horse Adoption Center at Palomino Valley near Reno. He says that it doesn't take a ton of data to know when horses are in trouble. Wyatt has processed tens of thousands of horses in his seven years at the horse corrals. "The worst conditioned animals that I can recall came out of Nellis due to lack of forage, lack of water," Wyatt says. "A lot of them are so weak, if they get down they don't have the strength to get up. You don't have to do a lot of counting when you start looking at animals that are in such poor condition that they are starving."

Dave Catoor handles most of the horse gathers as a contractor for the BLM. "Down at Nellis there were colts that were just dried as prunes, not one but dozens of them," Catoor says. "Coyotes had ripped some of their hind legs apart, the back end of 'em. Their little mouths were full of mud, their noses caked with mud. We had to rinse the mud out before you could feed them. You got the choice of letting them starve to death or bring them some feed and water. It's just that simple."

Many strategies have been tried, and few have succeeded. Using unadoptable horses to sell for slaughter (a humane and self-supporting program) was ruled unacceptable. Selling horses at a cost (for the gather and other expenses to get them ready for auction) was more than the market could bear. The Adopt a Mustang or Burro program—at $125 per horse, $75 per burro—quickly became yet another government giveaway.

Prisoners were used to train horses, but that was not cost-effective. Unadoptable horses, held and fed in sanctuaries until they die, cost millions annually. Gathers were stopped or delayed by animal rights groups, adding misery to already suffering horses, and often court costs which were charged to taxpayers. When the BLM started waiving fees for multiple adoptions to move horses more cheaply, a cry of "foul" was heard all the way to Washington, D.C., because some of the horses were quickly moved to slaughter.

The Dispute

The solution isn't easy, but the fact is that there are too many wild horses for the resources. Based on an average annual reproduction rate of 18 percent, the BLM estimated back in 1990 that of the 37,000 horses roaming public lands at that time, and counting the average numbers being gathered annually, there will be 159,000 horses on the range by 2001.

This is the big dispute: What are the right numbers, and what do they mean?

With all the warring factions regarding wild horses, there is agreement that mustangs should be left on the range. The question is where, and how many? API says keep 'em coming, let them reproduce at will and self-destruct. Lappin says keep as many as we can keep healthy. The BLM says whatever it takes to keep the range in thriving ecological balance. Ranchers say a few are okay, if they can stay in business.

There is strong emotion connected to equines. More than 27 million people over age 12 ride horses each year and there are a quarter-million young people involved in 4-H horse projects. Congress appropriated a quarter-million dollars to make an accurate count of America's wild horses in 1992. The BLM, using two helicopters and 20 years of experience, counted 33,000 horses in Nevada. There are close to 50,000 throughout the West. But even these numbers don't satisfy some folks.

© KEN MILLER

TOP: When a water source dries up and turns to mud, foals get stuck and die the hard way. BELOW: This old, wild mare is sick and hungry.

© KEN MILLER

The Horses

Two-thirds of the nation's wild horses can be found in Nevada, an unnatural place for horses that would prefer to be on the plains. They like grass and water, and within the past few years have had difficulty finding either in the Silver State. A seven-year drought has caused major hardship in the West, and hundreds of horses have died agonizing deaths from starvation and dehydration in Nevada, partly due to inadequate funding for gathers and court delays.

There are serious crises out there on the range. Water holes have dried up. Cattle have been removed from many of the ranges, so there are fewer people out there able or willing to pump or truck in water for horses and wildlife. When livestock were removed from the Nevada Test Site in the '60s, there were 1,000 horses on the range. By 1991 there were an estimated 10,000 horses, most under duress. Foals were abandoned by their mothers, which had no milk, and the distance to water was too far for the foals to go. Studs were fighting for mares. Mares were fighting for their lives. Springs were drying up, leaving muddy bogs that trapped the weak animals until they died.

Others, trying to get water, suffocated on the mud, their stomachs filling with silt which turned into cement in their bellies and couldn't pass through. Others, having to wander too far to get enough to eat, couldn't make it back to water, so they died, too, very slowly, of dehydration.

The Ranchers

When the Wild, Free-Roaming Horse and Burro Act was passed in 1971, there were 126 horses on Joe Fallini's range southeast of Tonopah, Nevada. Fallini's father encouraged him to claim the horses in 1971, but Joe declined. "The government will take care of the horses," he said. Joe Fallini was wrong. By 1984 there were 2,306 horses fighting for forage and water along with his cattle on the range his family had worked for generations.

Fallini runs 2,100 head of cattle on the Twin Springs Ranch on 663,000 acres of private and leased ground. On many parts of the ranch he has been practicing rest-rotation and deferred-grazing systems to help improve the range. "But there got to be so damn many horses on us that we had to haul water. We had to open up our winter range because we couldn't pump enough on the summer range."

© C.J. HADLEY

Wild horses from the range near Tonopah, Nevada. There are lots of bays and sorrels and an occasional appaloosa, roan, palomino, paint or pinto.

Fallini asked the BLM to do something about it. Ten years ago he reported that colts were getting trapped in the mud. "It's survival of the fittest. I've seen eight or nine of them and I thought they were dead, but the larger ones would step on them and I'd see them flinch. I felt sorry for the damn things and reported it to the bureau. A week later, 42 were dead."

Fallini sued the BLM and the court ruled in his favor because the animals had been found in areas not allocated for horses. The BLM removed all but 200 head.

"They just about broke us is what they done, and that's why we had to sue them or just walk off," Fallini says. "Just the water for the horses over the years cost us $921,586 and they wonder why we got upset. But if we had not paid for the water, everything would have choked to death including our cattle."

The Challenge

At one point the BLM thought the wild-horse problem would go away. Tonopah Resource Area wildlife biologist Ted Angle admits they were in denial for quite a while. And for decades challenges for the BLM have increased. "The world is getting so rights conscious these days," Angle says. "It seems that no matter what we try to do, there is someone there to try to block it. There's a high price to be paid for the environmental awareness we have in this country and as long as we continue to feed this habit and spend more money than we take in, we will continue to have this type situation. I think there's gonna be a time when people are going to say, Whoa!"

Many observers say there needs to be sale authority for the BLM. No other animal besides the horse is under such protection or constraints. Wildlife can be controlled by hunting. Some bison are sold. Livestock is controlled by permit and season of range use. Horses worth $500 and more are sold by the government for $125; some are sold later for a profit, as meat. The law needs to be amended so that sick, lame and old excess horses can be sold at auction to help pay for the program.

"Is it better for a horse to be adopted by someone who is overmatched and who has a few square yards for the horse to spend the rest of its life on and who may send it to slaughter after a year anyway?" Fred Wyatt asks. "Or would it be better for the animal to be humanely destroyed?"

The BLM has made mistakes, mostly because it is run from the Potomac and politics have directed its western action. But its main concern nowadays is controlling and protecting the horses. Because of special interest, communication is grim on the western range, especially when it concerns mustangs.

Wild Horse Annie would know what to do. With a soft touch she would bring the groups together with facts and logic. She would fight to change the law to humanely deal with unadoptables. She would make sure the horses, wildlife, recreationists, ranchers and farmers could coexist. She would encourage federal agencies to continue to improve the resource, and she would agree that wild-horse numbers must be controlled. But, mostly, Wild Horse Annie would make sure that her beloved mustangs continue to be protected, and that they stay healthy, happy, and free. ■

SPRING 1994

SURVIVAL BATTLE

A ranching family vs. the kangaroo rat.

By Bill Evans

About 2 a.m. on October 27, Andy and Cindy Domenigoni came to an awful realization: the "California Fire" sweeping through Riverside County was heading straight for their ranch near Winchester. They raced into action, saddling horses and moving their cattle to the only pasture that was free of vegetation. Miraculously, the herd didn't spook, and they were able to hold it there more than two hours as the inferno roared around them.

At times, the smoke and dust were so thick the couple lost sight of one another while riding side by side. At times, things got even worse. "Gusts of wind jettisoned flames at us from 200 yards away," Cindy said. "It was a horrifying experience."

Relief came at dawn: the first rays of sunlight revealed the fire to be moving on. Andy and Cindy headed wearily back to the home they had left hours earlier, wondering if it would still be standing. When it came into view, they breathed sighs of relief, but the devastation around them was immense. Riding through the blackened landscape, they felt as though they were crossing some barren planet lost in space. The fire had charred all but 300 acres of their 3,000-acre ranch.

As they surveyed the damage, it was made even more painful by their realization it might have been avoidable. For it seems likely that Andy and Cindy Domenigoni were victimized not by a random blaze, but by the Endangered Species Act. This act's provisions had prevented them from disking a firebreak which might have protected their property and prevented imposed costs still with them today. And, ironically, those provisions failed even to help the kangaroo rat they were designed to protect.

© JEFF FOOTT/TOM STACK & ASSOCIATES

The kangaroo rat can also be hurt by management of the Endangered Species Act.

The Domenigoni ranch dates back to 1879, and ranch owners and ranchland inhabitants, like the kangaroo rat, were good neighbors. As Riverside County Farm Bureau environmental specialist Dennis Hollingsworth points out, the rat got along just fine under the regimen generations of Domenigonis imposed upon the land over the past century.

© SCOTT MONACO

After the California Fire, Andy and Cindy Domenigoni were happy to save their house, their cattle, and themselves.

Unfortunately, after this rodent was identified as an endangered species in 1988, the ranch became part of a 77,000-acre preserve study area and the Domenigonis were forced to take 800 acres of land out of production. In addition, they were prevented from protecting their property by disking a firebreak at the same time production restrictions were increasing the danger of fire. The Domenigoni land abuts kangaroo rat preserves on federal, state, and water district land, which land managers had begun leasing to ranchers after the cessation of controlled burning. The result was the predictable explosion of native vegetation.

In 1992, the county fire marshall identified the area as an extreme fire hazard. The Domenigonis wanted to disk a firebreak, but the U.S. Fish & Wildlife Service (FWS) in Carlsbad warned that, if they did, they would face possible felony charges. It seems wildlife managers believed disking might disturb the kangaroo rats in their burrows. Instead, FWS recommended the Domenigonis mow away the brush. According to the California Department of Forestry, mowing may fail to provide fire protection in many cases, and, according to the Domenigonis, trying to safely mow 11 miles of fenceline to control brush build-up is impractical.

PHOTOS © SCOTT MONACO

Domenigoni's water tanks once supported by railroad ties have collapsed and a twisted, blackened mass of metal is all that's left of a squeeze chute. Andy and Cindy's losses are huge.

When the fire actually occurred, some of the rigid rules were ignored. Neighboring rancher Mike Rowe jumped on a tractor and disked a firebreak as the flames approached his home. Even though the FWS threatened prosecution, they have backed off. According to agency biologist John Bradley, a provision in the law exempts persons acting to save their lives.

It is unfortunate that the exemption doesn't include "livelihoods," as a tour of the Domenigoni ranch reveals. The family's financial losses could exceed $400,000, due to lack of production and land taken out of use. But, even worse, now there is no pasture or feed to support animals. Half of their calf crop has been sold, along with half of their breeding stock. And even that's not all. The loss of vegetation means that if rains come, with no cover, the topsoil could be washed away and gullies could be cut into the hillsides. Andy and Cindy are trying to re-seed as much as they can. Unfortunately, and perhaps predictably, the price of some seed quadrupled after the fire.

The Endangered Species Act has produced horror stories similar to the Domenigonis all across the country since Congress approved it in 1973. As Oregon Sen. Mark Hatfield puts it: "There is no question that the Act is being applied in a manner far beyond what any of us envisioned 20 years ago."

If the Domenigonis' experience has any value at all, perhaps it is as an additional argument against provisions of the Endangered Species Act which sometimes hurt not only landowners (and eventually, perhaps, U.S. taxpayers), but the animals they are intended to protect. According to biologist Bradley, it was not fire which left the Domenigoni ranchland bereft of kangaroo rats. "Rather," he said, "they probably moved from the area after the act idled the land and the brush grew too thick."

Asked if that means measures to protect endangered species are not always good for those species, Bradley said that leaving the land alone is not necessarily good. Perhaps there is another lesson to be drawn as well: attempts to manage every form of life on the planet are by their very nature destructive, and destined to fail in a way that may prove costly to us all." ■

Devastation is everywhere. Charred and scarred fence posts punctuate miles and miles of fenceline and they no longer constitute a barrier: the slightest pressure and they break.

WINTER 1998

FISH FRY

Chasing the extinct on the Black Rock.

By Carolyn Dufurrena

Ten thousand years ago, Nevada's desert playas shimmered with lake water. From the shadow of Lassen Peak in the Sierra Nevada to Winnemucca, from the Walker River all the way north to Oregon, more than 8,000 square miles of Nevada valleys rippled blue in a glacial summer only a few degrees, scientists say, cooler than today. Melting mountain ice flows in the high Sierra, the Rubies, the Pine Forest, a few inches more rain each year, filled the valleys hundreds of feet deep. The beaches and bays of Lake Lahontan snaked around what is now the Carson Sink, the Black Rock Desert, the watersheds of the Quinn River, the Little Humboldt. Waves cut terraces as much as 600 feet above the current level of its valley floors. Mammoths roamed the shorelines, fish swam in the depths.

As lovely as that picture paints, the flooding and receding of Nevada's Pleistocene Lake Lahontan was as brutal a series of events as it was beautiful. The second of the four flood periods brought a chemical change to the lake water so violent that "no fish or mollusk" could live in it. Evidence remains of volcanic ash and pumice choking the waters. Between and after these high stands, the lake's desiccation and erosion was complete. Rivers carved deep through the lake beds, drawing gravel channels far out into the centers of the now-dry basins. After the highest and most recent stand, the lake completely dried up in about 300 years. Entire populations of mammals slogged and stuck in the alkaline mud of the Black Rock basin searching for food; the cutthroat trout that swam freely over the thousands of miles of Nevada lake took refuge in the channels, swam up the canyons into the mountains where spring-fed creeks sustained them until the next time the lake should fill.

Like all species that survive in times of stress and serious environmental change, the Lahontan cutthroat trout adapted to its extreme evolutionary history.

"The fish is now extremely tolerant of water temperature changes, low oxygen levels and dissolved salts in its watery world," says Gary Vinyard of the University of Nevada, Reno. "They're a very tolerant fish, well adapted to very harsh conditions." Their flexibility is one of the reasons they have survived this long.

The Lahontan cutthroat trout (LCT) had been thought to be officially extinct from the desert basins of Nevada. Then, in 1984, a biologist with the Nevada Department of Wildlife (NDOW), hopping across a creek in the rough

Summit Lake, Black Rock Desert, Nevada.

volcanic tablelands of the Sheldon Antelope Refuge west of Summit Lake, thought he saw...well... A flurry of excitement ensued.

An armada of federal agency vehicles, and one old Jeep carrying Julie Wilson, the landowner's daughter, and me, approached the headwaters of Virgin Creek in the torpid first week of August 1984. Access from the upper meadow (part of Harry Wilson's Alkali Ranch) was tough—head-high sagebrush over alkali powder, steep rhyolite canyon walls narrowing the options. The stream was dark brown, lukewarm to the touch, almost still, blocked from free flow to the valley floor below by a series of beaver ponds. The men were in a jolly mood. In addition to their electroshocker, designed to render the fish unconscious for examination, they all had their fly rods. Sure enough, that electroshocker's batteries were dead and there was nothing to do but to reel the specimens in, one at a time.

And so they did. Shallow live traps were set in the creek to hold the fish until the men were ready to bring them out that evening. Seventeen wildlife biologists fished the heck out of that virgin creek, and caught many specimens that were cutthroats in all physical characteristics. They kept them in the live traps all day, and packed them out the canyon that evening in frame-pack garbage cans with oxygen bottles. Sadly, the stress of being hauled out from under their cool banks, confined to the warm, oxygen-deprived water in the fish traps all day, and then jostled in bubbling chaos up the canyon, was too much for most of them. By day's end, there were hundreds of fish neatly laid out (big to little) on the grass in the meadow at the headwaters, not having survived the trip out of the canyon.

The survivors were sent away to be ground up for DNA analysis. Electrophoresis would prove whether or not the fish were really the extinct cutthroats. For the biologists knew that a fish could look like a cutthroat, and still have a few of those nonAryan rainbow genes.

In fact, a few months and another expedition later, it was discovered that the alleged cutthroats were tainted by the genes of rainbows. So what if they were 23 inches long and fought like crazy, an obviously viable population of big, little and medium-sized fish in a drainage that would never make the first cut for "A River Runs Through It." It didn't fit the model. Still, the creek was closed to fishing and the landowner's cattle excluded from the drainage, so the population could be watched. A few years later the landowner was bought out, and the gates locked. No one seems to know the status of the creek or the fish now, but the U.S. Fish & Wildlife Service (FWS) has the key to the gate.

The political machine that grew out of the Endangered Species Act evolved quickly. Over the next decade, regulations proliferated to protect the habitat and enhance the survivability of the cutthroats. Researchers freely admit that Lahontan cutthroats are well adapted to the relatively warm, alkaline stream waters characteristic of the Great Basin. After all, the fish evolved there. Yet, various environmental groups, federal agencies, and NDOW officials lobbied relentlessly for more and more stringent grazing regulations to cool and cover the steams in which the threatened species had lived for the last 8,000 years.

"There are certainly benefits to having a species listed as threatened or endangered," explains NDOW's head man, Rich Heap. "There's a lot of money out there for research available to universities and government contractors" to study various aspects of the target creature. Heap cites another example of an endangered species, the cui-ui, of which there are now "somewhere between two and six million fish. But they're still not delisted."

Now science has determined that the strains of cutthroats found in various watersheds in western Nevada are slightly different from each other. The Humboldt River strain is a tad different from the Quinn River strain, and now there is evidence that even within those watersheds, individual streams may contain genetic variations.

The Lahontan Cutthroat Trout Recovery Plan was written by FWS officials. The plan calls for restocking LCT in about 150 miles of stream in the Winnemucca-Gerlach area. NDOW actually manages the fish in the creeks. To make matters even more complicated, the Bureau of Land Management (BLM), which administers the public lands, must implement the regulations generated for preservation of the habitat. Thus, BLM takes the heat for implementing the agenda of other federal and state agencies and NDOW appears to answer to no one. Ron Wenker is BLM's Winnemucca district manager. "It tends to be a bit controversial," he says dryly, master of understatement that he is.

I went to the BLM looking for a success story, an example of a rancher who could work with the new regulations on the threatened species and still survive. The BLM has spent the last eight years writing habitat management plans for allotments that contain potential habitat for Lahontan cutthroat. "Unfortunately, many of the ranches in question sold during that period," Wenker told me. Other operators had problems accepting yet another tier of federal grazing restrictions that called for utilization of only 10 percent of available grasses and the necessity to move livestock at the drop of a hat when utilization levels were reached.

But that's not Wenker's biggest frustration. He fought his fights, and used every ounce of his not inconsiderable diplomatic expertise to ready his district for the arrival of

The Black Rock Desert. The flooding and receding of Nevada's Pleistocene Lake Lahontan was as brutal a series of events as it was beautiful. Rivers carved deep through the lake beds, drawing gravel channels far out into the centers of the now-dry basins.

the Lahontan cutthroat trout, which were to be planted in various and sundry drainages throughout the Winnemucca District. The problem? No fish. Heap explains that the holdup is FWS: "It just won't let us plant any fish." NDOW would like to plant genetically pure Lahontan cutthroats right away, whether it gets them from a hatchery or transplants them from another native population. Rich Heap explains that they plan to start killing the populations of fish that live in their target streams in September.

"We'll put Rotenone in the creeks, which suffocates the fish by keeping them from absorbing oxygen through their gills. Then next summer we'd like to start planting Lahontan cutthroat trout."

Heap wants to plant about 100 fingerlings each year. Unfortunately, he can't quite say where these fish will come from. He says if they "can just get one creek planted," they'll make steady progress. He explains that NDOW will monitor the streams on a yearly basis to see that their habitat is acceptable. They will take their electroshockers to count the fish (even though the counting will probably kill some of them), and presumably to check for rogue rainbows hauled in by disgruntled fishermen.

Lahontan cutthroats in the Humboldt River drainage are open to regular fishing; they are not in the Quinn River-Black Rock basins. So it's fine to harvest the fish on one side of the mountain but on the other side they must be conserved. The fish look the same.

The Lahontan cutthroat is threatened primarily by genetic mutation from other populations of fish, which are being planted in the streams by, you guessed it, Nevada Department of Wildlife. Historically, NDOW has planted all kinds of nonnative species in various places all over Nevada, for the enjoyment of sportsmen and to the detriment of native populations. Almost incredibly, NDOW still plants rainbows in McDermitt Creek, which has one of the last pure populations of LCT in its headwaters. Its solution? Have the BLM install fish barriers, at $50,000 or so each (from BLM's budget, not NDOW's), so the two populations can't mix.

Who cares? Fishermen in Nevada don't care so deeply about having pure Lahontan cutthroats in their streams. Heap agrees: "I don't think fishermen care what kind of fish they catch, as long as they catch a lot of them." Fish researchers care deeply about what kinds of fish are in the streams, and have characterized NDOW as a bunch of "knuckle-dragging Neanderthals" for its management of the fisheries in Nevada. (Of course, it's the academics who have the government contracts.) The ranchers who make their daily living on the public lands also care deeply, but for different reasons. It costs them money. The Whitehorse Ranch on the Oregon/Nevada border forfeited over $250,000 to the Lahontan cutthroat over three years of grazing cuts so that the fish could have more willows.

The cutthroats will need their legendary adaptability more now than ever. They can look forward to yearly monitoring, being shocked, counted, tagged, transplanted and, eventually, probably caught and released. It was a lot easier on them when all they had to contend with was a few cows eating the grass by their creeks and wandering through their spawning gravel. Back when they were still extinct. ■

WINTER 1999

GRIZZLY PICNIC

The strike was sudden but by no means subtle, for a grizzly bear in a sheep camp creates a commotion not unlike that of a great white shark cruising amid swimmers off the shores of Martha's Vineyard. By Richard Menzies

Bears are curious and may approach to determine what you are," says *Earthwalk Press*. "Remain quiet and make no abrupt moves; try not to show fear. Once you're identified, the bear may leave. A grizzly possesses keen sense of smell, good hearing, but poor eyesight. It will often rise on its hind legs to investigate. If it does, it may be helpful to speak softly in a steady monotone; this may reassure the bear you aren't a threat."

Then again, the grizzly may decide that since you pose no threat, he might as well eat you. In which case, you'd better reach for a gun and fast. But not too fast. Unless it can be proved the bear struck the first blow, you will wind up in a heap of legal trouble. That's because *Ursus arctos horribilis* is on the endangered species list, and to harm one except in defense of one's life is a federal felony.

"The only time you can shoot one," explains Barbara Franklin of the U.S. Forest Service, "would be if he had a hold of your leg and was eatin' you."

Ranger Franklin and I were standing on a high forested ridge in the Gros Ventre Mountains, about 60 miles south of Yellowstone National Park. At our feet lay an eviscerated ewe, one of at least half a dozen sheep that only hours earlier had met a most horrific demise. The grizzly had snatched only his favorite body parts—the brisket and udder—then left her to bleed to death in the dust.

The strike was sudden but by no means subtle, for a grizzly bear in a sheep camp creates a commotion not unlike that of a great white shark cruising amid swimmers off the shores of Martha's Vineyard. Horses bolt, dogs bark, and sheep scatter like buckshot—crashing through deadfalls, tumbling off cliffs, running until their legs and lungs give out. Meantime, herdsman Andy Charley can do little but try to lie still in his tent, a can of pepper spray in one hand and his Holy Bible in the other. And speak softly in a low monotone, much the same as government agents will the following morning when they come to assess the damage.

Among the first to arrive is Wyoming state game warden Chris Queen, whose unenviable task it is to autopsy the mutilated ewe, then drag her through the brush to where his All Terrain Vehicle waits, already heaped high with dead lambs. Looking on are Dick Thoman and his sister Mary, sheep ranchers and reluctant caterers for this particular grizzly bear's picnic.

"You know," sighs Dick, "the sad part about this endangered species, the grizzly bear, is that if you came here and you tried to steal something from this sheep camp and I shot you, I could probably get off by saying I was defending my personal property. But if a bear comes and takes our sheep, which is also our personal property, and I shoot the bear...well, that's a whole different case."

Mary continues the thought: "So we're just caught here; we can't do anything to defend ourselves. We have to sit here and helplessly watch it kill our animals. And wait for [game wardens] to get their act together enough to get it out of here, and by then some more animals suffer. And you gotta go back and see the walking dead; I mean, that's

"We can't do anything to protect ourselves. We have to sit here and helplessly watch it kill our animals."

even worse. There's a sheep down in there with her udder eaten off, and here's the little lamb following her, and there's nothing we can do—nothing—just sit here and wait. And then hope that we can find them all to submit the claim. That's the hardest part for us. It seems something's gone wrong in this country."

When Dick and Mary tell of hard times, they know whereof they speak. Only three weeks earlier their father Bill Thoman had been killed in an accident. The 77-year-old mainstay of the family ranch died on the job, about 16 hours into a working day that typically began at four o'clock in the morning and didn't end till 10 at night. The day after his death, Bill's kids observed what Dick describes as "probably one of the toughest memorials of all times, and that was that we had to go haul some sheep. We had all these sheep in the corral and the trucks lined up. The sheepherders were all ready to go, so we had a pretty tough call. But finally we just opted to go ahead—and hell, it was a pretty tough thing to do. But...you just gotta keep going."

It wasn't the first tragedy that struck the Thoman family. In 1974, Dick and Mary's 23-year-old sister Catherine drowned in a river while riding her horse. Six years later, their brother Bill was killed in a trucking accident, leaving behind a widow and two sons.

Today, Bill's widow Mickey and daughters Mary and Laurie hold down what's left of the home ranch near Kem-

merer. As often as they can get away, they're joined by another Thoman son, Bob, who runs a farm on the far side of the Wind Rivers, and also daughter Kristy, who lives in Big Piney.

When he isn't counting dead sheep, Dick Thoman runs a small trucking company, while Mary, who holds a Ph.D. in vocational education and school administration, earns her keep as a sales director with Mary Kay Cosmetics. "It's sort of a weird thing," she explains, "but it's the only thing I can do with a ranch schedule."

As children, all the siblings took an active part in the livestock operation that's sustained three generations of Thomans. Winters they hit the books in a small ranch school; summers they lived in the saddle, riding the family's Elk Ridge grazing allotment in the Bridger-Teton National Forest.

Brother and sister Dick and Mary Thoman at their sheep wagon/camp trailer.

Back in the 1950s, the Thomans were forced to sell almost 1,000 acres of their home ranch in order to make room for the Fontenelle Dam and Reservoir. In 1980 the Interior Department took the rest of it, which today is known as the Seedskadee National Wildlife Refuge. Raising sheep was becoming more challenging all the time—then three summers ago the first bear attacks began.

Over the course of three months, 54 ewes and 62 lambs were confirmed as bear kills. Six black bears were shot; four grizzlies were taken prisoner and transported out of the area by wildlife officers. The following summer the casualty list swelled to 200 ewes and 220 lambs. When it came time to truck the herd south for the winter, the Thomans came up two semitrailer truckloads short.

"It was like I told the forest ranger this morning," says Dick. "I said, 'You know, we can't tolerate these types of losses here in the sheep industry.' So she alluded to the fact that it was about two days' trail to where we could load the sheep on a truck. And apparently that was one of my options. The other one was, maybe, that they would let us use an allotment that was supposed to be in rest. Well, that messes up the grazing system."

The Thomans worry that if they retreat from Elk Ridge, they run the risk of losing their grazing allotment. And, according to the terms of the Endangered Species Act, should they take any direct action against the bear that's wreaking havoc on their livestock, they would most certainly lose it.

"We can't even shoot across the draw at a bear heading towards the sheep," explains Mary. "They would get you for harassment of an endangered species. So you can't try to head the bear off or do anything except sit here and watch them eat your animals. Even if it's your pet horse, your pet dog."

Aggrieved ranchers can appeal to the Wyoming State Department of Game and Fish for financial compensation—but once again, the rules of the game seem to be stacked in favor of the predator. For example, one can't simply subtract the number of sheep that come down off the mountain in the fall from the number that went up in June and then submit a bill for the difference. Rather, each dead sheep must be found, and it must be found within 24 hours while the cause of death can still be determined. In thick brush and tall timber that's no easy task—by Dick Thoman's estimate, only about one in three bear kills is ever found. And even if all the carcasses could be found, he complains that the current system doesn't take into account all the other negative effects of a bear attack.

"The economic loss that we suffer isn't just the animals that they kill," he says. "The sheep are stressed. There's a number of those animals that're gonna be crippled up, broken legs. Later on in the summer they'll show up with an abscess or a rupture, and those are gonna have to be culled out and sold from the herd. The mothers that are killed, their lambs are gonna be left behind. They'll be less weight, lesser value than what the rest of them are at shipping time."

There is no financial compensation available for time spent driving back and forth across Wyoming, no consideration for the many hours the Thomans must spend filling out and filing the requisite forms. Nor is there much in the way of a settlement at the end of the process. For instance, after losing $60,000 worth of sheep in 1997, Mary says she submitted an itemized claim to the commission in the amount of $27,000. After looking it over, the state offered to pay $6,600.

Mary appealed the judgment to an arbitration board, and was eventually reimbursed $19,500—"which is still less than the $27,000 we submitted for, which is a whole lot less than the $60,000 that we lost."

Short of a military counterstrike, what the Thomans would most like to see is a reevaluation of the 1993 Grizzly

Wyoming state game warden Chris Queen surveys the carnage left by a grizzly attack. Over the course of three months, 54 ewes and 62 lambs were confirmed as bear kills. Six black bears were shot; four grizzlies were taken prisoner and transported out of the area by wildlife officers. The following summer the casualty list swelled to 200 ewes and 220 lambs. When it came time to truck the herd south for the winter, the Thomans came up two semi-trailer truckoads short.

PHOTOS © RICHARD MENZIES

Bear Recovery Plan. According to the plan, only the area within the recovery zone will be managed primarily for grizzly habitat. Yet the bears that are currently snacking on the Thomans' livestock are 25 miles outside of the recovery zone. And since grizzly bears, unlike tourists, don't thrive in a crowded environment, trucking them back to Yellowstone doesn't appear to be a workable solution.

"All the grizzly bear studies I've read," says Mary, "say that they don't like to have more than one per 25 square miles. That's a normal territorial area, and I told the commission, 'You have more bears in there according to any study than it's possible to have. How could we help but have a loss when you have 'em that thick in here?' You know, we have more than one bear per square mile up here."

And before the bears get any thicker or spread out any farther, perhaps now would be as good a time as any to ask just what they'll start eating once they've polished off all the sheep and cattle? Another question: Who's going to fatten up all those doomed recreationists once all the food suppliers have been put out of business by predators?

"What I can't understand," says Dick Thoman, "is two percent of the population feeds this nation, right? Why should we have to fight and struggle so hard to feed the rest of the nation? The world? We could fold up tomorrow, and our neighbors, and so forth and so on, until pretty soon we eliminate the food supply. And when the food's gone, then what? You gotta look at the economics of this thing—weigh it out, dollar for dollar, what this little sheep operation contributes to the economy compared to one stupid grizzly bear. I mean, this is not just a nine-to-five job for me. I can't go home after five o'clock and have a beer and laugh about it with everyone else. Because... this is our life." ■

UPDATE: On September 10, 2009, a grizzly bear seriously mauled a sheepherder who works for Thoman Ranch near Fontenelle, Wyoming. The attack occurred after midnight on the Thomans' Forest Service grazing allotment in the Gros Ventre Wilderness.

The herder, Marcello Tejeda, and Jorge Mesa, were awakened by the sounds of a bear attacking the sheep. Tejeda rushed out with a flashlight, expecting to find a black bear. The herders were unarmed because the Thoman family had been advised not to give the men guns since they might shoot a wolf or grizzly bear in just such a situation, incurring the wrath of the federal government as it enforces the Endangered Species Act.

The bear, which had a cub, had already started killing sheep and was attacking the livestock guardian dogs. The bear turned on Tejeda and started mauling him. Mesa grabbed pepper spray and with the help of the dogs was finally successful in driving the bear away from Tejeda.

Mesa used a cell phone—which luckily had service—and called for help. The injured herder had to be taken six miles on a back road to meet the ambulance. He was life-flighted to Eastern Idaho Regional Medical Center in Idaho Falls, where he was listed in serious condition. Tejeda received a seven-inch gash on top of his head, two punctures to the left side of his chest, a punctured lung, three claw wounds to the right side of his abdomen and a puncture wound to his right wrist. He was lucky to survive.

In addition to the attack on Tejeda, scores of sheep have been killed by wolves and grizzly bears this summer in the Upper Green River Valley. The Thomans' neighbor reported that nine guard dogs had been killed in August and September by the large predators.

The Thoman family has been ranching in the area since before 1900 and their sheep have grazed on these allotments since 1978. "It isn't like we just sprang up," Mary Thoman said.

FALL 1999

For generations, all the Cundall family has been involved in ranching, but from pioneer beginnings on the plains of Nebraska to a pair of ranches on the prairie slopes of Wyoming, corporate interests overwhelmed their family operations. The opportunity on the last truly large working ranch in western Montana seemed perfect for them, a dream come true. But then came the power company, and then the federal government, and then there were…

WOLVES AT THE DOOR!

By Tim Findley

Twenty-three-year-old Jeston Cundall looked out that February morning in 1996 from the apartment he and his new bride shared above the spectacular Lost Trail arena, out across the snowy nearest pasture to where one of their cows had died the day before. His day's work was before him, and Jeston was planning in his mind when, strangely, the dead carcass seemed to be moving, as if it were being pulled by something. Jeston raced down the steps and toward the fence for a better look. Unbelieving of what he was seeing, he shouted back for his wife Sharee, who had been raised in this country. It was Sharee, in her natural youthful enthusiasm, who first made the identification. Watching wide-eyed with her husband at the stark contrasts between snow and shapes, she said to him, "Holy cow, it's a wolf!"

Jeston took a better look through the fixed scope on his .22 magnum. Not just one wolf, but two, a female and a large male, were dragging the 1,200-pound cow toward the distant fence. In that fateful moment, Jeston only

watched through his scope. The rifle remained locked.

Some will tell you there always have been, and always will be, wolves in this part of Montana northwest of Kalispell and only 60 miles south of the Canadian border. Look an old-timer like Bud Elberud in the eye and he might deny ever having come on one close enough to be bothering his cattle, but he leaves no doubt about what he'd do if he did. "Then again," he says, "I wouldn't even tell my wife about it."

Certainly there were wolves here when Pleasant Valley was first settled in the 1890s. In those days, one or two professionals were likely to be kept busy hunting down marauders of all sorts, including wolves, grizzlies, coyotes and mountain lions. Even though they certainly never took them all, by the mid-1970s, wolves and grizzlies were both on the endangered species list and protected from a bullet by a potential $100,000 fine and jail time for anybody who even took a wild shot. After that, the code here, as elsewhere in the West, was "shoot, shovel, and shut up." The wolves were assumed to be gone, moved north into Canada where in the presence of packs thought to total some 50,000 wolves or more, ranchers still have a legal right to protect their herds. Around here, nobody said much about them.

"Holy cow... it's a wolf!"

Lost Trail Ranch is a consolidation of at least two former homesteads in this lush valley. It almost had a town once, made up of outlaws, renegades and railroad hands who built the near-forgotten line meant to connect Kalispell and the tiny town of Marion with Libby to the west. It was a much calmer and spectacularly beautiful place when a rich Los Angeles developer enthralled by his experience on a dude ranch bought the Lost Trail and its 8,000 acres as an intended gift for his preteen daughter in 1990. He acquired two stately mansion-sized Victorian houses along with the broad soft green pastures fed from the headwaters of the Fisher River all the way up to the tree lines owned by the Plum Creek Timber Company. It was an achingly beautiful place and the new owner, Dick Randall, set about adding to its charm with miles of new fences and gate posts, fresh bright paint on all the buildings, restored cabins with new foundations, and even what he called a "calving shed" that was the size of a respectable county arena, replete with bleachers.

Randall is the grandson of one of the pioneer cattlemen who first brought white-faced steers to Texas, but he is a developer, not a rancher. Even as the obvious economic anchor to the entire valley, Lost Trail was meant by the owner to be a working view estate where the real chores were handled by a manager.

In Wheatland, Wyoming, Jerry Cundall and his family could not boast of quite such opulent arrangements, but theirs was a comfortable place built up by Jerry and his father after they moved on from their original land in Nebraska. Jerry's wife Sherma had grown up on her family's own ranch east of Walsenburg, Colorado. By then, the Cundalls had four strikingly handsome children, three boys and a girl, who all expressed their own special interest in livestock and agriculture. They were a strong family with values as simple and sturdy as the rural West where they all were raised. But on two separate ranches in Wyoming they found themselves in conflict with corporate and government interests meaning to gain control over the water.

It was almost by coincidence of friends who knew friends that after two failures in finding a manager for Lost Trail, the rich developer was led to a perfect match in an entire family willing to take over operations of his Montana treasure. To the Cundalls, it was an unimagined dream come true. They were promised the job would last at least 10 years and that their entire family would find the perfect setting for the ambitions they all shared. Jerry set about to build the kind of cow-calf operation the owner wanted, improving on the year-to-year grazing leases on 20,000 acres of the neighboring Plum Creek timberland. At its peak, before environmentalist pressure demanded reductions on the leasehold, the Lost Trail ran about 900 head. Young Jeston and his bride found managing the horses and the nearby pastures perfectly suited to their interests. His sister Cheyenne, soon to go off to college back in Wyoming, delighted in working with the livestock. Teenager Josh loved the tractors and machinery, and even more than that his seemingly endless solitary treks on hunting or fishing trips in all directions. Jade and his wife Molly kept an interest in the haying and daily operations. Their mother Sherma was perhaps happiest of all with her grandly preserved double-storied and porched home, around which she carefully planted and nurtured a brightly blooming showplace garden. It was perfect.

Wolves had almost nothing to do with it. In 1989, before the Cundalls arrived, the U.S. Fish & Wildlife Service (FWS) had stunned the neighbors in Pleasant Valley by announcing that a pack of wolves had formed there, "by natural recurrence." Doubtful ranchers were informed that the animals would be monitored and that any losses would be reimbursed.

"We tried to tell them it wouldn't be good for any of us or for the wolves either," said Martin Anderson of the Big Meadows cooperative which borders Lost Trail, "but there wasn't a damn thing we could do about it."

Within months, the wolves had caused the predictable

These wolves were in sight of the Cundalls' ranch house.

trouble. Between September 1989 and June 1990, at least 13 calves and two cows in the valley were acknowledged by federal authorities as having been killed by wolves. There is a story frequently told in Pleasant Valley of one older rancher who spotted a wolf on the frozen surface of Dahl Lake and fired a shot over its head. To the rancher's shock, instead of running in the opposite direction, the frightened wolf ran directly at the rancher and then cowered down at his feet. Around the same time, a rancher, thinking he was aiming at a coyote, killed what was up to then one of the largest wolves recorded within the lower 48, a 130-pound male.

Concerned by the loss of livestock, the feds set up traps to capture, without harming, the wolves in Pleasant Valley. A group of environmental activists, some on trail bikes, moved into the valley behind them and sprang every trap they could find. Even so, all of the wolves said to have "recurred" in 1989 were dead or relocated by the time the Cundalls arrived at Lost Trail in 1990.

Five years later, the winter of 1995-96 would carry on with some of the deepest snows and continued high water in local memory. State and federal officials agreed with the account of locals that the exceptionally heavy winter had seriously depleted the population of white-tailed deer in the region—the most likely natural prey of wolves. Yet it was in the coldest midst of that winter when Jeston Cundall and his "holy cow" bride spotted the wolf pair in a pasture barely 100 yards from the barn. Officially, the government and animal rights activists pronounced that this pair had simply migrated down from Canada. If so, they had blundered into a range made by that year's winter less likely than in many years to provide their natural food source.

"Does it add up? Does it make sense? I don't know," said Jerry Cundall. It was up to Jerry to make the decision after his son first spotted the wolves dragging away a dead Lost Trail cow. He didn't think about it for long, and he didn't discuss it with some of his older neighbors before Jerry instinctively followed his honest streak and reported the wolf sighting to Montana Fish & Game.

"Well," said Bud Elberud, "it might not have been the smartest thing to do, but I guess I understand it." Cundall himself acknowledges that if he had known what was likely to happen otherwise, he might well have decided to deal with the wolves himself. But with his call to authorities, the bureaucratic wheels were put in motion.

FWS experts, using a helicopter and trackers, set up new traps for the wolves. They captured the female in what was meant to be a noninjuring leg snare, but by the time they found her she had already tried to chew her leg free.

"So, one day, Carter Neimier [FWS wolf expert] drives up and says he's got the wolf," remembered Josh Cundall. "He asked if I'd like to see her, and I said, 'Sure,' and I followed him down to his truck. He had the wolf on the front seat, right beside him. She was drugged, but I still thought that was pretty crazy. He just said they were easier to control that way."

The wolf, found to be pregnant, was treated for her injuries and then fitted with a radio tracking collar and released back into Pleasant Valley to whelp her pups. Without really meaning to, Jerry Cundall's honesty had virtually assured the return of a wolf pack to Pleasant Valley.

If it were only just about wolves and letting them find their share of nature, there is probably no one familiar with this region of Montana who would object to seeing more of what is already a cherished wild all around them. If it were even that wolves behaved in much the same way as they do in Canada where the sight or scent of two-legged beasts sets them fleeing, perhaps the arguments would be lessened. But the wolves of Pleasant Valley seemed to understand the difference south of the border.

Ellen Hargrave, a wise-cracking '60s survivor out of Kansas who still rolls her own with Zig Zag papers, today operates the Hargrave Cattle and Guest Ranch with her equally unceremonious husband Leo. They run some cattle on the 1,400 acres, primarily for the dudes, but seriously

PHOTOS BY SHERMA CUNDALL

enough to make an income. The first time her foreman Ryan Reynolds came upon the big black wolf, it was after dark and he just kind of stumbled up to it near the calving corral. "I saw its eyes first, and then it just stood there and snarled at me," said Reynolds. Another employee, a young woman given to nature trails, came across one of the wolves on the road one evening. "She stopped and got out to look at it, and that wolf just stopped and looked right back at her," said Hargrave.

In almost no encounter of the many told by neighbors around Pleasant Valley did the wolves seem at all impressed by two-legged creatures. Through that summer of '96, and on into the next two years, the wolves were spotted occasionally. The Cundalls at Lost Trail began adding up the disappearances among the herd at the end of each grazing season—22 cows and 30 calves were missing by the time the snow began flying in 1998. Other outfits told of similar losses—13 calves off the Baker place, three cows and seven calves off Bob Monk's range. Some losses are always expected, but this many seemed extraordinary. The wolves were seen even near the small elementary school in the valley. Like others in the ranching families, Martin Anderson of Big Meadows insisted that his 10-year-old stepdaughter not play on the nearby hillsides any more.

"I saw its eyes first, and then it just stood there and snarled at me."

Any wolf lover anywhere will tell you it's myth. Wolves aren't killers, they will say. The wolves just hunt for survival, and only among the weakest animals, probably most likely to die anyway. Friends of wolves will tell you wolves pose no threat to humans.

By the official federal records, the alpha pair which appeared in Pleasant Valley in 1996 produced only one pup that season. The deer population was slow to recover from the hard winter, adding to the predators' difficulties. By early winter 1997, the pack was said to consist only of three adults and one pup. In 1998, with officially still a "paucity" of natural prey in the region, the pack was reported to have had "a large litter."

By then, Sherma Cundall had other worries on her mind. The promise of 10 years or more on the Lost Trail was beginning to fade with Randall's own financial problems in Los Angeles and with his concern that his daughter's love of the ranch itself might lead her away from better ambitions. In any case, the Montana Power Company had recently shown interest in Dahl Lake, a shallow, algae-clogged pond at the eastern extreme of the ranch that was slowly evolving into a peat bog. It was fenced from the cattle and generally unused, but it was large enough for the power company to have interest in "saving" it as wetland which could serve as mediation for what the government said was loss of wetland created by the company's dam on Flathead Lake to the southeast. Dahl Lake alone might have been no great loss to the magnificent expanse of Lost Trail, but the absentee owner saw in the power company's offer a $5 million chance to dispose of it all.

That was Sherma Cundall's biggest worry. She kept a diary as she saw it moving closer and closer to the same nightmare her family had experienced before in Wyoming. The power company didn't want a ranch. It wanted to be off the hook with the federal government. When the deal was made with the Lost Trail owner to buy the place, the power company wouldn't even listen to the Cundalls when they suggested other buyers. Montana Power wanted only to sell the whole place, the last great working ranch in western Montana, to the FWS, which had no intention of going into the ranching business. The Cundalls would have to leave.

"More packing today, books and things," begins Sherma's diary on January 11, 1999. "Jeston and two friends walked out behind the barn and discovered 10 wolves eating a roping calf. They ran them up the hill and then left. Later, Don Bernal from Libby and his son and two other relatives came up to rope. All 10 wolves were back in the corral and had attacked the pen of calves. One calf was completely eaten and only his bones remained. The second still alive, but so badly ripped up he had to be shot, and a third had teeth marks all over his rear and was so sore he could hardly walk. Jeston doctored him and he seems okay now."

For the few remaining months the Cundalls were still in charge of Lost Trail, the wolves seemed almost to sense that it was ending. From Sherma's diary, January 15:

"The wolves came back, killed and ate another 450-pound calf in the same pasture after running the whole bunch through the fence. All 10 wolves were still there when the boys went to do chores this morning."

© TIM FINDLEY

The Cundall family, from left: Josh, Jerry, Sherma, Jeston (holding daughter Myla), Sharee, Molly, Jade and Marta the dog.

Although they had never informed the Cundalls or anybody else in Pleasant Valley about it, federal agents knew the pack now numbered at least 13 individual wolves and presented a formidable threat to all the livestock in the valley.

"The wolves have nothing to be afraid of," Sherma wrote. "As a result they just trot off and watch us. It makes for great picture taking, but it is very unnerving!"

Now, the sightings in Pleasant Valley and nearby Lost Prairie took on more disturbing proportions. Calves and cows were being attacked in winter pastures, virtually at the doors of every ranch. The Cundalls had brought from Wyoming their two Great Pyrenees dogs, gentle white giants known to protect sheep and cattle herds. Jerry Cundall made a point of "bonding" the two dogs, Rush and Marta, to the herd, and up to now they seemed to be a deterrent to the wolves.

But the winter of 1998-99 would be drastically different. "We became very concerned for Rush and Marta after the January incident," Sherma wrote. "They would be no match for 10 wolves. Several times, the dogs showed up at the house or barn, exhausted and very visibly terrified.... On one occasion, the male would not even leave the porch for three days."

There was still more to trouble the people of Pleasant Valley that winter. FWS had moved with surprising bureaucratic speed to produce its report on what it now called the proposed Lost Trail National Wildlife Refuge. The feds had made a show of inviting all the ranching neighbors to "scoping" meetings where their views could be heard and squeaked onto butcher-paper tablets by the felt tip of a facilitator, but most of the ranchers knew the futility of that exercise. Now they were being presented with a federal report on the options that left only one really likely—Lost Trail, the economic engine of their valley, was to be a federal refuge, returned, somehow, to a more "natural" condition. Already, a former federal bison manager had moved into the big main house and evicted the Cundalls to the apartment over the arena-sized calving shed.

Wolves were only one species the new federal managers proposed to protect by their new refuge. There were also grizzlies which occasionally passed through the range, and eagles, and lynx. And now, for the first time, there appeared the surrogate species being used throughout the Pacific Northwest much as the spotted owl was to halt logging. These headwaters of the Fisher River, the federal report said, were home to the threatened bull trout.

At Big Meadows, Martin Anderson expressed it to the nodding agreement of neighbors around his kitchen table: "Who in their right mind would want the federal government for a neighbor?"

Still, even if anything could be done to save Lost Trail, in that winter the battle was more concentrated on saving the herds.

"Joe Fontaine [FWS] and his crew came up the 18th [of January] with plane and helicopter and removed four of the wolves to Spotted Bear," wrote Sherma Cundall. "Upon arrival here, they announced that the pack was located several miles to the west of us, eating on an elk calf. When they got there to examine the kill, it was not an elk calf but a 600-pound Big Meadows calf."

Federal agency people could no longer deny that the wolves were feeding on cattle. They distributed radio trackers to some of the neighbors so they could monitor the presence of the pack. Bob Monk was among the first to receive one. Monk, 79, has lived in the valley since 1946. In 53 years, he had only seen two wolves, but by that point, the indirect damage done to his and his wife Donna's future was even greater than a season's loss of calves.

"At my age," Monk said, "I make my most reliable living by leasing out pasture to others who bring their cattle in. It's a fair income, keeps us going. But word gets around about the wolves either taking cows or running them through fences. Nobody in their right mind is going to bring their cattle up here."

"Nobody in their right mind is going to bring their cattle up here."

At Lost Trail, they began calving on February 13. Just five days later, Sherma Cundall glanced out her window and saw Marta running toward her with a terrified look in her eye. Sherma and Jeston's wife Sharee went out to the fence where the other dog Rush was barking frantically at something to the north of him. "And there they were, not 300 yards away," wrote Sherma. "Six wolves, two of them dragging a newborn calf under the fence."

There was nothing they could do except to take pictures and shout at the wolves in hopes of frightening them off enough to recover the dead calf as evidence. The wolves didn't go far, and the Cundalls could see them on the hillslope watching calmly as Jerry covered the calf remains with a tarp. As evening fell, Jerry Cundall moved all the cows and heifers into a corral, except one cow which had only dropped her calf late that afternoon and was not yet ready to move. She had bedded the calf down between a large rock and a tree for some protection. Jerry drove out in his pickup just after dark to check on them and found two wolves lunging at and harassing the cow. Not until Cundall was within 50 feet of them did the wolves even pay attention to his spotlight.

With Sherma's help carrying the calf, Jerry walked the cow back to the barn. By morning, they found her weak and bleeding from the mouth. She died that afternoon. A vet who examined her found her lungs had burst, probably from terror and shock. The calf died the next morning.

Now with their own government-provided monitor, the Cundalls kept track of the pack that remained almost continuously within half a mile of their house. Government agents responded by saying they had shot and killed one young female and two males. That left three wolves, including the alpha pair, still within easy monitoring range. The cows and calves, needing to be turned out to the drier hillside, remained in the wet pen.

The answer provided by the United States was a siren hung from a tree that periodically sounded by a timer, and a curious little propane-powered cannon that the Cundalls were advised to fire off now and then in various directions. That February and March, Pleasant Valley echoed with booming retorts of cannon volleys and the penetrating periodic whine of the siren. It terrified the dogs, which hid in the barn. The wolves ignored it.

"Some of the older folks told us that the wolves might be attracted by the shots," said Jerry. "They get used to thinking it might mean someone has brought down some meat." But by then, the absence of game in Pleasant Valley was evident to everyone, and it could not just be the winter that was to blame. At least 70 head of cattle were killed or missing. Defenders of Wildlife, which supposedly compensates ranchers, has so far only agreed that there is evidence to pay for three.

"It was demeaning just trying to talk to [the Defenders] about it," said Ellen Hargrave.

Finally, in late April, the last three remaining wolves were killed by federal Animal Damage Control shooters. The Cundalls took time out in May to attend the graduation of their daughter from the University of Wyoming. They had much work ahead of them. The federal government had given them until June 1 to be completely out of Lost Trail. They planned to move to a nearby academy for troubled youth, where Sherma will teach, but for a few weeks the entire family will have to live in a motel at McGregor Lake. Josh, who so loved the tractors and his treks in the woods, plans to look for a job as a hand in Wyoming. Jeston and Sharee will look for work around Kalispell. Jade and Molly haven't decided.

Was it all just coincidence, just another sign of our changing times? Did the wolves just find their way from Canada and, as the feds describe it, "recolonize" Pleasant Valley? Maybe, but Bob Monk shares the story of being approached repeatedly in 1983, five years before that first pack appeared, by representatives of The Nature Conservancy wanting to buy his "wetlands." The report of Fish & Wildlife on Lost Trail Refuge reveals that, unknown to Dick Randall, federal authorities had identified Dahl Lake as a site for preservation in 1985, well before it was supposedly "found" by the power company.

In the map of their proposed new refuge, FWS marks

Gray wolf feeding pups in Montana.

Lost Trail like a large puzzle piece filling in a blank space of formerly private land between Kootenai National Forest on the north and west, Lolo National Forest on the south, and Flathead National Forest on the east. The proposed action to create the refuge, says the federal report, is to mitigate damage elsewhere, and "to restore floodplain acreage to its historic role; and to enhance the survival prospects of endangered and threatened species in the area."

From the time The Nature Conservancy made its overtures to Monk in 1983, to the surveys of possible wetlands in 1985, and up until 1989 when most local ranchers believe a pack was "reintroduced" in the valley by government agents, no wolves had been seen. Was it merely coincidence that at the start of the second term of Babbitt's environmentalist Interior Department, Canadian wolves decided to "recolonize" Pleasant Valley during its worst winter in recent memory?

In the week of May that the Cundalls were gone for their daughter's graduation, Martin Anderson and at least two others in the region spotted that lone black wolf again in the open meadows. As usual, the animal seemed unafraid of humans.

Lost Trail was the last large ranch of its kind in western Montana. It cannot be replaced and is unlikely now to ever be restored by anyone with enough care for the land to see that the grass will not be overgrown and left to strangle or that the fine fences and carefully tended buildings will not fade, or, as the government has already planned for some, be torn down.

Jerry Cundall will try to maintain the 150 head he has left on his year-to-year grazing lease with Plum Creek, but it's doubtful how long that can last. As a working ranch, Lost Trail is over and done, and with it, perhaps, the heritage of all Pleasant Valley. "I'm disappointed," admitted Dick Randall, "but the truth is I don't know anyone who could have made it work to produce an income in these times."

For lots of reasons, some of them economic, some of them political, times have changed in western Montana. Old-timers, both here and elsewhere in the West, will assure you of one thing, however: There will always be wolves. ■

FALL 2001

Listen to the Songbirds...and bring on the Cows

Conventional wisdom said birds and bovines don't mix.

By Dan Dagget

In 1994 Dave Ogilvie started water flowing once again through some old dirt irrigation ditches on the U Bar in New Mexico. At the time Ogilvie rewatered those ditches, he noticed that water leaking through their dirt walls began to reinvigorate trees living along their banks. The trees sent out new shoots. Seedlings started appearing. Among that new growth, Ogilvie noticed flashes of red, yellow, and blue as a variety of songbirds took up residence in the revitalized patches of cottonwood, box elder, and Russian olive.

A year later, the Southwestern willow flycatcher was listed as endangered under the Endangered Species Act (ESA). Grazing was blamed for bringing this songbird to the brink of extinction. Cattle, it was claimed, denuded the riparian areas the birds needed to exist. Conventional wisdom said these birds were absolutely unable to coexist with cattle.

Ogilvie wondered if some of the birds on the U Bar could be flycatchers. He knew that 643 miles of river and adjacent land in the Gila drainage (including the riverside land on the U Bar) had been identified as possible habitat for the bird. Since some of the people calling for protection of the species were also calling for the removal of cattle from this land, Ogilvie was worried. He hired a biologist to do a bird survey. The biologist found Southwestern willow flycatchers—and the largest population yet discovered: 64 pairs of endangered birds were counted on the U Bar in 1995, while 38 were counted along California's Kern River, the next most populous site.

Those high numbers caught the attention of Dr. Scott Stoleson, wildlife biologist for the U.S. Forest Service and Rocky Mountain Research Station in Albuquerque. Unlike some of his peers who stuck to their prejudices that flycatchers and cows couldn't mix, Stoleson undertook a

© JAY DUSARD

The U Bar Ranch cattle share a riparian area with more endanged songbirds than anywhere else.

detailed study at the U Bar. Those studies have indicated that it is neither an accident nor an anomaly that these birds thrive on the ranch in the presence of their purported nemesis. In fact, it seems that cattle ranching, as practiced on the U Bar, promotes and sustains the kind of habitat these endangered birds prefer.

Stoleson found that rather than the dense, undisturbed stands of willows these birds are said to need, the flycatchers were nesting in mature cottonwoods and box elders with a relatively open understory and water nearby. That's exactly the kind of habitat found on the U Bar. The trees are nurtured by the leaky ditches. They reach maturity protected from wildfire by the cattle which clear away the flammable understory. The ditches provide the nearby water which Stoleson's observations reveal is the second most significant factor in the birds' choice of a nest site.

U Bar flycatchers even break with the most entrenched preconception of all—that they cannot coexist with cattle. Stoleson's data shows that areas on the U Bar grazed by cattle support more flycatchers than those that aren't grazed. Not a lot more, but enough to refute the preconception.

From 64 pairs in 1995, the U Bar population of Southwestern willow flycatchers grew to a high of 200 in 1999.

© JEAN-LUC CARTRON, UNIVERSITY OF NEW MEXICO

The willow flycatcher has shown that grazing and agricultural operations can be used to heal ecosystems. Their testimony has been dismissed in favor of archaic preconceptions that the only way humans can restore nature is to leave it alone.

"At that time," Stoleson says, "the ranch was home to 40 percent of the entire known population."

As impressive as that is, it's just part of the U Bar's success story. The ranch riparian area serves as home to the highest density of songbird territories in North America—an average of 1,300 per 100 acres. (The next most dense site supports 1,100.) On the U Bar stretch of the Gila, 99 percent of the fish are native species and only one percent are nonnative. The average for other streams in the Southwest is closer to the opposite. The U Bar, which Ogilvie leases from the copper-mining giant Phelps Dodge, supports the largest population of one threatened fish, the spikedace, and among the largest populations of another, the loach minnow. Both of these species are listed by The Nature Conservancy as among the 500 most endangered species in the United States. Other threatened, endangered or significant species doing well on the U Bar include the common blackhawk (largest known population), Abert's towhee, Bell's vireo, Gila woodpecker, Gila chub, desert sucker and Sonoran sucker.

What these rare creatures seem to be telling us in the most significant way they can—by making their homes and proliferating on the U Bar stretch of the Gila—is that this riparian area on a cattle ranch is managed in the way best suited to ensure their survival and promote their recovery. The people who are putting together the official recovery plan for the Southwestern willow flycatcher, however, have a different take on the matter. The Draft Southwestern Willow Flycatcher Recovery Plan produced for the U.S. Fish & Wildlife Service (FWS) states that its approach is "to determine…the degree and the conditions under which livestock grazing is compatible or incompatible with flycatcher recovery." Having stated that, the draft plan then goes on to call for "the total exclusion of livestock grazing from those riparian areas that are deemed necessary to recover the flycatcher where livestock grazing has been identified as a principal stressor."

On the way to this conclusion, the draft plan mentions the U Bar and acknowledges that "information reviewed here also suggests some degree of compatibility between grazing and flycatcher recovery." Based on this and a stated desire to "avoid recommending undue or unnecessary restrictions on a widespread, traditional land-use industry," the draft plan leaves the door open for some grazing in some areas under certain conditions. In those cases it offers guidelines for how that grazing would be conducted.

It would be reasonable to expect these grazing guidelines to be based on David Ogilvie's practices. After all, his Southwestern willow flycatcher recovery project is the most successful yet. It even outperforms the draft plan's ace in the hole—removing all grazing. The U Bar has three times as many flycatchers as the most successful preserve and 10 times as many as some. But instead of using Ogilvie's holistic goal-directed management as a model, the draft plan would have grazers conduct their activities according to a set of rules drawn up by the technical subgroup. The fact that the draft plan's grazing guidelines are not based on Ogilvie's management means none of the Plan's $104 million will be spent recreating the most successful flycatcher recovery project known. In fact, since the plan's rules would serve as obstacles to applying a goal-based management approach like Ogilvie's, you could say the plan's millions would be spent making sure the U Bar's success will never be repeated.

The U Bar is "an extremely unique situation," says Greg Beatty, of FWS's Phoenix office. "Much of the rest of the flycatcher's habitat is very different."

Federal agent Beatty is right. The U Bar is unique, but that uniqueness is not a matter of physical characteristics. What is unique about the U Bar is that it is managed according to goals, not rules, and that its success is so outstanding. As I write this, the ongoing Southwestern willow flycatcher count for 2001 on the U Bar stands at 138. Two similar-sized preserves that border the U Bar have seven flycatchers between them.

If this situation were taking place in any other area of human activity, it would inevitably result in a scandal. If a sports star were outscoring his teammates by 138 to 7, and the coach announced he was going to bench the star and use the play of the underachievers as a model for the whole team, the fans would be screaming for the coach's head. They would accuse him of pursuing another agenda besides winning.

That's what appears to be happening here. The draft plan's "other agenda" is habitat protection. The writers of the plan have made the assumption that habitat protection is the best route to flycatcher recovery. David Ogilvie's success makes it clear that we don't need to remove people from the land to bring the Southwestern willow flycatcher back from the brink of extinction. Nor do we need to further cripple the agricultural economies of rural communities.

Beatty pointed out that if the practice of using cattle grazing and ranch management to create or restore flycatcher habitat is ever going to be accepted widely, other successes in other locations are going to be necessary. As for obstacles presented by the draft plan, "Do it on private land," suggested Beatty. "The Endangered Species Act, and therefore the draft plan, don't apply on private land."

David Ogilvie knows from experience that any action on private land that involves federal money or adjacent federal land or involves land between the high-water marks of a stream requires consultation with FWS and therefore comes under the ESA. As an example, Ogilvie points to the fact that the first in a series of projects on private land that would expand the U Bar's exceptional habitat has already come under FWS scrutiny and been delayed and reduced in scope.

© JAY DUSARD

Forest Service wildlife biologist Scott Stolesen, left, with rancher Dave Ogilvie, center, and environmentalist Dan Dagget. Diverse interests are working together for the birds.

Working with U Bar owner Phelps Dodge Inc., the Quivira Coalition and EcoResults, David Ogilvie and Scott Stoleson are collaborating to use pole plantings, off-road vehicle exclusions, restorative grazing practices, and re-watered dirt ditches to further expand the Southwestern willow flycatcher's most successful recovery by as much as 150 acres.

That is, if the Southwestern Willow Flycatcher Recovery Plan, as it is finally approved, doesn't stop them. ■

FALL 2002

The Real American Wolfman

Ed Bangs knows how to straddle the double yellow line.
By Tim Findley

By day, on such an average sunny afternoon as this, he seems no more than just another federal bureaucrat. A little more dedicated to fitness than most, perhaps, as he leaves his daily noon-hour workout in the gym, but still just a slim average-looking man of 50 dressed in a casual shirt and khakis. He is headed back to his modest corner office in the IBM building where the federal government has rented space, and almost no one in the consciously upscale neighborhood of coffee shops and boutiques in the revised old brownstones of downtown Helena, Montana, takes any particular notice of him.

They don't know him from the deep woods of the northern Rockies or the numbingly trackless winter plains of Yellowstone valleys where his silent patience signals fear. They have never seen him approaching a lonely ranch house in a clearing far back from the timber where a family has been anxiously watching for hours. They are unaware that this is an amorphous character feared and hated by many on both sides of the issue of predatory blood.

"Tim Findley, from *RANGE*," Ed Bangs shouted in greeting from the end of the hall as I stepped off the elevator. I had announced myself to no one, and though I was on time for our meeting, it seemed surprising that he would recognize me well before I could him.

Bangs is full of unintended surprises. Fifteen years ago, when he was made chief of the U.S. Fish & Wildlife Service (FWS) Gray Wolf Recovery Program, he was the darling of dreaming intellectuals who fantasized on romantic wild packs returning to lurk in almost any mountainscape less civilized than Central Park. Now those same people fill their websites with vigilante calls for outrage against Bangs and his "killing spree." Hardly five years ago, he was seen by ranchers as a cold-eyed devil unmoved by the sight of torn and bloody carcasses in calving pens. Now it is he they turn to as an expert when their need is for retribution.

Ed Bangs has become something of a shape-shifter, charming but unpredictable. What else would you expect of a survival expert from the wilderness of Alaska whose favorite pastimes are poetry and modern dance? Don't get that wrong; Bangs is not like a Grizzly Adams in tights. He is a hardy outdoor man and the father of two who is no more afraid of a wolf than he is of an hysterical PETA representative. That is probably why the government saw him as so intellectually suited for a job that seems to straddle the double yellow line.

"Oh, yeah," Bangs agrees, "we're in the middle. I mean, we get run over by people from both sides all the time. But what I tell them is that the whole wolf issue has nothing to do with wolves. It has to do with human values. The average mountain lion kills twice as much big game as a wolf in a year, and lions even attack humans, unlike wolves. There are thousands of mountain lions and a relative few wolves, but wolves stir up these powerful human emotions, so it becomes a big political knock-down-drag-out issue."

"If you look at what we predicted and what has happened, you can say we're done with wolf recovery now."
Ed Bangs

Raised in a working family in Ventura, California, Bangs followed an impulse to earn a bachelor's degree in game management from Utah State University and then added a master's in wildlife management from the University of Nevada, Reno, home of—what else?—the Wolfpack. For 13 years, he was in what he called "the perfect job" as a federal game manager on the Kenai Refuge in Alaska, tracking, hunting, teaching bear and gun safety and spending as many hours on skis or in small planes as he did in his office. Still, in the spirit of Jack London, he found time to produce two- dozen articles on his wildlife experiences. But in 1988, just about the same time that a pack of wolves found their way south of the Canadian border and began establishing new dens in Montana, Bangs' wife decided their family needed a little more of civilization. Helena would do.

In Montana, Bangs and wolves soon became synonymous. As project leader for wolf recovery in the state, Bangs began the trapping and monitoring program for FWS, touring the northern regions to encounter angry ranchers, visiting local colleges and community centers to offer calming presentations on the presence—and protection—of the legendary predators.

"There are all these dark tales and fears, but the truth is that there is no record of a wild wolf having attacked anybody in the United States," he says. "We'd even see wolves wandering along in the middle of cattle herds, paying no attention to them at all. The wild ones just didn't seem to recognize cattle as something they could eat."

That would change, especially as the new Clinton administration and Bruce Babbitt began to see the wolf as emblematic of their desire to restore wilderness, beginning in the premier park showplace of Yellowstone.

"I met Babbitt a couple of times," Bangs says, "but whatever he was saying was all Babbitt himself. Like all Interior secretaries he had his own ideas, and all he ever really said to me was 'Good job.'"

Bangs had none of the romantic notions Babbitt expressed of the "green fire" being restored in the eyes of wolves once hunted to near extinction in the lower 48. At Kenai, the job of game managers before Bangs had been to kill wolves, sometimes even from helicopters, and elsewhere in Alaska it was common for them to be shot whenever they threatened livestock or protected wildlife. Wolves, to Bangs, were like big and not particularly smart dogs—understandable but not overpowering in either their image or skills.

"Most often we would find them watching from a distance. Just watching," Bangs says. "That was part of what made them seem frightening."

But with the political imprimatur of Babbitt, the message was sent out to the public that wolves would soon return a certain unsuspecting thrill to Yellowstone and a new balance to nature. Bangs was given the job of completing a congressionally ordered Environmental Impact Statement on their reintroduction.

The Interior secretary had posed and toyed with drug-calmed captive wolves brought from Canada and fed in pens prior to release. He had never seen a wolf in the wild as Bangs had, and he didn't care whether wolves had a taste for beef or not. The report to the secretary affirmed that it would be possible to introduce wolf packs into Yellowstone, but it also cautioned that the supposedly endangered predator would quickly reproduce and establish new territories that would go beyond the park. Eventually seven packs, or at least mating pairs, were brought in for release.

With 17 million acres of national forest near the park, but less than half of that suitable to wolves, Bangs predicted that "sooner rather than later," the packs would expand their territories onto private land. He knew he would eventually be killing some of the same wolves he had "saved" in the release program.

"The wild ones just didn't seem to recognize cattle as something they could eat."

"If you look at what we predicted and what has happened, you can say we're done with wolf recovery now," Bangs says. "By December we will have met all our recovery goals. Even now, I spend most of my time these days working toward delisting [of the wolf from the Endangered Species Act] by seeing that they stay recovered and that we make some transition to state management."

That, in Bangs' view, would include not only the right of ranchers to protect their cattle (as they can now), but a hunting season on wolves, which Bangs predicts and supports as "the best thing that could happen." Only the killing of wolves by humans put the carnivores on the endangered list to start with. Impossible as it may be for their friends in the city to take, Bangs believes that only a managed program including hunting can keep them off it.

Bruce Babbitt in his cynical way knew as well as Bangs does that depredation by wolves has a miniscule impact on the overall cattle industry, but Bangs was not following a political agenda as he tracked the rapid expansion of the packs into neighboring regions. "It's nothing to the industry," Bangs says, "but to the individual family or small rancher, wolf depredation can mean disaster. We understand that and we take it very seriously."

In his report on the Yellowstone and Idaho releases, Bangs had predicted that 10 percent of the wolves turned out would eventually have to be killed because of such attacks. Up to now, the figure is actually only about five percent, but it has caused howls of protest from fanatical followers of the packs.

Recognizing the public relations value, environmental groups virtually adopted every pack of wolves released under Bangs' program, and monitored their fate on the Internet as if keeping up with backwoods family members. Now they rage about the dirty work of killing the predators that attack domestic livestock "in wolf territory."

However much he may be correct that wild wolves did not even initially recognize cattle as food, Bangs acknowledges that at least some packs have learned better. Weeks now seldom pass when he is not contacted by a rancher seeking a permit to shoot a molesting wolf or when Bangs himself is not called out to investigate another claim.

He can find them. He can sometimes even call them into view, but Bangs will feel no particular emotions about the wolves as either romantic legends or rogue killers. His job is management, and he carries it out with almost fearless efficiency.

"We were gun netting one time and this New Zealand guy working with us had a wolf and shouted over to me, 'Ed, can you hold this for a minute!' I took hold of the wolf by the back of its neck, thinking the Kiwi had tranquilized it. A couple of minutes later, another helicopter landed nearby to tell me something, and this wolf goes nuts. In an instant I'm holding the animal by its face, not its neck, and boom, he bit into my wrist and I thought I could hear all the bones breaking. I turned loose of him and he turned loose of me, and we just stared at each other." The wolf was recaptured, tagged and released. Bangs later went to the emergency room. No bones broken, just puncture wounds.

Of such survived encounters are other legends born. Bangs has surely heard them all. Earlier this year, he was invited to Sweden, where in the dim arctic forests perhaps the scariest stories were first told and still endure. Wolves had virtually disappeared from Scandinavia as well, until packs appeared recently from Finland and Russia, touching off debates among livestock and wildlife managers much like in the United States.

"There is evidence in Sweden that wolves may have attacked people even recently," Bangs says, "but some of those attacks may have been by hybrid wolf dogs or rabid wolves."

And there is where myth and wild reality may somehow strangely converge. Bangs and nearly all experts agree that the far more dangerous creature, and one even the Humane Society agrees should be eliminated, is the hybrid wolf dog—the ferocious pet someone thought could be born of mating wild and domestic species. Apart from Bangs' territory, in the southwestern United States, hybrids are now suspected of being among Mexican gray wolves being reintroduced. If so, the hybrids are doomed.

Bangs, however, regards his own job as almost finished. "His" wolves have expanded their territories and packs into and out of Yellowstone just as he predicted they would. An argument goes on that depredation has seriously reduced the elk herds in the park, but Bangs points to similar calf losses in the last few years among elk outside the wolf areas. The Yellowstone packs and those in central Idaho are established and certain. Their numbers alone will command consideration for delisting as endangered species, and then it will be up to the states to determine how best to live with a reestablished legend and a twisted political emblem. Reluctantly uneasy about taking over a federal headache, Montana, Idaho, and Wyoming are currently drafting their own wolf-management programs in anticipation of delisting.

"There will still be people who say there should be no wolves, but they are a tiny minority. There will be people arguing for wolves everywhere, and that's a tiny minority. We're going to have wolves. The question is how many can we have and what's a tolerable level. Wolves are very adaptable animals, but it's us who are going to have to decide where we're going to let them live and where they won't be tolerated," says Bangs, who himself still holds that ultimate authority.

He's divorced now and immensely proud of being a single parent to his two daughters. Urbane and articulate, he is a sort of man-about-town in Helena with a uniquely romantic job that regularly takes him off into the wilderness he loves. The little office he has in the IBM building can't avoid evidence of the exuberance of the federal printing office in splashing wolves across covers of their reports. But strangely, there are no pictures in his office of Bangs himself in an encounter with the canines.

We drove out north of Helena into a wooded canyon for a picture that might put him in a more natural setting, and I chose the site near a small stream.

"Oh yeah, this is fine," says the American wolfman. "In fact, there's a pack that has a den just over that mountain there."

I had to wonder how he could be so sure. ■

WINTER 2007

FATAL ENCOUNTER

When wild wolves become used to humans, bad things inevitably happen. By Laura Schneberger

Losing a child is an unnatural life event. Only those who have borne a similar loss can understand. Sadly, the family of 22-year-old Kenton Carnegie has joined that group.

Kenton was a third-year geological engineering graduate student at the University of Waterloo in Ontario, Canada. He worked at Points North Landing in Saskatchewan as part of his fall term co-op program. He was killed November 8, 2005, by a pack of wild Canadian gray wolves.

The wolf recovery and protection camp considers the incident to be a fluke, an anomaly. The tragic circumstances surrounding Kenton's death leave no peace or comfort for his family. A medical report lists the cause of death as "large canine bites, likely wolves." Overwhelming forensic and photographic evidence has been introduced. Four wolves were present at the scene. The investigating Royal Canadian Mounted Police officer told Kenton's father that it was necessary to fire warning shots to disperse those wolves to secure the scene. Yet the resolution of a biological investigation confirming the cause of death has not occurred. ■

FALL 2002

ENDANGERED?

What is, what isn't, who says.

Refuge

Deep in the hearts of Americans there is a sense of loss and responsibility for the natural environment. What we want is to save endangered species. By Tim Findley

I still remember seeing them myself that afternoon on the southern plains of Colorado when I was just a boy. We had heard them and searched that ache-blue sky for some sight of those long calls, like geese, but carrying over another breath or two as we paused and looked. They seemed invisible miles from us, and then at last when they appeared in a squadron of mighty wings on stretched white pencils of form, we stopped and cupped our hands over our eyes. Whooping cranes, an awesome and rare sight even then in the late 1950s, sailed over us as if they owned the sky.

With an instinct I have long since regretted and calmed, I felt that I wanted one of those incredibly magnificent birds, just to show I was a witness to it, almost as if to prove I had somehow stepped back in time. I knew they were well beyond the range of my .410, but with the rash insensitivity of youth, I fired a long leading, hopelessly wild blast. And then we all just watched, trying to implant in our minds a story we could tell forever, as they soared past our horizon, leaving long clear calls beyond when we could any further see them.

So I understood as I thought some others could not when the campaign to save the cranes really took hold in 1966. I even still felt guilty for firing that stupid shot. I had seen something that might never be seen again, as much as I wished, and I hated anyone who might be more successful than I was at taking a part of it away. That, as much as anything, is the story of how the Endangered Species Act began.

The Endangered Species Act (ESA) evolved in the United States through at least three distinct phases, each noted by a species that seemed to capture public imagination.

The endangered whooping crane (Grus americana) is the tallest of North American birds, standing nearly five feet tall with a wingspan of 7.5 feet. Males weigh on average 17 pounds, while females weigh about 14 pounds. Whooping cranes' lifespan is estimated to be 22 to 24 years in the wild.

Grus Americana

Robert Porter Allen was a dedicated ornithologist appointed by the National Audubon Society in 1946 to trace the migratory routes and nesting areas of whooping cranes known to winter in Texas. He would search thousands of miles, crisscrossing the remote wilderness of Canada and the Northwest Territories in his quest, until finally in 1954 a forest fire in the far northern edge of the province of Alberta drew his attention to the first confirmed nesting site of the bird scientifically classified as *Grus americana*. With some irony, it was in Wood Buffalo National Park, the unique region set aside in 1922 as a refuge for the bison.

By the time Allen found the nesting origin for the whooping crane, surely every schoolchild already knew the sad tale of the buffalo, brought to what many expected to be imminent extinction from the wanton slaughter of the 19th century. The shame of that was already part of popular culture in the flickering movies and the picture books retelling how the bison were eliminated from the Great Plains. Americans especially were aware that human excess and greed could destroy an entire species, and their guilt felt from that was evident from the buffalo on one side of a coin that held the image of the Sioux Chief Red Cloud on its opposite face. The message was respect, not conquest. Deeper in the hearts of Americans than of any other national cultures, there was already a sense of loss and responsibility for the natural environment.

Allen, truly a pioneer in environmental science, used his research work with the whooping crane to inspire Congress in 1966 to pass the Endangered Species Preservation Act. He called upon the secretary of Interior for the first time to make a list of endangered fish and wildlife and authorize U.S. Fish & Wildlife Service (FWS) to spend up to $15 million a year on preserving habitat, "insofar as it is practicable and consistent with their primary purpose." From this would come an essential element in the creation of FWS's "Redbook" on creatures endangered in America.

The whooping crane had long been protected by law from hunters, but the question to be answered was whether habitat protection could save a creature abundant in the Pleistocene era millions of years ago, but already in decline by the time of European discovery. As recently as 1950, natural storms had decimated one flock in Louisiana to a sole surviving bird named Mac, which was captured and relocated to the only other known wintering grounds of the birds in Texas. Mac was later found dead, apparently killed by other cranes.

Similar natural events including summer freezes and storms near the Arctic accounted for most of the continued losses in the precarious survival of Allen's discovery. Only the introduction of captive breeding and virtual hand raising of the cranes, including migration training with the use of ultralights, seemed likely to save them from extinction. Nearly 40 years later there is hope that some 200 whooping cranes known to exist may, with man's help, soon find their way from endangered status to threatened existence.

Nevertheless, the public inspiration found in an attempt to save the cranes would carry on into a vision that made much more seem possible. The buffalo might never return in such wild numbers but the televised work of Jacques Cousteau and others in the 1960s brought the sea and sea mammals into public consciousness as never before, and there, it seemed, was an almost religious awakening.

Eschrichtius Robustus

"For the first few days that we were here and at Santa Barbara, we watched them with great interest—calling out 'There she blows!' every time we saw the spout of one breaking the surface of the water, but soon they became so common we took little notice of them."—RICHARD HENRY DANA, "TWO YEARS BEFORE THE MAST," 1840

Mother and calf gray whale (Digital illustration)

The 19th-century literature of Dana, Herman Melville and others compounded a sense of the sea in overpowering metaphors and ultimate high adventure, but it was the underwater motion picture camera that provided the opportunity at last to look eye to eye at a living creature which seemed so obviously to understand.

The 1966 protection act had established a broad interest in saving certain species of native fish and wildlife but the terms of its authority were limited, and public attention was being drawn at the same time with even greater confidence to what could be done. In 1969, Congress replaced the old act with new terms that extended protection to invertebrates and increased prohibitions on illegal trade, prohibiting imports to the United States of products made from endangered species. Reaching out to sea and beyond, the 1969 version set the stage for a series of international conventions and the campaign to save the whales.

There was already great reason for optimism in such actions. Rachel Carson's "Silent Spring" in 1963 had vividly brought to awareness the dangers from uncontrolled use of pesticides, especially DDT. Empowered with new authority under the 1969 Act and with better knowledge of chemical effects, FWS began a campaign that in remarkably rapid time would seem to have "saved" not only the study species of the peregrine falcon but the veritable national symbol of the bald eagle. Even more than with the cranes, the efforts with raptors became success stories possible to be clearly seen in their achievements and ultimately inspiring in their aims. It was no wonder that so many saw the possibilities for rescuing the dominant creatures of the sea, beginning with the gray whale, *Eschrichtius robustus.*

It was also a time when long-ignored others assumed to be an academically quiet and gentle minority began to sense new power in the opportunity before them. The Nature Conservancy (TNC) was formed in 1951 among a group of scientists and researchers primarily interested in acquiring small regions for further study. But in 1970, the nonprofit organization used funds donated by newly awakened business and industrial foundations to purchase three islands off the coast of Virginia. It was the first major purchase by a once-small organization of scientists looking to study a pond. It has evolved into a secretive, major landholding and power-mongering cartel. Today TNC controls more than 12 million acres in the United States alone and 90 million acres worldwide.

With less financial success perhaps but with much the same enthusiasm, older organizations such as the National Audubon Society, the Wilderness Society and the Sierra Club expanded their public appeals in the easy times when suddenly everybody was an environmentalist.

Now, although international battles remain in the Asian Pacific, gray whales especially have come back in numbers that may exceed all historical records off the U.S. West Coast. The peregrine falcon and the bald eagle are no longer endangered and probably more cherished among humankind in general than ever. The eyes of the great marine mammals do, truly, seem to understand.

But the inspiration of those successes after passage of the 1969 act served as much to define what might be beyond legal reach as they suggested what might come in social—and political—rewards for a greater effort. New pressures were being imposed on politicians by groups that found new wealth in foundation grants from the ostensibly honest guilt of those who had exploited the earth to earn it. Protection of species, they argued with cash in hand, must go further.

Percina Tanasi

It was the U.S. Navy that complained most about listing whales, particularly the sperm whale, *Physeter macrocephalus,* as endangered, because oil from the species was still used in submarines. The test of wills, however, between the Navy and the Department of the Interior ultimately came out on the side of the whale and indirectly in the

Snail darter

politically potent creation of what many scholars say is the nation's most powerful law—the Endangered Species Act of 1973.

Passed with nearly unanimous bipartisan support and signed by its personal champion, President Richard Nixon, the new act closed old loopholes and spread into new areas. It created a category of threatened as well as endangered species and allowed an unlimited listing of animals, plants and invertebrates that might only be in danger in part of their range. It was not only illegal to kill or harm an endangered species; now even an unconscious act to disrupt a habitat could be regarded as a crime. The strengthening environmental movement could see the enormous implications of the act, even if many in Congress who were eager to be aboard the bandwagon of ecology could not.

The first widely publicized confrontation came over completion of a public works' dream beginning in the 1930s and about to culminate with closing the gates on the $100 million Tellico Dam on the Little Tennessee River. The 1973 law had sent scientists scrambling on a treasure hunt for rare species as if they had just been burst loose from a gigantic federal piñata. Species and subspecies everywhere were claimed from the edge of extinction, among them, the humble little snail darter, *Percina tanasi,* thought only to exist on the Little Tennessee.

Preposterous as it may have seemed to many, the little snail darter became the crowning proof of the power behind the Endangered Species Act when in 1978 the U.S. Supreme Court ruled that the "plain intent" of the law was to save all species possible, "whatever the cost." That included the $78 million already expended on Tellico Dam.

Now more uncomfortably aware of what had been set loose, Congress attempted in 1978 to establish a "god squad" committee that could exempt some species from extinction, but the political pressures were too great, and at their very first meeting the committee declined to exempt even the snail darter. Science, it seemed, had scored an important victory over mere social progress.

Yet even a defiant act by Tennessee lawmakers to complete the dam anyway was not what ultimately settled the issue. That happened when other scientists acting on their own found that the snail darter, to everyone's surprise, was not at all limited to the Little Tennessee. By 1984, with the dam full and operating, FWS downlisted the snail darter from endangered to threatened in its existence on many small streams of the Tennessee Valley.

Even so, the scientific treasure nuggets of unheard of plants, animals and insects were still scattered for the finding all over the nation: a form of mint in San Diego stopped a Veterans Administration project; a subspecies of squirrel blocked the Catholic Church from a huge telescope project in Arizona; a fly stopped a hospital and a mouse blocked a subdivision in California. All real stories, and despite the outcome at Tellico, most with costly consequences to the planners and developers. The mightiest law of the land exerted its power everywhere and brought a stillness to the general inspiration remembered from the eyes of a whale.

Strix Occidentalis Caurina

The Endangered Species Act of 1973 was a beast of its own being, evolving beyond itself into proportions few were willing to predict. All that was really known was that once it took hold it was almost impossible to stop. Yet it was established in the American psyche. Even with the extremes and the errors that could be seen from the case of the snail darter, the sense of a new, more enlightened morality toward other species prevailed. The planet, and every precious bit of life upon it, was clearly worth saving. To argue against that was to risk political suicide.

Under successive Republican administrations, the FWS Redbook of species in danger added still more careful lines, while attempts were made to protect some private property rights by allowing a "take" of some localized species, provided its habitat was assured elsewhere. It was a feeble adjustment that would soon seem meaningless.

In 1989, Sierra Club Legal Defense analyst Andy Stahl stood in the pit of a university lecture hall in Oregon and directed himself to what he assumed to be a loyal crowd of activists, one of whom was videotaping the Sierra Club leader's remarks.

"I've often thought, thank God the spotted owl evolved," Stahl said, nearly giggling at his own revelation, "because if it hadn't, we would have had to genetically engineer it."

The spotted owl, *Strix occidentalis caurina,* was "perfect" he said. He compared the owl to a slide of Disney's "Bambi," knowing its innocent features would pull at shallow American emotions, and he delighted most in what he said was scientific discovery that the owl could only survive in old-growth forests.

It was not the owl the Sierra Club wanted to save. It was the old-growth and even managed-growth forest of the

Spotted owl

© GREG VAUGHN/TOM STACK & ASSOCIATES

Pacific Northwest that was the prize environmentalists intended to protect. The spotted owl, Stahl readily admitted, was merely the surrogate for their cause. No other species had ever been used in quite the same way. The owl wasn't bound by a single nest or limited to a specific stream. It couldn't be assured of survival by some other stand of trees. Its range could cover hundreds of miles, crossing over more than 25 million acres of Northwest forests. Anywhere it could thrive, its habitat had to be protected.

Pressured by environmentalists holding increasingly important jobs in the Department of the Interior, FWS listed the spotted owl as threatened in 1990. Within three years, hundreds of lumber mills were shut down and thousands of workers were displaced from their jobs in the timber industry and related employment. The response by excited environmentalists was to deluge federal authorities with petitions for listing still more species and demanding even more expanded habitat protection.

Bambi had gone bad, real bad.

Newly emerging organizations like Arizona's Center for Biological Diversity made it its specialty to find more overlooked species and petition for their listing. Beyond that, the openings provided in the evolution of the act since 1966 provided for habitat protection in some areas not even related to species identified upstream or miles away. The criterion recognized by FWS was to protect not species in immediate danger, but those that might someday be put at risk. Working in questionable legal relationship with such groups as The Nature Conservancy and the Environmental Defense Fund, the federal agency began pressuring private landholders to sell wetlands and water rights often only remotely connected to habitat protection of specific species. The act even provided for the reintroduction of species, particularly predators such as wolves and grizzly bears, into suitable habitats from which they had once been eliminated.

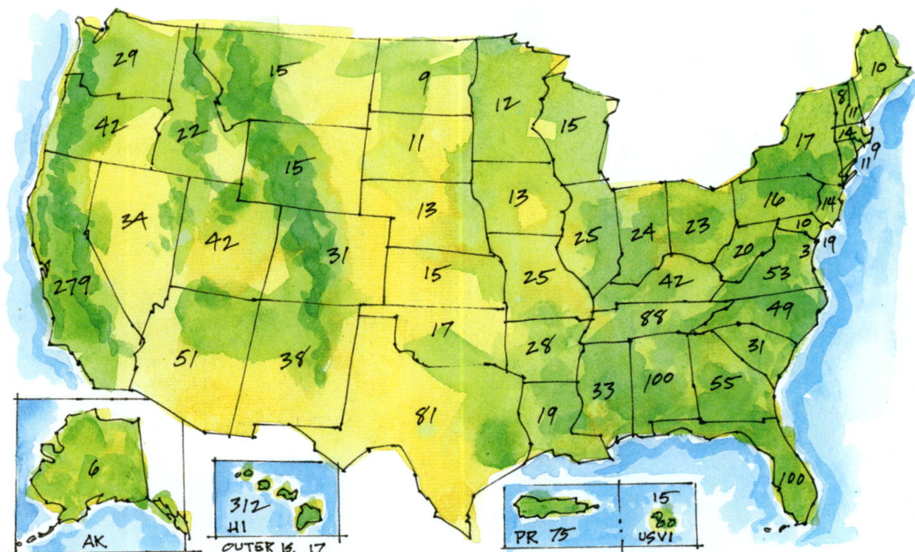

Listed species' range by state/territory as of July 2, 2002—1,258. Omits "similarity of appearance" and experimental populations. Does not map whales and non-nesting sea turtles in coastal waters. Numbers are not additive; a species often occurs in multiple states. Information courtesy U.S. Fish & Wildlife Service.

Bruce Babbitt, long contemptuous of any legislative challenge to what he regarded as his baronial domain, almost mockingly said, "I am certain that the members of Congress who passed the Endangered Species Act didn't understand the American West."

By 1995, Babbitt's Interior Department was so overwhelmed with species proposed for listing and lawsuits filed by environmental groups that the Clinton administration tried to offset the pressure by exempting some small-property holders. But in that same year, the U.S. Supreme Court in the "Sweet Home" decision in Oregon ruled that any alteration of a listed species' habitat could bring a prison sentence. Finally, that year, Congress imposed a moratorium on further listings.

Yet Babbitt would not accept any limitations on his most powerful tool and the most potent public relations device of his environmental backers. In 1998 he gloated before a news conference, claiming that his people proved conclusively that the Endangered Species Act "works.... In the near future many species will be flying, splashing and leaping off the list." Babbitt proclaimed: "They made it. They are graduating." He provided a list of two-dozen species seemingly on the verge of imminent recovery. Five species on the list were already extinct. Eight were listed by mistake in the first place, and four others were discovered not to have been distinct species at all.

Babbitt had been sucked in by a blunder in his own public affairs office, but it didn't matter. The almighty Interior secretary stood by his own fantasies like Mussolini claiming Ethiopia. It was politics, not science, and if there was any doubt about what worked, Babbitt also cited the probably accurate estimate that 86 percent of Americans supported policies on the protection of endangered species.

Most probably still believe the spotted owl is endangered, even though a preponderance of newer research and evidence suggests the Sierra Club "science" was cooked to make it seem the owl could only survive in old-growth forests. Having served its purpose as a surrogate to halt logging, the remarkably prolific owl is now seldom mentioned even by the Sierra Club itself.

By the time Babbitt made his 1998 graduation speech, more than 1,100 species were on the list. Although many of them, including the spotted owl, have since been found to exist in far greater numbers than previously thought, the act itself makes it virtually impossible to easily delist any but those acknowledged as a mistake in the first place. Only 11 species have been removed from the list as recovered. These include the gray whale, the peregrine falcon and the American alligator, as well as similar species that ultimately survive because of hunting restrictions and changes in the use of pesticides. Dozens if not hundreds of other species are under consideration for delisting or downlisting, but the cumbersome process imposed on the

Act by lawsuits and other actions now requires years of verification that the species is no longer endangered or threatened. More than 4,000 "species of concern" still await decision on petitions to add them to the list.

In 1971, the speechwriters for then assistant secretary of the U.S. Fish & Wildlife Service, Nathaniel P. Reed, reached deep for eloquence in saying, "America has matured to the point that we are no longer willing to sacrifice the end product of eons of evolution—a species or subspecies of wildlife—on the altar of the god called Progress without putting up one darned good fight." Yet the evolution of the Endangered Species Act is marked far less by sure science of survival than it is by the cynical, if more certain, craving for political opportunism. No imposed limitation on property or regulated restriction of public use under the act has ever been credited with saving a single species in the United States. It remains a powerful and popular law of the land based in its limited success on the increasingly common good sense that nature should no longer be taken for granted.

On that fall afternoon in Colorado we were just hunting, as boys then often did. With all I have learned since, I still don't think it would have changed my thoughts immediately after I fired that wild shot. "God," I whispered to myself. "I'm glad I missed." ■

FALL 2002

WHAT'S WRONG with ESA? WHAT ISN'T?

A virulent tool in the rape of rural America.

By Jeff Goodson

The Endangered Species Act is broken. It has utterly failed in what it set out to do, and 30 years of lawsuits have transformed it from a simple environmental law into the most virulent tool in the rape of rural America. There are a lot of problems with the ESA. What follow are the most important:

Species That Aren't Species

The ESA was originally designed to protect species from extinction. The term "species," however, has since been twisted from a biological into a legal term. Today it's so broadly defined as to include simple population segments—a definition used to list common species like the gray wolf and Canadian lynx.

Species That Aren't Endangered

Likewise, "endangered" no longer means in danger of extinction; today it includes threats in any part of a species' range. A number of listed organisms aren't biologically endangered at all—they're just rare in the United States. The lynx, for example, has the largest range of any wildcat in the world; more than 18,000 lynx skins were traded from 1995-99.

The Definition of Take

The ESA prohibits the "take" of endangered species. Take means to capture or kill, but the U.S. Fish & Wildlife Service (FWS) interprets the term to include everything from common ranching, farming and construction activities to backyard playgrounds. Even a simple walk in the woods can now qualify as take.

Junk Science

FWS says it uses the best available data when it lists endangered species. The dirty little secret among professional biologists is that a lot of it is junk science—and not just the population estimates used at listing. In 1998, a federal claims court found that the U.S. Forest Service used bad spotted-owl data to block logging in California, and last year the National Academy of Sciences found no scientific basis for cutting off water to Klamath farmers. Earlier this year, the National Marine Fisheries Service had to rescind critical habitat designation for 19 fish populations after admitting that "we just designate everything as critical, without an analysis of how much habitat" is actually needed.

Biological Fraud

Less common than junk science is outright biological fraud. In the latest known incident, seven government biologists planted captive-lynx fur in two national forests during a

Lynx

© DAVE WATTS/TOM STACK & ASSOCIATES

federal endangered species' survey and then fraudulently submitted the samples for DNA analysis.

Irreversible Decisions

No matter how bad the science, delisting a species is almost impossible. In 30 years, only nine U.S. species have been delisted because of taxonomic revision or new information. One of them, the Concho water snake, was listed in 1986 after a college professor convinced FWS that only 600 to 800 survived. Ten years and $1.5 million later, the agency finally delisted this snake when up to 70,000 were found slithering around.

Biased Administration

Lawyers use the term "arbitrary and capricious" to describe government bias in program administration. Administration of the ESA may be more arbitrary and capricious than any environmental program in America. The most recent ruling was from a federal judge in Oregon, who found that wild and common hatchery salmon of the same species were treated differently at listing.

Expensive Compliance

ESA compliance is a high-dollar proposition. On private property, Section 10 of the act usually requires expensive habitat conservation plans and the donation of mitigation land. On the public domain, compliance may be impossible altogether except through costly litigation.

Irrelevant People

In 1978, environmentalists used the snail darter to try and stop Tennessee's Tellico Dam. The lawsuit went to the U.S. Supreme Court, which confirmed that Congress didn't care about people when it passed the ESA. To this day, FWS argues that it cannot assess impact on people during the listing process.

Economic Damage

The Supreme Court's Tellico Dam opinion stated that "the plain intent of Congress...was to halt and reverse the trend toward species extinction, whatever the cost." Since then, the ESA has left a trail of economic damage from the Northwest (spotted owl) to the Southeast (red-cockaded woodpecker) and everywhere in between—from the Klamath Basin (salmon and steelhead) and Southern California (California gnatcatcher), to Arizona (Mount Graham red squirrel), Oklahoma (burying beetle), and central Texas (golden-cheeked warbler, black-capped vireo and cave invertebrates). After 30 years, even the FWS recognizes the damage. In an exceptionally rare printed admission in 2001, the agency stated that "the halt on logging late-successional forests...during the early 1990s had a dramatic impact on people who depended on Bureau of Land Management and Forest Service timber supply for work."

Lockdown of the Public Lands

The ESA is the tool of choice for locking down the public domain. As environmentalists Andy Kerr and Mark Salvo recently noted in *RANGE,* Spring 2002: "Pending and imminent ESA actions to protect the mountain plover, mountain quail, sage grouse (the spotted owl of the Sagebrush Sea), yellow-billed cuckoo and other species will dramatically affect public-lands livestock grazing." Most communities battered by the ESA had thrived for generations off sustained multiple use of the public lands. Ranching, farming and logging communities in the Northwest, Southwest and Southeast have been especially hard hit.

Litigation Abuse

Dozens of ESA lawsuits are active at any given time, filed by organizations like the Center for Biological Diversity, the Sierra Club and the Natural Resources Defense Council. The granddaddy of ESA litigation, Jasper Carlton of the Biodiversity Legal Foundation, filed a single lawsuit in 1992 on behalf of 443 species. A few years later he was simultaneously pursuing individual lawsuits to force list the lynx, wolverine, fisher, grizzly bear, Spalding's catchfly, painted rock snail and Amargosa toad. As Carlton put it: "Instead of one lawsuit, we bring 10, 15, 20 lawsuits."

Abuse as a Property Control Tool

For environmentalists, force-listing species through litigation is a favorite property-control tactic. Jasper Carlton once complained that FWS was "avoiding listing species that are wide-ranging and have implications for landscape-scale protection: lynx, wolverine, fisher, bull trout." Since then, environmentalists have greened the federal agency and front burnered the strategy of suing to list species with landscape implications. These include not just terrestrial species, but aquatic species that can be used to control stream flow and water quality on a watershed scale. Of 85 species identified last year as candidates for listing in the continental United States, over half are aquatic.

Children Playing God

It's bad enough that the ESA empowers FWS to play God, but the individuals who make those profound decisions are neither elected nor accountable. Many aren't even professional biologists with the experience and seasoning necessary to judiciously defend the biology on which their decisions are based. A federal biologist in Austin, Texas, once had the audacity to tell a landowner that the loss of his 750-acre ranch would mean the extinction of a bird found in dozens of Texas counties.

Unjust Compensation

The Fifth Amendment of the Bill of Rights states, "nor shall private property be taken for public use without just compensation." Environmental lawyers hotly debate the meaning of "take" in this constitutional context. But the simple truth is that when the government takes the use of property, it takes the property. Landowners everywhere have had government take the use of their property through the ESA without just compensation.

Environmental Damage

Another dirty little secret about the ESA is the extent of environmental damage it causes. In central Texas, golden-cheeked warbler habitat wastes massive volumes of groundwater. A handful of aquatic species has rendered 45 million acre-feet of the Edwards Aquifer as inaccessible as Pluto. Those listings are ultimately responsible for the environmental impact of every infrastructure project required to produce the water to replace it. Likewise, managing for old-growth forest to protect some species demonstrably increases wildfire damage. It can also threaten highly endangered species like Kirtland's warbler that rely on pre-climax vegetation, and drive less common pre-climax species to the edge of extinction.

Incentive to Kill

Not surprisingly, the property and natural resource damage inflicted by the ESA generates a profound incentive to "shoot, shovel and shut up." No landowners in their right minds want endangered species habitat damaging their property and natural resources, and smart landowners ensure that that habitat either doesn't develop or doesn't survive.

It Doesn't Work

At the end of the day, the biggest problem with the Endangered Species Act is that it doesn't work. FWS says the ultimate goal of the ESA is the recovery and subsequent preservation of endangered species and the ecosystems on which they depend. Today, after 30 years, there are 1,258 U.S. species on the endangered species list. Incredibly, only seven have recovered.

As long as the ESA establishes an incentive to kill, it will fail as conservation law. Habitat will be conserved and species will be saved when landowners have an incentive to conserve, and they get just compensation when the use of their land is taken for the public use of species preservation. ■

FALL 2006

OWL BE DAMNED

How and why the government failed so miserably in its costly attempt to protect spotted owls is a sordid tale.

By Jim Petersen

Last January, the U.S. Fish & Wildlife Service published a call for proposals for development of a recovery plan for the northern spotted owl. It's about time. The owl was added to the nation's burgeoning list of threatened and endangered species nearly 16 years ago. That it took so long helps explain why only 10 of 1,264 species listed under the 32-year-old federal Endangered Species Act (ESA) have ever recovered.

If my gut sense is correct, the owl won't be number 11. It is already doomed across much of its range, and the reason is well-known among field biologists who have been observing the bird for 20 years. More aggressive barred owls are pushing them out of their 21-million-acre home range, or killing them, or both.

Barred owls (not to be confused with common barn owls) migrated west from their native East Coast environs a century or more ago. No one knows why, and until they started killing already threatened spotted owls, no one cared. Now they do. Just how long it will take the barred owls to finish off their brethren isn't known, but the situation has become so precarious that a federal biologist recently opined that shooting barred owls might be the only way to save spotted owls.

© THERISA STACK/TOM STACK & ASSOC.

Barred owls (shown here) are pushing spotted owls out of their home range.

How and why the government failed so miserably in its costly attempt to protect spotted owls is a sordid tale that illustrates what happens when science is politicized. It begins with the fact that protecting owls was never the objective. Saving old-growth forests from chainsaws was. The owl was simply a surrogate—a stand-in for forests that do not themselves qualify for ESA protection. But if a link could be established between harvesting in old-growth forests and declining spotted owl numbers, the bird might well qualify for listing—a line of thinking that in 1988 led Andy Stahl, then a resource analyst with the Sierra Club Legal Defense Fund, to famously declare, "Thank goodness the spotted owl evolved in the Northwest, for if it hadn't, we'd have to genetically engineer it. It's the perfect species for use as a surrogate."

Indeed it was. But to back their play, the Sierra Club, the Audubon Society and their friends in the Clinton administration needed a good story for the judge. They found it in three obscure reports: a 1976 master's thesis written by wildlife-biology major Eric Forsman at Oregon State University; Mr. Forsman's 1980 doctoral dissertation; and a 1984 report written by Forsman and two other biologists. All three reports suggested a strong link between declining owl populations and harvesting in old-growth forests. Unfortunately, this hypothesis has never been tested. So despite 16 years of research, no link between old-growth harvesting and declining owl populations has ever been established.

Salmon

We know little about the relationship between harvesting and owl populations. One such study—privately funded—infers an inverse relationship between harvesting and owls. In other words, in areas where some harvesting has occurred owl numbers are increasing a bit, or at least holding their own, while numbers are declining in areas where no harvesting has occurred.

This news will come as no surprise to Oregon, Washington and California timberland owners who are legally required to provide habitat for owls. Their lands, which are actively managed, are home to the highest reproductive rates ever recorded for spotted owls. Why is this?

One possible answer is that the anecdotal evidence on which the listing decision was based is incomplete. No one denies the presence of owls in old-growth forests, but what about the owls that are prospering in managed forests and in forests where little old growth remains? Could it be that spotted owls are more resourceful than we think?

We don't know. And the reason we don't know is that 16 years ago some federal scientists chose to politicize their hypothesis rather than test it rigorously. They flatly rejected critiques from biometricians, who questioned the statistical validity of evidence on which the listing decision was based, and declared with by-god certainty that once the old-growth harvest stopped, owl populations would begin to recover.

Some biologists believe that spotted owls still have a fighting chance for survival east of the Cascades in Oregon and Washington. But there is a problem here: white fir is pushing native Douglas fir out of these forests in the same way barred owls are pushing spotted owls out of their home range. Minus a long-term thinning program opposed by many of the same environmental groups that pushed the owl's threatened species listing, the birds will probably vanish from these forests too.

No doubt one or more environmental groups will use the government's call for recovery plans to demand that even more habitat be set aside for spotted owls. When that demand is made, Congress must be forcefully reminded of a recent U.S. Forest Service estimate that an additional 1.1 million acres of federal forestland in the Pacific Northwest have grown into old-growth status since the owl's listing—and that despite this growth, spotted owl numbers continue to decline.

Senators especially must be reminded by voters of these facts, because they have yet to endorse changes in the Endangered Species Act ratified by the House of Representatives last fall. Among other things, the House version mandates immediate development and implementation of recovery plans for all listed species. To avoid repeats of the spotted owl fiasco, it will be necessary for the scientists involved to peer-review listing proposals representing all sides of inevitably controversial questions.

It should not take 16 years to write a recovery plan. The fact that it did ought to prompt some very pointed questions by concerned citizens everywhere about what went on behind locked doors in Portland, Oregon's, U.S. Bank Tower. The building was nicknamed the Tower of Power by the government scientists who gathered there in the spring of 1990—beyond public and congressional scrutiny—to sift through the pieces of their story. Congress should ask for their notes, but shouldn't expect much to be revealed. I'm told they were shredded daily. ■

VOICES DAVID FOREMAN, EARTH FIRST!

"We must make this an insecure and inhospitable place for capitalists and their projects.... We must reclaim the roads and plowed land, halt dam construction, tear down existing dams, free shackled rivers and return to wilderness millions of tens of millions of acres of presently settled land."

During courtship, the male sage grouse spreads its long tail feathers into a spiky fan. Sage grouse live in the western sagebrush plains, where they feed on insects, berries and shoots.

FALL 2008

Chicken Little and the Polar Bear

Policy based on biased information and poor decisions leads to human misery. By Michael S. Coffman, Ph.D.

Remember the media coverage last March of the disintegrating Wilkins Ice Shelf in the Antarctic? They told us that the disintegration was merely another example of how man-caused global warming was devastating the Antarctic, and by extension, the Arctic and Greenland ice packs and glaciers. The average viewer came away with the idea that all Antarctica was melting. The implication was that species like the polar bear were threatened with extinction, and melting ice would flood the world's coastlines and islands.

A whopping "220 square miles of the ice shelf collapsed," warns Ted Scambos, a glaciologist at the National Snow and Ice Data Center at the University of Colorado at Boulder. Jim Elliot, who captured video of the disintegration, says, "Big hefty chunks of ice, the size of small houses, look as though they've been thrown around like rubble. It's like an explosion."

The media used powerful adjectives like "collapse," "explosion," "threatened," and "hanging by a thread" to dramatize the event to cataclysmic levels. What was not reported was that the 220 square miles represented only 2.67 percent of the entire Wilkins Ice Shelf and only 0.01 percent of the entire Antarctic ice cover. Within that context, the media reporting is obviously Chicken Little hyperbole. Dismayed by the exaggerated reporting, Joseph D'Aleo, former director of meteorology at the Weather Channel and current executive director of Icecap.com, says that the breakup was more comparable to "an icicle falling from a snow-and-ice-covered roof."

Unfortunately, the media and alarmist scientists are not content with putting this issue into perspective. To their credit, they admitted the breakup will not raise the sea level because floating ice had already displaced all the water it was going to. But they then somberly reported that research reveals the area surrounding the Wilkins Ice Shelf had warmed an incredible 4.5 degrees Fahrenheit since the 1950s—faster than any place on earth. The reader or viewer is left with the idea that such warming is also melting continental ice, which will cause ocean levels to rise 20 feet or more as Al Gore incorrectly but graphically depicts in his video, "An Inconvenient Truth."

This cataclysmic scenario just isn't going to happen. What the media and global-warming alarmists fail to tell the public is that all the ice-shelf disintegration in the past decade is confined to northwestern Antarctica, especially the Antarctic Peninsula. The disintegration of ice shelves in this region is due to a warming of the ocean, not of the atmosphere. The rest of Antarctica has been cooling and accumulating ice since the early 1970s. This is exactly the opposite of what the man-caused global-warming theory predicts should occur.

There is another problem with this cataclysmic warming/melting hyperbole. Research published in 2007 reveals that the ocean warming is likely due to volcanic activity, not global warming. In January 2008, one volcano was even found to be actively warming the underside of the glaciers overlying it, causing them to melt from the bottom up and advance much faster than would otherwise be expected. Also not reported is the fact that some 3,000 scientific temperature-measuring robots plying the oceans have found that earth's oceans are cooling, not warming, as the

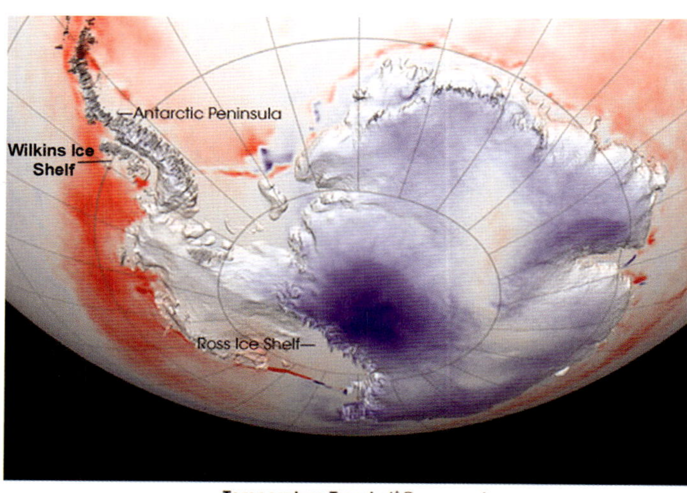

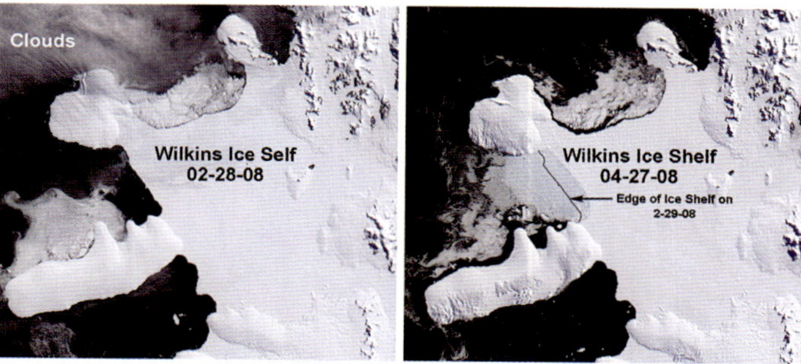

The breakup of the Wilkins Ice Shelf in Antarctica during March 2009. The media and alarmist scientists give the public the impression that Antarctica is warming so fast that it is causing catastrophic melting, when in fact the warming is only occurring in the ocean along the western Antarctic Peninsula. This warming is probably caused by volcanic activity, not global warming. Almost all of Antarctica is cooling. SOURCE: *NASA Earth Observatory*

man-caused global-warming theory demands. Of course, none of this is ever reported by the media or acknowledged by the alarmist scientists. So there is no way the average reader/viewer can put the issue into context.

Most people are acutely aware that the winter of 2007/2008 was the coldest in nearly three decades. They are still reeling from their heating bills. There is a reason for that. The earth's temperature plummeted by about 1.3 degrees Fahrenheit, ironically wiping out all the warming of the last 100 years. Although this does not mean we are heading for the next ice age, Antarctica's sea ice nonetheless reached record levels. As I write in May, the 2008 Antarctic winter has not yet reached its midpoint and already the sea ice is on track to break the 2007 record. Likewise, formation of the North Pole's sea ice this year was much faster and thicker than in recent years, and the 2008 polar summer melting should be less than it has been in the immediate past.

That is good news for the polar bear; its populations have been at record numbers the past few years—even with the melting polar sea ice. Yet, in spite of all the good news, the U.S. Fish & Wildlife Service (FWS) bowed to hysterical environmentalist pressure this May and listed the polar bear as a threatened species. There is little to no scientific evidence to list the polar bear. Sen. Inhofe (R-Oklahoma) says, "the decision to list the polar bear as 'threatened' appears to be based more on politics than science."

Environmentalists have been salivating for years over the prospect of listing the polar bear as endangered so they can use the Endangered Species Act as a weapon to limit the U.S. economy. Watch for an avalanche of lawsuits.

Why did the FWS list the polar bear with no science to back it up? In what can only be described as a leap of irrationality, the FWS justified its decision on computer models that predict rampant warming and continued melting of polar sea ice. These are the same computer models that admittedly have a 100-percent error level and were shown last year to predict warming that has not been demonstrated in real life. ■

Polar bear

Consensus? What Consensus?

We have all heard the litany in the news that 2,500 scientists working in conjunction with the United Nations Intergovernmental Panel on Climate Change (IPCC) agree with a 90-percent certainty that man is causing potentially catastrophic global warming. They even received the Nobel Peace Prize, along with Al Gore, for their exemplary work in the field. This, we are told, is a solid consensus having very few dissenters. The problem is that this so-called consensus is a myth—it never existed.

In early 1992, 47 of the top climatologists in the world signed a petition during an annual conference on climatology held in Heidelberg, Germany, decrying "the unsupported assumption that catastrophic global warming follows from the burning of fossil fuels and requires immediate action." Back in 1992, 47 Ph.D. climatologists represented a sizable chunk of all the climatologists in the world. The press ignored it.

Stung by the press's rebuke, the signers redoubled their efforts and were successful in obtaining 424 signers at the Rio de Janeiro Earth Summit, also in 1992. Known as the Heidelberg Appeal, it once again was ignored by the media, even though the number of signers eventually reached 4,000, including 72 Nobel prizewinners in science.

Several other petitions over the years met with the same fate. They were all ignored by the media. Then, in 2001, the Oregon Institute of Science and Medicine (OISM) launched the Petition Project, spearheaded by Dr. Frederick Seitz, past president of the National Academy of Sciences and of Rockefeller University. The Petition Project amassed 17,800 signatures; all signers had degrees in the physical sciences. This time the media did take notice, but not in the way one might expect.

For every scientist who even slightly favored the IPCC conclusions, 792 signed the petition saying there was no convincing evidence that there is man-made catastrophic global warming. For every Ph.D. who endorsed the IPCC report, 1,800 signed the petition refuting it. If anything, there is a scientific consensus that man is not responsible for global warming.

Instead of reporting that nearly 18,000 scientists refuted the man-caused global-warming theory, the media trumpeted alleged flaws in the petition. The petition drive was accused of filling the petition with duplicate signers. That allegation was proven false. Not surprisingly, many scientists happened to have the same name. Other names that seemed to be phony—such as Michael [J.] Fox, the actor, and Perry Mason, the fictional lawyer in a TV series—were actually real, credentialed scientists. No retraction was ever made by the media, nor did they even acknowledge the authenticity of either the signers or the petition.

Outraged with the sheer duplicity of the press and global-warming alarmists, OISM launched the same petition again in 2008. It used a subset of the mailing list of American Men and Women of Science—a who's who of science—to mail the petition, requesting that the recipient sign the petition if he/she agreed that Kyoto Accord was a danger to humanity.

The results show that 31,072 scientists, 9,021 of whom are Ph.D.s, signed the petition. Every signature has been vetted for authenticity.

Ironically, using the Freedom of Information Act, it has been proven that the so-called 2,500 scientists the IPCC claims make up its "consensus," are really not scientists at all. Of that total, only 308 scientists reviewed the 2007 IPCC report. Many of them disagreed, some strongly so. Not surprisingly, all their comments were rejected and not included in the report. The remaining 2,192 so-called scientists come from all walks of life: politicians, government bureaucrats, social workers and, apparently, even a hotel manager. Fewer than 40 of the 308 scientists were generally supportive of the hypothesis, and fewer than five actually endorsed the report. Yet the report was hailed by the media as the consensus of thousands of scientists.

Let's put this in perspective. For every scientist who even slightly favored the IPCC conclusions, 792 signed the petition saying there is no convincing evidence that there is man-made catastrophic global warming. For every Ph.D. who endorsed the IPCC report, 1,800 signed the petition refuting it. If anything, there is a scientific consensus that man is not responsible for global warming. What did the mainstream media do with this potentially explosive story? They ignored it, as usual. Only the conservative media and FOX News highlighted this phenomenal story.

It seems that the mainstream media and, by extension, the people who depend on it for accurate news, would rather believe a lie than the truth. This realization led Dr. Ross McKittrick, who discredited the hockey-stick theory of the 2001 IPCC report, to lament, "We are now at the stage where mere facts, reason, and truth are powerless in the face of the global-warming propaganda."

It is a scary thought, but he is correct. Ignorance and propaganda now form the basis of our policy on climate change and on many other environmental issues. We are treading a dangerous path. ■

UPDATE, September 2009: The winter icesheets for both poles continues to grow. In Antarctica, the icecap is near record levels. The 2009 summer melt of the Arctic icecap is less than either 2008 or 2007, which is showing a continuing recovery of the icecap. The polar bears are doing just fine.—MC

SPRING 2009

TRACK of the CAT

Cougar politics and predator policy make people fair game. By Laura Schneberger

In New Mexico, 2008 could have been called the year of the cat. Hands-off predator management began showing consequences. A modest preventative lion control program in place since 1985 was scrapped by the state's game commission on October 2, thanks to pressure from Wild Earth Guardians. It was a bizarre ending to a scary year.

In May, Las Cruces residents were warned to be cautious because a lion had killed a poodle in the backyard of a suburban home. On May 17 in the Sandia Mountains, Jose Salazar Sr. and his wife Charlotte, 38 weeks pregnant, took their children on a hike at the popular Balsam Glade trail near the Sandia Peak Ski Basin. Charlotte and Jose held the younger children and walked along the trail, while five-year-old Jose Jr. trotted along a few yards ahead of them, a situation that later garnered criticism from animal activists. Charlotte suddenly heard her son yelling. She looked up and saw him lying across the trail with a big cat on top of him. "He was fighting, flailing his arms, while the cat was biting and clawing his back and shoulders," she says. "Then the cat grabbed him by the head and took off down the mountain."

The boy's father leaped into action, sprinting down the steep hillside while his wife screamed not to lose sight of the cat and their son. The chase ended about 300 feet down the slope when the cat lost its grip and stopped. Jose made a last leap at the animal.

"In just the instant when my son's scalp tore and the cat lost its grip, my husband got there," says Charlotte. The cat looked up, dodged and ran.

Thankfully, litte Jose was lying where the lion dropped him. His father scooped him up and ran up the mountain. Hoping to spare his wife from seeing their injured child whose scalp slid off the back of his head and lay on Jose's hand, the young father used his Sunday shirt and a pocket knife to bandage the wounds. The family regrouped, carried the children back down the trail and called 911.

© DAVE WATTS/TOM STACK & ASSOCIATES

The air ambulance met the couple at the Sandia Peak ski area parking lot, and the boy was airlifted to the hospital. The child's injuries resulted in several surgeries to clean and repair punctures to his arms, shoulder, neck and face, deep lacerations to his back, and reattachment of his scalp.

While the injured boy was in and out of surgery the following day, his mother at his bedside, Jose Sr. guided New Mexico Department of Game & Fish (G&F) officers along the trail to confirm the site of the attack. They located one of the child's boots near the scene. His other boot was found 30 feet downhill and appeared to be covered with saliva. It had numerous punctures. Jose was horrified to see that there were dozens of families exploring the exact same area. The trail was still open to the public.

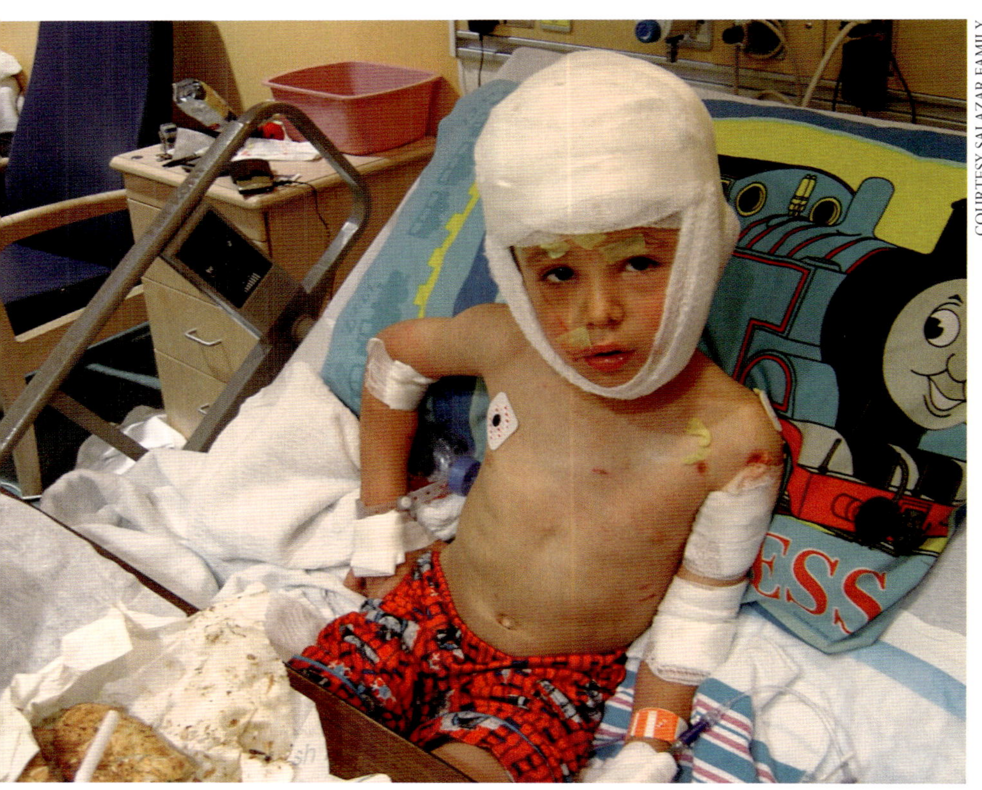

COURTESY SALAZAR FAMILY

Jose Salazar Jr. was saved by his father from the lion attack. Approximately 10 aggressive human/mountain lion encounters have occurred each year since the 1970s. More than 40 were confirmed in 2008.

With media on the scene, G&F officers reported the injuries the boy had suffered as serious scratches. Jose called his wife and, fearing a second attack on yet another family, they agreed to make a statement to the media. They felt the agency had downplayed the incident, and government officials publicly speculated that it could have been a small bear, despite the Salazars' insistence it was a cat.

The trail finally was closed three days later. Game officers collected little Jose's shirt, boots and hair from the attack site and sent them to the University of New Mexico for analysis. DNA samples extracted from the chewed boot were identified as human and *Puma concolor*—mountain lion. For several months the director of Game & Fish and several commissioners persisted in informing the public that the attack was not a confirmed lion attack until Charlotte made public the DNA test results. The lion involved in the incident has still not been captured.

Four weeks after little Jose's encounter, New Mexico had another attack, this one fatal. In mid-June the people of Piños Altos in southwest New Mexico were tying up phone lines comparing stories of lion sightings in their small community. The brother of 55-year-old Piños Altos resident Robert Nawojski was on the phone trying to reach him, but Robert wasn't answering. Walter Nawojski, who expected to meet his autistic brother for a hike later in the week, decided to report him missing.

On Friday, June 20, search and rescue teams, looking for Robert, encountered an aggressive lion near his home. They also found what seemed to be a human body buried in what lion hunters identify as a kill cache. G&F field officers and state police were called in. The lion was hit with some buckshot but escaped. Officers were able to examine and recover Robert's body from what family members say were five different caches. The Medical Examiner determined he had been killed June 16 or 17 by a large cat.

USDA Wildlife Services (WS), formerly known as Animal Damage Control, were called to the scene. Local officers with lion-hunting experience discovered more than one set of fresh tracks. Snares were set and a week after Robert's body was found, WS officers snared a lion. It was an average-sized adult male lion, about three years old and healthy, weighing approximately 125 pounds. It had four small holes in its back that appeared to be from buckshot. It was considered to be the lion at the scene where Robert's body was found. A second lion was caught several weeks later in the same area.

Unfortunately, Robert's death was not a wakeup call. State officials instead insinuated that Robert was somehow responsible for the attack because he was eccentric. Environmentalists say the encounters were due to the community being in the lion's territory. Piños Altos is an old mining town founded in 1859. In the town's 149-year history, no record exists of lions stalking humans until 2008.

In late September, 29-year-old Adam Wheat was hiking

Mountain lion

near the Taos ski lodge, when he was attacked by a lion. The lion hit Adam squarely in the chest, knocking him down. A physically fit young man, he was lucky enough to land with his hand on a rock and he pounded on the cat until it let him go. He hiked two miles, drove to his place of business and found someone to take him to the hospital. The lion that attacked Wheat was not found.

In the wake of the attack on their son, Charlotte and Jose Salazar learned that encounters had been on the rise across the state. Approximately 10 aggressive encounters had occurred each year since the '70s. More than 40 were confirmed in 2008.

Charlotte says, "It's disturbing that the New Mexico Game Commission is following the same tired recommendations of extreme animal rights and environmental organizations, which feel the solution is just more education for the public on how to live with and fend off mountain lions, instead of proactively and properly managing their growing numbers."

The lion control program scrapped on October 2 was called a "scorched earth cougar killing policy" by Wild Earth Guardians (WEG). The preventative lion control program began in January 1985. Its purpose was to find a cost-effective method to manage mountain lions that made a habit of preying on local livestock in Game Management Unit 30 located in southeastern New Mexico. The costs began at around $30,000 per year and by 2008 had increased to approximately $40,000 per year. The contractor was responsible for furnishing equipment, transportation, fuel and supplies. He was not provided state health insurance or retirement benefits.

Unit 30 borders the Guadalupe Mountains and Carlsbad Caverns national parks. The program targeted only excess problem lions that migrated from the wildlife refuges, forced out by more dominant cats. Ranchers in the region had clearly demonstrated confirmed depredations amounting to losses of 350 to 400 sheep per year, along with confirmed horse kills and aggressive human encounters. These resulted in severe personal and economic challenges to the communities.

On October 2, despite three and a half hours of testimony by both ranchers and the general public, the game commissioners voted overwhelmingly to stop the depredation control program. The Salazars attended the meeting to oppose any further restrictions on lion hunting and managed lion control in New Mexico. Like the rest of those who testified, they were ignored by game commissioners.

Locals don't have much confidence that game wardens will help the situation. Internal planning documents on depredation regulations rewritten in 2005 allow game managers to remove funding for predator management and replace it with more public education. This is supposed to include providing information on how the public can reduce the likelihood of conflicts between cougars and people.

Unfortunately, nobody has told the cougars about the education program. ■

FORESTRY

CONIFERS, ARAPAHOE NATIONAL FOREST, COLORADO

WINTER 1997

SOMETHING'S WRONG in LIBBY, MONTANA

And it's happening all across rural America where well-intended environmental laws have become battering rams in the hands of ecomaniacs. By Bruce Vincent

Something is wrong in Libby, Montana. Something's wrong in Arizona and New Mexico, in Georgia and Indiana, in eastern Oregon and southern Idaho. The target is rural America. The weapons are spotted owls, grizzlies, woodpeckers, bats, the Appalachian rattlesnake, grazing "reform," wetlands "protection" and mining law "reform." The casualties are the resource-providing families, communities, and cultures of the West and, tragically, the very environment society claims to be protecting.

All across rural America, families have for generations made their livelihoods by practicing good stewardship of the environment and by providing resources for humankind from the environment. These families (and our resource providing culture) are being displaced by a society that has been led to believe that the only way to protect our environment is to lock people out of it. Our natural resources are now being mismanaged by professional litigants in court instead of professionally managed by trained scientists and practitioners on the ground.

Whether you live in a farming, ranching, mining, logging or fishing community, the stories from rural America are strikingly similar. We share a culture built upon providing resources for society. We share a bond with and a respect of the earth and its blessings. In 1996 we also share some problems. I know most about timber towns, but our story could be from anywhere.

I am a fourth-generation logger from Libby—a small timber community in the mountains of northwest Montana. I graduated from high school in Libby and then went to college in Portland, Ore., in 1973. I logged during the summers to pay for school and met and married my wife PJ during one of those summers. After 10 years of school (slowed by marriage and having kids) I had a bachelor's degree in civil engineering and a master's in business administration—and an intense desire to raise our four children in the rural environment I had enjoyed as a kid. PJ and I moved back to Libby in February 1984 to join the family logging company.

Small family logging outfits are exactly the same as small family ranches or farms. It takes a husband and wife with both shoulders to the wheel to make it work—and for decades our family has done just that. Until four years ago our company employed 65 other families. We now employ just ourselves and four others. If the reason for this collapse in our family business was because we have just about whacked down the last trees in our area, as most Americans believe, then we would have to "cowboy up" and take our lickings for mismanagement of the forest. The truth is that we have more trees in northwestern Montana than we did in 1911. Unfortunately, some folks have a vision for our area that simply doesn't include the people who live here or human manipulation of the environment. Their vision is being incrementally implemented through a host of legislative, regulatory, and legal maneuvers and abuses carried out under the banner of "saving the planet."

My introduction to the quagmire of public land management was nine years ago when the U.S. Fish & Wildlife Service (FWS) announced a grizzly bear augmentation plan for the Cabinet-Yaak ecosystem. I knew what a grizzly bear

PHOTO COURTESY VINCENT FAMILY

The Vincent boys, from left, Bruce's brothers Scott, Steve and Will, father Vaughn, and son Chas.

was—it is part of the romance of living in Montana—but I didn't know what an ecosystem was or what augmentation meant so my wife and I attended a public hearing on the issue and our lives changed.

The people of Libby were told the government was going to artificially recover the area's existing grizzly bear population back to its historic level. When we asked how many bears have historically lived in our ecosystem, the FWS agent said, "We have no idea." When we asked what level they were going to recover to, the FWS agent said, "Well, we've at least got to have a viable genetic pool." When we asked how many grizzly bears constitutes a viable genetic pool, the FWS agent said, "We have no idea. But we think 90 or 120 bears would be a cool start." When we asked how many grizzly bears currently live in our area, the agent said, 'We have no idea. But we think there are four.'"

My wife, who is originally from San Jose, California, came unglued when she learned we had four bears in our backyard and the federal agency was going to add 116 more. When we discovered that our home was in the "human-grizzly conflict zone" we asked if we were going to be able to send our kids out to fish in the creek behind the house like I had my whole life. "Well, you might have to modify a few of your behaviors," the recovery coordinator responded. We were told to tie bells on our children when we send them out to play so that the bears would hear the bells and run the other way. We were told that if there's a problem with a bad bear then the FWS would deal with it. Do you know how they tell the difference between a good bear and a bad bear? Bad bears have bells in their poop!

© JOE MCDONALD/TOM STACK & ASSOCIATES

"When we asked how many bears have historically lived in our ecosystem the FWS agent said, "We have no idea."

Jasper Carlton from Boulder, Colorado, represents the Fund for Animals. Carlton came to Libby armed with the Endangered Species Act, 13 lawsuits, and a vision to turn Kootenai National Forest into a public park at the expense of the timber town's economy. We have federal laws that he is legally abusing to implement his vision—at a terrific cost to forest families and forests.

The Kootenai National Forest provides us with 70 percent of our economic base. We've been logging for 90 years but Jasper Carlton is pursuing his vision with vigor and the pile of litigation and appeals he and others set in motion paralyzed the Forest Service managers. By 1993 we had lost 60 percent of our timber economic base. The mill that used to employ 1,000 people closed October 13, 1993. The Louisiana-Pacific world-class, state-of-the-art small log processing plant also closed down because they have no wood despite the 10 to 14 billion board feet of dead lodgepole pines standing around Libby. The mills didn't close because the trees aren't there but because we can't access them—and that could prove harmful to the forest itself.

We live in a forest system that has millions of acres of lodgepole pine trees. For eons our lodgepole stands have matured, died, and regenerated through catastrophic fire loss every 80 to 120 years. The last time that forest recycling happened in Libby was in 1910 when three million acres burned up between Libby and Spokane in three days. That forest is 86 years old and has had a Northern Pine Beetle epidemic in it for 15 years. Further, due to fire suppression and a failure to "thin" the materials that should have burned up during the past 86 years we have what forest scientists call a fuel loading problem—500 tons per acre in some places. Since the normal load of fuel is around 50 tons, the next fire could burn so unnaturally hot that it will incinerate rather than regenerate. It could take centuries instead of decades to regenerate our children's forest because we are pretending that natural management after 100 years of human management will be benign.

Although something is wrong in Libby, we are hardly alone. It is clear that something is wrong when a nation is persuaded into believing that its economy is the enemy of the environment.

Something is wrong when a nation is persuaded into believing that groups like EarthFirst! have a right, maybe even a responsibility to do what they do. Their book, "Eco-Defense, a Field Guide to Monkey-Wrenching," is a recipe book on how to commit murder and mayhem against those of us who make our livings from the land. It has pictures, diagrams, and step by step instructions for blowing up our equipment. Worse yet, when these guys practice what they preach the media makes their actions sound like white-collar crimes to save the planet instead of the terrorism it really is.

There is a thin line between environmental sensitivity and environmental insanity—and in this nation we are crossing the line over and over again. Before we fix the mess that we are in we must first understand how we got here.

Americans became environmentally aware during the '60s when, for the first time, visions of the Cuyahoga River burning through downtown Cleveland, fish floating wrong-side up in Lake Erie, and Los Angeles air turning purple with pollution filled our living rooms. Television was the new home companion. With a heightened awareness of environmental dangers, our society empowered groups like The Audubon Society, Sierra Club, and Wilderness Society to help in the effort to stop the degradation of our planet. This movement helped to pass the Clean Air Act, Clean Water Act, Multiple Use Sustained Yield Act, Endangered

Species Act and other good, well-intended laws designed to take care of home. But something has happened to those laws and to the environmental movement.

Those people we empowered 30 years ago found out they could make a lot of money selling the under-informed urban population of this nation "The Big Lie"—that preservation equals conservation. For 30 years, America has been told that the only way to protect the environment is to preserve it, by locking man out. Those who have grown up on the land know we don't have to pick between preserve and destroy—we know that conservation lies between these two extremes. It is conservation that rural Americans depend upon for our livelihood and society depends on for its well-being. But America doesn't know what conservation is.

America is 85 percent urban, three generations from the farm and kids think meat and milk come from Safeway and lumber comes from Ernst. Their environmental information comes from television in 20-second sound bites, and this source is incredibly dangerous in complex issues like resource management.

© TOM STACK/TOM STACK & ASSOCIATES

For instance, America learned about the spotted owl not from a forester while on a walk in the forest—but from the evening news. The visual backdrop for a 20-second video presentation on the spotted owl is...the world's butt-ugliest clear-cut with the very last tree falling in it. Explaining the clear cut to America is some Neanderthal logger with knuckles dragging the ground and snoose driveling down his chin, and he says, "God I like to make stumps," and he's wearing an "Eat an Owl" T-shirt. Or they find a three-piece suit and tie from Weyerhaeuser and in front of a 30-story building in downtown Portland, the suit says, "America wants wood fiber, and by God, we provide it." That, sadly, is our story. The next 20-second sound bite is given by a yuppie standing in front of a babbling brook with a pristine mountain top behind him, and with a flag in one hand and a bald eagle in the other, he says, "All I want is clean air and water for my children." Then he quickly points out that those people in the last sound bite are greedy, corporate bastards intent on profit alone. And that's the end of the story.

Every industry—farming, ranching, mining, logging—is treated the same. We aren't perfect, but we're the best resource providers this nation or this planet has ever known and we work to improve our methods every day. The truth is, if we don't change the environmental steamroller that's destroying our resource communities, then we're going to be the greatest threat to the global environment through misguided lockup of our own. If we destroy the industries of this nation, we're going to be running them out of here and into the waiting arms of developing countries that have a need for cash and do not have the economic luxury to be environmentally sensitive. We can import softwood from Siberia and beef from Argentina and Brazil, but it will be produced by methods rural Americans abandoned 30 years ago. Becoming a nation that imports raw products and exports environmental havoc is not the environmental legacy I want to leave to my kids.

The environmental movement was timely and necessary in its formation, but it is now 30 years old—as are the laws and regulations it spawned. The movement has failed to mature beyond the crisis and conflict orientation that started it and continues to fund it. Now, the movement that began because of environmental policy failure at the ground level is causing real environmental failure at the ground level.

When I get tired, to get going again I think about what happened to my dad (and a whole generation of farmers, ranchers and miners) 30 years ago. When I was in the third grade my principal told my dad I had scored high on the Iowa basics test and if I ended up being a logger it was his fault. The message was clear to Dad: I was going to be too smart to be a dumb old logger like him. That night I overheard a conversation between my parents through paper-thin walls in which, for the first time, my dad looked down at his hands, saw calluses, saw dirt under his fingernails, and for the first time in his life was ashamed of the heritage that he had hoped to pass on to the fourth generation. A terrible mistake was made by my principal and by society at large when they perched a misplaced mantle of guilt on my father's shoulders.

My dad doesn't have two degrees hanging on the wall, but he has more sustainable environmental information in his head than he could have gotten with a doctorate from Yale. His education is based upon experiential knowledge from 40 years of working in the environment we are debating about. He knows how to take academic resource management theory and turn it into reality on the ground. I'm proud of my father, and if my children care to take the reins of resource providing from the fourth generation—after they go to college—they will do it with their head held high.

It is time that the leading export of our rural areas stops being our young, well-educated, well-rounded children. If we're going to figure out how to provide food, clothing and shelter for 10 billion people, then we bloody well better have our smart kids back on our farms, our ranches and in our logging jobs. It's going to take some pretty smart kids doing some pretty creative things to provide for that mass of humanity without destroying the planet.

America is tired of hearing only the doom and gloom of what is wrong and ready to start hearing about what can be right. We need to build a coalition of our resource cultures and tell America that there is a way to provide food, clothing and shelter without damage. We need to tell them that the current approach—pitting the consumer against the producer, the economy against the environment, jobs versus owls, crops versus clean water, public good versus private property—is not going to work. It is time for a new, more mature, more realistic environmental movement to step into the conflict and begin to find solutions, and that is us.

Our new environmentalism movement will only succeed if we remember three final truths. First, democracy works—but it is not a spectator sport. Second, when people lead, leaders follow. And third, the world is run by those who show up.

Ralph Waldo Emerson said that what lies before us and what lies behind us are of little consequence compared to what lies within us. And I think within us is still the pioneering spirit that built the country and will help secure our place in its future. We are not fighting for yesterday, but we are fighting for tomorrow with our cultural values intact. ■

FALL 2006

Forestry on the Brink

The great lie. By Tim Findley

Looking down from 30,000 feet, the great forests of the Northwest begin to roll away behind you from where the Rockies meet the plains. It is like crossing an infinite carpet of deeper and deeper greens etched faintly by shaded highways and roads, open only now and then to the clearings of towns or farming valleys. So immense is it as you are carried at hundreds of miles an hour toward the Pacific that many seeing it for the first time have been made to wonder at their own belief in the great lie.

The forests are not vanishing. The epic of vast untrodden wilderness cannot be gone. The mystery is still there, the lost sense of curving river meadows and deep, dark canyons cannot help but inspire imagination even from so great a height.

Yet the truth is surprising in its contradiction. If we could fly back in time to the 15th-century period of first European discoveries, our window view would seem little different—except to the trained eye able to recognize that there were not more trees in that presumed pristine time, but less. And that what we witness now after two most recent decades of mistruth is not a plan to recover the forests, but a misguided plot to murder them.

In the 21st century, we fly over a productive, ever renewable resource our own people are forbidden to harvest, and with each passing year we are losing more and more of the skills it would take to do so. The forest from on high seems so bounteous, but it is actually choking on itself in the thick clutter of unchecked growth. Clutched in impossible tangles, much of it suggests more of terror than tranquility. It is a fire waiting to happen. More in despair than peace is the dead dry evidence among the standing trees of insect infection killing at will.

We are wasting our forests, but it is not due to logging and harvesting. We are ruining our natural wealth with political arrogance and indifference too far out of reach to bring to earth.

"If the question is to thin or to burn," said a Forest Service official to *RANGE* in 2000 with a statement that stands today, "then the answer is burn."

Later that year on our imaginary flight you could have seen the smoke that covered hundreds of square miles in the Bitterroot fire of Montana and Idaho that still lies largely in infested ruin.

American forests have never been threatened by overlogging more than they are today by lies and mismanagement. ■

FALL 2006

ASH & SMOKE

We do not have too few trees. We have too many trees, of the wrong size, of the wrong type, and in the wrong places. By Bruce Vincent

In 1998, I wrote a story for *RANGE* called "Something's Wrong In Libby, Montana," which discussed the possible collapse of the forest-management culture in our rural public-land-dependent towns in the West. What has happened since that article was printed?

The numbers are sobering. According to Paul Ehringer & Associates of Eugene, Oregon, 430 sawmills have closed in the West since 1988. The job losses in the milling and logging industries exceed 50,000.

BITTERROOT NATIONAL FOREST, AUG. 6, 2000. COURTESY JOHN MCCOLGAN

Where I live in Lincoln County, Montana, (population 18,000) we've lost five sawmills and more than 1,500 timber jobs. If the collapse is due to forest mismanagement, and/or the evening newscasts have been correct—"We're running out of trees"—then the collapse would be easier to stomach.

The real reason for the collapse of public timberland management in the West is not a lack of trees, but a lack of understanding. Will Rogers was right when he said: "It ain't what you don't know that's a problem. It's what you know that ain't so that's a problem." When it comes to forest management, the public knows a lot that ain't so, and that lack of understanding is saving our forests and forest communities to death.

Many of the trees we enjoy today should have been killed by fires during the last 100 years. But with the advent of Smokey the Bear in the early 1900s, we minimized the impact of fire in our ecosystems. We now know this was a mistake. We should let fires burn the forest a bit at a time. After nearly a century of fire suppression, we now have a mammoth "fuel loading" problem.

Contrary to popular opinion, we do not have too few trees. We have too many trees of the wrong size, of the wrong type, and in the wrong places. When today's forests catch fire, they burn as never before because the fuel load of dead and down timber is, in many places, over 500 percent of normal. The fires have way too much fuel to burn. Each summer, catastrophically hot forest fires engulf and consume vast watersheds of overstocked and overstressed trees.

None of this is news. The General Accounting Office identified the problem in 1990. It reported that there were over 190 million acres of forestland in the West where the biggest ecological threat is a single wildfire. These unnaturally hot blazes race across the landscape, burning homes, threatening communities, toasting wildlife and habitat, pulverizing watersheds and boiling streams.

There is a better way. We have the technology to do fuel-reduction projects that would let us remove some of this fuel, take the chosen trees to wood-processing plants in our communities, turn these "tubes of carbon" into consumable products for a consuming society, and then reintroduce fire into our fuel-reduced ecosystem.

Unfortunately, the environmental-conflict industry has spent the last decade litigating to stop this human intervention and force our rural communities into allowing nature to take its destructive course.

Thankfully, the policy discussion of forest management has changed in the last several years. It changed when tens of thousands of Southern Californians stood on the roofs of their million-dollar homes with six-dollar hoses trying to fight the blazes roaring out of their million-dollar viewsheds. The policy discussion changed because the residents of Arizona, Colorado, Oregon and California have all witnessed the largest fires in their histories in the last five years and, as the old song goes, "We've only just begun."

With the reality of natural management burning down to the edges of the San Bernardino Airport, President Bush's Healthy Forest Initiative passed both chambers of Congress and was signed into law in 2003. Unfortunately, attempts to implement this commonsense legislation have faced lawsuits from the professional litigants within the environmental-conflict industry. Very little positive action has happened in the forest near communities like those in

FOREST PHOTOS © DAVE SKINNER. INSET: JIM PETERSEN.

LEFT: Mortality was near 100 percent in this lodgepole pine beetle infestation near Elk City in northern Idaho's Nez Percé National Forest, yet nothing was salvaged or replanted because environmental litigants blocked every Forest Service attempt to repair nature's wrath. INSET: Pine beetle. ABOVE: This ponderosa pine thinning on private land in eastern Oregon is an excellent example of the kind of thinning work so desperately needed in federal forests in the interior West.

northwest Montana. For many, such as those employed at the Owens & Hurst Mill in Eureka, implementation was too late.

Will the timber culture ever return to Libby? I think so, but reality is a relentless dictator. The fact is that the Kootenai National Forest has 2.5 million acres of trees. Each year, this forest grows 492 million board feet of wood while 300 million board feet of timber dies due to windthrow, insects and disease. If we do not remove some of this fuel, we are simply stacking 300 million board feet of firewood in our forest, in our watersheds, around our communities and around our homes.

If we have not learned what science is telling us before that time, then possibly from the ashes will arise some sanity that will not ignore the realities of nature or the needs of humanity. Perhaps we will recognize the need to provide for our domestic consumption of wood fiber rather than importing 65 percent of our wood-fiber needs from other nations with less environmental sensitivity than our own. Perhaps we will see a new generation of forest stewards move back into our area with the courage to invest in the multimillion-dollar machinery necessary to implement modern forest-management theory with the support of society rather than its scorn.

Perhaps. But if society waits for the realities of ash and smoke to dictate a positive step toward sanity in forest management, then our forest ecosystems and our forest social and economic systems will continue to pay a terrible price. ■

NOTES from an old STUMP JUMPER

Requiem. By Jim Hurst

I look out my office window at a site similar to a bombed-out munitiions factory in World War II Germany and I have to ask myself, "What went wrong?" Seeing a once productive and efficient mill destroyed by the cutting torches of dismantlers is a gruesome sight witnessed far too often in rural communities adjacent to our national forests.

In our case what went wrong is the fact that we had no control over our own destiny and no help from Washington. Environmental groups, many funded by green trusts and foundations, torpedoed the timber program on the Kootenai National Forest. Our case is not unique. It illustrates what happens when outsiders make decisions and we are powerless to intervene. Rural dwellers who own private property should also beware, as government takings "for the good of the nation" will most likely accelerate in the coming years.

Rural Americans must organize or face oblivion. How it'll be done and who does it remains to be seen. One thing I know is that there is no room for exremists, self-promoters or large egoes. Reasonable people with strength in numbers can effect positive change for rural Americans. That's the rack I'm willing to hang my hat on. ■

FALL 2006

TREES ARE THE ANSWER

A world without forests is as unthinkable as a day without wood. By Patrick Moore, Ph.D.

Without a doubt, wood is the most renewable material used to build and maintain our civilization. Forestry is the most sustainable of all the primary industries. This should give wood a lot of green ecopoints in the environmental movement's ledger.

Unfortunately, this doesn't seem to be the case. Greenpeace has gone before the U.N.'s InterGovernmental Panel on Forests, calling on countries to reduce the amount of wood they use and to adopt "environmentally appropriate substitutes" instead. No list of substitutes is provided. The Sierra Club is calling for "zero cut" and an end to all commercial forestry on federal public lands in the United States. The Rainforest Action Network wants a 75 percent reduction in wood use in North America by the year 2015. I think it is fair to summarize this approach as "cut fewer trees, use less wood."

It is my firm belief, as a lifelong environmentalist and ecologist, that this is an anti-environmental policy. Putting aside, for a moment, the importance of forestry for our economy and communities on purely environmental grounds, the policy of use-less-wood is anti-environmental.

Why is this the case?

Twenty-five percent of all the wood used in the world is for building things such as houses and furniture. Every available substitute is nonrenewable and requires a great deal more energy consumption to produce. That is because wood is produced in a factory called the forest by renewable solar energy. Wood is essentially the material embodiment of solar energy. Nonrenewable building materials such as steel, cement, and plastic must be produced in real factories such as steel mills, cement works, and oil refineries. This usually requires large inputs of fossil fuels, inevitably resulting in high carbon-dioxide emissions. So, for 70 percent of the wood used each year for energy and building, switching to substitutes nearly always results in increased carbon-dioxide emissions, contrary to climate-change policy.

Fifteen percent of the wood harvested is used to manufacture pulp and paper mainly for printing, packaging, and sanitary purposes. Fully half of this wood is derived from the wastes from sawmills, which produce the solid wood products for building. Most of the remaining supply is from tree plantations, many of which are established on land that was previously cleared for agriculture. So even if we did stop using wood to make pulp and paper, it would not have the effect of "saving" many forests.

I have spent the last 15 years trying to understand the relationship between forestry and the environment, to separate fact from fiction, myth from reality. Since 1991 I have chaired the Sustainable Forestry Committee of the Forest Alliance of British Columbia. The general public is being given the impression, by supposedly reputable sources such

Planted Douglas fir seedlings, Port Gamble, Washington.

New growth on clear-cut, southern Oregon.

as *The New York Times* and *National Geographic*, that forestry is a major cause of species extinction when there is actually no evidence to support that position.

Forestry seldom, if ever, causes species to become extinct. We tend to think that forests need our help to recover after destruction, whether by fire or logging. This is not the case. Forests have been recovering by themselves, without any assistance, from fires, volcanoes, landslides, floods and ice ages, ever since forests began more than 350 million years ago.

Consider the fact that 10,000 years ago all Canada and Russia were covered by a huge sheet of ice, under which nothing lived, certainly not trees. Today, Canada and Russia account for 30 percent of all the forests on earth, grown back from bare rock. Go to Alaska where the glaciers are retreating due to the present warming trend, and you will see that from the moment the rocks are laid bare to the sun, it is only 80 years until a thriving new ecosystem is growing there, including young trees.

Fire has always been the main cause of forest destruction, or "disturbance" as ecologists like to call it in order to use a more neutral term. But fire is natural, we are told, and does not destroy the forest ecosystem like logging, which is unnatural. Nature never comes with logging trucks and takes the trees away.

All kinds of rhetoric are used to give the impression that logging is somehow fundamentally different from other forms of forest disturbance. There is no truth to this. It is true that logging is different from fire, but fire is also very different from a volcano, which in turn is very different from an ice age. In fact, no two fires are ever the same. These are differences of degree, however, not kind. Forests are just as capable of recovering from destruction by logging as they are from any other form of disturbance. All that is necessary for renewal is that the disturbance is ended: the fire is out, the volcano stops erupting, the ice retreats, or the loggers go back down the road and allow the forest to begin growing back, which it will begin to do almost immediately.

In the context of my experience I say: "Give me an acre of land anywhere on earth, tell me to grow something there with which I can make paper, which would also be best for biodiversity, and I will plant trees every single time, without exception."

I believe that trees are the answer to many questions about our future on earth. These include: How can we best advance to a more sustainable economy based on renewable fuels and materials? How can we improve literacy and sanitation in developing countries while reversing deforestation and protecting wildlife at the same time? How can we reduce the amount of greenhouse gases emitted to the atmosphere, carbon dioxide in particular? How can we increase the amount of land that will support a greater diversity of species? How can we help prevent soil erosion and provide clean air and water? How can we make this world more beautiful and green?

© DAVE SKINNER

Little remains in the devastating aftermath of the 500,000-acre Biscuit Fire on southern Oregon's Siskiyou National Forest. Less than one percent of the commercial timber killed by the 2002 fire has been salvaged. The rest has been tied up in litigation or declared off-limits to salvage.

The answer is: By growing more trees and using more wood as a substitute for nonrenewable fossil fuels and materials such as steel, concrete and plastic, and as paper products for printing, packaging, and sanitation.

The fact is, a world without forests is as unthinkable as a day without wood. And it's time that politicians, environmentalists, foresters, teachers, journalists and the general public got that balance right. Because we must get it right if we are going to achieve sustainability in the 21st century.

May the forest be with you. ■

TAKINGS

KLAMATH BASIN, OREGON © LARRY TURNER

WINTER 1999

A ROAD RUNS THROUGH IT

The feds seem to be using a tiny town surrounded by wilderness to make a point. But what is the point?
By Tim Findley

It was truly a fine fish, a firm 24 inches of glorious Lahontan cutthroat brought up from somewhere midway down in the cold azure depths of Pyramid Lake.

All the others on the boat—the Paiute game wardens and the U.S. Fish & Wildlife Service (FWS) honchos and Bruce Babbitt's friends—agreed it was a nice catch, worthy almost of some of the trophies taken here years ago before the Paiute depleted their own fishery. They smiled and took pictures and shook the boss's hand after the Interior secretary ceremoniously returned his prize to its native waters.

As usual, though, it was Babbitt himself who insisted on having the last, and most flamboyant, words on his achievement. "Nevada has a flashy side. So does the Lahontan. It seems to say to the brown desert: 'Look here! See my silver sequins, my pink pinstripes! Try to top that!'" Babbitt gushed in a letter to the *Reno Gazette-Journal,* recalling the moment and thanking all who made it possible. It had helped convince him, he said, that "the economy is the environment" and that the future of the West lies in providing more such experiences for hordes of Americans "hungry for the outdoors."

ILLUSTRATION © JOHN BARDWELL

The letter, and variations of it repeated all over the West in 1998 by the Interior secretary, was part of what Jamie Mills of the Newlands Water Protective Association called Babbitt's summerlong "Sermon On The Trout."

Bruce Babbitt, so they say in Washington, is back. He sulked awhile and even thought about quitting after the still-unsettled scolding he took from Congress late in 1998 over campaign funding influences. But Babbitt's people say he has put all that behind him and is once again on the trail of feeding the nation's need for an environment unsullied by such "mistakes" as dams and irrigation districts.

He wrote of hearing "cash registers ring with angling dollars," and of restaurants filled with fishermen, "linked by the magic of water," all apart from such outworn uses as "an aging concrete plug called Derby [irrigation diversion] Dam" on the Truckee River.

Hungry though they may be, however, it will be some time yet before Babbitt's FWS will allow the flocking fishermen to actually feed themselves on the officially threatened Lahontan cutthroat. And while Babbitt roved around the Northwest last summer swinging sledgehammers at small dams, FWS was doing its own part to make things a little more miserable for people who actually do earn a living in the outdoors.

Nowhere was that more apparent than alongside the ankle-deep stream of the Jarbidge River in northeast Nevada. The Jarbidge has its moments, especially in spring after a heavy winter when the runoff fills the narrow aspen canyons near its headwaters and sends it flushing rocks, limbs, logs and all in a headlong rush down to the Bruneau and on through rolling prairies of southern Idaho until it finally links up with the great Snake River on its way to the Pacific. It's that notable descendency that gives Nevada's Jarbidge the respectable title of being part of a federally recognized "navigable" waterway, even if most years it's more like the sort of river Mark Twain used to say you needed to jump across three or four times before getting thirsty enough to drink it dry.

What the Jarbidge really is in its Nevada origin is a portrait-pretty little trout stream worthy of an angler's ode to spiritual tranquility. There's maybe just one thing wrong with its movie-star good looks—a road runs right by it.

Not a big, well-traveled road with asphalt lanes and guard-railed curves. Just a winding lane and a half of rocky dirt highway in its best places, and a little less than that where it cuts off into South Canyon on its way up to the wilderness area. It's in that stretch of road used for recreation and fire control where the federal government, with the help of strong environmentalist pressure, has decided to expand its reach by halting repairs to the flood-damaged road in the name of the newly endangered bull trout.

Otis Tipton, the chubby-cheeked supervisor of road maintenance in this part of Elko County, seems like a nice friendly boy a lot younger than he really is, and he still

PHOTOS © TIM FINDLEY

Otis Tipton, the supervisor of road maintenance for Jarbidge, Nevada, still seems hurt that his careful crossing of the Jarbidge River on a rented bulldozer ended up in an infamous September "grilling." Tipton, center, was scolded by the feds but backed by just about everyone in town. Below: *Jack Creechley, John Williams and John Berndt are standing in the middle of the old mining town. They helped Otis move trout by hand out of old flood-made pools in the Jarbidge River, before he made the crossing in the rented bulldozer. They didn't see any bull trout.*

looks almost personally hurt by it all, like a kid who didn't mean to step on the puppy. Tipton went to a lot of trouble making sure the bulldozer he rented was extra clean. He checked and double-checked to make sure there were no leaks of oil or gas or grease before he drove it across the river—and only through the water that one time to get around the Forest Service roadblock.

But that did it, the stern people from FWS say. Tipton got the water muddy and probably threatened the bull trout with extinction, they said. And the bottom line is, he didn't even apply for a "rolling stock" permit before he went ahead and did it.

The folks from Nevada's Division of Environmental Protection questioned Tipton pretty hard about that, making him take them right back to the site and explain himself in front of God, bureaucrats, and very nearly the entire town of Jarbidge, most of whom turned out for the September grilling of Tipton in South Canyon.

The townspeople, all 65 of them in the summer population, may confidently be said to be completely on the side of Tipton in this dispute, and in some ways just as confused by all the trouble. Since the roadwork happened July 22, somebody from the Sierra Club has put a message on its Internet site calling Elko County officials "elected thugs." Somebody else has claimed that Jarbidge is trying to rekindle the whole Sagebrush Rebellion, and one TV report even suggested that the townsfolk in Jarbidge might have links to the Montana militia.

Jarbidge Justice of the Peace John Williams blinks at that one and sticks his thumbs in the bib of his blue-striped railroad coveralls. "Bull trout," he says with no enigma. "Always did think they were good eatin.'"

It was a few fortunately farsighted individuals like the 74-year-old Williams who probably saved the uniquely treasured town of Jarbidge from going to the ghosts after all the mines finally shut down in the 1930s. From then on, there really wasn't much reason other than pure love of the place to stay in the tiny town with its old log cabins and porch-covered wood sidewalks. You can still find western relics like it elsewhere in places such as Silverton or Kellogg, or Angels Camp or Virginia City. But Jarbidge is about the only natural town of its type left that is still at least 100 miles on a mostly dirt road in either direction from anyplace serious enough to expect daily mail service. Mail still only makes it to the post office in Jarbidge three times a week, less sometimes in the winter. Casual tourists don't know about the place, and probably couldn't find it unless they seriously studied a map and had plenty of patience to keep looking beyond an attention-getting 8,500-foot mountain pass. Fishermen, hunters and some true lovers of the West the way it was know about Jarbidge. Up to now, that has worked out just fine for the family-sized locals lucky enough to live there, cradled in a canyon like a lost, but living, memory.

Just after Memorial Day in 1995, the Jarbidge busted loose with one of those rare, rock-throwing floods they call "events." It rampaged down the canyon, roaring through several prepared camp and picnic sites and taking out a big chunk of South Canyon road alongside the fork they call Pine Creek. Some two miles down from the trailhead leading into the federal wilderness area, the Forest Service dropped two big logs across the road and nailed on a sign declaring it closed.

Up until then, since at least 1909, when the Elkoro Mining Company was making this the most active gold region in the state, it was understood that there was mutual agreement over it being a county road through federally administered public land. After the flood, Elko County sought state funds to help repair the road, but was given a low priority in relief money needed elsewhere in the state. Generously, the Forest Service offered to employ federal

Fixing the road by hand, just above the pretty little Jarbidge River.

emergency funds to pay for the repairs to the road along with the campsites. Elko County was happy to accept the offer.

But as the Forest Service stalled on its promise through the rest of that year, and on past the next, and the next, it began to become apparent that something else was up on the Jarbidge.

In 1994, the Alliance for the Wild Rockies, based in Missoula, Montana, had filed a lawsuit to force listing the bull trout as threatened or endangered all the way from Puget Sound to the extreme of its range and its only known refuge on the rim of Nevada's Great Basin—the Jarbidge. The real object of the environmentalists was to use the bull trout in the same way the spotted owl had been used to successfully halt logging in the Pacific Northwest.

By March 1998, Nevada at least had agreed to limit the bull as a catch-and-release threatened species on the Jarbidge. But the demands to save the fish from habitat degradation caused by logging, dam building, overfishing and the introduction of nonnative species wasn't getting anywhere quickly with the feds until Otis Tipton at last fired up that spanking clean Cat last July.

It was really only a desperate and emergency move that caused him to do it, Elko County officials testified later. After stalling for three years, the Forest Service let it be known that it had no intention of repairing the road, or the campsites either. Where it had dropped its log roadblock amounted to at least a three-mile extension of the hikers-only wilderness area. "It was either fix it ourselves, or lose the road," said an attorney for the county.

Beyond just the obvious need of the road for fire, and even flood protection, the high-water spring of '95 had overwhelmed campsites and wiped out relief stations. Jack Creechley and his wife Dot own the Outdoor Inn, the town's main business and general social center. Jack wasn't the first to notice streamers of toilet paper hanging from some trees as the Forest Service clenched, summer after summer. Like it or not, the wilderness was getting closer to the little town.

That Tipton neglected to acquire the necessary rolling-stock permit for the work from state environmental officials was only something overlooked in the emergency to get it done before another winter. But just one day after he started his work, the FWS demanded the state issue a cease-and-desist order against Elko County and consider thousands of dollars in penalties for what it said was serious sedimentation of the river caused by Tipton's rented bulldozer. To his amazement, the feds even accused Tipton of changing the natural stream channel by attempting to repair the washout.

It was so serious FWS was moved to declare an emergency and immediately list the bull trout as endangered in the Jarbidge. It's a fine of $1,000 to be caught bothering one, and possible criminal penalties of jail time and up to $100,000 for continuing to mess with the bull.

As it happened, Jack Creechley, along with John Williams and some other folks from town, had gone up to watch Tipton work that day and had even moved some trout—none of them bulls—out of the old flood-made pools and back into the main stream. It was about as radical an act as they've ever done, unless you count hauling that huge oak back bar all the way up from the Golden Nugget in Las Vegas to the Outdoor Inn a decade or so ago.

Jack Klippenstein, a retired heavy equipment operator from Reno who has been fishing along the Jarbidge since 1971, testified that he missed all the morning action with the bulldozer by taking the 10-minute drive into town. When he got back to his campsite below the work later that afternoon, he said, the water was clear as ever and he caught his five-fish limit for supper—none of them bull trout. "It didn't hurt or help the river," Klippenstein said in a puzzled way at all the trouble. "It helped the road, but it didn't hurt the river or the fish."

Tipton wasn't able to get much done anyway before he was ordered to stop, but what he did in a couple of hundred yards served to halt further erosion along the washout. It is true, however, that no one has actually seen a bull trout there since.

Not, maybe, that there really aren't any bull trout there. Williams, who sometimes exaggerates, especially about fishing, insists he's caught one now and then on worms over the last half century. But fly-fishing Creechley never has in nearly 30 years, and neither has anybody else he knows—except maybe John Williams.

The bull is actually a char that eats other little trout. Its predatory nature, in fact, once helped establish a bounty on catching them. But the furious opponents of the roadwork, led most lately by Trout Unlimited and Friends of the Swan, insist the pink-spotted bull is likely to be the biggest and best fish caught in streams like the Jarbidge. And, of course, the one most imperiled by any attempts to do so, intentional or not.

Tony Lesperance, Elko County commissioner, who has long been known not to mind much being called a rebel when it comes to dealings with the federal government, said, "They can list the damn moon if they want to, we're going ahead with opening up the road because the county has its police powers."

That was about the same opinion come to by the Nevada Environmental Commission. Its chairman and state engineer Mike Turnipseed said he was "fed up" with all the wasted time. "This is Nevada," he said. "We're Nevadans and this is our resource."

© TIM FINDLEY

They called it the Liberty Rock, and on July 4, 2000, more than 100 strong men pulled the Forest Service's last obstacle from South Canyon Road, reclaiming it for the people of Elko County.

After hearing all the evidence and interviewing Tipton again both at the site and in Elko, Turnipseed's commission came to the conclusion that Tipton should have gotten a rolling-stock permit, but that he meant no harm by forgetting it, and that he actually did more good than harm to the river by returning it to its natural channel. They directed the county to apply for a state permit immediately and maybe pay a token fine before getting on with the rest of the work.

The state environmental commissioners are aware, however, that their decision will simply, as Turnipseed put it, "get us off the hook." The real battle is yet to come, because now the Forest Service claims it, not Elko County, owns the road, and it's backed up by Trout Unlimited and others who have written letters proclaiming the road can't be fixed without violating the law that protects the endangered bull. Bruce Babbitt, wandering around the West with a sledgehammer last summer, at one point offered to personally mediate the dispute. By then, officials in Elko County and people in Jarbidge in particular knew a lot better than to bite on that bait.

Late in August, in a stuffy little room at the opposite end of the Great Basin, FWS officials conceded to a crowded gathering of Lahontan Valley farmers what has seemed obvious to the farmers for years—that the cui-ui sucker fish in Pyramid Lake is not nearly so endangered as the feds originally thought when they made it the first finny creature on the list in 1966.

In fact, the FWS representatives admitted their initial "modeling" of the cui-ui's problems and the way to solve them were all wrong. The fish lives longer than they thought—a spawning female was found to be 51 years old. The initial count of them was not accurate—somebody forgot that sucker fish travel along the bottom while they were counting fish nearer the surface. And it turns out that thousands of the fish were being killed by the methods of chutes and ladders imposed by the government to save them.

Did that mean the cui-ui, chief cause of all the trouble for some 30 years between Pyramid Lake Paiutes and the farmers, was no longer "endangered"? Far to the contrary. Numbers of the fish, past or present, have little to do with it, FWS people said. The cui-ui was not listed as endangered because of any scientific evidence, they admitted. It was "nominated" for its cultural importance to the Paiute. And no matter what new modeling might show, the sucker will remain on the endangered species list for at least another five years until it can be determined for certain that it is likely to survive into the 22nd century.

Like the cui-ui, the bull trout was nominated in the Jarbidge as an emergency measure to save its existence, whether or not local folks might agree that it really needed saving or was even there at all.

Bruce Babbitt, in his inspired letter to the *Reno Gazette-Journal* last summer, expressed the feelings of many in such disputes. "I reeled in a bit of the New West," he expounded. "What I saw, in the technicolor swirl of that Lahontan cutthroat, was a deepening iridescence, the strengthening pulse of a Great Basin ecosystem on the mend."

Such purple prose from the secretary, back from his own near extinction. Not so easily spoken, however, in Jarbidge, where county authorities concede it is unlikely that the South Pass road can be fixed again this year before the snow flies. ■

UPDATE: Jarbidge is the prettiest town in the Silver State. It celebrated its centennial in August 2009 with crowds brought to the remote wilderness village in part by years of attempts by federal authorities and environmental activists to close roads to the town. It had a standby army of supporters all over the nation since the 2001 federal attempt.

WINTER 2001

The GREAT AMERICAN LAND GRAB

The Clinton administration's lands-locked legacy may be undone before it is even fully recognized as a sinister plan to manipulate the population and the economy of the United States. By Tim Findley

At the beginning of the Clinton administration in 1993, the U.S. government owned more than 630 million acres of the nation's landmass, most of it west of the Rockies. Combined with state-owned land, military bases and Indian reservations, it represented the largest percentage of government-controlled property of any non-Communist country in the world, including Russia.

Although challenged in the 1970s by the so-called Sagebrush Rebellion, most in the West remained satisfied with the multiple use of federal land that allowed production and profit from timber, mining and grazing under federal management. Because most of the land remained remote, but open to recreation, "ownership" was seldom at issue among political leaders or the generally urban populations on the coasts.

"Environmentalism" had been steadily rising as a cause among urban activists since it was inherited as part of the general mistrust of the industrial establishment in the 1960s. By the late 1980s, aided by the influx of funding from foundations that usually derived their wealth from the underpinnings of the establishment itself, the cause of protecting the environment from pollution and destruction had become a morally based crusade with detractors limited to questioning some methods but seldom the cause itself.

In 1990, the Sierra Club, using Wisconsin-based research, identified what would become the icon of the movement and its inspiration in the use of litigation. The "endangered" northern spotted owl rapidly emerged as the surrogate species for halting logging on federal properties, first among "old-growth" forests in California, and eventually extending to at least 70 percent of forests throughout the West previously open to harvest.

Newly elected President Bill Clinton and Vice President Al Gore acknowledged the economic impact of this on the timber industry in a series of summit meetings that promised, but never delivered on, a new partnership that would allow timber harvesting to continue under terms that were more environmentally cautious.

Between the promises made at those summit meetings and the summer of 2000, more than 300 timber mills were closed in the northwestern states alone, some at the cost of economic catastrophe to entire towns. At least 130,000 people with jobs related to the timber industry were temporarily or permanently put out of work, effectively devastating an industry worth some $4 billion to the national economy.

More importantly, the use of surrogate species, like the spotted owl, to establish zones of critical habitat made the Endangered Species Act the most powerful tool of executive authority in restricting land use. Since 1990, timber harvest on federal land has declined from 12 billion board feet a year to barely 2.5 billion board feet in 2000.

In 1990, 596 species were listed as threatened or endangered in the United States. By 1999, the list had grown to 1,205. In the West alone, critical habitat for those species is estimated to extend over more than 80 million acres. At the same time, active reintroduction of predatory species, primarily wolves and grizzly bears, was a federal priority in at least four western states. Recovery of both species proved so rapid that the endangered status of both is being reconsidered.

Established on record for its strong environmental stance by Vice President Gore's campaign-conscious book, "Earth in the Balance" (1992), the Clinton administration put aside its own choice of Bill Richardson as secretary of Interior to accept the recommendation of the intimidating League of Conservation Voters (LCV) to name its president and former Arizona Gov. Bruce Babbitt to the job.

Babbitt, himself a failed presidential candidate in 1988 and grandson to an Arizona cattle baron, expressed his contempt for western livestock producers and vowed to the LCV, "We must identify our enemies and drive them into oblivion." He set upon a course aimed at revising and limiting the use of federal land for grazing purposes, while at the same time demanding new restrictions on mining and resource exploration on federal properties. Thwarted by congressional resistance to his arbitrary revisions of law and regulations, Babbitt bluntly announced he would avoid Congress and carry out his program by executive authority.

Primarily due to allotment reductions and wilderness expansion, livestock production on public lands in the West has declined by more than 20 percent under the Clinton administration. By the end of his first term in office, Clinton claimed to have established an unparalleled record in the preservation and protection of the environment. The 1996 report of the Department of Interior hailed new acquisition or extended control over more than 141 million acres, most of it in the West. It amounts to an area roughly the size of West Virginia and was added to the more than one million square miles of the West already in federal ownership.

Although those acquisitions were accomplished largely in piecemeal steps often involving wetlands and forest habitats, the Clinton administration took an unprecedented campaign advantage in 1996 by using the 1906 Antiquities Act to declare 1.7 million acres of Utah's Grand Staircase-Escalante a National Heritage Site, restricted from any exploitative use, including extraction of what is thought to be one of only two deposits of the most valuable low-sulfur coal in the world. The other deposit in China is being mined by an Indonesian company that was a contributor to the Clinton campaign. In 1999 alone, the federal government removed more than 2.3 million acres from access to mineral exploration. These withdrawal notices were taken in spite of congressional refusal to grant Babbitt's demand to revise mining laws.

THE WEST IN 2001: SHRINKING PRIVATE LANDS AND EXPANDING WILDERNESS HABITAT. "GROPING OUR WAY BACK TO 1492?" OR IS IT SOMETHING CLOSER TO GEORGE ORWELL'S "1984"?

The heritage-site declaration of the Grand Staircase was done without consultation with or notification to any elected representative in the state of Utah, including its two U.S. senators. Following his reelection, President Clinton once again named Babbitt as his secretary of the Interior and entrusted him with what was to become the most intense and controversial period of federal expansion of control over U.S. lands in history.

While millions of acres of lands in the West were either added to federal ownership or further restricted in their use, only one significant region was divested of federal ownership. That was the Elk Hills Naval Oil Reserve in California, a 47,000-acre site with a daily production of 60,000 barrels of oil and 400 million cubic feet of natural gas, previously kept in strategic reserve. In 1997, under the guidance of Vice President Al Gore, Elk Hills was sold by sealed bid to Occidental Petroleum Corporation for $3.65 billion in cash. It was the largest privatization of federal land in U.S. history. The vice president's father and former U.S. senator, Al Gore Sr., was, prior to his death in 1998, the vice president of Occidental. The Gore family is a significant stockholder in the company.

At the time of the Elk Hills sale, Patricia Fry Godley, U.S. Department of Energy assistant secretary, said, "This sale helps get the government out of the oil and gas business." Consumer costs for gasoline and heating fuel reached record prices in the United States within two years of the transaction, and U.S. Naval authorities expressed concern about shortages of fuel reserves for military operations.

Despite promises of "partnership in stewardship" promoted by Babbitt's Interior Department, the second term witnessed even further restrictions on multiple use of federal lands in the West and was marked by Babbitt's own defiance of congressional or legislative authority in policy. "The clock is ticking," Babbitt told one congressional committee in warning that he would not wait for their approval for expanded federal control.

Regardless of local opposition, eight more heritage sites were declared, with the vice president given the duty and personal recognition for his own presidential campaign by announcing the last four during a campaign stop in Washington state. Total acquisition in those lands amounted to at least 10 million acres, but Babbitt made clear that his recommendation to the president would include at least four more sites. The administration also put forward legislation seeking at least $1 billion in funding for future federal-land acquisition.

Throughout this time, since logging was halted by litigation in the 1990s, forest experts within the government itself had repeatedly warned that the ban on harvesting even dead or diseased timber was leading to a potential disaster in 40 million acres of federal forests overgrown and overloaded in tinder-dry fuels.

The first major fire of 2000 was touched off by the federal government itself in an attempt to eliminate some of this fuel. The Park Service burned over 50,000 acres near Los Alamos, New Mexico, and destroyed 260 private homes. The superintendent in charge was removed from his job but later given a new post at higher pay overseeing the nearly adjacent 96,000-acre Baca Ranch which the federal government acquired earlier this year at a price of $101 million. This amount is estimated by private analysis to be twice the actual value of the land.

When lightning-sparked fires broke out in the summer of 2000 in the Bitterroot National Forest and many other parts of Montana, and in even greater stretches of Idaho, Secretary Babbitt blamed it on "the worst drought since the 1930s," although that was not an accurate statement of conditions. Despite valiant and heroic work by federal firefighters and others, more than six million acres were consumed in the West in the most disastrous fire season in more than 75 years.

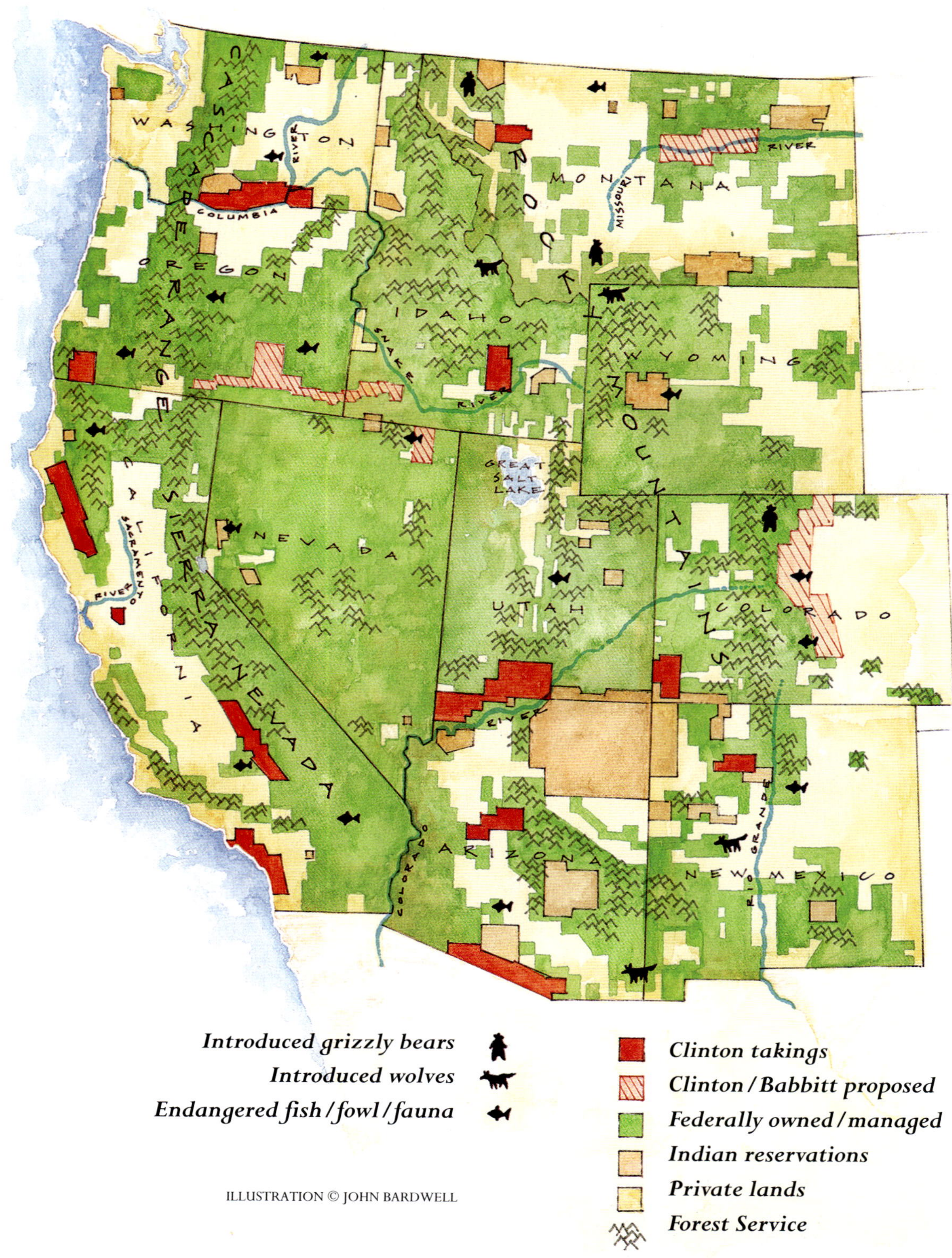

ILLUSTRATION © JOHN BARDWELL

Secretary Babbitt, speaking for the Clinton administration, accused Montana Gov. Marc Racicot of "running for a cabinet post" (in the next administration) by suggesting federal policies were in part responsible for the wildfires.

In its budget submission for 1999-2000, some $20 million was diverted from federal funds to combat wildfires into the president's Lands Legacy fund for new federal acquisitions. The U.S. Forest Service, nominally an agency of the Department of Agriculture, nevertheless was directed by Babbitt's own choice for BLM boss, Michael Dombeck. Despite the dire warnings of fire in neglected forests, Dombeck had argued that economic losses in the timber industry would be offset by $100 billion in mysteriously collected recreation revenues by 2001. At the same time, he announced plans to halt all road construction and eliminate existing roads on 40 to 60 million acres of the national forests.

Dombeck's deputy chief for forest management, Jim Furnish, told *RANGE* in 1999, "If the choice is to allow more harvest or to allow it to burn, then it's burn." Following the summer fires, Babbitt and Dombeck said it would require more than $1.7 billion to begin restoration of the devastated areas, including $117 million to clear dead trees and brush. Environmental groups publicly objected to the funding for clearing debris.

Once Bruce Babbitt had established his position on behalf of environmentalists in the Department of Interior, he soon brought in others dedicated to the movement, including George Frampton, former president of the Wilderness Society, who rose to become President Clinton's chief environmental advisor.

Frampton and others given positions by Babbitt and Gore were well aware of the most radical proposal put forward by environmentalists in these last 10 years. Attributed to "EarthFirst!" extremist David Foreman, but actually the work of a consortium of organizations including the never-touched Nature Conservancy, the Wildlands Project proposes to control and restrict human activity on no less than 50 percent of the U.S. landmass, virtually all in the West. It is an almost unbelievable scheme to favor wildlife over human habitation and predatory domination over any domestic use.

Fully implemented, it suggests a reduction in human population of the West by one-third. It claims to have the backing of the U.N. Council on Biodiversity and the Clinton administration. As much ego-ideology as it is the "deep ecology" it claims to be, the Wildlands Project was described by Foreman as "groping our way back to 1492."

Except as it is acknowledged by its creators to involve a region covering at least half the size of the continental United States, the Wildlands Project is difficult to display on a map because of its spider-vein corridors proposed for the exclusive use of migrating wildlife. The plan, given some credence in the United Nations, shocked members of the U.S. Senate who subsequently put aside any vote on the U.N. Biodiversity Treaty.

The Clinton administration takes pride in establishing a record to exceed that of Theodore Roosevelt in setting aside public lands for the future. Others observe that Roosevelt was himself experienced with the West and familiar with its people, while Clinton, even on a staged vacation trip to Wyoming, acknowledged being uncomfortable in the wild, and his Interior secretary admits he is unpopular in the rural West. While Roosevelt set aside the Grand Canyon and other lands for the appreciation of all Americans, Clinton's actions have been characterized by further restricting access to public lands.

If there is a comparison to be made, the critics say, it might be between Clinton and actions of Presidents Andrew Jackson and Ulysses S. Grant in taking native Indian lands as public property, while restricting the Native Americans themselves to limited reservations. ■

Federal land acquisitions or expansion of control under President Bill Clinton

Grand Staircase-Escalante, Utah—1.7 million acres
Grand Canyon Parashant, Arizona—1.1 million acres
Aqua Fria, Arizona—71,000 acres
Pinnacles, California—8,000 acres
California Coastal—840 miles (offshore coastline)
Hanford Reach, Washington—200,000 acres
Cascade/Siskiyou, Oregon—52,000 acres
Canyons of the Ancients, Colorado—164,000 acres
Ironwood Forest, Arizona—134,000 acres
Sequoia National Forest, California—328,000 acres

Additionally proposed monuments

Craters of the Moon, Idaho—661,000 acres
Vermillion Cliffs, Arizona & Utah—293,000 acres
Missouri Breaks, Montana (1)
Steens Mountain, Oregon (2)
Santa Rosa Peak, California (3)

Federal Purchase (Lands Legacy)

Baca Ranch, New Mexico—96,000 acres
Mojave Desert, California—405,000 acres (4)

(1) 149 miles of the Missouri shoreline in Montana are in the Breaks. A region of protection has been proposed on a minimum of 230,000 acres. Much of that expands into currently used grazing areas.

(2) Environmentalists demanded up to six million acres around the highest peak in south-central Oregon. Pressure from Secretary Babbitt on state authorities would set a minimum of 143,000 acres aside from grazing or other uses.

(3) A minimum of 31,000 acres in the mountain itself, although checkerboarded with private inholdings and expanded with unclear "buffer zones" in federal demands.

(4) The total purchase since 1994 of 6.6 million acres in the California Desert Protection Act is the largest acquisition of private land in BLM history. The purchase was made possible with the help of $15 million from the nonprofit Wildlands Conservancy.

Additional acquisitions include some two million acres for habitat protection of endangered species and Clean Water Act restrictions, as well as more than a million acres in areas of critical concern and wilderness designations. Proposed habitat buffer zones extending up to 100 miles from river shorelines alone amount to over 150,000 river miles. It should be noted that in every case when a National Heritage Site was enacted by the Clinton administration, the amount of land acquired proved greater than expected, in some cases twice as much as had been suggested. ■

SUMMER 2001

DAVID & GOLIATH

When Big Brother decided to hold Wayne Hage and his rights hostage, this articulate, tenacious, driven rancher decided to fight back—and he's winning.

By Tim Findley

Truth be known, Old Yeller and me don't get along that well even on the best of days. That truck has a definite '70s attitude, all consumption and little consideration of others. So, pulling into Tonopah, Nevada, at the start of a high-desert snowstorm, it seemed unlikely that we'd be going much further that day in pursuit of the elusive Wayne Hage.

Local kids had already been given a snow day off by school authorities knowing what was coming on the bus routes out to distant ranches, and plows were ahead of the shovels in piling the slush along the curbs and sidewalks. Only one last warming den I could find on the main drag was even still open, casting out a pale amber welcome in the steadily darkening afternoon. When it's weather like that, there's no hope of reaching the Hage ranch by telephone either.

© TIM FINDLEY

Hage is out there, pretty much alone. But like his Viking ancestors confronting a Celtic stone wall, he is given to storming the issue, no quarter given, none expected. In the West today, if you haven't heard of Wayne Hage, you haven't learned to listen.

Checking around on one last remote chance of getting lucky, I was told that, no, Hage was not in town. But I was informed and soon confirmed that his wife, former Idaho Rep. Helen Chenoweth Hage, was there. At the laundromat.

Put now aside all those pressures for political correctness and your new-age indignation. Helen Chenoweth Hage earned commanding respect in her three terms in Congress, leaving her seat only as she had promised as a self-imposed term limit, and in spite of pleas throughout the West that she at least be offered a cabinet post. Forget the fact that her political moxie and no-nonsense charm made her probably the most admired, and often most controversial, representative of western rights in Washington, D.C., during all the dim years of Clinton-Babbitt. Put your mind on Tonopah in a snowstorm and know that somebody still has to do the laundry.

It is 60 miles out from Tonopah on roads few tourists travel to Hage's Pine Creek Ranch. When there is a blizzard blowing up, it seems a little farther. Along with the laundry, I was grateful it was the former congresswoman, and not me, busting her four-wheeler through tracks at first a few inches, then soon a foot or so deep in steady snow that in some places blotted out any trace of road at all. "Can you see it?" she asked, merrily blasting along as if I could.

Wayne Hage and Helen Chenoweth have been married for just about a year and a half now. In the context of whatever you want to call the struggle in the West—Wise Use Movement, property rights rebellion, local authority, whatever—it is, among the informed and even among some uninformed, the trophy union of the time. Sort of like Wild Bill Hickok and Calamity Jane.

Wayne was waiting at the end of what I could see of the road when we arrived. It would not be his way to admit it, but I had to conclude that he had been watching for quite some time before he spotted the dark form of her S.U.V. at last coming through that sheet of storm.

Hage is a Nordic type, Norwegian by heritage, with a kind of icy intellect that's not unfriendly, but does expect you to have read the assignment. Like his Viking ancestors confronting a Celtic stone wall, Hage is given to storming the issue, no quarter given, none expected. In the West today, if you haven't heard of Wayne Hage, you haven't learned to listen.

If, less than a year after he acquired his 700,000-acre spread in Nevada's Monitor Valley in 1978, the U.S. Forest Service and federal allies in the environmental movement had not begun their relentless pressure to buy or force him out, Hage might be known today only by his slightly grumpy approach to cowboy poetry. And by something of the same token, if federal marshals had not displayed such murderous intent on Randy Weaver and his family in what would become the Ruby Ridge part of her congressional district, Helen Chenoweth might have gone on as a highly successful but publicly unnoticed management consultant and sometime lobbyist on western issues.

But in perhaps its most positive success of the period, it was the nemesis federal government that brought them together with mutual admiration—two scholarly but savvy people as much alike sometimes as Freud and Fulton.

© TIM FINDLEY

Wayne Hage and his wife Helen Chenoweth Hage spend time between the Nevada ranch and the Stewards of the Range office in Boise. The Hage case could open up a whole new vista on the issue of western property rights. He and his family have been fighting for justice for almost a decade.

Wayne will sit you down on the long side from the head of their big table he commands in the ranch house that both are remodeling these days. Hospitality and warm food abounds, but you soon learn to think about the question before you ask it.

"Well, okay," Hage is likely to begin, "let me explain that to you, and I'll walk you through it."

Helen, who happens to think her husband is "the smartest man I've ever met," has also learned to notice the flicker of caged fear in the eyes of guests being invited to walk through yet another trek of Hage knowledge stepping off usually from somewhere near the American Revolution.

Wayne Hage, who happens to think his wife is "the brightest politician I've ever met—because she knows how to listen," can, in truth, be tiresome. Even he agrees that probably half the people listening to him and nodding their heads don't really get it at all, and that another third are just pretending they do. God knows he tries, but it takes a lot of patient comprehension.

If there is only one thing Hage would want understood, it's this: there is no such thing as public lands. The very phrase "public land" should be abolished from the lexicon of people like him who are willing and capable of taking on the issue of federal lands in the West. Put on some good shoes, it's a long walk through it.

When the U.S. Park Service first came to Hage wanting to buy his ranch for a new park, they offered him about half what it is worth. "And when I asked 'What about my grazing allotments' they shook their heads and said, 'Oh, no, that's public land.' I already knew better than that, but they didn't—yet."

If they couldn't buy it with their bargain offer, the feds seemed just as determined to snatch Pine Creek and the Monitor Valley some other way. First, incredibly, as a national defense site for the MX missile project, a cold-war fiasco that would have ICBMs running around the range on railroad tracks like the rabbit at the dog track. The MX went down in flames of controversy and sinister implications that stretched into some of the best-known names and political careers in the state. Hage didn't need to look for allies or even lawyers in that fight. They found him.

The U.S. Forest Service and federal allies in the environmental movement have put relentless pressure on Hage to buy or force him out.

With the beginning of the Clinton administration, the covetous eyes of federal authority found new focus on the Hage property. Now it was new grazing regulations and claims to water rights covering his allotments that they used to turn the ratchet tighter on the stubborn Norwegian with a master's degree in science and a book full of research on his property rights. When Hage refused to cave in to the ranch-killer pressure, federal agents confiscated his cattle for illegal grazing on public land.

"There is no such thing as 'public' land," says Hage. "Since at least 1890, it has been established as split-estate federal land. The government retains the mineral rights, but surface property rights to forage and water and access are established in lawfully adjudicated grazing allotments and recorded as state law. It is federal land, but I own the surface property rights."

It is at about this point that many in the long cast of western characters to whom Hage has explained it begin to shuffle a little in their seats. Hage has been singled out in the unprecedented seizure of his cattle and his allotment rights. Even if he might have chosen it that way, he was being forced to go it alone in his stance against a federal taking of his property without compensation.

Wayne Hage and his second wife, former Rep. Helen Chenoweth, became celebrities and talked to groups across the country about the Hage case and private property rights. No one fought harder.

The second most important thing Hage wants his guests to get is that you do, of course, take the bastards to court—but you take them to the right court.

"The inclination every time is to go to federal district court to defend your rights to justice," Hage says. "But the federal district can't decide that. It can't fix a property rights' dispute; it's not their jurisdiction. All it can do is decide on the rules and regulations. The issue is the property—was it yours and did they take it?—and the only court that can decide that is the United States Court of Claims" [now called the U.S. Court of Appeals for the Federal Circuit]. In his federal case, Hage is not the defendant. It's the U.S. government that is accused of taking his property, and what is clearly at issue is that it was and is his property, on which he pays his taxes, that the federal government is trying to steal.

It's federal, not public land—a split estate—and your rights can be confirmed in the federal court of claims. If you get that much, you've earned the right to some knowing nods at the long table in the ranch house. But Hage has more, much more. He is, in fact, winning, and it may make a significant difference in western history. "Let me walk you through that," says Wayne. And Helen has such a pretty smile.

Hage is very aware that other ranchers and property-right holders instinctively seek a "silver bullet" solution in some far foreseen U.S. Supreme Court decision. But if that ever comes, it is likely to be a *coup de grace* to federal authorities already badly wounded by Hage's victories in the federal court of claims before Judge Loren Smith.

"We have yet to lose on a single issue," Hage says, "and bit by bit we are breaking down 100 years of federal misinformation on so-called public lands."

So far, the court has found for Hage in concluding that the U.S. Forest Service did take his property and did set out to destroy the economic viability of his ranch. His allotments, covering some 600,000 acres, are part of his property, the court has said, and there has been preliminary agreement that Hage owns the water, forage and access rights to that property, although the scope and extent of those rights remain at some issue.

The stage is thus set for the key decision that could open up a whole new vista on the issue of western property rights. Hage doesn't deny that the U.S. Constitution permits the federal government to seize his property, but not, under terms of the Fifth Amendment, without just compensation. The key decision expected from the court this year is how was the property taken and what is its value?

Already, Hage confides, there have been subtle, second-hand attempts to settle the matter in figures that bounce heavily around $10 million. Even for an interim taking that would cover the nine or 10 years that Hage has been deprived of his ranch's productive capacity, the amount might exceed that, and a more punishing ruling on a full taking could double it. Hage stands to win. Big time.

He's no Viking dummy ready to start the feast, however. Hage and his lawyers know the case will go on in political as well as legal arenas as environmentalists especially attempt to drum up hysteria over the "loss of public lands."

"Johanna Wald of Natural Resources Defense Council has been quoted as saying, 'We know we're going to have to buy these allotments,'" Hage points out, and similar buy-out, force-out strategies were produced at this year's green-fed RangeNet 2000 symposium against grazing, oddly in a way acknowledging the truth to Hage's position on split-estate property.

But for those in the western property rights' movement

PHOTOS COURTESY HAGE FAMILY

After Wayne died, the family carried on, with young Wayne running the outfit. From left: Wayne Hage and his wife Yelena, Margaret (Hage) Byfield and husband Dan, Helen Chenoweth-Hage, David and Laura (Hage) Perkins, Jeff and Ramona (Hage) Morrison, and Jace and Ruth (Hage) Agee. This is Pine Creek Ranch's backyard. Helen died five months after Wayne on their anniversary, October 2, 2006. "This conflict," Judge Smith wrote, "is a drama worthy of a tragic opera with heroic characters; however, this is a court of law. Its duty is to decide cases in accordance with the law as that law is received from the cases which bind us, and the statutes, and the Constitution which the Court is bound by its oath to follow."

willing to listen, Hage advises persistent patience along with careful planning. "A right undefended is a right waived," he says. "The protection of property rights is fundamentally the preservation of civil liberties."

Only, don't go beating your shields at the wrong time or in the wrong place, Hage advises. Some ranchers have already waited past the six-year statute of limitations on takings' cases. Others persist in trying their luck hopelessly in federal district courts.

"It's like if you have an ignition problem with your car and you take it to the transmission shop," Hage begins. "That's the wrong place. They can't fix it. Let me walk you through this…." It is no easy stroll from there into what Hage ultimately sees as an attempt to create a Treasury-saving corporate state covering federal land. But two points a night—the federal split estate and the U.S. Court of Claims—are fair achievements in following Wayne Hage. And besides, Helen at that point kindly offers a glass of wine to finish the evening.

It has stopped snowing by morning in the Toiyabes and across Monitor Valley, where from the crest of Table Mountain one of Hage's kids once called it "the edge of the world." Two feet of a silent white blanket spread as far as the eye could see up to the distant peaks still embraced by clouds. The vision part of the view.

Though they grudgingly acknowledge his intellect, the usually liberal press continue to cast Wayne Hage as part of the Sagebrush Rebellion, something they imagine as a kind of horse-barn conference meant to stampede across the public lands. It wasn't, and Hage never was part of that privatization attempt anyway. They don't quite understand Hage, and though they think they do, they don't quite understand his wife either. Helen Chenoweth was an attractive single lady when she served Idaho in Washington, D.C. Among other unfair characterizations, the media there once called her "The Poster Girl for the Militia Movement," which she definitely was not.

Together now they work with Hage's Stewards of the Range foundation, carrying on a struggle Hage sees as nowhere near over. They commute as much between Idaho and Nevada as more ordinary folks might between home and the supermarket. Neither Wayne nor Helen play upon the celebrity status they've earned. Talk between them is more often about picking up more one-by-eights for bookshelves to finish the remodeling project.

But strolling out hand in hand after breakfast through the fresh snow along the corrals, they do seem a legendary pair. Like Hickok and Calamity Jane.

And, whaddya know, it is Valentine's Day. ■

UPDATE: In the nearly 20 years Hage fought for his rights in Nevada's Monitor Valley, he never lost a case in the Court of Claims. His first wife and mother of his children, Jean, died midway in the struggle and he was nearly driven bankrupt as he carried on the fight with his second wife Helen Chenoweth. Yet in a cruel irony of fate, neither would survive for the ultimate victory. Wayne lost to cancer in 2006, Helen to a Jeep accident only six months later. The $4 million awarded due to takings, plus more than a decade of interest, has yet to be awarded to Hage's estate.

we place on wildness.

Doesn't this suggest a cultural bias?

NOSS: Fifty percent is an estimate I made years ago of the proportion of an average region that would need to be managed for conservation in order to meet well-accepted conservation goals. The question "how much is enough?" should be answered empirically rather than dogmatically. If we consider empirical research on this question, it turns out I was pretty much on the mark with my 50 percent hypothesis. Studies done by researchers in North America, Australia, Africa, and elsewhere have found that's about what it takes. Most of the estimates fall in the range of 25 to 75 percent. It takes more land in some regions than in others to meet the same goals, because regions differ in their biogeography. For example, regions with high endemism (that is, many narrowly distributed species), such as much of California, require more area to meet the goal of representing populations of all species in a reserve network than a region with more widely distributed species, such as the northern Rockies. And, of course, states such as Iowa and Illinois have so little natural habitat left (only around two to three percent) that opportunities for meeting conservation goals are limited without extensive habitat restoration. We have to set the standards lower.

"Carnivores are emblematic of wildness, something that is spiritually and aesthetically important to many people, but which is lacking in so much of the modern world."

The Wildlands Project, however, does not restrict its vision to areas west of the 100th meridian. We and other conservationists have ambitious plans for the East as well. For example, state government agencies in Florida and New Jersey, of all places, are attempting to protect a third or more of their land in conservation areas. That's much more than most western states that have much more public land.

RANGE: Such a radical proposal attached to the "shock value" tactics of David Foreman and Earth First! might be put aside as fantasy, but you place substantial scientific credentials of your own in conjunction with what many regard as the demagogic terrorist methods of Foreman. Are you comfortable with that?

NOSS:: Well, Tim, the Dave Foreman of the 1980s Earth First! days was a bit different from the Dave Foreman of today. Isn't that true of anyone? His conservation goals remain basically the same (I generally agreed with him then and I agree with him now), but his tactics have changed. Curiously, Dave's a lifelong Republican. He's hardly a terrorist, and I resent your use of that word. Save the terrorist word for murderers like Osama bin Laden and Timothy McVeigh.

I came into the conservation movement as a naturalist, one who studies nature. I saw the beautiful woods I played in as a kid in southern Ohio destroyed by developers. I went to college to become a biologist, hoping to apply my skills to the conservation of nature. Today we call this field conservation biology, which I define as science in the service of conservation. Conservation biology is mission oriented, as are medical science, range science, engineering, and other applied sciences. We are interested in solving problems, not just knowledge for the sake of knowledge. Many prominent conservation biologists and other scholars have served on the board of the Wildlands Project, and many more (at least thousands, I would guess) are very comfortable with our approach. Indeed, one reason we founded the Wildlands Project was to forge a link between activists and scientists interested in large-scale conservation.

RANGE: Clearly the acquisitions of public and private lands appropriate to the Wildlands plan is ongoing by funded conservation trusts led by The Nature Conservancy. Is TNC in part clearing the way for such connectivity and what you call "linkages" in the West?

NOSS: TNC has their own ecoregional plans; they don't follow ours. However, it is true that over the last few years, TNC's planning has taken on a regional focus much like ours, and they use many of the same scientific methods. I think it's clear that the Wildlands Project has had a significant influence on TNC and other major conservation groups. In addition, research in conservation biology has demonstrated that a collection of small, isolated reserves (TNC's old approach) just doesn't cut it in the long term—you need large, interconnected networks of protected areas. Small, disconnected reserves lose native species rapidly over time, are invaded by alien weeds, and are more difficult and expensive to manage. Most private land trusts, on the other hand, have shown little interest in biology—they've been more interested in protecting "open space." But that's beginning to change as these organizations get better educated staffs.

RANGE: As you have observed in speeches, the primary danger today even to such major predators as wolves and grizzly bears is not hunting, but roadkills. Are you suggesting in this project that even transcontinental highways be altered in some way or closed to accommodate the corridors?

NOSS: In some regions, even surprising places such as the central Canadian Rockies, direct roadkill is the largest documented source of mortality for large carnivores. How-

© LINDA DUFURRENA

Evening light on Pine Forest switchback towards Blue Lake and Onion Reservoir in northern Nevada's Pine Forest Range.

ever, in many other places, human persecution (legal or illegal hunting) remains the major cause of death. But here, too, roads figure prominently in the problem, because they provide access to people with guns. The higher the density of roads, the lower the probability that wolves, bears, and other animals can survive. This has been documented worldwide.

Regarding major highways, we are not so impractical to suggest they be closed. However, we do recommend underpasses, land bridges, and other wildlife crossings be constructed at strategic locations—places where animals regularly get struck—to protect wildlife as they move across the landscape. New highways should be built only if they take the movement needs of wildlife into account. Wildlife crossings have been built in several states, for example Colorado, California, and Florida, as well as extensively in Europe. Yes, it's costly, but not close to the cost of building the road in the first place. Ironically, in some cases building a new road can be a good thing. Near where I live in Florida, the state is proposing to build a new limited-access highway that will be elevated for seven miles to protect black bears, other wildlife, and sensitive wetlands. The new highway will replace a busy two-lane road that is responsible for most of the black bear roadkills in the state.

"New highways should be built only if they take the movement needs of wildlife into account."

RANGE: Do you not agree that the economic impact of such a project would be disastrous to the western United States and even to the nation as a whole?

NOSS: Absolutely not. The cost would be trivial compared to many things our society spends big money on (for example, welfare, missiles, and highways). In many cases wilderness preservation enhances local economies by stimulating tourism and business investments and relocations. This has been demonstrated convincingly by Professor Tom Power at the University of Montana, among others. Reintroducing wolves to Yellowstone has given the local economy a shot in the arm. The state of Florida has been spending more than $300 million per year for nearly two decades buying land for conservation, so that the state will remain attractive to tourists and businesses.

RANGE: Assuming such a plan is implemented, who would administer and manage it? The government? Or a nongovernment agency? Who should have police powers in controlling use?

NOSS: We're not talking about any kind of centralized administration and management of wildlands networks. Despite the claims of the wise-use alarmists on the Internet, we are in no way aligned with the United Nations and their fictitious black helicopters. To the extent that new wilderness areas, national parks, national wildlife refuges, etc., are added to the system, they would be managed by the federal agencies in charge, as they are today. Other lands would be managed by land trusts, other private organizations, or by the same willing landowners (ranchers, farmers, and others) who manage them today. But we think there should be added incentives, such as big tax breaks, for managing land in a way friendly to nature. There would be no "police power" other than the law enforcement system already in place.

RANGE: Did you once say that westerners are part of the "slothful and ignorant populace" who disagree with you? Do you not recognize the elitism contained in the proposal itself?

NOSS: I don't remember saying that, but if I did I would have been joking. I wouldn't use the word "slothful" in a derogatory sense, because I like sloths. On the other hand, I do believe that ecological ignorance on the part of the public is one of our greatest problems. Most people, particularly in the cities, don't have a clue how nature operates. However, this problem is hardly unique to the West. In fact, studies have shown that easterners are more ignorant about wildlife, on average, than westerners. As for elitism, if it is elitist to place a high value on ecological education and on compassion for the land and living things, then yes, I'm an elitist. But I certainly don't hold any special grudges against westerners. I've spent most of my professional career in the West and the South, where I feel more comfortable than with uptight easterners.

"I would favor tax breaks for couples with two or fewer children and tax penalties for those with three or more."

RANGE: What if you're wrong? None of us may live long enough to know, but what if species are more adaptable than you seem to think? What if the growing general acceptance of ecological relationships assures a natural balance in the future better than any imposed plan could do? And what, conversely, if such enforced intervention as the Wildlands Project leads to ultimately dire consequences on social freedom: do you care about that?

NOSS: I do care. The proposals of the Wildlands Project are science based. But even the best science (which we strive for) carries a moderate-to-high level of uncertainty. Sure enough, some research suggests that particular species are more adaptable to human activities than we once thought. The pileated woodpecker, for example, declined with forest fragmentation across much of the country, but now seems to be doing fairly well in fragmented landscapes, as long as enough big trees are around for foraging and nesting. It adapted. However, probably more species are turning out to be more sensitive to human landscape modification than we thought, but we won't know for sure unless we monitor their populations across many generations. In the face of such uncertainty, scientists recommend following the precautionary principle, where we try to pursue policies and management practices that pose the least risk to nature and human society. Sometimes there are conflicts, of course, and tradeoffs must be made. The available evidence suggests that the extinction crisis is our greatest global problem. Therefore, in the face of uncertainty I would risk erring on the side of protecting too much land rather than too little.

Although this may conflict with economic development in some cases, it need not conflict with personal liberties. Big corporations pose a much greater threat to liberty than conservationists. Like many in the Wildlands Project, I consider myself a conservative—an old-style, Teddy Roosevelt-kind of conservative. I'm libertarian in many of my views, especially with respect to personal behavior. For example, it's my own damn business whether or not I wear a seat belt. But given the high level of selfishness that humans display, we need policies and laws to protect nature, just like we need laws to protect human life and dignity from the depredations of other humans.

RANGE: Certainly as an optional question for you, but one still most troubling for many: statements by Foreman and others have suggested that returning so much area to a pre-Columbian state can only be accomplished by some form of population control, bluntly eliminating some portion of human existence. This is a chilling statement with obvious derivations. Can you comment on it?

NOSS: I don't think the implications are so obvious, Tim. Globally, human population growth is the biggest threat to nature and to human liberty and peace. Second in importance is the growing rate of per capita resource consumption. What kind of world do we want to live in? A world with swarming people pressed shoulder to shoulder or a world with wide open spaces and clean air to breathe? Population control need not require draconian measures—in fact, I would oppose such measures. Rather, it's a matter of providing incentives and disincentives. Rather than giving people tax breaks for every additional child they have—which we do now and President Bush wants to increase—I would favor tax breaks for those couples with two or fewer children and tax penalties for those with three or more. I think such a tax policy, combined with strict limits on immigration, would take care of our population problem in the United States. Likewise, destructive technologies (for instance, those wasteful of fossil fuels) should be taxed heavily and sustainable technologies, such as solar and wind energy, should be promoted. "Conservative" and "conservation" spring from the same root, and it's about time today's so-called conservatives figured that out. ■

These giant swaths are the areas targeted by the Wildlands Project and they seem to slowly expand and run together to cover ever more land. Why not the center of the country? Dr. Noss says states such as Iowa and Illinois have too little natural habitat left, so "we have to set the standards lower." This map no longer appears on the Wildands Project website.

TAKING LIBERTY

How private property in America is being abolished.
By Michael S. Coffman, Ph.D.

One hour before the U.S. Senate was to adopt the United Nations Treaty on Biodiversity, Sen. Kay Bailey Hutchison (R-Texas) went to the floor with a 300-plus-page draft copy of Chapter 10 of the United Nations Global Biodiversity Assessment and a four-by-six-foot poster.

The poster showed the lower 48 states overlaid with hundreds of red islands representing wilderness areas interconnected by thousands of red ribbons called corridors, all surrounded by yellow buffer zones. Small green patches were "human occupation zones." The agenda was so outrageous it would have been discounted, except that Sen. Hutchison had the proof in her hands. The date was September 29, 1994, and the agenda was called the Wildlands Project.

Senate majority leader George Mitchell (D-Maine), along with several other senators, withdrew the scheduled cloture vote on the treaty and a vote was never taken. That should have been the end of it, but in reality it was only the beginning.

While environmental concerns may be legitimate in some cases, many of the accusations made by environmental nongovernment organizations (NGOs) today are nothing more than perceptions created to indoctrinate the public and cause unfounded fear that generates income for the NGO. Environmental fear has become a multibillion-dollar business that preys on unknowing urbanites. Seventy-seven percent of all Americans live in about three percent of America's land area classed as urban by the U.S. Bureau of Census. The number only climbs to a little over six percent when all developed areas are included. Activist NGOs have found it easy to leverage legitimate environmental concerns into profitable campaigns that have marginal or negative environmental benefits.

Because urbanites outvote rural residents by a three-to-one margin, they can pass laws that harm rural residents in the belief we need more government land and open space. Yet, most environmental laws strip rural citizens of their ability to use proven management practices to provide goods and services to urbanites. As a result, groceries, appliances, lumber and other commodities cost more.

The higher cost of goods and services is not the most dangerous threat to America. Our founding fathers recognized the critical nature of private property rights as they were firsthand witnesses to the abuse of power that occurs

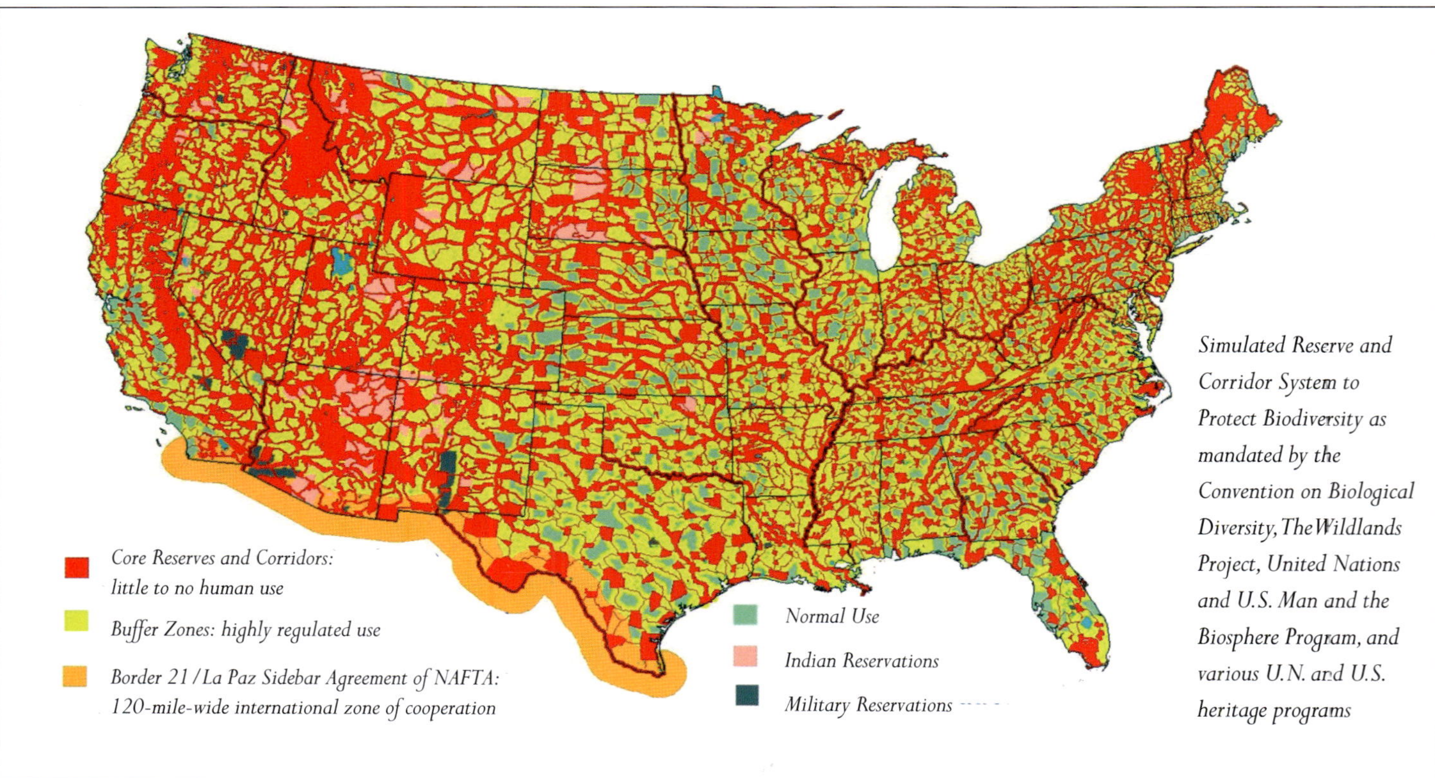

Taken from the United Nations Convention on Biological Diversity, Article 8a-e; United Nations Global Biodiversity Assessment, Section 13.3.2.2.3; U.S. Man and the Biosphere Strategic Plan, U.N. / U.S. Heritage Corridor Program, "The Wildlands Project," WildEarth, 1992.

when government controls private property. James Madison and others even claimed that the entire purpose of government is to protect private property. They knew that private property is the foundation to liberty and wealth creation.

Hernando de Soto, a Peruvian citizen, completed a massive study for the World Bank in the early 2000s, the findings of which were published in "The Mystery of Capital." De Soto's team studied many nations for several years to determine why capitalism triumphs in the West and fails in Third World nations. He found that strong property rights are the basis of liberty and wealth creation—just as was claimed by America's founding fathers.

For instance, equity loans on personal homes provide the funding for 70 percent of all small business starts in the United States. Small businesses are the economic backbone of America. This would not be possible without strong property rights. In turn, unencumbered legal property rights allow banks the security needed to make the loan in a few days or weeks.

This is not the case in Third World nations. Because of arbitrary regulations and corresponding corruption, de Soto found that it takes 10 to 20 years and many payoffs to register property ownership in these countries. Hence, impoverished citizens do not register their ownership so their property rights are not legally established. De Soto calls this real but unregistered property "dead capital" because its equity is not available for investment. No equity means no capital to build wealth. Since citizens cannot build wealth, neither can the nation, condemned to perpetual poverty no matter how many socialist income-redistribution plans are imposed by the United Nations.

Loss of liberty to faceless bureaucrats who use a corrupt and arbitrary regulatory system to their own advantage is happening to more and more rural citizens in the United States.

Rural citizens are not alone. A growing number of communities are faced with arbitrary regulations under the umbrella of "smart growth" and "urban-growth boundaries." Depending on who draws the arbitrary boundary, low-value agricultural land can instantly be worth millions. Immediately across the urban-growth boundary, these arbitrary regulations prohibit development and the value of the land remains low. Within 100 yards, one landowner reaps millions and another gets nothing. Arbitrary regulation—no matter how noble the intent—always breeds corruption.

Studies conducted by the Harvard Institute of Economic Research clearly show this enormous economic impact. Quarter-acre lots in cities with minimum smart-growth regulations average \$10,000 to \$40,000 per lot, while similar lots in cities imposing heavy smart-growth regulations average \$200,000 to \$600,000 per lot. There is a strong correlation between the time it takes to get a permit and the cost of the land, just as de Soto found in Third World nations.

"The collective needs of nonhuman species must take precedence over the needs and desires of humans."

WILDLANDS PROJECT COAUTHOR REED NOSS EXPLAINS THEIR INTENT

Harvard economists Edward L. Glaeser and Joseph Gyourko, in their paper "The Impact of Zoning on Housing Affordability" (March 2002), emphasized that the entire increase was due to smart-growth regulations. These "feel-good" regulations represent a huge drag on future urban economy.

Little did I know when I prepared the map Sen. Hutchison used on the Senate floor, that environmental operatives were already in key positions of our government, ready to implement the antiproperty rights directives of the United Nations Treaty on Biodiversity. Although the treaty did not pass the Senate, they were able to shift gears, developing the authority necessary to implement the Wildlands agenda under an administrative cloak that didn't require congressional approval. It has been just over 10 years since they actively began transforming America into Wildlands. What is most frightening is how much they have accomplished in that short period.

For anyone who doubts that environmentalists are serious about destroying private property in America, redistributing the wealth, and reducing the use of our natural resources, those doubts should be put to rest. They are more than halfway there.

Under the Wildlands Project, the United States would be transformed from a land where people can live where they choose and travel freely, to a Wildlands-dominated landscape where people live in designated population centers with limited travel allowed through highly restricted corridors. The Wildlands Project is the master plan for both the United Nations' Agenda 21 and Biodiversity Treaty. In classic socialist utopian idealism, Agenda 21 defines how every human being must live in order to save Mother Earth. The Wildlands Project represents a grandiose design to transform at least half the land area of the continental United States into an immense "eco-park" cleansed of modern industry and private property.

Wildlands Project coauthor Reed Noss explains their intent: "The collective needs of nonhuman species must take precedence over the needs and desires of humans."

While many key laws like the Endangered Species Act (ESA), Clean Water Act and dozens of others that would facilitate implementation of the Wildlands agenda were already in place, environmentalists needed to identify areas that had no protection in order to begin converting land to conform to their agenda. The Clinton administration undertook two major programs with no congressional oversight during the 1990s to identify and begin targeting these areas. They were the Gap Analysis Program (GAP) and the Roadless Area Rule.

The GAP process starts by analyzing existing protected

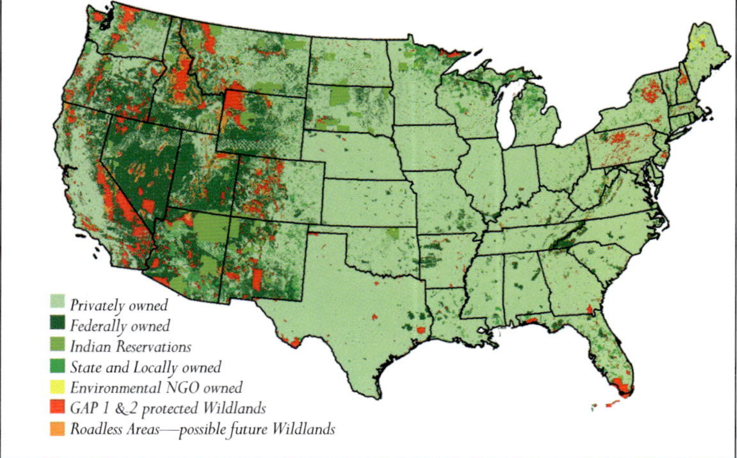

Areas identified as GAP Classes 1 & 2 protected Wildlands and designated roadless areas on U.S. Forest Service land.

government land, then overlays geographical data of vegetation habitat, animal distribution and property ownership. Land ownership is further divided into stewardship classes: (1) is "fully protected" (such as wilderness areas); (2) is "mostly protected" (national parks and many wildlife refuges); (3) is "partially protected" (national landmarks and multiple-use areas like U.S. Forest Service lands); and (4) is "no known land protection" (usually private land). Classes 1 and 2 are often combined.

Although GAP sounds innocent, even noble, it is designed for the sole purpose of defining where gaps exist between already-protected areas and those that require protection. These gaps are huge in Midwestern and Eastern states where very little government land exists. Federal, state or local governments already own more than 40 percent of the land area in the United States; however, most of this federally owned land is in the West.

The only way to close these gaps is by taking private property through condemnation, conservation easements or uncompensated regulations. In most cases, access to this land represents a rural family's livelihood and GAP represents a direct threat to their way of life.

The second federal program implemented at the end of the Clinton administration is the U.S. Forest Service Roadless Area Conservation Rule (RA). RA established blanket, nationwide prohibitions generally limiting timber harvest, road construction and reconstruction within 58.5 million acres of inventoried roadless areas on national forests and grasslands. The lives of thousands of people depend on these historically available resources for their living in forestry, livestock production and mining for critically needed minerals. This was one of the first major efforts to convert already restricted government lands into Wildlands status, and accelerated the process of extinguishing the use of private lands within these areas.

On July 14, 2003, the U.S. District Court for the District of Wyoming issued a permanent injunction and set aside the roadless rule. However, the U.S. Forest Service issued a new rule on May 5, 2005, that allows the roadless rule to be imposed with the permission of the governor of each state.

Already existing laws such as the ESA have made it easier for environmentalists to push their Wildlands agenda. By threatening landowners with species listings or habitat designations, they can force private property owners into signing conservation easements, or into giving away a large portion of their property to the government or to a land trust as mitigation in order to use just a small portion of their land.

The government owns 60 percent of Oregon and 42 percent of Washington, so the immediate focus in the Pacific Northwest has been to complete the conversion of these lands into Wildlands and target the private lands within these areas. The ESA has so far been the biggest tool for accomplishing this goal. The designation of the spotted owl gave the environmentalists the surrogate they needed. The spotted owl's "habitat" occupies everything west of the Cascade mountain range's centerline, which includes large tracts of private property. The intention was never to save the bird, but to make ghost towns out of entire communities.

The federal government, State of Oregon and environmental NGOs collaborated to completely shut down agriculture in the Klamath Basin of south-central Oregon in 2001. Federal agents misrepresented the amount of water needed for endangered suckerfish in Klamath Lake, resulting in the loss of all irrigation water to farmers in the basin and turning farmland into dustbowls. The environmental NGOs fulfilled their mission.

Even though their land essentially became worthless, the State of Oregon did nothing to help the farmers. Thousands of Klamath residents lost their jobs, and businesses that supported farming faced financial ruin. Later that summer, the National Academy of Sciences reviewed the data supporting the court decision and found "no clear evidence" that high lake levels benefited the fish or "convincing scientific justification" for not allowing the farmers to continue to use the water for irrigation. In fact, evidence showed that the suckerfish seemed to do better when the farmers used the lake water for irrigation. In reality, an arbitrary ESA decision based on highly questionable science brought economic devastation to an entire region.

On the eastern side of the Cascade Mountain Range, the federal GAP analysis showed that large tracts of land were already protected or nearly protected, but there were still many ranchers, miners and foresters who used these lands and held legitimate property rights. A concerted effort was made through the Clinton administration to begin the transformation of this region through the Interior Columbia Basin Ecosystem Management Project in 1993.

The project attempted to develop cooperative management strategies between federal, state and local governments to control land use over the 64-million-acre Columbia Basin Ecosystem east of the Cascade mountains into Idaho, western Montana and northwest Wyoming. Citizens strongly opposed it and in 2003, after a 10-year study, only federal agencies and NGOs continued the program.

Individuals living within populated areas of the Northwest are also beginning to feel the effects of the Wildlands agenda to move urban growth into designated "human occupation zones." For example, in 1979 planners drew an Urban Growth Boundary line around Portland, Oregon, to control urban sprawl. Land values within the smart-growth boundary skyrocketed. Land values outside plummeted.

Smart growth causes severe economic hardship. In 1990, two out of three families could afford a home in the Portland area. That figure dove to one out of three by 2000. The problem became so bad that in 2004 the citizens of Oregon overwhelmingly passed Measure 37, requiring just compensation for landowners suffering from smart-growth regulations and other land-control restrictions.

Except for parts of Florida and the southern Appalachians, the Southeast generally has very little federal, state and local government land that activists can use to lobby for creating Wildlands. So, to speed the process up and help identify private land for Wildlands protection, Region 4 of the U.S. Environmental Protection Agency (EPA) and the University of Florida's GeoPlan Center conducted a GAP analysis called the Southeastern Ecological Framework Project in 1999-2000.

The project prioritized ecological areas in the Southeast that need protection. Because GAP gives such a high priority to ecosystems over people, more than 60 percent of the Southeast—nearly all rural areas and private land—was identified as having a high protection priority.

Florida has already undertaken a number of statewide initiatives to implement the Wildlands Project under a variety of names, of which the Greenways Planning Project and Save Our Rivers Program are the largest. During the 1990s these programs were under the umbrella of the Preservation 2000 Act, changed by the Florida Legislature in 2000 to Florida Forever. The goal was to place as much as 80 percent of Florida into Wildlands reserves and corridors, which they call hubs and linkages.

By 1999, Florida had purchased 1.3 million acres through the Save Our Rivers Program. After 2000, the same program targeted new lands for acquisition by "green-lining" a huge area of land. Green-lining typically locks the land value at rock-bottom prices, denying the landowner any chance for receiving highest and best value for his land, thereby skimming the landowner's equity for the government.

By 2005, Florida had purchased another 800,000 acres throughout the state increasing state ownership from 29 to 37 percent.

The state used conservation easements to acquire development rights on an additional 315,000 acres at about one-third the cost of what the state would have had to pay to buy the land outright. The landowners often sell the easement for quick cash, figuring the land will never have much future value. Or the landowner sells the easement because regulations have made it increasingly difficult to make a living on or to otherwise use the land.

Florida is cannibalizing its private land in the name of protecting nature. It is not the only state in the East that is doing so. Delaware, Maryland, New Jersey, Rhode Island and New York are also following closely in Florida's footsteps. These states are also identifying greenway hubs and linkages for the Wildlands Project.

Local communities will always need regulations that focus on true harm, nuisance and public health. A healthy economy is required to protect the environment. If the local, state or U.S. economy declines because arbitrary regulations limit or remove private property from production, it is highly probable that the very efforts to protect the environment will eventually cause its decline.

The end result will not be the eco-utopia the greens envision. It will be a land owned by government and elite land trusts. In truth, the Wildlands agenda is not about whether America's land and resources will be used for human benefit; it is about who will own them. Private property rights are as important to the environment as they are to people. ■

SPRING 2007

DARK MOON RISING

Surrendering sovereignty.

By Tim Findley

Has North America been sold? Did it go for a bargain price secretly agreed to by the three most powerful politicians on the continent, without a Howdy, a Hola, or a Hail Britannia to the people who elected them?

Under the plan, more than 500 million people are meant to be literally incorporated into the North American Union as early as 2010. They are expected to share natural resources, military defense, and a universal system of education that will alter long-held values, customs, and traditions and even change their languages. Law enforcement, health care, and cultural activities as well as virtually all trade will be financed with the new currency of the North Americans: the "Amero."

Nowhere would the impact be greater than in the American West, cut off as a virtual subcontinent by an artificial, but impassable, barrier of a colossal superhighway cutting through the central "heartland" of the United States between the meaningless borders of Canada and Mexico.

It is not a computer program or an academic exercise. It is the essence of the "informal" agreement reached by the so-called trinational leaders of the continent to surrender the sovereignty of their nations to a gigantic corporate cartel.

Will the people of the United States, Mexico, and Canada resist it? In spite of their own illusions about democracy and representative government, can they resist? The arrogant architects of the North American Union are almost certain they cannot.

The concept of America is already gone in the description of a new North America that leaves the borders between the three nations as little more than speed bumps, and in its "deep integration" plans to control the lives of individuals in once unimaginable ways, as if Orwell was a new chapter discovered in their secular bible.

Is it a new world or a dark moon rising? Is there blood on its rim?

Breaking the Heartland

It was an animated conversation among friends and neighbors at a local diner, something about traffic congestion and road repair. Coffee talk, much like Analiese Kunert had heard all her life in San Antonio. But as she listened, Analiese felt a deep chill. They were talking about a monstrous new development called the Trans-Texas Corridor, and she realized from their description that it is meant to cross directly over the 30 acres with its cherished hacienda built in 1798 that is the home to her and her husband and their two young children.

AP PHOTO/HARRY CABLUCK

Texas Gov. Rick Perry prepares to deliver remarks as he announces details of a state transportation plan on Monday, January 28, 2002, in Austin, Texas. The artist's rendering at left illustrates the Trans-Texas Corridor plan, said by some to improve the state's transportation needs of the future.

Santa Ana's cavalry had once camped there. All the flags flown in Texas may have fluttered there in their own time, and arrowheads still found by visiting children attest to an even longer history. Never in more than two centuries have the 18- to 20-inch-thick stone walls been breached.

But the Trans-Texas, she hears, cannot be stopped.

Like most Texans, the Kunerts regarded Rick Perry's grandiose speeches in 2001 about meeting the future of growth in Texas to be campaign rhetoric. Analiese had not really noticed in 2004 when, in the middle of his first full term, the governor accepted a $7 billion investment of the Spanish corporation Cintra and declared it, "One of the most significant days in transportation history."

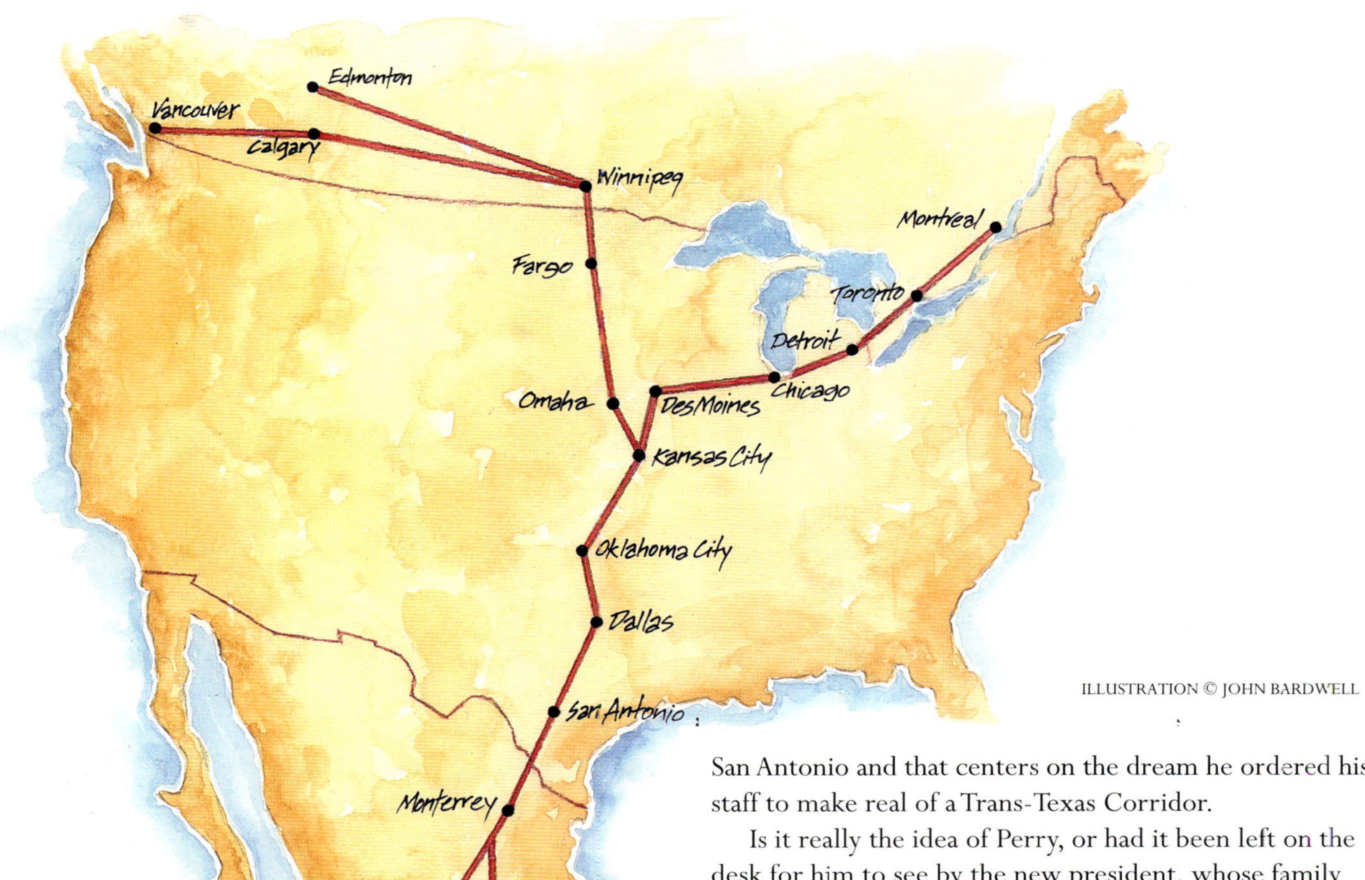

ILLUSTRATION © JOHN BARDWELL

Speaking like a coach with a winning score in the Sugar Bowl, Perry said the Spanish investment "will not only bring the Trans-Texas Corridor from conception to completion; it will change forever the way we build roads in Texas."

Whether or not they even knew the game was being played, no coffee-table cabinet was meant to have anything to say about it, and property owners like the Kunerts were best advised to accept a fair price and get out of the way.

Gov. Perry had been a rancher and an Air Force C-130 pilot, but he had learned his political skills rising up through the Texas Legislature to become lieutenant governor in time to take over the governor's mansion for the remaining two years left in the term of newly elected president of the United States, George W. Bush.

Winning a full term on his own in 2002, Perry carried on with a momentum already established in his agenda of addressing expected growth with a transportation policy that always favors expanding highways out of Laredo past San Antonio and that centers on the dream he ordered his staff to make real of a Trans-Texas Corridor.

Is it really the idea of Perry, or had it been left on the desk for him to see by the new president, whose family enjoys far better international contacts than the rancher-made-good Republican who followed G.W. into the top Texas job?

Whatever, Perry left no doubt among his appointees, especially Transportation Commission Chairman Ric Williamson, about what he expects to be his legacy.

"Once the governor decided where we needed to head, he wanted to remove it from the political flow of the state. He wanted it to become policy as opposed to politics, and that was one of the reasons for us to move so fast. And we've done an admirable job," Williamson told his commission in June 2002.

Legislation making a Trans-Texas Corridor a separate project in state policy was rammed through the Texas Legislature in 2003 with little notice. Among those who would usher Cintra to the head of a very short line of contractors willing to build such a yellow brick road was Perry's legislative liaison, Dan Shelley, a former lobbyist who also formerly served as a consultant to Cintra. Once Cintra had beaten out even a Halliburton subsidiary for the project, Shelley left the governor's office and accepted a lucrative contract to serve as a lobbyist for the Madrid conglomerate. Although state policy prohibits him from lobbying the governor's office for a year, last summer Shelley invited four state lawmakers on a junket to Canada to visit a Cintra toll road near Toronto. The trip was cancelled after the

Dallas Morning News started asking questions.

State insiders buzzed with rumors, and even *TIME* magazine dipped briefly into the issue but soon withdrew after suggesting a "boondoggle" was in the works in Texas.

Analiese Kunert has paid no attention to all that. She assumed it would be easy to defend her own historic property at the scoping meeting scheduled by Texas Department of Transportation (TxDOT) officials in South San Antonio, but she found the meeting in a high-school cafeteria crammed with an audience so large that authorities

PHOTO COURTESY KUNERT FAMILY

The Kunerts' cherished hacienda, built in 1798, is in the way of a monstrous new development called the Trans-Texas Corridor. Analiese and Robert Kunert, shown with daughter Chloe and son Zachary, say that never in more than two centuries have the thick stone walls been breached. But Trans-Texas, they hear, cannot be stopped, and property owners like them are told to accept a fair price and get out of the way.

locked the doors to keep an almost equally large crowd waiting outside.

"They said they'd let us speak," Analiese recalls, "but I could see it was almost hopeless. Instead, they ran a half-hour presentation on it, once in English, and then a second time in Spanish. Then they let people talk for three minutes each, but they didn't really answer any questions, and most of us didn't know quite what to say. It was like a done deal."

She was stunned. Many of her neighbors, including retired rancher Jimmy Lamberth, were angry. "It didn't even have anything to do with highway congestion," he says. "The thing is meant to go around all the big cities, and we'd just be nearest on the route from Mexico."

Lamberth, a lifelong rancher, had watched TxDOT work before in establishing farm-to-market highways in the state, but he was astonished by a proposed toll turnpike that would end up cutting off even some of those highways. "I saw [TxDOT] recently working on Highway 281 to solve a problem with cross traffic," he says. "They installed stoplights on the freeway, even though they had money for overpasses. They just didn't want to compete with the toll road."

To Chris Stall, the city manager of the midsized town of Columbus, Texas, the whole concept at first sounded like science fiction. The aliens must have landed. "It would roll right over our town without an exit or an on ramp," Stall says, "leaving us isolated not only from business, but from existing roads to our own markets."

What Perry and TxDOT presented to them seemed almost unbelievable in its 10 to 12 lanes of highway, with high-speed passenger and freight rail lines attached, along with pipelines for fuel, water, fiber optics and electric power. Concessions of fuel, food, lodging, shops, and emergency services would be self-contained in the median. And all of it would cut nonstop through the state in a swath the width of four football fields.

Like Sherman through Georgia, it would consume at least 146 acres for every mile it made to the Oklahoma border, ultimately covering more than 4,000 miles of Texas in the largest network of toll roads ever known. That, it soon becomes clear, was what Perry meant when he said it would be a "new way of building roads" in his state. Not the size of it or the materials involved, but the fact that it would be a SuperToll highway with most of the profits for at least half a century going to Cintra.

"Governor Perry and his friends spend a great deal of time researching ideas to create more revenue," says TxDOT's Williamson. "The corridor is primarily a revenue producer."

Ultimately the project is estimated to cost a staggering $186 billion, more than the entire amount spent on the interstate highway system, which the governor apparently means to get up front from private financiers. Ironically, although Cintra calls itself the transportation arm of its parent conglomerate Grupo Ferrovial, the company is best known in Europe not for highway building, but for the management of parking lots.

"Santa Ana has come back," Analiese Kunert says grimly. Still, she and others cling to hope that state law and even political pressure will allow citizens some leeway to redirect the monolith ahead of its reach over some of the most valuable agricultural land in the state.

"If you aggressively invite the private sector to be your partner, you can't tell them where to build the road," TxDOT Commission Chairman Williamson stated at another meeting in May. Even new state law passed by the voters last year to limit the use of eminent domain for acquisition of private property holds no authority over specifically exempted state highway projects and the Super-Corridor in particular with its "quick claim" clause granted in the legislation.

"People on the south end of San Antonio were furious," says Analiese Kunert, "but people on the north side still say they never even heard of it."

It is a fair description of the spotty prairie fires flaming up in grassroots opposition to Perry's plans while the Legislature remains confused and disorganized on the issue, in part because to many it still seems unbelievable.

Perry regards himself as a visionary. From his first campaign enthusiasms, the former state legislator and lieutenant governor has always wanted the historic corridor to emerge along the route of Interstate 35 out of Laredo, just across the border from the Mexican truck bottleneck in Nuevo Laredo. Nuevo Laredo is a town so hopelessly corrupt and gang infested that the chief of police resigned saying he could not enforce the law, and the city newspaper, raked periodically by automatic gunfire, published a front-page statement in 2005 saying that for the sake of their employees' lives, it would no longer do any investigative reporting. Essentially, terror is in charge where Texas intends to provide five or six lanes going north—suggested speed, 85 miles per hour until you either run out of gas or, under the NAFTA [North American Free Trade Agreement] scheme, reach Kansas City.

There has been no approval or even serious discussion in the U.S. Congress of a NAFTA-Plus SuperCorridor through the middle of the United States linking Canada and Mexico. The idea only formally exists in the supposedly nonprofit nongovernmental organization of North America's SuperCorridor Coalition Inc. (NASCO). Formed in 1994 and funded with at least $2.25 million in U.S. transportation funds for "technology integration," NASCO is run by a trinational board of directors that includes transportation officials from the United States, Canada and Mexico. The president of the board is a Kansas City attorney. Two of the members are deputy directors of the Texas Department of Transportation.

"There are no plans to build a new NAFTA Superhighway," the nonprofit group claims. "It exists today as I-35."

Follow the money. It goes to Laredo and bears north along the Trans-Texas Corridor, following the route of Interstate 35. ■

Kansas City, Here They Come

In Ottawa, Canada, Vicente Fox's successor, Felipe Calderon, was meeting with Canadian Prime Minister Stephen Harper, himself relatively new to the chief executive's job since Liberal Prime Minister Paul Martin was cast out in a shadow of corruption and scandal at the beginning of 2006. The Mexican president-elect had come to Ottawa ostensibly to discuss progress in the North American Free Trade Agreement (NAFTA) with the new Canadian leader, but there was obviously more on the agenda.

At a joint appearance, Calderon looked to Harper in comparing the border fence to "the Berlin Wall—a grave error." Harper tried to avoid serious political risk, noting "concerns for safe and secure borders," but suggesting there should be no "unnecessary barriers, not just to trade but to the ordinary exchange of tourism and social relationships between our countries."

AP PHOTO/HARRY CABLUCK

David Zachry, standing on the left, president and CEO of Zachry Construction Corp., shakes hands with Texas Gov. Rick Perry after the state and a private company signed a transportation contract on Friday, March 11, 2005, in Austin, Texas. Standing between them in the background is Mary Peters, Federal Highway administrator. Seated on the left is Rafael del Pino, chairman of Grupo Ferrovial, who shakes hands with Michael Behrens, executive director of the Texas Department of Transportation. The agreement is a step forward for the Trans-Texas Corridor, an 800-mile traffic and trade route between Oklahoma and Mexico.

Neither Calderon nor Harper had played a direct role in the trinational deal made in Waco, Texas, to put in motion what was being called "NAFTA Plus." But Calderon knew he would have to face the same violent chaos at his December inauguration as had already prevented Fox from even making a farewell speech to his Congress. And Harper, the Canadian Conservative Party leader, had only that year succeeded scandal-scorched Liberal leader Martin as prime minister. Both leaders knew the stakes were too high for Bush not to come clean, as Harper put it, on the border issue.

The 43rd president of the United States looked uncomfortable as he signed the legislation in a well-covered photo opportunity. This wasn't what President Bush wanted, but he needed something to deflect a predicted loss of his own party's majority in the approaching election. Signing on to the fence was a cynical and ultimately useless bow to poll pressure, but Bush crossed his fingers and moved the pen.

Quietly, by closed channels, he advised his counterparts in Mexico City and Ottawa that the American people have "short memories" for such things. By Thanksgiving, he had already eliminated funding for an actual fence and slipped the issue off the table, where it was unlikely to be found again among the opposition of Democrats.

Still, he could not yet come clean on Waco and the promise it implied to make both U.S. borders little more than vague in a visionary North American Union (NAU) linking all three countries with a gigantic SuperCorridor of high-speed travel and trade from the Yucatán to the Yukon.

If Bush wasn't ready to take the heat for that, neither Calderon nor Harper would either. The three presidents had signed nothing at Baylor University in Waco or later at the Bush ranch in Crawford, Texas, that they would have to answer for to their legislatures.

Waco, as it would be called, was just a three-way handshake on the Security and Prosperity Partnership of North America (SPP)—one match for three big cigars that might alter the history and culture of the Western Hemisphere. And most of the people in all three countries don't know a thing about it.

"Our partnership," as a Texas White House press release called it, "...will help consolidate our action into a North American framework to confront security and economic challenges, and promote the full potential of our people, addressing disparities and increasing opportunities for all."

Journalist Jerome Corsi, who was nearly alone in questioning the deal, says when he asked SPP director Geri Word why there was so much secrecy, she replied, "We did not want to get the contact people of the working groups distracted by calls from the public."

A second summit, this one attended by Harper for Canada, was arranged in Cancún, Mexico, in March 2006 to discuss the objectives identified by their SPP "working groups."

Robert A. Pastor, an American University professor regarded as the father of the NAU for his 2001 book, "Toward a North American Community," served in a capacity with the U.S. Council on Foreign Relations (CFR) to convene both the Waco and Cancún meetings.

Pastor wrote in a 2004 CFR publication: "Countries are benefited when they change these [national sovereignty] policies, and evidence suggests that North Americans are ready for a new relationship that renders this old definition of sovereignty obsolete."

AP PHOTO/ARNULFO FRANCO

Dr. Robert A. Pastor is vice president of international affairs and professor of international relations at American University in Washington, D.C. Pastor helped Pres. Jimmy Carter (above,center) hand over the Panama Canal to Panama in 1977. He is known as "the father of the North American Union."

Journalist Corsi found part of his answer in Pastor's news conference after Cancún introducing the CFR report, "Building a North American Community." Pastor said the trinational working groups of two-dozen top-level global thinkers had concluded a new institution to be essential to the deal. "And that would be a North American advisory council made up of eminent individuals, appointed for terms that are longer than those of the governments, and staggered over time." In other words, it would be a permanent, non-accountable elite bureaucracy that would advise the elected leaders of Canada, the United States, and Mexico as parts of a new North American community.

"And hopefully," Pastor went on, "the three leaders would turn to this North American council and say, 'Look, we're getting wonderful advice on what we should do about North America as a whole. Why don't you prepare a plan for us on education, on agriculture, on the environment, and we would consider that even as we consider the advice of our government.'"

It was an incredible statement on behalf of a secretive body of eminent appointees that virtually challenged the sovereignty of all three major nations on the North American continent.

Pastor was no real friend to George W. Bush, being a lifelong Democrat who actively supported John Kerry in the 2004 elections. Researcher Patrick Wood tracked Pastor's career back to a CFR task force that engineered President Jimmy Carter's gift of the Panama Canal in 1976 to Latin Americans who soon turned management of the vital, U.S.-built link between the Atlantic and Pacific oceans to a front company for the People's Republic of China.

Today, 90 percent of port operations on both sides of the canal are operated by the Chinese, but the real jewels of Hutchinson Whampoa, based in Hong Kong, may be the ports of Manzanillo and Lazaro Cardenas on the southwest coast of Mexico. Huge container vessels from Asia arrive there on a regular basis with all the consumer goods, from shoes and furniture and clothing and electronics, that are simply no longer produced in the United States.

From those Chinese-operated ports, consumer goods meant for WalMart and other outlets in the United States move north by rail and by Mexican trucks toward the bottleneck at Nuevo Laredo, south of San Antonio. That is part of the secret of NAFTA Plus and the SuperCorridor linked through Texas to what is already planned as a huge hub of immigration and trade where Interstate 35 meets Kansas City.

NAFTA itself was created in 1994 with first-ever "fast track" authority granted by Congress to President William Clinton, after only eight hours of debate and with no public approval. The European Union, by contrast, required more than 10 years of arduous and still-contentious public discussion before creating its amalgam of 21 states. Europeans were given an opportunity to vote on it. The French and the Dutch rejected it.

The Mexican business newsletter, *Frontera Norte Sur,* quoted Isidoro Ruiz Agaiz, a federal deputy in the lower house of the Mexican Congress, as saying a deal has been made with the city council of Kansas City, Missouri, that will circumvent the customs' monopoly held by brokers in Laredo, Texas, with a SmartPort in Kansas City where Mexican authorities would inspect freight bound south of the border.

"I don't know where these ideas get started," scoffs Kansas Republican Sen. Pat Roberts. "This is one of those blogosphere things that makes you wonder what's going on." He says he was unaware of any authorization bill for a SuperCorridor. So far none exists, but Roberts, in addition to being a Kansas senator, is also chairman of the Senate Intelligence Committee. It is surprising that he, like most other members of Congress, simply ignored an international agreement like the SPP.

But whether U.S. politicians or the major media are willing or able to recognize it, a series of meetings and high-level deals among self-professed intellectuals and bottom-line corporate executives have steadily moved Pastor's North American Union closer to an ominous reality.

The official website of the federally funded but "nonprofit" organization North America SuperCorridor Coalition Inc., (NASCO) says: "From the largest border crossing in North America [Detroit], to the second-largest border crossing of Laredo, Texas, Nuevo Laredo, Mexico, extending to the deepwater ports of Manzanillo and Lazaro Cardenas, Mexico, and to Manitoba, Canada, the impressive, trinational NASCO membership truly reflects the international scope of the corridor and the region it impacts."

It simply awaits doing on the route NASCO has already mapped and seen begun with the matching Trans-Texas Corridor toll road.

Mexico's advantages from it seem relatively obvious in the long-awaited surge of Mexican trucks past U.S. Teamster objections into the all-consuming gut of the United States, and with fuel pipelines that could carry still more of Mexican oil to its largest customer. Canadian advantages had apparently been well explored by former Prime Minister Martin, who owns the largest West Coast shipping line in Canada and has dealt closely with Chinese and Asian markets. Canada, especially in its western regions, is still rich in natural resources, including water that could be shifted south in another pipeline to dry regions and timber

AP PHOTO/J. SCOTT APPLEWHITE

Canadian Prime Minister Paul Martin, right, and Mexico's President Vicente Fox, left, shake hands as U.S. President George W. Bush, center, looks on following their meetings and a joint news conference at Baylor University in Waco, Texas, Wednesday, March 23, 2005. Relations have been strained between the U.S. and its closest neighbors and two biggest trading partners with trade, security and immigration issues as points of contention.

that could be moved all the way to Asia. Fiberoptic communications lines and eventually bullet trains carrying passengers and freight would be added to the 10 to 12 lanes racing across the midcontinent.

In theory at least, the United States would come out best with an assured flow of consumer goods, regardless of corporate abandonment of high-priced U.S. labor. So long as Mexicans or Chinese or other Asians will work for much less, the working class of the United States could be satisfied as retailers selling the goods to each other.

They would pay in a new denomination replacing the dollar, which Pastor and others have suggested be called the "Amero," linking all the people of North America to a common currency—and maybe all working people on the continent to a common drudgery.

The NAU and a NAFTA-Plus SuperCorridor are not imaginary black helicopters. They are part of a disturbing scheme by intellectual elites with their corporate partners acting as if they are a royal court of kings and consorts beyond the reach of the common masses. ■

FALL 2009

CAP and TRADE LOOMS LARGE

Will it save the planet or condemn us to serfdom and poverty? By Michael S. Coffman, Ph.D.

By a vote of 219-212 on June 26, the U.S. House of Representatives passed the mind-numbing 1,200-page American Clean Energy Security Act of 2009 (H.R. 2454). Since it was first introduced on May 15, very little discussion was allowed. "We're taking decisive and historic action," said the committee chairman, Henry Waxman (D-California). Waxman is responsible for piloting the bill through the House along with his co-sponsor, Ed Markey (D-Massachusetts). While Waxman may be right that the bill is decisive and historic, most economists claim it is a massive energy tax under the guise of environmental protection. It will give us large reductions in our standard of living, huge job losses and a radical turn toward big government with a corresponding loss of individual freedom.

The Waxman-Markey bill is a cap-and-trade bill similar to what most European nations imposed in 2005. It imposes a declining ceiling, or cap, on greenhouse-gas emissions—primarily carbon dioxide (CO_2)— over the next 40 years. This reduction amounts to three percent below 2005 levels by 2012, 17 percent by 2020, 42 percent by 2030, and 83 percent by 2050. Each regulated industry is given a percentage of the allocated "allowances" defined for the cap that year. The remaining percentage will be auctioned off, with revenues going to the federal government. In other words, it is a hidden tax.

It allows industries like the electric-power sector to buy and sell carbon credits. Thus, a company can continue to emit high levels of CO_2 above the cap by buying credits from more-efficient companies which keep emissions below the cap. That's the theory. The application is far worse. Carbon credits can be bought and sold on the stock market, where megaprofits will be made by speculators and hedge funds—the same characters who brought us the global economic crisis.

The Congressional Budget Office (CBO) projects the cost per family to only be $175 per year. EPA's estimate is even lower. However, the Heritage Foundation analyzed the CBO/EPA computations and found that they conveniently left out major economic costs. Although the Heritage

PHOTO COURTESY OF ECSC PICTURES

Wind power is supposed to take the place of fossil fuel in generating electrical power. The problem is that the wind only blows 25 percent of the time and has to be subsidized by taxpayers at a cost of $24 per megawatt hour. Coal, natural gas and nuclear received only 44 cents, 25 cents and $1.59, respectively.

Foundation stopped short of accusing these government agencies of cooking the books to minimize the economic costs, its own computations showed the cost to be a minimum of $1,288 per year for an average family of three and $1,900 for a family of four.

Worse, the Heritage Foundation's projections do not include losses due to unintended consequences and lost-opportunity costs. When these are included, the costs for a family of four escalate to an average of $2,979 per year over the 2012-2035 time frame. By 2035, the cost is $3,609 per year. In the meantime, the federal government will have raked in $6.5 trillion. Waxman-Markey dwarfs TARP and the Stimulus Plan. Of course, the poor get hit the hardest.

Spain has been building solar and wind farms for almost 10 years and has found that for every renewable green job created, 2.2 jobs are lost. Green jobs come at a cost of $754,000 per job. Like wind power, the U.S. currently subsidizes solar power at more than $24 per megawatt hour. This Spanish solar farm produces eight megawatts per hour.

In practice, increased energy costs would be much higher in the East, Midwest and Rust Belt, where energy-intensive, coal-fired power producers and fuel-oil heating predominate. Not surprisingly, congressional Democrats representing these regions are cool to the idea that their constituents would be hit the hardest. To get them onboard, Waxman diluted the bill, giving special allowances and exemptions to the utilities in these states to soften the blow. The bill also allows up to 1.5 billion tons of international emission reductions, or "offsets," to companies that they can purchase instead of reducing their own emissions each year. An additional one billion tons of offsets are also available for purchase from U.S. sources that capture and sequester CO_2 in some manner.

Eventually the exemptions phase out and the full weight of a 40-percent reduction of carbon emissions hits the U.S. economy like a tsunami.

The operative word here is "purchase." These companies can purchase these offsets or credits, the cost of which is passed on to the consumer, with absolutely no reduction in carbon emissions. It is a scam of unbelievable proportions. Companies like Al Gore's Generation Investment Management Fund are purchasing companies like Camco International Ltd. that sequester carbon. These parasites are positioning themselves to earn billions in profit from the scam at the expense of the consumer, with absolutely no benefit to society or the environment.

By June, there were four of these lobbyists for every congressman proclaiming how the nation must have this legislation to stop global warming. Nowhere in their dazzling propaganda, however, does it mention that at the very best, such a draconian hit on our economy would lower earth's temperature by less than 0.09 degrees Celsius by 2050. This gives new meaning to economic pain with no climate gain.

The exemptions and offsets so diluted the bill that environmentalists decried that there would be no net reduction in CO_2 emissions until 2030. Therein lies the weakness of cap and trade. It is a system begging for corruption. Politicians can grant special dispensations to those they favor, and penalize those they don't. Faceless bureaucrats arbitrarily define the emission caps for specific industries and businesses. Pass a few bucks under the table and you get special treatment.

This type of corruption is what has happened in the European Union. So many exemptions have been made to favored industries that it has turned the entire carbon emission reduction effort into a fiasco. Not only has there been no reduction in the EU's carbon emissions in the four years the EU has imposed cap and trade, but emission rates have actually accelerated at a faster rate than those of the United States. Nations are even giving rebates to industries with skyrocketing energy costs in an attempt to keep them from fleeing to foreign soils. Meanwhile, all these machinations cost huge sums of money. Who pays for it? Taxpayers and consumers.

Eventually (after the crop of politicians who passed it retire or die) the exemptions phase out and the full weight of a 40-percent reduction of carbon emissions hits the U.S. economy like a tsunami. Waxman, Markey and Obama are way ahead of the ball on this one. They have choreographed everything so that renewable energy provides the energy lost by capping fossil-fuel emissions. President Obama has promised he will spend $15 to $20 billion a year to make it happen.

Renewable Energy

Cap-and-trade advocates claim that wind and solar energy will make up the difference in the loss of fossil-fuel energy. All that is required is that we increase wind and solar energy from less than two percent of our energy needs today to 15 to 20 percent by 2020. There are some big problems with this. The wind only blows about 25 percent of the time and the sun doesn't shine at night. While battery technology has made tremendous advances in the past 15 years, there is no technology known today that can store enough energy to compensate while wind towers lie idle and solar panels are inactive.

So, what is going to power your air conditioner when the wind stops blowing on a sultry summer day? Or run your furnace when it is 20 degrees below zero outside? The only way to guarantee the power we must have to sustain our economy and lifestyles is to back it up with fossil-fuel generating plants—the same CO_2-belching ones we have today. A percentage of those have to be in operation 24/7 to immediately take over supplying the needed energy when the wind suddenly dies or the sun goes behind a cloud. Sure, natural gas-generating facilities can start producing energy from a dead start, but natural gas electrical generation is much more expensive to operate than coal. Even if gas were competitive, there isn't enough natural gas to make up for the loss of coal-energy generation. Congress made sure of that this past March when it cavalierly tied up 9.3 trillion cubic feet of natural gas permanently with the Omnibus Public Land Management Act of 2009. (See "Has Congress Gone Mad," *RANGE*, Summer '09.)

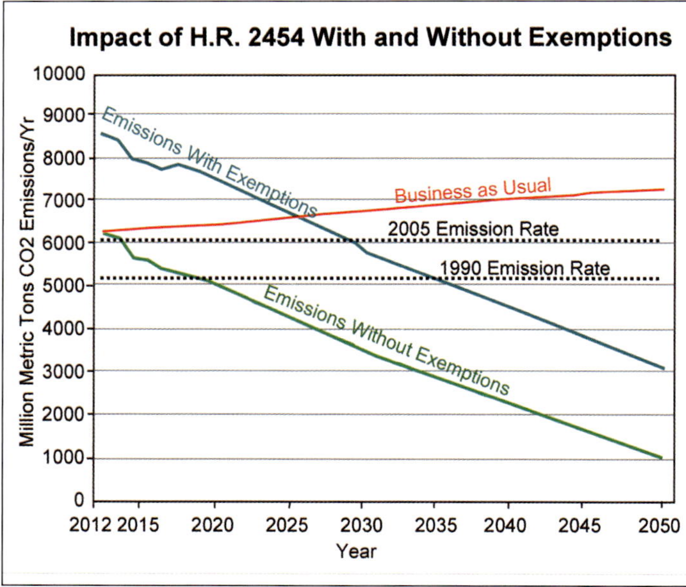

The impact on CO_2 emissions before and after Waxman watered down H.R. 2454 to get the needed votes from the Midwestern and Eastern Democrats. Like typical politicians, the new bill postpones the harshest impacts until Waxman and Markey are no longer in office.

Wind and solar energy have a host of other problems as well. The obvious one is that if we have to keep a significant percentage of the fossil-fuel plants ramped up and ready to take over in seconds, then we are still emitting a lot of CO_2. This nonproductive cost is deadweight and has to be added to the cost of wind and solar. Wear and tear for wind turbines is high and solar photocells get dirty, resulting in substantial maintenance costs. These problems tend to defeat the entire purpose of renewable energy.

Another consideration is that wind and solar farms will not be placed where they could be easily connected to the existing electrical grid. To connect them to the grid adds huge front-end costs. There are significant environmental impacts as well. Birds die when they fly into wind-turbine blades, and solar farms take up square miles of critical habitat for some critter or another. To think that environmentalists won't fight construction efforts tooth and nail is naïve.

Then there is the NIMBY factor—Not In My Backyard. Just ask the Kennedy clan and other elites on Cape Cod who demand that the wind farm off the Cape be removed because it spoils their view. These are but a few of the problems.

The untold difficulty with renewable energy is that it is expensive. Comparing costs is made more difficult by less-than-truthful reporting of total costs by wind and solar interests. Although highly variable across the United States, the Energy Information Administration reported last year that both wind and solar were subsidized at a rate of $24 per megawatt hour, while coal, natural gas and nuclear received only $0.44, $0.25, and $1.59, respectively. Worse, these subsidies do not include the costs of coal-fired power plants that have to stay in operation as a backup to wind and solar. Both wind and solar must be heavily subsidized to stay in business. Once again, guess

© MIKE COFFMAN

Fatal Consequences

Václav Klaus, newly reelected president of the Czech Republic and current president of the European Union, gave a stern warning to the world during the March 2009 International Conference on Climate Change in New York City. He warned that it is "irrational" to blindly attack technologies using carbon-based energy without first developing economically feasible replacements. There is no known way "industrial economies can survive on expensive, unreliable" renewable energy. Not only is replacement with renewable irrational, but it can have "fatal consequences."

President Klaus condemned the blind acceptance by politicians that the United Nations Intergovernmental Panel on Climate Change's "publications represent the [best] science" on global warming. They do not. "These documents do not represent science, but politics and environmental activism." The IPCC deliberately includes only science that supports its preconceived man-caused theory and ignores key peer-reviewed science that refutes it.

"Very respectable scientists," he says, "tell us quite persuasively that . . . there is no one unique, unprecedented climate change" due to man-caused greenhouse-gas emissions. Klaus has a Ph.D. in economics and has studied this issue in depth. "The climate system of our planet has a significant internal [natural] variability." Furthermore, he claims, the "hypothesis of anthropogenic [man-made] global warming is based . . . exclusively on the results of experiments with the very imperfect computer models." The believers in this hypothesis, he notes, "are not able to explain why the global temperature increased from 1918 to 1940, decreased from 1940 to 1976, increased from 1976 to 1998, and decreased from 1998 to the present, irrespective of the fact that the people have been adding increasing amounts of CO_2 to the atmosphere."

Klaus asked this question during 2008's conference, "What is endangered? Climate or freedom? My answer is clear and resolute. It's our freedom, and I might add, our prosperity." He concluded his talk in 2009 by warning, "The environmentalists speak about 'saving the planet.' From what? And from whom? One thing I know for sure: we have to save it—and us—from them."—Michael S. Coffman, Ph.D.

who pays for these subsidies?

Undeterred by these concerns, President Obama claims that we should follow the example of Spain, which is now producing nearly 20 percent of its energy needs from renewables. During the campaign, Obama claimed that he would create five million new green, clean jobs in our transition to renewable energy. So, let's see how these countries have fared by converting to renewable energy.

A study by King Juan Carlos University in Spain found that 2.2 jobs were destroyed in other areas of the economy for every green job created by government decree. Further, it cost $754,000 for every green job created. Applying simple math, Obama's five million new green jobs will only come at a cost of 11 million existing jobs. Worse, 90 percent of those green jobs are construction jobs that will be lost once the infrastructure nears completion. The study concluded that Spain's renewable policies were "terribly economically counterproductive." The authors warn the United States that "the Spanish/EU-style 'green jobs' agenda now being promoted in the United States in fact destroys jobs."

Wind and solar can certainly play a niche role in America's energy supply, and may eventually play a significant role if the technology is developed to mitigate most of its seemingly endless limitations. But as Václav Klaus, president of the EU and the Czech Republic, warns, "These technologies have not yet been invented. . . . There is no known and economically feasible method or technology by which industrial economies can survive on expensive, unreliable, clean, green, renewable energy."

Implementation of the Waxman-Markey bill would seriously harm the economy of the United States, cause the unemployment of six million people, and substantially reduce every family's standard of living.

Perhaps this wrenching transformation of our society could be justified if the doom-and-gloom forecasts of catastrophic consequences of man-caused global warming were correct. However, readers of *RANGE* know that more than 32,000 scientists in the United States alone are now saying there is no convincing scientific evidence that man is causing global warming. Thousands of leading scientists around the world have radically changed their minds because emerging science is increasingly negating the man-caused theory.

Science is also showing that CO_2 is a miracle gas that has increased global food production by over 12 percent. It will continue to do so at an increasing rate. At best, passing the Waxman-Markey bill is not in the nation's best interest. At worst, it is insanity. It is all pain and no climate gain.

The next step is for the Senate to take up the bill passed by the House. This is likely to happen in late summer or early fall. If you have never written your senator before, it is essential you do so now. The consequences are too severe to let this legislation pass. ■

ENVIROS

BALD EAGLES IN ALASKA © EBERHARD BRUNNER

SUMMER/FALL 1993

The SUPERSTAR and the LADY

John Muir and Mary Austin had different views as to what was right and wrong in nature.
By Barney Nelson, Ph.D.

In the early 1900s both John Muir and Mary Austin were writing about sheep grazing in Yosemite, but from opposing viewpoints. Muir called sheep "hoofed locusts" and preached for their removal from the mountain meadow cathedrals. Austin, on the other hand, implied that grazing by sheep, like all creatures who "use the face of the earth to better it," was causing the very flowers and meadows which Muir wanted to protect.

Nature writing was so popular and lucrative during this period that writers competed with one another in two categories: wildness and nobility. Calling himself a "true mountaineer," Muir stared down bears, gloried in earthquakes, clung to swaying pines during thunderstorms, rode an avalanche down a mountain, and even wrote with eagle-feather quill pens. In him the California mountains produced the most nobility: leadership, spirituality, exceptional ethics, and persuasive force. He said a minister would preach a better sermon, and a lawyer deliver better arguments after a trip into the high country.

COURTESY NATIONAL PARK SERVICE, J. MUIR HISTORICAL SITE

While both Muir and Austin indulged in hero worship, Austin places the wild and noble laurel wreath on the shepherds' heads.

However, Muir must not have considered humility and truth as ethical concerns. Egotistically, he calls Henry David Thoreau's stay at Walden Pond "a mere saunter." In 1888, Muir climbed Mount Rainier with a well-organized 12-man expedition, complete with packhorses. He claims blithely that he "did not mean to climb it, but got excited and soon was on top." On another occasion, hearing Clarence Starr King praised for a daredevil climb of Mount Tyndall, Muir said, "When I climbed Tyndall, I ran up and back before breakfast."

Nature writers, both then and now, traditionally assume a wild persona and are allowed, both by critics and readers, to use poetic license (stretching the truth) and hyperbole (exaggeration) in order to heighten interest and the reader's sense of vicarious adventure. However, during Muir's day this physical competition between writers began to get out of hand, and seemed to climax in 1913 when Joseph Knowles stripped naked and walked off into the forest in a cold drizzle in front of a fleet of newspaper reporters. He reportedly lived off the land, lured a bear into a pit, clubbed it, made himself a coat, and wrote a book which sold 300,000 copies before his comfy cabin stocked with canned goods and clothes was discovered.

Austin is one of the few female naturalist writers of the day. Her book, "The Flock," appeared in 1906, right in the middle of Muir's peak writing years. She almost seems to have written her book to correct misinformation about sheep and shepherds published by Muir, whom she knew personally. Their "facts" are at opposite poles almost point for point.

Austin's book deals with the story of sheep grazing in California. She says sheep had been grazing the mountain meadows for more than 100 summers in numbers ranging into the hundreds of thousands, grazing through pastures in early spring as growth began, and back again in the fall after seeds had dropped, an ideal situation for both sheep and plant. She says sheep droppings had been fertilizing the flowers, and asks, "Is it not the custom [everywhere] to put sheep on worn-out lands to renew them?" California shepherds, she points out, came from countries where sheep, flowers, steep mountain pastures, and crystal streams have coexisted for thousands of years.

Born in the Midwest, Mary Austin's father and only sister died when she was 10. In 1888, graduating with a degree in science from Blackburn College, Austin headed to California with her mother to homestead in the San Joaquin Valley. She lived a stark life, often near starvation, amid farmers, sheepherders, cattle ranchers and Indians, all of whom had become close friends and companions.

In "The Flock," Austin assumes a humble persona of naive reporter, happily tagging along behind the sheepherders as they climbed into the meadows with their

SHEEPHERDER WATCHES OVER THE FLOCK © LINDA DUFURRENA

flocks. While both Muir and Austin indulged in hero worship, Austin places the wild and noble laurel wreath on the shepherds' heads. She says the world needs livestock not that we "should have mutton" but that we "should have men." She says when the men return from the mountains they are handsome, tan and bearded. She says the job "sorted" and "selected" the best men, "cleared" their eyes, and "tightened the slack corners" of their mouths. At the end of the trail, they would finally be "worth talking to." About herself she said only that it had taken her "an hour of stiff climbing" up a glacier to reach a shepherd's camp.

Muir's persona fearlessly and capably guides Roosevelt, Emerson, Burroughs, botanists, naturalists and the college educated into the vast mountains. Austin's persona humbly hangs around the homey campfires of Mexican, Indian, and Basque, picking their brains for insight and understanding. Muir says he could have become a millionaire but chose to become a tramp, words he incidentally wrote from his 17-room, redwood-paneled, marble-fireplace home. Austin calls herself simply a lady writing a book.

Muir's persona looks down his clean, moral nose at the ignorant, ill-mannered sheepherder, who wears "everlasting clothing," which he describes as pants waterproofed by congealed fat and gravy juices, impregnated with bits of nature. These greasy clothes do make the sheepherder a collector of specimens, says Muir humorously, but "far from being a naturalist."

These greasy clothes do make the sheepherder a collector of specimens, says Muir humorously, but "far from being a naturalist."

Austin calls the sort of judgment which ridicules sheepherders simple prejudice and says the fact "that most sheepherders are foreigners accounts largely for the abomination in which they are held and the prejudice that attaches to the term." Austin preferred the company of Shoshones, Paiutes and settlers from Old Mexico to her white neighbors because, she said, their carefree natures contrasted with "people whose creeds are chiefly restrictions against other people's way of life."

While being out in wild nature supplies Muir's persona with a deep appreciation of nature, this does not seem to work on his shepherd, who gains no appreciation of the wild beautiful nature which surrounds him. Says Austin, again because of language, the shepherd simply finds it difficult to put his appreciation into words.

The apparent argument between their authorial personas seems to become almost heated as they trade opposing facts. Muir's sheepherder carries a six shooter; Austin says they never carry guns because "a gun does not go easily in a *cayaca*." Muir says their food is "usually far from delicate"; Austin goes into rapture over the wonderful meals she has eaten at a shepherd's fire. Muir makes fun of the sheepherder's desire to sleep next to the sheep "as if determined to take ammoniacal snuff all night." Austin says, "The smell of sheep is to the herder as the smack and savor of any man's work." Muir describes sheepherders forcing sheep to wade and swim streams; Austin says sheep men always built tottering bridges over streams because sheep were such fastidious drinkers, they would die of thirst rather than drink from a fouled stream.

"All outdoors contrive to nourish imagination and [sheepherders] have in full what we oftenest barely brush wings with."

Austin also pooh-poohs the idea of risk in the Sierra saying the city dwellers are often incredulous that the shepherds "go about" these mountains "unhurt and unoffended by the wild."The Sierra, she says, are a maze of sheep trails, footpaths, and camps. Tucked away at the edge of most large meadows is food, shelter and firewood. Western hospitality traditionally welcomed anyone to these supplies which took any true risk out of traveling light, a fact often overlooked by today's young hikers who, trying to follow in Muir's footsteps, succumb to exposure and exhaustion.

Austin says shepherds were masters at reading weather signs by clouds and sky color, so they seldom suffered from weather stress. Wildcats, cougars, coyotes, and bears, she said, were merely "incidents of the day's work, like putting on stiff boots." Bears often strolled harmlessly over sleeping shepherds at night or burned their paws trying to rob frying pans. "Or so it was," she says pointedly, "in the days before the summer camper found the country."

The two authors even disagree over the sheep's natural wildness. Muir says domestic sheep cannot exist without the herder. Their stupidity and flock mentality, he says, makes them easy prey for predators. Austin, taking an opposite stance, says sheep problems with predators are caused by close herding. She relates an incident at El Tejon during the drought of 1876, when 58,000 head of starving sheep were simply turned loose in December to die. The flocks slowly disapeared into the bear-, cougar-, and wolf-infested mountains. The next fall, when rains had finally replenished the winter meadows, 53,000 head of healthy sheep trailed themselves back down from the mountains.

One chapter of Austin's book even takes on Yosemite National Park, saying even the rangers sympathized with lawbreaking shepherds and looked the other way while they snuck back into their old summer haunts, because the rangers "despised…the work of warding sheep off the grass in order that silly tourists might wonder at the meadows full of bloom."

Either John Muir or Mary Austin must be wrong about sheep. Was one author lying or did prejudice and stigmatism taint perspectives? If indeed a duel was being fought between the two authors, Austin lost the battle. Muir's persona "worked" on the reader and Austin's did not. Instead of drawing the reader into a shared vicarious experience, Austin shuts the reader out. Muir's persona says to the reader, "Come along with me into these mountains; only you and I truly appreciate the wilderness." Only Muir and the reader recognized each plant; only Muir and the reader could ride an avalanche. Everyone else, even tourists, did not appreciate the "glorious objects about them," but the readers, identifying with Muir, did not see themselves as tourists.

Readers were put off by Austin's persona because it shut them out by emphasizing the superiority of natural men over urban readers. Austin's persona tells the reader, "Stay away. You and I are not fit for the wilderness, leave it with these healthy shepherds who best know how to take care of it and who have given their lives to it." And perhaps this was her intent. Even as a child, Mary Austin was admonished by her mother not to "antagonize people," but to try to "draw people to you." Mary would reply stubbornly, "And what would I do with the people after I have drawn them to me?"

This was something John Muir may not have thought of. Today over two million travelers stand in line every year to see the views of Yosemite. The "beautiful" well kept "gardens" full of flowers, "grass up to a bear's hips," and "champagne water," which Muir encountered during his first summer in Yosemite Valley with the sheep, have been replaced by two hotels, four swimming pools, five grocery and general stores, five souvenir shops, two golf courses, six gas stations, a bank, a hospital, campsites for 6,000 people, and a vast motel and parking-lot complex.

Today in Yosemite lodgepole pines have invaded the meadows, white fir and incense cedar are crowding the great sequoias. Seedlings of these invaders used to be grazed by sheep and burned by fires set by shepherds in order to improve pastures. The same kind of fires the Paiute and Shoshone set to improve hunting meadows. One of Muir's modern critics, with old stigmatisms attached, even calls John "a shepherd and the people his sheep." ■

FALL 1995

BUTCHERING THOREAU

Modern scholars are slicing a literary classic to eliminate cows. By Barney Nelson.

I saw a cartoon the other day, published by the "The Far Side" folks. A cow was sitting in the witness chair with a stern judge presiding and a badgering prosecuting attorney in her face. The attorney said they had figured out *how* she did it, but the question now was *why*. The cow is currently on trial for everything from shrinking our national-park playgrounds to depleting the ozone. Somehow, Henry David Thoreau gets credit for starting this mess but that was never his intention.

While teaching a new class called Environmental Literature at Sul Ross State University in Alpine, Texas, I was about to assign Thoreau's classic American lit essay, "Walking." One of our textbooks (American Environmentalism: Readings in Conservation History, Third Edition, 1990, by Roderick Frazier Nash) had a shortened version, which Nash had renamed, "The Value of Wildness." I read Nash's version and, at first, it seemed okay. But there were many little innocent-looking ellipses where passages had been removed. Curious about what was missing, I compared it with Thoreau's original.

I was shocked! Nash, a respected University of California history scholar, had carefully left out all references to horses, cows, farming and pastures. His deletions and one misplaced paragraph had changed the essay's focus from how wildness as a saving grace lurks beneath the surface of all things domestic, to California-style anti-agriculture propaganda.

Thoreau's original version attempts to define the word "wildness" and how important it is to the sanity and happiness of modern man. When Thoreau finds himself "leaving the city more and more" and heading into the wilderness for a walk, he says, "We have a wild savage in us." This wildness that he struggles to define cannot be bred out, beat out, preached out, or domesticated out of any animal, including the human. He says the earth possesses a terrifying wildness that will be our eventual salvation.

Today Thoreau is considered some kind of mountain-man hero who built a cabin with his own two hands and lived alone in the wilderness, something most of us are too domesticated to do. But we skip over the details. Thoreau was actually quite unhealthy, his wilderness cabin was less than a mile out of Concord, Massachusetts, and he walked home for chocolate pie almost every afternoon. But he tried to explain how wildness *can* be found even in a frail man like himself, even in our libraries.

Traditionally, Americans have looked with disdain on all things domestic because we want to stand for freedom. Desk jobs, air-conditioned tractors and push-button conveniences have stripped us of our self-respect. As a result, people seem to be projecting their own worst faults onto cows. Cows can seem quite lazy on a warm afternoon. They belch as they lie around chewing their cuds and their flatulence is blamed for destroying the atmosphere. Elk and buffalo, of course, like more-ethical, healthier, and wilder humans have better manners. Only slovenly, TV-watching, beer-drinking couch potatoes and cows would defecate in

Thoreau rejoiced in the fact that the cow had not lost this wildness. He loved "to see the domestic animals reassert their native rights—any evidence that they have not wholly lost their original wild habits and vigor."

pristine water, leave trails up and down stream banks, draw flies and get cranky as they age. Cows and modern humans must be dumber than elk and buffalo, much less noble, much less environmentally aware.

But the cow was not born domestic. In "Walking," Thoreau reminds us she was in fact descended, like people, from the savage. One cow ancestor, the wild European aurochs, became extinct in 1627; another, the wild white ursus, in 1859. Other ancestors are either threatened or endangered: the Asian yak, the banteng of Indonesia, the guar of India, even the European wisent.

Thoreau rejoiced in the fact that the cow had not lost this wildness. Looking to nature for ways to understand human problems, he observed that each generation of "horses and steers have to be broken before they can be made the slaves of men." He said, "[t]he seeds of instinct are preserved under the thick hides of cattle and horses, like seeds in the bowels of the earth, an indefinite period." And he loved "to see the domestic animals reassert their native rights—any evidence that they have not wholly lost their original wild habits and vigor."

Thoreau begins his essay, "I wish to speak a word for Nature, for absolute freedom and wildness." So do I. I grew up and spent my adult life on ranches in Arizona and Texas. I have cried holding calves in my arms while they died, and I've eaten a bunch of them without guilt. I have worked cattle in places where, when I heard a twig snap, I had a few tense moments in which to decide whether to run for my life or give chase. Some of those old wild, sharp-horned, brush-popper cows came out of a manzanita thicket like a freight train, aiming for my horse's belly. I've helped pull weak cows out of deep mud where they had bogged down, only to have them try to kill me for my efforts. Thoreau in his sissy-sounding words called it "sportiveness in cattle" and said it was usually "unexpected."

I've been on ranches where phantom cows lived long, happy lives, never caught or branded. Constantly pursued by some of the West's finest cowboys, these cattle have learned to leave very faint tracks. I've seen mule deer in Texas that were shot at every deer season, and often by poachers between, which did not run from an approaching pickup, horse or foot traveler. Nobody in a pickup and few people horseback ever catch a glimpse of renegade cattle. Foot travelers better hope they don't.

I've helped pull calves from wild heifers which would run off and leave their calves to die because they smelled like a human. Like all wild animals, cows react to changes in weather, showing restlessness and nervousness when a storm is brewing. I've seen 300 heifers sniff the breeze off a "blue norther," throw kinks in their tails and stampede. Or, as Thoreau would say, they were "running about and frisking in unwieldy sport" as they "shook their heads, raised their tails and rushed up and down a hill."

Thoreau enjoyed seeing his "neighbor's cow [break] out of her pasture early in the spring and boldly [swim] the river" like the buffalo. Like buffalo, I've seen cattle hump up with their snow-covered backs against the wind and wait patiently for the three-day thaw they seemed to know was coming. I've seen them break ice for a drink and drift into a storm in order to get through it faster. History is full of tales of abandoned cowherds left to die in a blizzard and found alive with new calves the following spring—although sometimes neither they nor caribou make it.

Maybe catching should be the measure of an animal's wildness? I've known some cows that couldn't be gathered. On the other hand, I've known both elk and bison that could be rounded up easily. I've been licked in the face by a tame wolf and have shot into a pack of wild dogs to save my life. I've known pet mountain lions and feral "domestic" cats. In "Brute Neighbors," Thoreau says, "The most domestic cat, which has lain on a rug all her days, appears quite at home in the woods."

I once raised a wild chicken that roosted alone with the coons for several years; Thoreau knew a partridge that acted like a hen. About cattle, he said he "perceived by their horns, as well as by their activity, their relation to the deer tribe."

Perhaps the number of times an animal has killed a man should determine wildness. The cow wins the race a hundred times over. I once knew a crippled cow that couldn't stand, yet hooked a cowboy carrying a bucket of water to her. She pounded, slashed, and scraped him through the brush and rocks for several long minutes before he was finally able to crawl for his life. As Thoreau would say, she was "not yet subdued to man."

Maybe eating feed poured out by humans should be the measure of wildness? Cows must be taught to eat hay or feed cubes. This doesn't come naturally. On some desert ranches where cows are never taught, a drought can wipe out an entire herd. I've seen antelope come to the feed ground to eat but have known cows which starved themselves to death once corralled. I have friends who spend their winters feeding Yellowstone's elk, hauling hay on sleds with teams of horses. Today buffalo, elk, and musk oxen are often branded, vaccinated, castrated, dehorned, kept in pens or fenced pastures and harvested, just like their former wild cousin the cow.

Cows are often called stupid when they step on a cowboy's foot, when they take his horse away from him, when they blow snot down his neck while he's trying to brand their calf. They are called stupid when they get old, smoothmouthed, stiffjointed and refuse to get on the truck that will permanently take them away from their pastures. They are called stupid when they silently lose a tracker in noisy, slippery shale, or lie down and disappear behind a foot-high bush. They are called stupid when they out-hear, out-see, and out-smell their tracker. College-educated cowboys humbly admit they have been outsmarted by a stupid cow.

All of this is wildness.

It was in this "Walking" essay that Thoreau wrote, "In wildness is the preservation of the world." He is often misquoted as having said, "In wilderness is the preservation of the world."

Nash also adds to this mistaken interpretation in his book, writing, "Thoreau spoke a half-century before most Americans were prepared to listen sympathetically to his message. Nevertheless, his philosophy survived to become the intellectual foundation of the wilderness preservation movement."

However, Thoreau's contemporaries read his original essay instead of the Nash version. That may be the reason they did not listen and rush out to preserve wilderness. Thoreau's classic essay focuses on the idea that wildness is something we cannot lose. He says civilization can hide it, oppression can stifle it, and education can tame it, but scratch the surface and wildness springs eternal. He says wildness can be found in the forests and in wilderness, but he also lists numerous other places: in domestic animals, in "tawny" grammar, in less "civilized" cultures, in libraries, in architecture, underneath calluses, in the migratory instincts of birds, in the simplest and obscurest of men, in soil, in the smell on a trapper's coat, in tan skin, in both bogs and spades, in the sound of a bugle on a summer night, and in the humble act of walking. He says that wildness is imported by cities and that men plow and sail for it. He did not say wildness needed our condescending protection; he said wildness would protect us. Nash does Thoreau and American literature a sad disservice by narrowing these big classic ideas down into preservation politics. ■

THOREAU'S VERSION OF THOREAU

One vivid example of the way Nash changed Thoreau's meaning occurs in the following paired passages. Thoreau's version explains "wildness" through skin color:

"A tanned skin is something more than respectable, and perhaps olive is a fitter color than white for a man—a denizen of the woods. 'The pale white man!' I do not wonder that the African pitied him. Darwin the naturalist says, 'A white man bathing by the side of a Tahitian was like a plant bleached by the gardener's art, compared with a fine, dark green one, growing vigorously in the open fields.'

Ben Johnson exclaims,
"How near to good is what is fair!"
So I would say,
"How near to good is what is wild!"

NASH'S VERSION OF THOREAU

Nash deletes Thoreau's original paragraph. Then he inserts a paragraph that actually appears several pages later in the essay. Through his manipulation, Nash is able to give his own version a preservationist and anti-agricultural flavor that Thoreau never intended:

"I would not have every man nor every part of a man cultivated, any more than I would have every acre of earth cultivated: part will be tillage, but the greater part will be meadow and forest, not only serving an immediate use, but preparing a mould against a distant future, by the annual decay of the vegetation which it supports....

Ben Johnson exclaims,
"How near to good is what is fair!"
So I would say,
"How near to good is what is wild!"

This moved paragraph originally appears right after Thoreau's sentence, "Not even does the moon shine every night, but gives place to darkness." Thoreau follows it with the idea that even grammar rules should sometimes be broken in order to allow for freedom of expression. Through his metaphoric comparisons between forests and cultivated fields, moonlight and darkness, proper grammar and lingo, Thoreau was explaining how he believed the world needed and already contained some sort of a balance between this "wildness" he was attempting to define and the constraints placed upon us all by society, education, government and religion.

SPRING 1997

THE MISSION

Has Jon Marvel's passion for Idaho become a nightmare for federal lands ranchers? By Linda Hesthag

Jon Marvel loves open land. Like many transplanted Easterners, he has a great appreciation for Idaho's millions of acres of wilderness and mountains. He hikes. He has run every river in the state. He and his wife have made Idaho their home for 27 years. That is why this Hailey architect spends 50 percent of his time investigating and often protesting federal lands management decisions.

Marvel says his goal is to preserve and restore Idaho's natural beauty for future generations. It is a goal that most Idahoans share. What has created controversy are his tactics and his attacks on western ranching culture. It is clear that he would like to see all the cows removed from public lands.

Marvel's primary weapon is the Bureau of Land Management (BLM) and Forest Service's own grazing regulations. As an "interested public," he can protest and appeal decisions made by the federal government on a large portion of Idaho's public leases. When Marvel believes public land is being mismanaged—and even when he doesn't—he simply files a protest or an appeal with the federal government. Everything, including positive management changes and decisions made by ranchers and federal land managers, can easily be blocked by individuals with nothing at stake. Anyone in America can be an interested public on federal lands.

© LINDA HESTHAG ELLWEIN

According to Bob Mitchell, BLM legal advisor, Marvel and his group, the Idaho Watersheds Project [later named Western Watersheds Project], have filed hundreds of protests over the last two years. For the family rancher, the consequences of such an appeal and subsequent legal ramifications are usually catastrophic.

Few would argue that abuses have occurred over the last 120 years on federal land, often by those with no generational stakes in it. But many would come to the defense 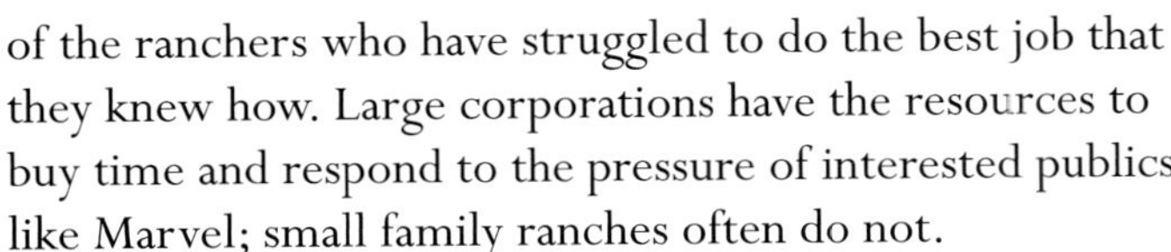 of the ranchers who have struggled to do the best job that they knew how. Large corporations have the resources to buy time and respond to the pressure of interested publics like Marvel; small family ranches often do not.

Marvel was born in Wilmington, Delaware, and began visiting Idaho at the age of 13. He and his brother used to work summers on the trail crew at Sun Valley. He moved to Idaho after college and attended graduate school in Eugene, Oregon. He was 22 when he moved to Idaho full-time.

Marvel and his group have been very successful at making national headlines by constantly attacking what they believe are poor grazing practices. This has created great opposition from the ranching community.

Even though Marvel's views are insulting to ranchers, his attitudes toward public lands are representative of many new residents of the West. But his disdain for the people and culture makes many people, including other environmental activists, cringe. Some fellow environmentalists feel Marvel's motives are often unclear and that his approach is too antagonistic and threatening. Others say he is motivated by ego and his goal is to get all cows off public lands. He has heckled at public meetings and even stuck out his tongue at an auctioneer during a recent state lands auction.

Since Marvel's activism affects so many people—ranchers, federal and state government officials and fellow environmentalists—many believe it would be good for Idaho if he would participate in a collaborative investigation of Idaho's ecosystem on the ground. These community projects, working without emotion or ego, are benefiting everyone.

Many critics complain that Marvel is costing the federal government and the state a lot more money than he's bringing in from a few grazing leases as a result of the mountains of paperwork required to respond to him.

"This last year the paperwork from his one group has tied me to my desk 90 percent of the time," say range conservationist John Biar from Idaho's Jarbidge area. "I rarely get out on the ground anymore. It's hard to manage a million acres from a desk."

Ranchers believe that natural resources are our only true source of wealth. The challenge is to harvest sustainably. Many environmentalists feel nature should be allowed to take its own course, without interference from man.

Environmentalist Kathy Baer is program director for the Sawtooth Wildlife Council in Stanley. She has a broader view. "I have recently come to believe that the real answers lie with those people who work the land," she says. "They are the ones who can restore the balance between nature and society." ■

© LARRY TURNER

Eastern Oregon ranch.

Q&A

Who is Jon Marvel? What is his vision for Idaho? Here are a few glimpses:

What do you appreciate about Idaho?

I like the environment here, that there's so much open land that we're not barred from entering because it is publicly owned. This is something in the East we don't have very much of, at least where I grew up [Wilmington, Delaware].

What influence do you think the ranch culture has had on Idaho?

I think it's been extraordinarily influential in Idaho and the rest of the West, because it's a gregarious and domineering kind of culture.... The history of livestock ranching in the West is one of conglomeration and growth into massive units of operation as opposed to the Ma and Pa operations. And, of course, the days of the commons when there was no organization on the public lands, it was first come, first served. The Johnson County cattle wars in Wyoming were indicative of the kind of independent, take-charge, aggressively grabbing whatever they could. In a way it's a culture that is dysfunctional in relationship to the rest of society.

Why do you say it is dysfunctional?

Well, because it's taken what it's wanted without asking permission and without considering the concerns of others. That continues to this day. Public lands ranching is one of the more aggressive forms of capitalism, a very directed effort to control the use of millions of acres for the benefit of a very few.

So is the issue control of that land?

There are many issues involved here. That's certainly one of them. And I think many ranchers to this day who are public lands users believe that at some level the land is theirs.

Is your purpose with the Idaho Watersheds Project to run ranchers out of business?

No, no, I think that they're running themselves out of business. Our goal is to have a healthy functioning environment that sustains the greatest good for the greatest number of people, as well as the wildlife dependent on that environment. There's no question that I believe that reducing the number of cows and sheep on public lands will help achieve those goals and I think that possibly may result in many ranch operations ceasing to be in business. But that's not our goal.

What are the positive effects that the ranch culture has had on the state?

I can't think of any. I find that the negatives so outweigh the positive. Their arrogance, their lies, their manipulation of politics, their control of the state legislature and the governor's office. Their environmentally destructive practices, their dependence on social welfare through the Taylor Grazing Act, and other subsequent acts. The way they treat people they disagree with. All those things add up to a huge preponderance against them as a culture.

How do you feel about hunting?

Well, I think hunting is a good thing; it benefits many families just in terms of food supply. In Idaho we are fortunate to have plentiful species out there. I think that people who own land and live adjacent to public lands where wildlife roam, which belongs to all of us, have to factor into their business a risk factor that they will lose some portion of their production to these animals which formerly, in many cases, had access to those areas as prime winter habitat and were excluded by the introduction of livestock and homesteading.

So, if those areas develop as subdivisions, you would feel the same way?

Yes. However, I do support the establishment of land trusts and the maintenance of open land, where it can be accomplished. One thing we might point out is we don't see any initiative taken by the cattle association or the wool growers. They whine a lot about subdivisions and private land development but they don't do anything about it. Ranchers are constantly subdividing in places like Lemhi and Custer counties. I understand the Colorado Cattle Association has actually created a land trust to benefit ranchers where they can make contributions of easements or in-fee land to protect open spaces. What's the matter with Idaho ranchers? They don't do it. It's a big complaint for them, but the complaint really is they don't want us meddling with their operation because they use subdivision as a threat.

If you could choose between working cooperatively and going the route you're going, which one would you prefer?

I'm perfectly willing to collaborate and cooperate with people, and often have. As you know, I went down to meet [ranchers] Jay Black and Joel Hermann on the Ecogroup Winter Camp Youth Allotment. Carl Austin, down at Oakley, called me [because] he was concerned we were going to bid on state leases he held, and I went down and saw...where he was actively working to protect Goose Creek and the tributaries on the state lease. We issued a press release...saying that we would not apply for his leases because he was working so hard to do a good job there and we couldn't even get that in the newspapers. Nobody would even publish that.

You often talk about desertification. What do you think is the primary cause?

Cattle didn't coevolve with a droughty, arid, hot and then very cold environment. They're a swamp animal. I think that desertification has been caused by livestock mismanagement. Well, I think cattle are really an unsuitable species for the arid West, and I think there are large aspects of mismanagement that have occurred—or no management may be a better way to describe it.

Some scientists say that if grasses in a brittle environment are totally rested, without any animal impact whatsoever, that the soil caps over and forms a cryptobiotic crust that can create more erosion due to runoff and the inability for water to absorb into the soil. Do you think that's true?

Well, this is a classic Allan Savory theory [of the Center for Holistic Management] and if you read the articles and the collected information that [enviro scientist] Joy Belsky has put together about this, the word is bull****. That's the simplest way to describe it.

If it was possible on those same areas to increase organic matter in the soil and increase the plant communities and biodiversity, including species and age groups, would that, in your opinion, be more beneficial than the crust?

Absolutely not. I presume the next question is, "Aren't livestock a way to accomplish that?" And I would say no. There is no evidence to support Wayne Burkhardt [Ph.D., range science], or anybody else, saying that the systems we have in the arid Great Basin and the Snake River Plain are coincident with large ungulate grazing and coevolved with them. And, even if there were evidence, and even if Wayne Burkhardt and Allan Savory and their friends were correct in this, it would make no difference in my understanding of public lands ranching as being inappropriate for Idaho or the arid West, because there are many other reasons besides that, that should be driving these people out of business. So, I'm even willing to say, for a moment anyway, all right, they're right. But it doesn't matter.

What about the economic impact on public lands ranchers?

There's no reason to sustain a culture that is dependent on us as a welfare handout source and which has the arrogance that this particular one does. If they canned the arrogance and started to talk openly...then we might get somewhere. But [when they whine], we've been here for 100 years and blah, blah, blah...I like it. I really like it. Because I know that their foot is half in the grave right now, if they keep talking like that. And that's good. Because they won't know until it caves in underneath them, what hit 'em. ■

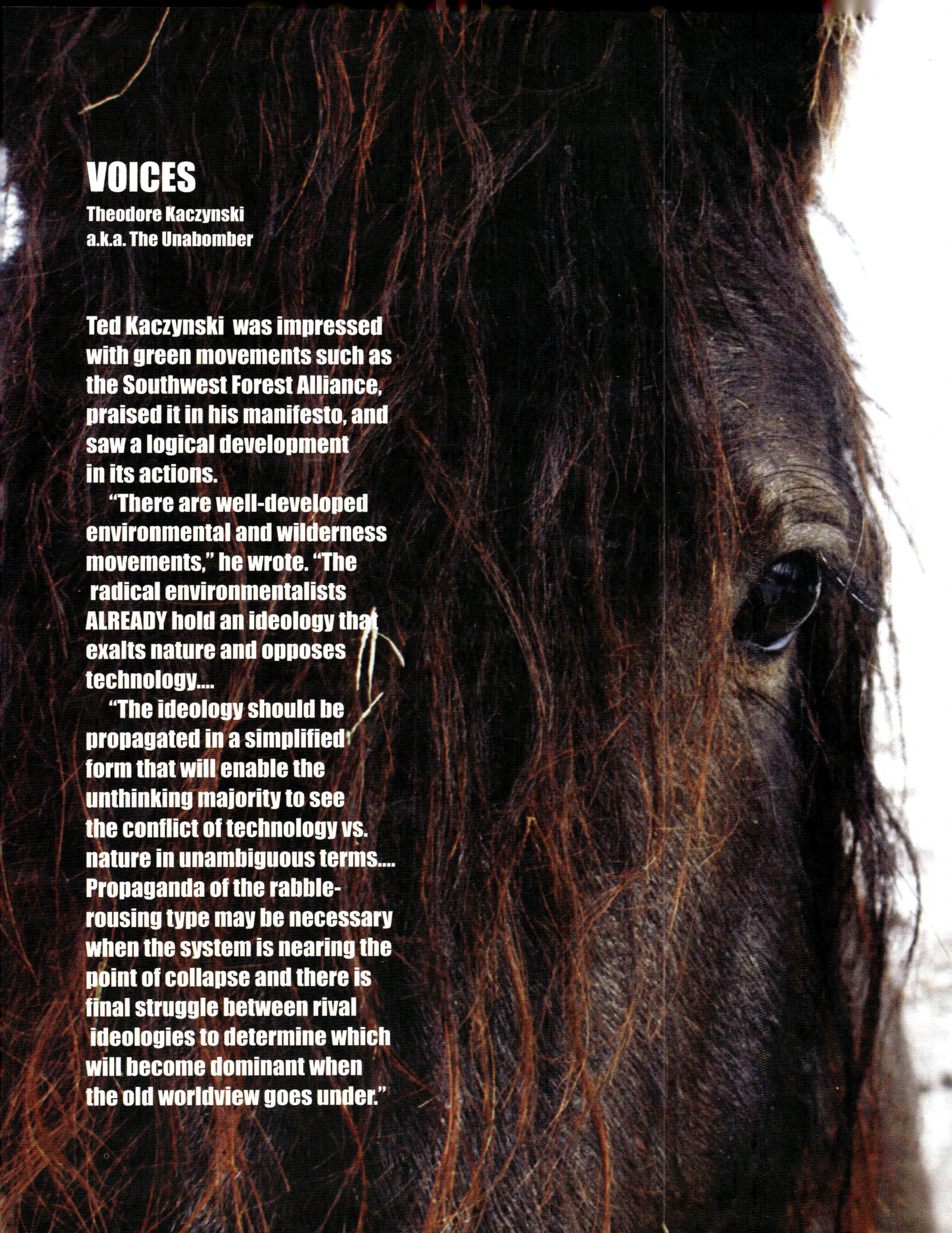

VOICES

Theodore Kaczynski
a.k.a. The Unabomber

Ted Kaczynski was impressed with green movements such as the Southwest Forest Alliance, praised it in his manifesto, and saw a logical development in its actions.

"There are well-developed environmental and wilderness movements," he wrote. "The radical environmentalists ALREADY hold an ideology that exalts nature and opposes technology....

"The ideology should be propagated in a simplified form that will enable the unthinking majority to see the conflict of technology vs. nature in unambiguous terms.... Propaganda of the rabble-rousing type may be necessary when the system is nearing the point of collapse and there is final struggle between rival ideologies to determine which will become dominant when the old worldview goes under."

SPRING 2003

NATURE'S LANDLORD

The story of the world's most powerful environmental group: The Nature Conservancy.
By Tim Findley

Unless we as a people are willing to accept the continued loss of not only private property and individual rights, but of large portions of our national culture and customs as well, The Nature Conservancy must be brought to heel. Right now, it is a well-fed and generally admired beast leading us in a wild run that is as destructive in its seemingly friendly character as it is in its seldom-seen attacks. This is no errant clumsy puppy we can finally calm. It is a runaway predator that will turn on us in defense of its territory.

The Nature Conservancy (TNC) is the wolf we raised ourselves, the grizzly we fed from the table. The monster we made with indifference. If it is left to go on growing, it will be the master and we the obedient slaves.

If left unchecked, The Nature Conservancy will be the master and we the obedient slaves.

Americans who presume to know the subject from national press accounts and even from their personal experience with our 10th largest nonprofit organization will be outraged by such a suggestion. To them, TNC's aims and accomplishments are as obvious in the millions of square miles of forests and wetlands "saved" by TNC as they are in the simple stunning beauty of a single butterfly that might not otherwise exist. Whatever small abuses may have occurred, well-meaning Americans will argue, those are nothing in comparison to what TNC has preserved for future generations.

Yet it is just those future generations we should be concerned about in bringing some accountability to a small group of people with grossly exaggerated power and authority over fundamental elements of a free society.

The Beginning

In less than half a century, TNC would control 90 million acres worldwide.

George Fell sat all alone at the corner of a long polished table in the Washington, D.C., library of the American Nature Study Society. This was the last office left open to him, and his work spilled out from a heavy leather briefcase. It scattered across the table. A hundred separate regions were depicted there. Places where nature alone still strongly held dominance. Fell was determined to save those places, whatever it took, and part of those files held a guidebook on how he might do it: financial records of corporations glutted with wartime profits, federal documents on land acquisitions, and data on tax shelters for charitable trusts.

Many, but not all his friends in the Ecologists Union had deserted him, rejecting what they saw as his crass mixture of political pressure with scholastic science. Fell was largely alone, living on the wages of his wife, a medical technician, but he had a plan.

It was 1951. Most of American society, including even the scientific community given new respect since the end of the war, was preoccupied with the gorging opportunities of victory and peace. Korea was troublesome, but the real message was in expanding wealth and unimaginable advances in public technology. George Fell clanged a different, unharmonious tone, suggesting pause in a period of development, study over pragmatic success, and most of all a step from the towers of scientific academia into the slippery ground of political pressure and subtle extortion as the means to an end.

If even he could have imagined it then, what Fell was about to create could have come from a story line in "The Twilight Zone." Less than a half century later, it would be by far the most powerful environmental organization in history, capable of manipulating governments, including that of the United States, endowed with assets amounting to nearly $3 billion, and exempt from taxes. It would be directly in control of some 90 million acres worldwide, with more than 12 million acres, an area the size of Switzerland, in the United States alone. Its private data bank contained unsurpassed information on the dispersal of plant and animal species in all 50 states and at least one-third of the rest of the world. And yet, even with its tentacles reaching into the most influential elements of international power, it remained secretive, virtually untouchable by legal oversight, its motives and its methods only vaguely understood as somehow being associated

Stillwater Marshes near Fallon, Nevada, on the Pacific Flyway and the reason The Nature Conservancy rode into town to "save the birds." What they did is attain water rights that left behind lifeless farms unable to support even weeds.

with science.

As it happened, 1951 was the year Steve McCormick was born. In February 2001, a half century after Fell began forming his cadre at that library table, McCormick stood in the richly appointed Arlington, Virginia, headquarters of The Nature Conservancy and accepted the godfatherly introduction from Anthony P. Grassi, the venerable but seldom-seen chairman of the board of governors of TNC. McCormick, Grassi suggested, was "born for the job" as chief executive officer of the richest environmental organization on earth and the 10th best-funded nonprofit organization in the United States, just behind Stanford and Harvard universities, and well ahead of U.S. Catholic Charities.

"It's not enough," said McCormick.

Firmly set as it was, deep in the foundations of American wealth and power, The Nature Conservancy had teetered just slightly at its highest point when John Sawhill unexpectedly died in 2000 after serving for its 10 most successful years as chief executive. Little power struggles had troubled the organization before, all the way back to Fell's time when others began to catch on to the practicality of his scheme to sustain the organization by using donated funds to buy selected properties, and then sell or trade those properties to the government.

But by the time the eclectic and slightly eccentric-seeming McCormick stood at the precipice of power so long held by old-school ties, the awesome opportunities before him reached deeper and wider into the sources of real wealth in America and the world than anyone could have imagined. Philanthropic foundations based on almost obscene accumulations of mogul wealth from energy, technology, and industrial development still held billions of dollars necessary to be transferred, some say "laundered," through charities for tax purposes.

As the founders of TNC discovered in the '50s, the really big money from such charitable foundations as the Pew Charitable Trusts (Sun Oil), Rockefeller Foundation, Charles Stewart Mott Foundation (GM, sugar, banking), General Motors, The Ford Foundation, and dozens of others had seldom, if ever, gone directly to poor people. It went to work for secondary providers such as research by the Cancer Society or relief by the Red Cross—recipient groups that could show altruistic results without really altering the overbalance of power between the wealthy and the poor. The Nature Conservancy provided a perfectly useful new purpose, not only "saving" stretches of nature, but then transferring the land to the government for "public" purposes that would not challenge the resource holdings behind the foundations themselves. The government might manage these new public lands, but the real power of

PHOTO COURTESY THE NATURE CONSERVANCY

By the time the eclectic and slightly eccentric-seeming Steve McCormick stood at the precipice of power so long held by old-school ties, the awesome opportunities before him reached deeper and wider into the sources of real wealth in America and the world than anyone could have imagined.

old money accumulated in a period of exploitation would remain in its control without new competition.

For TNC, the method established a continuously revolving source of funds—donations to government, purchase to donations—that only grew larger as those in the organization realized new ways to refine Fell's concept under the shelter of its tax-exempt status acquired in 1950.

Soon, the governing board of TNC was formed of bankers, investors, and foundation heads themselves. It was disguised somewhat with the creation of boards of trustees set up in eight regions with chapters in every state, and run with the figurehead presence of "trustee members" from government and the media, including Attorney General Janet Reno, retired Army Gen. H. Norman Schwarzkopf, and media leviathan Gerald Levin of Time Warner Inc., among many other prominent names.

Particularly in the 1990s as policies of the Clinton administration and the greens' choice of Interior Secretary Bruce Babbitt cleared the way, The Nature Conservancy could report astonishing growth in its own nontaxable assets. But those millions leading into billions hardly told the story. By then, The Nature Conservancy could tap into almost limitless funds virtually at will. Money was far less important than power.

"We've raised a lot of money," said McCormick. "Well, that, in itself, is not a measure of success. We've been growing a lot. That is not a measure of success."

While he was president of New York University between 1975 and 1979, *The New York Times* credited John Sawhill with creating a "miracle of higher education" in turning around the struggling academic and financial condition of the nation's largest private university. If that had been a single miracle of higher education in the '70s, Sawhill must have found beatitude from his increase of TNC assets by more than five times in the 1990s.

Sawhill was a straight-laced egghead with an eye for opportunity, an academic with degrees in economics but a career interest in energy, serving in cabinet-level jobs in the federal energy offices of presidents Carter, Nixon and Ford. He was a worldwide consultant on energy resources with a particular interest in nuclear development when he took power over TNC, by then already managed by potent corporate heads familiar to Sawhill's exclusive clubs. With his experience and his influence, he was hardly more than a tweak away from fine-tuning the nonprofit organization into a uniquely powerful international shadow government, unaccountable to any electorate—not to the people of the United States, and not even to its own one-million-plus membership.

At perhaps the peak of its public recognition in 1996, Sawhill and TNC took over much of New York City's Central Park for a private party celebrating "the world's last great places" and honoring Ted Turner, their only real competitor in ownership of U.S. land, as the organization's "Big Fish." The honorary chairs and masters of ceremonies for the exclusive $750-a-plate event included Peter Jennings, Dan Rather, Diane Sawyer, Paula Zahn, Charlie Rose, Mike Wallace and Charles Osgood—in short, the celebrity cream of national media. It was an awesome display not so much of the lands accumulated in the cause of conservation as it was of the influence clearly held in the name of The Nature Conservancy.

To underscore the obvious bias, CBS commentator Andy Rooney, another "honorary chair" of the party, snarled at a young and skeptical *RANGE* reporter covering the event. "The Conservancy obviously does good work.

You need to study journalism."

Its membership doesn't elect the board of governors of The Nature Conservancy, and Sawhill really didn't need to convince anybody of the group's good works with his elaborate party. By then, Sawhill also held posts in the Clinton administration as an advisor on the Council for Sustainable Development and the Council on Environmental Quality. He wasn't really looking for new members with thin wallets and big ideals. His successor, Steven McCormick, would make it known he doesn't even want them.

"Frankly, most politicians don't pay any attention [to TNC membership] because 1.2 million people are not that many," McCormick told *The Sacramento Bee.* He wouldn't waste more effort on mailings trolling for 25-buck members, but would instead fish in the deep water with personal appeals to the real high rollers in American business. "It's just a greater return," he said.

◆ ◆ ◆

George Fell, those 50 years ago, was somewhat limited in his vision by the places he admired most in the eastern United States. The Ecologists Union had expanded scientific thinking into the interrelationship of species, but there was still a romantic strain of nature-loving Thoreau in the heart of their concept. Not yet, not even after Fell succeeded in winning his first big contribution from Virginia's Old Dominion Foundation to buy New York's 700-acre Mianus River Gorge, had TNC taken on its own cynical description of itself as "nature's landlord."

But McCormick, "born for the job" in San Francisco, did little else but hone his skills for that concept. After earning an unusual degree from Berkeley in agricultural economics, he went to work for the San Francisco-based California chapter of TNC almost immediately after graduating from law school in 1976, and by 1984 was TNC's executive director for California.

Sawhill and his predecessor in the national office, Patrick Noonan, were building an empire of ideal illusion, expanding acquisitions and loading its revenue base with huge contributions beginning with $25 million from the Richard King Mellon Foundation (Mellon National Bank) in 1983 that was up to then the largest such grant ever made for conservation purposes. In 1988, *National Geographic Magazine* devoted a major feature to the organization, and seated *National Geo* executives among TNC's figurehead trustees. New inroads were made in Latin America under TNC's Parks in Peril program, offering ready cash along with neglected land and resource surveys to flimsy national governments.

But McCormick by then had his own fish of sorts to fry in California where TNC faced the good-intentioned competition of the older and more established Sierra Club as well as dozens of other eagerly rising environmental groups. He could see the inevitable swing to the West of the movement, and quickly recognized the useful tactic of shifting from the mere acquisition of parcels of land to what he called Conservation by Design, spreading both financial and political control over even larger areas in a patient game of property chess that provided open space in the right places and brought the California chapter alone $300 million in private donations that made it easily the most powerful environmental organization contending in the great prize of the Golden State. With some help from Sawhill, McCormick began promoting his design as a new strategy for TNC's international operations.

As mysterious and shaded from view as was the national operation of TNC, McCormick's work from the West Coast was even less publicly visible or understood. The national organization had relied on the old money of the Mellons and the Fords. McCormick found he could delve into newer players, some of them obvious from the high-tech industry such as Hewlett Packard, but others aswirl in subsidiaries and fronts and limited corporations that lead to blind alleys in global finance. Almost instinctively, he recognized the politicians most vulnerable to matching their careers with TNC ambitions.

The Nature Conservancy, Inc.
Balance Sheet —
Fiscal Year Ending June 30, 2001

ASSETS	
Cash & Equivalent	$ 19,711,117
Accts Receivable	2,865,902
Pledges & Grants Rec'ble	97,544,629
Receivables / Other	30,702,166
Inventories for Sale or Use	0
Investments / Securities	878,787,475
Investments / Other	191,416,055
Fixed Assets	1,704,000,308
Other	8,557,160
TOTAL ASSETS	$ 2,934,584,812
TOTAL LIABILITIES	264,464,022
FUND BALANCE	$ 2,670,120,790

SOURCE: GuideStar financial website, Nature Conservancy, Inc. Financial Data Information, December 9, 2002. (Editor's Note: TNC's asset total is a million bucks off.)

"Steve recognizes that lasting conservation success will ultimately depend on vibrant partnerships among all sectors of society," said a TNC press release. "He champions innovation and experimentation, and does not shy away from the sort of bold land deals that come with big price tags—and the potential for big results."

ILLUSTRATIONS © JOHN BARDWELL

The governing board of TNC was formed of bankers, investors and foundation heads themselves. It was disguised somewhat with the creation of boards of trustees set up in eight regions with chapters in every state and run with figurehead presence of "trustee members" from government and the media, including retired General H. Norman Schwarzkopf (left) and media leviathan Gerald Levin of Time Warner, Inc.

Still, when Sawhill died without naming a successor, McCormick did not immediately step into his place. Sawhill died in May 2000, of complications from diabetes. That same month, McCormick resigned his post as head of the California chapter to become a partner in the Resources Law Group. That organization described itself as "specializing in representing public and private clients in the development of strategies to conserve natural resources and providing consultation to wealthy individuals on venture philanthropy for land conservation."

McCormick seemed to be striking out on his own. Something in the enigmatic structure of "nature's real estate agency" had trembled.

Only 3,000 people are on the TNC payroll. Most of them probably wouldn't know, and those who did probably wouldn't say, but something was uncertain in the process of choosing Sawhill's successor. "It's really a takeover of an existing organization with great integrity," Huey Johnson, former TNC western regional director, told *The Sacramento Bee*. "[McCormick] has made TNC a tool of government and companies with questionable environmental records."

Others, however, would say with at least equal alarm that it is the other way around. Building on Sawhill's fund-raising success, McCormick evidently has intentions of making the government and major corporations tools of The Nature Conservancy.

"Our mission speaks to preserving biological diversity, not creating nature preserves," McCormick said in complaint of the budget demands on TNC's own preserves, and in 50-year contrast to Fell's now modest-seeming hopes. "Land acquisition alone will not enable us to work at the scale we have to work at."

Walk any beach on either coast until you find a fence that prevents even the military from disturbing a potential nesting site of the threatened plover. There you will find The Nature Conservancy. Visit western farming regions in Nevada and California, especially where family farms are under relentless pressure to become "willing sellers" of their water rights, and you will see some of McCormick's work. Observe the heavy machinery and implications to agriculture from new U.S. Corps of Engineers' projects to rechannel western streams and rivers and you will find that the federal agency is being directed under an agreement with The Nature Conservancy. Find the charming nature trail securing the boundaries of the richest suburbs on the West Coast and it will likely have been built with help from TNC. Examine even the most radical environmental approach to shift the human population of the West into controlled core settlements bordering a vast corridor of wilderness from the Yucatán to the Yukon, and know that the "Wildlands" plan presented by Reed Noss and David Foreman was partly funded by The Nature Conservancy.

Anywhere TNC might be caught in a media spotlight, it ducks into the trees, but it is almost always the unseen Bigfoot behind every outrage in the battle over public land and private rights.

McCormick stepped into his $275,000-a-year job and made a tour of his empire, spread largely south into growing dominance over rainforests and wild savannahs, but reaching beyond those particularly useful landscapes into Africa and Asia, even into China. Governments had warmed to TNC and its data bank as potentates and dictators now bowed to McCormick.

For more than a decade by its own account, The Nature Conservancy has been seeking ways and means by which to establish control over forests and savannahs in Brazil as well as Costa Rica, Columbia, Guatemala, Bolivia, Belize and Panama. Millions of acres of land acquisitions accomplished in various ways, from reductions of national debt to the U.S. government to the swap of properties and outright purchase, have established TNC's authority in the region.

In February 2003, General Motors put up a matching grant totaling nearly half a million dollars to purchase more of the 30,000-acre Parana reserve in southern Brazil. The reserve was established by a $10 million grant from GM to The Nature Conservancy in 2000. Through its dominant Earth Foundation data bank, TNC can bring vast regions and scores of indigenous economies under its control and management. Here are a few examples: a million-and-a-half acres along the border of Panama and Columbia; at least 148,000 acres in Brazil; 260,000 acres in Belize (a fourth of that nation's total land area) that TNC says is now protected from conversion to agriculture; a half-million-acre portion of Guatemala comprising the largest "cloud forest" in Central America and requiring the relocation of indigenous people to a new farm managed by TNC.

Early in 2003 the influence of The Nature Conservancy led to the introduction in the U.S. Congress of the Tropical Forest Conservation Bill, offering to forgive $400 million in debt to the United States in exchange for agreements by Third World countries to save rain forests designated by TNC and offshoot conservation groups. Even other environmentalists worry that such debt-for-nature swaps might actually open the countries involved to further resource exploitation and undermine the democratic efforts of indigenous people to achieve self-determination.

In Peru, a deal was cut to absolve about $14 million of that nation's debt to the United States in return for control by TNC, Conservation International, and the World Wildlife Fund of more than 27.5 million acres of rain forest—a Peruvian "place" the size of Virginia. Few in the public of the United States—fewer still in Peru—knew anything of the deal costing the three U.S. environmental groups a cool pocket-pool of cash amounting to $1.1 million. The land reportedly contains great biological assets, including pink river dolphins and giant water lilies. It also holds vast resources in hardwood timber, oil, gas and fruit, which may be produced only under the supervision of TNC and the other environmentalist overseers.

No wonder McCormick was no longer impressed by TNC's accumulation of little "great places" in the United States that still went on at a rate of one new purchase every day.

To underscore the obvious bias [in the media], CBS commentator Andy Rooney, an "honorary chair" of TNC's "The World's Last Great Places" party in New York, snarled at a young and skeptical RANGE reporter covering the event:

"The Conservancy obviously does good work. You need to study journalism."

"Currently," McCormick scoffed, "80 percent of our resources go to a geography, principally the United States, that constitutes less than 20 percent of the world's biodiversity." Time has come, he said, to expand TNC's already astonishing international influence. Change the term "biodiversity" to "resources," and you will hear echoes of the mogul money at the heart of what is expanding as the world's largest real-estate cartel—or something more sinister. It would not have sold as a "Twilight Zone" script.

Even where TNC itself is not directly at the controls, the replications in land trusts and conservation schemes almost always owe their origins to imitating TNC without directly threatening it. That includes the U.N.-linked Conservation Union and Conservation International (CI) run by Peter Seligmann, who was a director of TNC until 1987 when he formed his mirror organization now covering 30 countries with assets in excess of $300 million. This year, CI launched a campaign of its own, lightly challenging TNC and McCormick with the celebrity leadership of actor Harrison Ford. Whatever the remaining integrity of the environmental movement may be worth, TNC has so far taken little notice of one more mere movie star as worthy of its attention.

So skilled and so experienced is The Nature Conservancy at the methods of disguising revenues in subsidiaries and limited partnerships, nonprofit fronts and federal grants, that perhaps no one really knows the true extent of its financial power. Few, however, would dare challenge it.

On its 50th anniversary, President George W. Bush wrote a congratulatory note to TNC saying, "The Nature Conservancy's accomplishments over the last five decades are remarkable."

Even he did not dare say frightening. ■

WATER RIGHTS & WRONGS

Graham Chisholm's job was to listen for the frailty.

Unless there is some other compelling reason, most local newspapers wouldn't report the way the man we'll call Joe died, especially not in the small family-conscious region of rural Nevada where he had spent his entire life and where most who knew him already understood how it happened anyway.

It had begun as a fairly nice morning up on what they call the bench overlooking Lahontan Valley to the east. Joe might have had reason to celebrate. Only the day before he had signed the last papers turning over his land and its water rights to the power company under the "willing seller" program to conserve the water of the Truckee River. It was a fair deal, giving Joe enough money to go wherever he wanted, to retire somewhere and forget about it all if he wanted. He walked out onto his back porch and stood watching for a while as the sun warmed the alfalfa fields stretching down the long slope. Then he shot himself.

Graham Chisholm wasn't much different from dozens of other Nature Conservancy operatives spread out all over the nation as John Sawhill began his confident drive on the "great places" still not in TNC hands. They were all young and well educated, but chosen more for their "activist" ambitions and sense of political charm than for any particular scientific knowledge about the environment or endangered species. "It was a choice," Chisholm said. "There was us, or there was the lawyers."

You couldn't blame Graham Chisholm or The Nature Conservancy for it, although ironically it was just this sort of sudden family tragedy that would have drawn Graham's attention only four or five years earlier when he first arrived in the Lahontan Valley offering neighborly help and understanding in all the confused stress imposed by a new federal "settlement" on use of the Truckee.

Chisholm wasn't much different from dozens of other Nature Conservancy operatives spread out all over the nation as John Sawhill began his confident drive on the "great places" still not in TNC's hands. They were all young and well educated, but chosen more for their activist ambitions and sense of political charm than for any particular scientific knowledge about the environment or endangered species.

Their job was to seek out the weaknesses in private barriers to restoring what TNC saw as vast ecological landscapes shaped back together in some cases one parcel at a time. It required them to become close to the people and their communities—to join their clubs and volunteer in social programs, and to listen, always listen, for their frailty.

Already, TNC had stumbled over its own ambition at least twice close enough to prompt federal attention. In Indiana, the operatives had taken advantage of a once nationally prominent neurologist then suffering in his last days with Alzheimer's disease. Helpful TNC operatives convinced him to change his will, leaving his entire estate and 95-acre farm to the nonprofit organization. The family was forced into court to win back the property in a trial exposing the cultlike deceit of "nature's landlord." Another case pitted an elderly woman against her stepchildren in a grab at a Colorado ranch. Still another drew national attention in 1993 when the Illinois state director of TNC, Albert Pyott, so coveted property near the Cypress Creek National Wildlife Refuge that he tried to intimidate the owner with a letter saying, "If your land is not acquired through voluntary negotiation, we will recommend its acquisition through condemnation."

Everywhere land could be put in question by new priorities of the Clinton administration especially, there was The Nature Conservancy. "We do work closely with the U.S. Fish & Wildlife Service," said TNC's William Weeks in 1991. "We buy these properties when they need to be bought, so that at some point we can become willing sellers [to the government]. This helps the government get around the problem of local opposition."

Although no one in the Lahontan Valley knew it then, that was almost precisely Graham Chisholm's job description as he nurtured his own way into influence in the Lahontan Valley, site of the nation's first western reclamation project in 1906, the place Teddy Roosevelt meant when he said he would "make the desert bloom."

◆ ◆ ◆

Sen. Harry Reid (D-Nevada) held his own peculiar

PHOTOS © TIM FINDLEY

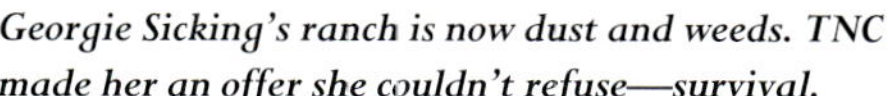

Georgie Sicking's ranch is now dust and weeds. TNC made her an offer she couldn't refuse—survival.

ambitions in land and power acquisition. Helped with advice from his close friend, Bruce Babbitt, Reid was already adept at swapping land in his own state in exchange for little gems of "great places" like the Virgin River northeast of Las Vegas. Reid was proud of the deal he brokered to "save" several miles of the river shores in trade for a spread of BLM land near the small town of Mesquite on the Utah border. The site is now a mini-Vegas with casinos and hotels and golf courses at the gateway of traffic into Nevada from Arizona. The shores of the Virgin River are safe for coyotes and rattlesnakes.

In the late '80s, Reid set out to accomplish the big political prize that eluded his predecessors in Nevada and even the attempts of President Ronald Reagan in bringing some settlement to the long dispute between California and Nevada over water splitting its course down the eastern and western flanks of the Sierra out of Lake Tahoe itself.

Settlement between the states was a relatively simple matter compared to solving the rubrics of promises made by the federal government 70 years earlier in diverting part of the flow of the Truckee away from land-locked Pyramid Lake into the two-river system of agricultural irrigation established by the landmark Reclamation Act. Reid would later rant in public hearings that the Lahontan farmers had "walked out" on his negotiations, but a congressional study concluded that the farmers had been "scapegoated" from the beginning by the deal Reid quietly set up between Sierra Pacific Power Company, the Pyramid Lake Tribe, and federal land managers to pick apart the water rights of the farmers. "They never had a chance," the report concluded.

Even then, there was no mention of the part played from the beginning by TNC, which had its eye on the great swamp-like sink of the Carson River at the eastern end of the valley where it simply vanished into the desert. These wetlands, protected first by the farmers themselves in the 1950s as a duck hunting region, needed to be restored by at least 25,000 acres, TNC concluded in declaring them another "great place."

Reid's Settlement Act passed by only a single vote as the last piece of legislation approved in the 101st Congress. Within days, there were already lawsuits and regulatory demands challenging the rights of Lahontan farmers to irrigation supplies.

Maybe it was just country courtesy, or maybe it was because local people thought he was an expert on the environment who would help them find a new solution, maybe it was because some were just afraid of offending him, but Graham Chisholm slid easily into the kind of respect afforded a visiting dignitary in a respectful small town. He was at the meetings of the Irrigation District and the County Commission; he volunteered his time with the Ag Center's committee testing local wells in the drought. He was there at the melon festival and the county fair, and cheerfully took his turn as the target in the dunking chair. And when the time came that some of the most concerned citizens began organizing a new group to defend local water rights, Graham was among the founding committee. It was always Graham, never "Mr. Chisholm" or "The Nature Conservancy representative." It was, by his preference, always Graham, the shyly informed college boy in his neatly pressed blue work shirt and faded jeans or chinos. Right down to what seemed almost a uniform requirement, Graham Chisholm carried out the handbook of TNC "partnership" creation. He knew everybody, shared meals with many of them, played with their kids, listened to their jokes and paid attention to their problems.

He impressed some, perhaps, and maybe scared some others with his description of the number of species visiting the wetlands from the western flyway and the conjec-

Thanks to The Nature Conservancy and Nevada Sen. Harry Reid, formerly productive farms like this in Fallon, Nevada no longer have water.

ture of scientists that still undiscovered cures to disease might be found among the plant life. But that was the generalized TNC hype on all wetlands. Chisholm could bring a botanist to speak at a meeting on short notice, but he himself was no expert. His graduate thesis in political science at the University of California, Berkeley, had been written on the formation of the radical Green Party in Germany.

Lawsuits and stringent new federal restrictions were taking their toll on the valley. If it were to survive as a viable agricultural community, local leaders agreed there would have to be sacrifices. They were in the depth of a killing seven-year drought that on its own was prompting many to sell just to survive. Under those pressures, there were no willing buyers beyond the government. In order to save what water they could, farmers agreed that other marginal lands would have to be given up in hopes of reaching some compromise. The president of the Irrigation District himself became one of the first willing sellers. After him, the elder leader of the valley's most long-standing family sold his land. Then another, and another whose children saw a better future in the money.

There was never enough, nor would there likely ever be enough in federal wetlands' funds to purchase what TNC had imposed as the goal of Reid's law. That was another reason Graham was there. Virtually none of the marginal lands sold for "appraised value" had any direct relationship to the actual wetlands. What was really purchased was the water rights that would be drained away, leaving ghost farms and pale, lifeless fields of laser-leveled ground unable even to support the growth of weeds.

Sen. Harry Reid's success at land swaps to help make possible the astonishing sprawl of America's fastest-growing city, Las Vegas, was accomplished in large part with financial backing of the Arizona corporation that had built Bugsy Siegel's first hotel, the Flamingo. Questioned for possible mob connections by federal authorities in the 1960s, Del Webb Corporation was by then out of the casino business, but it was still the Southwest's biggest builder of retirement communities and it counted among its former consultants Bruce Babbitt.

If there were not enough federal wetlands' funds to accomplish the aim in the Lahontan Valley, there was the desire of Del Webb for more land around Las Vegas, and just in case they needed to "get around the problem of local opposition" there was The Nature Conservancy to serve as the clean idealist handler of the deal.

At the end of 1995, Chisholm announced that TNC, with the partnership of Del Webb, had purchased "an old farmhouse" and adjoining property that it intended to convert as a "visitor center" for the Stillwater Wetlands. It was actually the empty five-year-old mansion of a broken-hearted young former farmer. Despite Chisholm's promises, it has never been used as a visitor center.

Well on the other side of the valley, but still with water rights in the system, 75-year-old Georgie Sicking said, "I had no choice really. They bought everything around me, including the irrigation ditch." It was an unusual expression of defeat for the gritty, self-reliant Sicking, a renowned cowboy poet, and perhaps the valley's most beloved character. "I'll be honest; I'm just tired of fighting with 'em," she said. "I feel like running. I never felt that way before." Graham graciously called her the night after she signed the Del Webb papers to ask if she was sure she got enough for the deal.

The county was at last growing tired of Graham and TNC as well, especially after TNC falsely claimed in its annual report that the city of Fallon had been a $1,000 contributor to its campaign. That, TNC explained, was the cost of a poster it had produced to show what the restored wetlands should look like, and copies of the poster went to the city.

Only, finally, when uncovered federal documents revealed that Chisholm had been a paid consultant to the U.S. Fish & Wildlife Service under a "memorandum of understanding" reached before Reid's negotiations were finalized did good-guy Graham at last fade from the scene in the Lahontan Valley.

He too had bigger fish to fry. His boss, Steve McCormick, was about to take over as CEO of The Nature Conservancy. He wanted Graham to take over his job as head of TNC's wealthiest chapter in California. ■

POLITICS

It may be tainted, "but t'aint enough."

Tip O'Neill made it the most common cliché of the American system in the 20th century: "All politics is local." O'Neill was perhaps the last great giant of Democratic leadership that could trace its power truly to the hearts of common people. Even contending with the overwhelming issues of the cold war, civil-rights struggles and Vietnam, the speaker of the House of Representatives always advised that people cared first about whether their neighborhood street was paved.

Democrats used the phrase, but strayed far from understanding it in their hungry plundering for greater campaign contributions beginning in the late 1970s. It was tin-plate-and-button worthless by the time Democrats rose back to real power under the integrity of such men as Bill Clinton and Bruce Babbitt.

As witnessed from campaign stops among logging families in the Northwest followed by indifference to them in office, the cause of the common man, particularly in the West, was no more than a flimsy façade. It was like a Hollywood town disguising the machinery that would tear it down as soon as the shot, or the election, was complete.

Given the unbelievable multimillions of dollars necessary to win a national public office, and sometimes even a local election, it might be said that The Nature Conservancy continues to buy up America at a bargain—$30 million here, another $10 million there, hundreds of thousands spread over more spots amounting to a chunk of property bigger than most states, it went on as if sanctioned by the Clinton administration. Seldom, if ever, could the money be traced to the politicians. By then, in the 1990s, TNC didn't need to buy national candidates. It already owned them.

ILLUSTRATIONS © JOHN BARDWELL

Tip O'Neill advised that people care first about their own neighborhoods. TNC begins there...

There is a sense of guilt in the American psyche, made even more apparent by the disparity of wealth in the world since the end of World War II. Common American tradition ran against unearned wealth and historic social abuses. There was a sense of guilt about our own achievements at the price of slavery and, as television brought a greater sense to it, at the price of what some portrayed as the last of Eden itself. Morally, intuitively, Americans held themselves responsible for the fate of the planet.

In 1973, The Nature Conservancy received a gift of 49,000 acres in Virginia's Dismal Swamp from the international paper and box-producing Union Camp Company. One reporter, sounding advanced for the time, questioned whether such a gift from a resource-exploiting corporation might be "tainted." Replied Patrick Noonan, "It may be tainted, but t'aint enough."

The wheels in motion by that time were being turned at TNC by its vice president for science, Robert E. Jenkins. Jenkins, with better scientific credentials than most of TNC's leadership, launched a bold and daring program that could prove to be the richest field of all for TNC. He proposed to produce a biological inventory of the entire United States, cataloging the existence of species and locations of natural communities in all 50 states under the TNC front of The National Heritage Network (now Nature Serve). Offered a database compiled without cost to the national budget, the U.S. government readily conceded to Jenkins' method as the standard for determining biodiversity on the continent.

The Nature Conservancy need never have looked back. Noonan was right. What had been "t'aint enough" was from then on plenty more. Federal land and scientific authorities didn't question TNC's findings and data. Congressional hearings hardly bothered to check the credentials of TNC representatives sent to testify on environmental issues.

One could, at an extreme, argue that it amounted to a coup capturing vital elements of the government's Interior policy. At the very least, it set in motion the powerful effects of the Endangered Species Act, regarded by some as the most powerful law in the nation. And perhaps most importantly, it established a basis of political influence that was very nearly outright extortion. Who would dare question TNC? No wonder major U.S. resource corporations sought their way onto TNC boards. It wasn't just guilt from past abuses. It was self-defense.

So, too, did national candidates not seek campaign help from TNC as much as they scrambled to be sure their campaign was on TNC's side.

To underscore this seeming mandate of national opinion, TNC reminded the political leadership of its own one million-plus membership and produced polls paid for by TNC shill companies showing that 85 percent of Americans who considered themselves environmentalists. The national media easily bought into the idea, and were supplied with gorgeous files of photos, films, and videos providing indisputable proof of the necessity to "save" the planet's fragile beauty. It was like showing a picture of an abandoned puppy, and it required no checking of sources.

The political credibility afforded TNC's indirect influence over U.S. Interior policy was not even a good measure of the enormity of its growing power. Financed in part by profits from lands sold to the government itself and able to call at will on funds from foundations and limited corporations almost eager to cover their own cash under an oak-leaf logo, TNC rather quickly became the richest environmental organization on earth.

It was no longer merely the 10th largest nonprofit organization in the United States. By the middle of the '90s it was recognized by what seemed a new term to most Americans—an NGO, or non-government organization. If that meant nothing to farmers and ranchers and rural dwellers beginning to see themselves as anachronisms in the surge of public opinion that TNC represented, it carried a great deal more weight in the "global consciousness" arising particularly after the end of the cold war.

In effect, TNC was serving as a shadow government of the United States in international forums discussing population control, energy distribution and basic human rights. No one from TNC was officially delegated to represent the United States. There was no official oversight on their actions. Whatever they did was unaccountable to any representative body of the American government. Yet now, when they spoke, it was with international authority that extended Jenkins' data bank on biodiversity over at least a third of the planet.

Multinational conferences sponsored by the United Nations or other coalitions of international interests began meeting in places like Rio de Janeiro, Brazil, or Kyoto, Japan, or Johannesburg, South Africa, to discuss the overwhelming issues confronting the planet—global warming, poverty, disease and overpopulation. The United States, in its own national interests, provided little more than ceremonial delegates with official power to the conferences. But the conferences stressed supposed global awareness ahead of national interests. Non-government organizations were far more compatible in finding solutions. Among them, clearly the most powerful was The Nature Conservancy.

In effect, TNC was thus serving as a shadow government of the United States in international forums discussing population control, energy distribution and basic human rights. No one from TNC was officially delegated to represent the United States. There was no official oversight on its actions. Whatever it did was unaccountable to any representative body of the American government. Yet now, when it spoke, it was with international authority that extended Jenkins' data bank on biodiversity over at least a third of the planet.

Almost incredibly, there still exists a Communist Party of the United States (CPUSA), which in its most recent diatribes attacks old American monopolies like DuPont and General Motors as being "the black hand of death to the environment." In the June 2002 newsletter of CPUSA, national secretary John Bactell rants against such capitalist abuse, then notes in one paragraph about beloved Cuba that "The Nature Conservancy is working in conjunction with the Chinese government on various projects to preserve regions of rich biodiversity."

You could say that a small group of people holding power over natural resources, agricultural production, and even free speech amounts to communism, but it can just as easily amount to fascism. It does not add up to freedom.

TNC, however, is well aware of American custom that all politics is local. That is why it patiently sells its position from "the grass roots" up, working to convince even the people it may victimize that they can act for the good of us all. "Partnership" is TNC's favored method of control. Only when that won't produce results quickly enough or largely enough would TNC resort to risking exposure of itself by making blatant campaign contributions.

After passage in March 2002 in California of a $2.6 billion bond measure for state parks, questions were raised about the largest single donor to that initiative campaign and to another donation two years earlier which provided $2.1 billion in state park funds. Both measures were sponsored by The Nature Conservancy. Its $1-million benefactor for campaign funds was identified first only as Rosebud and in the latest campaign as Wild Rose, but both came evidently from the same mysterious source.

Who was Rosebud? Defying state law, California TNC director Graham Chisholm refused to say. "We have a very clear relationship of trust with our donors who wish to remain anonymous," said the veteran of Nevada's Lahontan Valley "settlement." "That is fundamental to how we operate."

Both donations traced back to blind alleys of Limited Liability Corporations (LLC) based in Seattle. It financed victories for the two largest park bonds in California history with implications over millions of acres. Curiously coincidental perhaps is the fact that Rosebud is the last word spoken by the dying character based on William Randolf Hearst in Orson Wells' classic film, "Citizen Kane."

As it happens, the Hearst Corporation is currently involved in a land-buyout campaign that could cost taxpayers $100 million. A chief consultant to the Hearst Corporation is former U.S. Interior Secretary Bruce Babbitt. ■

THE BOARD

Probably the most powerful real-estate cartel the world has seen outside of empires.

The biggest mistake to be made in trying to understand The Nature Conservancy is to think of it as a passionate group of young scientists and scholastics rescuing imperiled landscapes and habitats at virtually the last minute with the help of dollars and dimes from schoolchildren and their liberal parents. It's the error most commonly conveyed by the national media, but that may not be by mistake.

The Nature Conservancy is run by a 39-member, self-nominating board of governors who represent some of the wealthiest and most powerful corporations in the United States. Only four of these members present obvious scientific credentials. The majority are presidents, vice presidents, chairmen, and chief operating officers of such mighty international business interests as ConAgra, Cisco Systems, Georgia-Pacific, Goldman Sachs, General Motors, Discovery Communications, Cargill and General Mills, American Electric Power Company, NASDAQ, the Orvis Company and DuPont. Harvard, Stanford, Rockefeller and Columbia Universities all have representative executives on the board.

Together, they represent what is most probably the most powerful real-estate cartel the world has ever seen outside the establishment of national empires. It is estimated that The Nature Conservancy continues to expand its holdings by at least one new acquisition every day. It could, for example, be conveyed in the manner of weekly newsreels during World War II showing the expansion of military occupation in bleeding globs of color across a map of the world. To imagine that such absorption of land and property is accomplished with donations and dues of even TNC's one million-plus members is absurd. Even studies by the U.S. Internal Revenue Service have concluded that such contributions are miniscule in comparison to what TNC accumulates from its own investments, grants (including some from the government), and profits from the sales of its lands—usually back to the government.

The organization reports a total income from fiscal year 2000 of nearly $787 million, but that seems almost modest in comparison to its total assets of over $2.8 billion—an amount exceeding the gross national product of some countries where it operates. And yet, The Nature Conservancy holds a tax-exempt status identical to a neighborhood library association.

The chairman of the Board of Governors, Anthony P. Grassi, is listed by TNC as president of the board of trustees of the New Canaan County, Connecticut, Country School. That's his retirement job. He was formerly chief financial and executive officer of First Boston Inc., and head of First Boston's investment banking and management committee, one of the most powerful investment groups in the world. Such big banks are found in more than one case these days at the dead end of tracing funds to TNC from their currently favorite source of Limited Liability Partnerships, a legal device making it more difficult to track the transfer of large amounts of money.

TNC's chief executive officer, Steve McCormick, made only a vague but highly grateful reference to one such group, Farallon Capital Management, an LLC, in crediting it with the most help in this year's $31 million purchase of the Baca Ranch in Colorado. Farallon leadership and organization traces back to First Boston and Goldman Sachs, both with convenient places among TNC's board of governors.

Still, though they can't take much credit for it, average donors and members of TNC can easily believe from the richly photographed publications produced by the organization that they are part of a noble aim to save nature. They don't even know how much TNC really controls or how potentially threatening its holdings may be. Since 1988, for example, TNC has held responsibility given the group by the government for management of 25 million acres of military property in the United States. Since 1961, it has expanded on an agreement with the U.S. Bureau of Land Management covering standards on the nation's public lands. And in 2001, TNC was granted responsibility for directing the U.S. Army Corps of Engineers in shifting the channels of American rivers and streams.

The 12 million acres that TNC acknowledges it owns in the United States is not half the truth of what it controls.

The first mistake is always in believing that it is an altruistic, nature-loving organization without a profiteer in its midst. How could there be? ■

THE LAND

As TNC "saves" land with your money, communities perish.

The Mianus River Gorge between New York and Connecticut remains a richly alluring place, laced with delicate shadows from eastern hemlock and ferns, soft seeming in its power. A place where fables still could easily be born.

Such gentle dreams are not so easily put in motion on the Texas City Prairie Reserve where petroleum pumps go on dipping their beaks and rocking back in rhythm like tasteless toys on the rim of rolling pasture that is home to half of the last 40 Attwater's prairie chickens known to exist on earth.

Concept to cocktail joke, that is the reality in the properties "saved" and preserved by The Nature Conservancy.

Perhaps the greatest secret held in the enigma of "nature's landlord" is that it is not really an environmental organization at all. It is a land-acquisition scheme, complex and highly elusive, but dedicated foremost to its own enrichment of wealth and power. And, as time has revealed, the ambition of the organization is not really for land, but for the ultimate management of human behavior.

For its 50 years of acting on behalf of what TNC itself proclaims to be "the last great places," the organization cannot legitimately claim to have scientifically saved anything that was facing certain extinction. It can, however, claim in multimillions of acres an amount of land it has excluded from use by all humans except those who meet TNC approval and can pay the price. It has preserved nature with all-time arrogance in the name of TNC itself.

George Fell's first benefactors at the beginning of TNC were associated with the staid and very wealthy Old Dominion College in Virginia. It was not unnatural in those times that their interest in conservation might focus on so near a parochial cause as the string of islands off the coast of their own state.

Along Virginia's eastern shore, running from Chesapeake Bay into the Atlantic, is a string of 18 barrier islands blessed with a rich and generally unspoiled diversity of shore life and habitat. These beaches, reachable only by boat, and the offshore waters once served as the economic resource for some 45,000 people living on Virginia's shores and dependent for their livelihoods on seafood and vegetable processing plants. It was what might be called today a sustainable system of food production and ecology. But in the 1970s, a company known as the Smith Island Development Corporation threatened to build a bridge from the mainland connecting to all the islands.

The Nature Conservancy's bright young man of that time, Patrick Noonan, stepped in with what would become characteristic TNC zeal to save such a last great place from the implied development. First to be rescued in the nonprofit group's series of purchases was the island and shallow-water income base off the eastern shore, now supposedly protected from human intrusion or development. Onshore, poverty deepened, particularly among largely minority labor put out of work when processing plants dependent on the nearby waters shut down. To replace them, there began appearing opulent new homes and duck clubs compatible with nature under terms of the Virginia Coast Reserve (VCR), the front established by The Nature Conservancy. In fact, even though locals knew about VCR and resisted the growing power of the nonprofit, they were unaware that other parcels purchased by the supposedly independent Offshore Islands Inc. and then "donated" to TNC were also part of the scheme. Offshore Islands Inc. only later admitted it was a shill company for TNC itself.

Twenty years into an economic disaster of its own making, TNC, now headed by Sawhill, vowed to fix it with an infusion of $2.25 million into the eastern-shore economy for "compatible" development of new business as in tourism, craft shops and small real estate under direction of the Virginia Eastern Shore Corporation, another TNC front.

It was an utter and undisguised failure. Doing it "TNC's way" simply didn't work. Millions were lost in failed investments. Local poverty only grew worse. But TNC hardly felt it. By then, nature's landlord owned 14 of the 18 islands, each served with opulent showplaces built for rich clients, all unaffordable to the people of the eastern shore.

"All of us will end up being servants to these God-damned rich people," one bitter resident told a reporter. By then, Patrick Noonan himself owned 14 parcels on the eastern shore.

In his book, "Trashing the Economy," researcher and writer Ron Arnold reports that no records can be found to establish that the Smith Island Development Corporation, which supposedly prompted TNC's action because of its bridge-building plan, ever really existed.

It is not really difficult to uncover outrageous contradictions and sad lies among the holdings of The Nature Conservancy. Given the rate at which it acquires property, it might be surprising not to stumble over abuses. Yet TNC remains untouched by any serious federal challenge to its status. Defectors from the organization wonder how it has not become even more reckless in its ruthless grab of what it wants.

The poster child of TNC's "partnership" approach to

preservation has been the Malpai Borderlands Group on the Arizona/New Mexico line and the Gray Ranch in New Mexico, where TNC wove one of its most complex webs out from a nest of some 360,000 acres "saved" from proposed development by Ted Turner himself. Outmaneuvering Turner, TNC spun their purchase into an unlimited reach over more than a million acres of public and private land captured in the complexities of more façades of organizations and tricky lines of no escape into the ultimate control of what Sawhill called, "models of ecosystem conservation."

It was a place already being eyed by Reed Noss and David Foreman as a "sky island" parcel of what seemed an impossible fantasy plot to remake most of the West into wilderness. Local ranchers, as parochial-minded and naively trusting of the government as any, would catch on only slowly, if at all.

Only now does Judy Keeler make better sense of what vaguely disturbed her that August day in 1990 when she and her husband came across a pickup parked inside the fences on their deeded land. The vehicle belonged to the U.S. Bureau of Land Management, but stuck over the federal emblem was the green oak leaf logo of The Nature Conservancy. The two BLM employees said they were conducting a survey of flora and fauna for TNC.

"We didn't even know what to ask," said Keeler. "We found out later they were doing the same thing on other adjoining ranches."

The survey would clearly be linked to an attempt to establish an Area of Critical Environmental Concern allowing even more federal authority over the region based on threatened or endangered species or habitats. Largely unknown to ranchers and property owners, the federal government had already ceded much of its own responsibility in making such judgments to the land-providing TNC under a so-called "cost-share" agreement relying heavily on the nonprofit's own data bank.

Within the next 10 years, U.S. Fish & Wildlife Service's long-held desire to establish an "Animas Wildlife Refuge" in the region would converge with TNC's own semisecret plan for an "International Peace Park" designed as a model of management by "nature's landlord." Another nonprofit formed for the purpose, the Animas Foundation, now controls more than half the original Gray Ranch, but is used primarily as a grass bank open to other ranchers to "rest" their own allotments.

There are some 25 other ranchers in the Malpai Borderlands Group formed in 1993 for mutual fire protection. Now they are bound to federal restrictions calling for them to take their cattle off grazing allotments for two years or

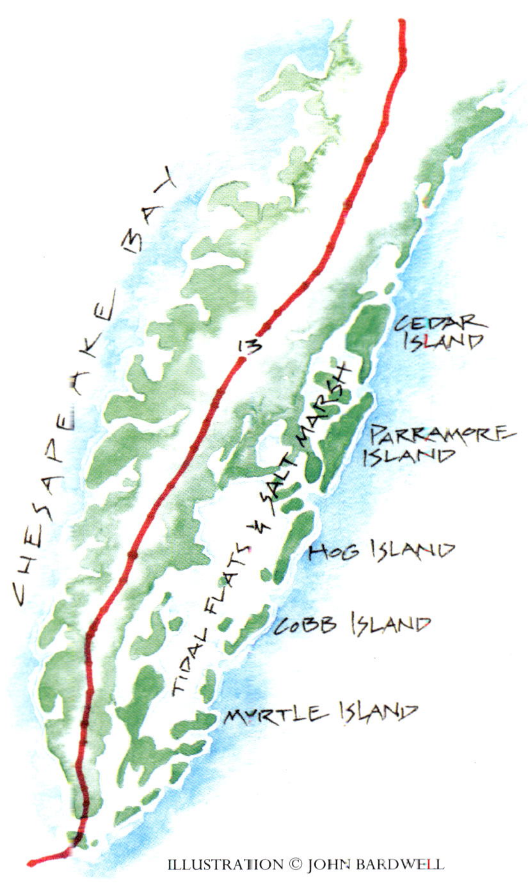

ILLUSTRATION © JOHN BARDWELL

Along Virginia's eastern shore is a string of 18 barrier islands blessed with a rich and unspoiled diversity of shore life and habitat. TNC "saved" the place from implied development but it was an economic disaster. Millions were lost in failed investments. Local poverty grew worse. But TNC hardly felt it. By then, "nature's landlord" owned 14 of the 18 islands, each served with opulent showplaces built for rich clients, all unaffordable to the original residents of the eastern shore....

more in order to allow controlled burns. If the ranchers make use of the grass bank, they are expected to pay it off by agreement to long-term conservation easements on their own property. Only a handful have accepted that deal so far, but pressure remains. The Nature Conservancy is in no hurry. Later more than sooner, perhaps, TNC will have it all. Meanwhile, Malpai is touted as a model of cooperation between government, environment and private interests, doing it the TNC way. Some say it resembles old Chicago.

Judy Keeler continues to ranch independently almost in the center of the one-million-acre Malpai region. She attends meetings, but her questions go unanswered.

"TNC didn't come into our area like friends," she said. "They came in with the attitude that they knew it all and were going to 'educate' us local ignoramuses on how to manage our ranches."

Especially since Bruce Babbitt took power over the Department of Interior in 1992, ranches falling into the hands of The Nature Conservancy have seemed like overripe fruit dropping from a shaken tree. Though it sends many of the properties into its revolving fund with the government, TNC could probably challenge even mighty Simplot in grazing land it has available for use.

In fact, TNC is directly and competitively in the livestock business, advertising its Conservation Beef as the alternative to production on what remaining ranches it has not already offered to buy, or trade, or convince the owners to donate for vague, but funereally rewarding public use.

"Beef with a mission," advertises TNC. "To save the best of the West for future generations." In a "Dear Friend" letter, W. William Weeks, TNC executive vice president, says, "The Nature Conservancy has worked with western ranch families for four years to help bring you Conservation Beef—a unique way to help preserve key landscapes in the great American West. We're proud of the results.

PHOTOS © CYNTHIA DELANEY

When The Nature Conservancy protects rain forests from human intrusion or development, it can have adverse effects on the indigenous people.

"We need only one more partner to make this project work: you.... Your purchase [of Conservation Beef] will help save great western landscapes for future generations."

Weeks, the author of TNC's book on policy and strategy, "Beyond the Ark," is a field marshal for TNC boss Steven McCormick in deal making in all directions. This includes new support for TNC by General Motors Inc., in exchange for vague research on climate change, and the agreement signed in 2001 between TNC and the U.S. Army Corps of Engineers for managing U.S. water resources in partnerships with local interests orchestrated by The Nature Conservancy.

America, as TNC likes to promote it, has been made environmentally conscious by TNC's selfless presence. Such altruism was part of what prompted Mobil Oil Corporation in 1995 to give TNC a 2,300-acre field of low-producing oil and gas reserves which also turned out to be one of the last known breeding grounds for the endangered Attwater prairie chicken.

All around the site near Houston the evident success of "big oil" hunches in steam-rising refineries and pipelines close to the collateral development of homes and offices that probably squeezed out most of the prairie chicken's habitat in the first place. But with the gift in hand, TNC did not set out to save the bird. It went to work restoring more oil and gas production on Mobil's forgotten field—sinking new wells, putting pumps back in operation and grazing Conservation Beef among the dipping machinery plunging into the earth.

"We believe the opportunity we have in Texas City to raise significant sums of money for conservation is one we cannot pass up, provided we can do this drilling without harming the prairie chickens and their habitat, and we are convinced," said Texas TNC spokesperson Niki McDaniel.

The nation's 10th largest charity has earned at least $5.5 million in oil and gas royalties so far from the field. There is no evidence that any major expenditure has been put into "saving" the prairie chicken.

Beneath the Gray Ranch at the center of TNC's much-heralded Malpai Group, by the way, is what some geologists consider to be a rich field of minerals, gas and oil. The rights to it were donated to TNC by Tenneco Corp. in the 1990s.

In New England, a political distance apart from the forest wars of the Pacific Northwest, The Nature Conservancy has acquired at least a million acres of timberland in Maine and New Hampshire put under secondary stress by the environmental campaign in the West. TNC continues to log most of that land in what it says is sustainable practice.

The spin-off of TNC, Conservation International, has

proudly announced that tropical forests it has acquired in Latin America will continue to produce coffee under exclusive agreements with Starbucks which will use low-impact harvesting methods and pass along the added expense to consumers.

Big game hunting, fishing expeditions, ecotourism and private real estate including farms are all available at the right price from Nature's Landlord. What protects nature is that "common" people can't afford any of it. ■

The Network

Big Brother, environmental espionage and The Nature Conservancy. By Jeff Goodson

There are few things that infuriate American landowners more than environmental espionage—the covert collection of environmental data on private property without the landowner's knowledge or consent. Usually focusing on biodiversity and water quality, the practice was virtually unknown until the 1970s. Since then, it has exploded with the support of state and federal agencies, environmental activists and the land trusts. Especially one land trust—The Nature Conservancy.

The Network

In 1974, TNC's science division began developing a sophisticated, decentralized biodiversity data system that could operate as a unified network. The system, created from scratch, would manage continually updated inventories of biological information using a standardized data-collection methodology and electronic data management system. The first Heritage Program data center was installed in South Carolina in 1974. By 1994 it was operational in nearly 300 facilities worldwide, including all 50 states, and known simply as the Network.

As the Network matured, the original emphasis on reserve selection and design broadened to include support for land-use planning, environmental-impact assessment and endangered-species management. By 1996 the Network was described as "the most comprehensive and frequently consulted source of information on biodiversity in the world," and was responding to 70,000 information requests a year. These came from federal, state and local natural-resource agencies, corporations, environmental organizations, researchers, academics, consultants and individuals.

Collaboration

Network development didn't come cheap, and the cost wasn't footed entirely by The Nature Conservancy. The system was nurtured in the early years by grants from the usual suspects—the Mellon, Hewlett and MacArthur foundations, and the Pew Charitable Trusts. These grants "successfully leveraged hundreds of millions of dollars in public funding, which helped expand the Network across the entire country."

The federal government played a major role in this growth, with critical support provided by the Bureau of Land Management, the Forest Service, Environmental Protection Agency and other federal agencies interested in using the system. Of special note was U.S. Fish & Wildlife Service support through its secretive Land Acquisition Priority System, and support from the National Biological Information Infrastructure. NBII, the federal program that today manages data on the nation's biological resources, says that it collaborates closely with TNC to "help provide increased, integrated access to selected data from TNC's central databases, including their rich geospatial data sets."

System Standardization

All Network data centers use a common TNC methodology for systematically collecting, storing and retrieving biological information, for gathering information on specific tracts of real estate, and for setting land-acquisition priorities. Information is continually reviewed and updated, and maintained in each data center. The system software can cross-reference, correlate and structure data, and make it quickly available to users anywhere. New technologies such as geographic information systems, global positioning systems, evolving remote sensing technology, and graphical database software are continuously integrated into the Network, maintaining its operational status as state of the art. Today, Network scientists everywhere "speak the same vocabulary, evaluate their work with the same yardsticks, share their ideas, compare notes, and exchange electronic data. There is an enormous sum of the parts."

Big Brother

On the ground, the Network is used to develop biodiversity inventories, identify critical areas in need of protection, generate strategic shopping lists, plan site actions, conduct biological and legal monitoring, and track information on specific real-estate tracts and transactions. As TNC puts it: "How rare? How threatened? We answer those questions...so we can decide which pieces of land to buy.... Once species are identified and ranked, the areas that shelter critically threatened species become the target of Conservancy projects."

The Network focuses on the status and specific locations

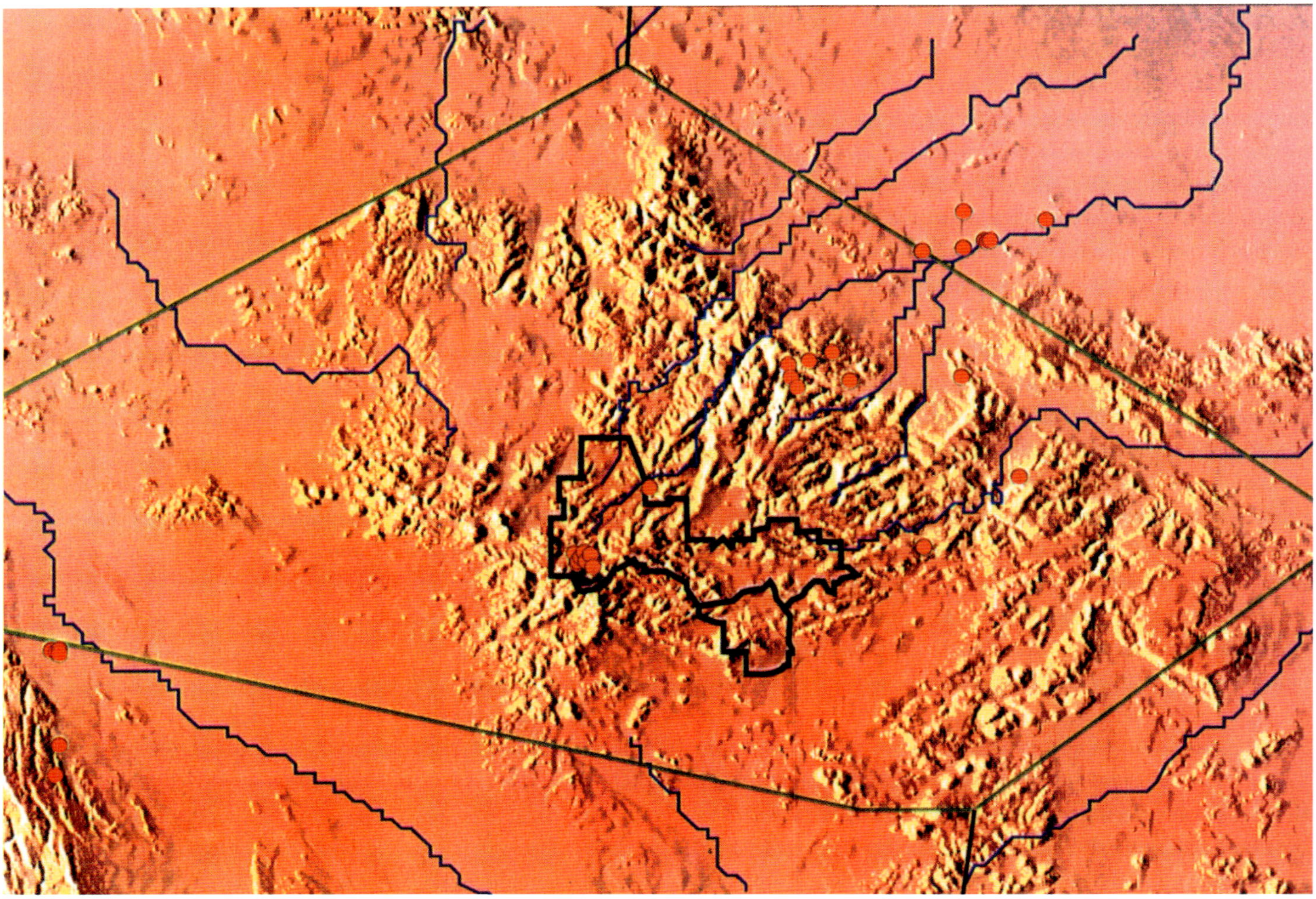

The Network at work in the Davis Mountains, Texas. Using proprietary data on rare plants and animals, The Nature Conservancy zooms in electronically on land they intend to target for acquisition. In the Davis Mountains, most property targeted by TNC is working ranchland. TNC biological data from private property may, or may not, have been collected with the landowner's knowledge and consent.

of plants, animals and ecological communities, and it now contains detailed information on more than 50,000 North American species and ecosystems. The system is designed to deal with local biota in extreme detail, and local data centers specialize in gathering raw biological data, conducting field inventories, and carrying out biological assessments. But there is also a centralized version of the Network's data-management system at TNC headquarters in Arlington, Virginia. That system contains hundreds of thousands of species' records, and is now by far the most comprehensive biodiversity database in the world.

Property Data

Once in the system, biodiversity data are integrated with local real-estate information. Networkers can examine voluminous and detailed information about sites of interest, including mappable data on specific land tracts, land transactions and property taxes. Tract information includes data on location, ownership, legal access, outstanding rights and interests, history, value, management, biological importance and intended use. Transaction files include data on land purchases, sales, leases, licenses, management agreements, easements, mortgages, mortgage releases and registrations. Tax files include information on legal descriptions, tax types, tax assessments, tax payments, amounts due and exemptions filed.

Outrage

Not surprisingly, the Network infuriates landowners—especially those with property that's targeted for acquisition. Much of that anger evolved from experience with the National Park Service's National Natural Landmarks program. NNL set out in 1962 to recognize "outstanding examples of the nation's natural landscape heritage," but evolved in the 1970s into an environmental espionage and land-targeting program. Before it went into moratorium in 1989 in response to landowner outrage, 587 NNLs had been designated nationwide, 3,029 sites had been proposed for designation, and thousands of additional sites, many of them private, had been covertly evaluated.

The National Park Service coordinated the NNL program "closely with those of other natural area programs, such as [that of] The Nature Conservancy." Many of the 363 sites evaluated in Texas, for example, were selected for evaluation precisely because they had already been identified in TNC files. More than 60 percent of all Texas sites were private, and many of them were evaluated without the landowner's knowledge or consent. There are literally dozens of comments in the raw program files about Texas landowners who may be "unreceptive to contact."

As NPS admitted in 1990 in the Federal Register: "[F]rom 1962 forward...some resource identifications, on-site evaluations, nominations, and designations have been done without appropriate notification and/or consent of the legal landowners.... Full sensitivity to landowner interests, including landowner notification and consent, has not always been demonstrated."

The Texas Fix

When the activities of the Texas Natural Heritage Program came to light in 1995, just a few years after the NNL moratorium, Texas landowners came unglued. Two bills were quickly passed and signed into law by then Gov. George W. Bush, requiring the Texas Parks and Wildlife Department to maintain the confidentiality of information collected on

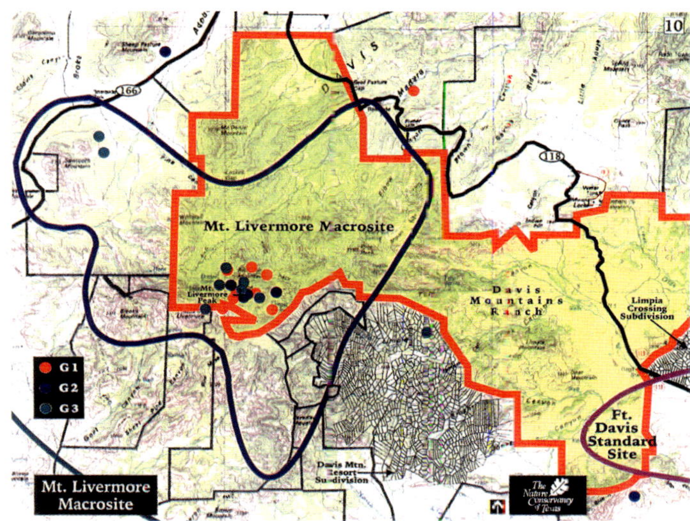

This map shows how a TNC target site is developed. The curved line lassoes a wide "primary" boundary within which ecological "fragmentation" will be minimized. Dots indicate the location of "rare" species of plants (10) and snails (2) although as many as 29 plants and 17 animals may be included.

private land. One (HB 2012) required TPWD to keep confidential any information pertaining to private property, whether it was collected at the request of a landowner seeking technical guidance or collected during the course of an investigation incidental to the enforcement of game and fish laws.

The second bill (HB 2133) limited the use of biodiversity information collected on private land to "the purposes of scientific investigations and research," and then only if authorized in writing by the landowner. Today, TPWD may not enter into the Network any data collected during a landowner-authorized investigation, and data cannot be reported or compiled in a way that identifies individual parcels of private property, without written landowner consent.

Epilogue

Spawned by The Nature Conservancy and nurtured with U.S. tax dollars, the Network has grown to jaw-slackening proportions. By the mid-1990s it was described as "the world's only operational example of a widespread, multi-node confederation of data centers and scientists engaged in a coordinated biodiversity inventory effort using standardized information management methods and technologies." Today, the Network describes itself as "a de facto national biological survey in the literal sense."

And so it is.

Landowners across America deserve the same kind of protection that Texas landowners enjoy from this kind of environmental espionage. If ever there were a time for national legislation to protect them, this is it. ■

SUMMER 2005

GOT'CHA!

A Fed-up Arizona family sues radical enviros for their lies—AND WINS! By Cindy Coping

"Our opponents don't use science, they subvert science," says Arizona rancher Jim Chilton. "Endangered species are just their tools to raise money and to impose their antiproduction philosophy."

Chilton wants to expose the way the Center for Biological Diversity (CBD) does business and is incensed over the lost livelihoods of tens of thousands of rural westerners: timber workers, ranchers and miners who lost productive, well-paid employment. "Too many other victims just couldn't defend themselves against relentless attacks by the Center for Biological Diversity or Forest Guardians."

PHOTOS COURTESY CHILTON FAMILY

This is Ruby Japanese Tank. CBD photographed a tiny corner, trying to prove that bullfrogs were taking over, thanks to cattle. Bullfrogs were introduced by Arizona Game & Fish and they eat the endangered Chiricahua leopard frog, which is being devastated by a fungus. "Cattle are not the problem with the Chiricahua," FWS told Jim Chilton. Wildlife and cattle have never seen this beautiful pond dry. It is fed by a spring. It was used by a Japanese farmer who grew and sold vegetables to miners in the 1890s. OPPOSITE: Heritage and integrity with deep roots spurred the Chiltons to fight back. FROM LEFT: Jim, father Ken, and brother Tom.

Brothers Jim and Tom Chilton and their father Ken, partners in Chilton Ranch and Cattle Company, recently won a defamation suit against CBD.

"Environmental activist organizations wear people down until they can no longer function," a witness in court asserted.

"That's exactly the problem," emphasizes Jim, who persevered through seven years of predatory political action, litigious attacks, slander and libel to protect the family's multigenerational heritage. "Ranching is not a job; it's a culture. It is a unique western American way of life and a national cultural treasure worthy of preservation. This [defamation] case is more about the truth, values and science than about money."

Jim, a fifth-generation Arizona rancher, and his ancestors have a long history of environmental stewardship. Since 1905 when the U.S. Forest Service (FS) replaced "open range" with regulated private allotments, the Chiltons have stocked their ranches conservatively and improved forage, infrastructure and herd quality. "You'll hit poor years," Ken says, "and you'll still have good grass cover."

In 1978 the Chilton Ranch and Cattle Company left northern Arizona where the family had raised cattle since 1888, and purchased the Diamond Bell Ranch southwest of Tucson. On their own initiative, they invited the Natural Resources Conservation Service to help create a range conservation plan for the Diamond Bell.

"We [still] needed a bigger place to support two generations," says Jim, "so when a good ranch came on the market in 1987 just 30 miles south of the Diamond Bell, we decided to buy it."

In 1991, Jim enlarged the ranch with purchase of the Montana Allotment in the Coronado National Forest between the Mexican border and Arivaca. He immediately implemented a rest-rotation grazing system in cooperation with the Forest Service. The system gives lowland pastures 20 months' rest out of 24 to increase perennial grass cover and rapidly recruit riparian vegetation. Today the allotment provides habitat for wildlife including javelina, deer, coatimundi, songbirds and Mearns quail.

Despite impressive stewardship, however, the Chiltons found themselves perpetually at odds with CBD, supposedly over three federally listed species: the Sonora chub, the lesser long-nosed bat and the Chiricahua leopard frog.

In wet years, the "threatened" Sonora chub minnows swim under the Mexican border fence and up an intermittent wash known as California Gulch. They venture only a few hundred yards into the United States because the border marks the end of perennial water and the extreme northern edge of their range. The Forest Service fenced and removed this tiny segment of California Gulch from the Montana Allotment in 1997 in response to a CBD lawsuit. Any fish that cross the border when the wash runs, die when the temporary water dries up in late spring. Although the leading researcher on the chub found the species secure and abundant in Mexico, it was listed because it was rare in the United States. In fact, most fish are rare in dry washes.

The lesser long-nosed bat is another south-of-the-border species. Adult males never travel north into the United

States. Pregnant females migrate each spring to a few locations in southern Arizona where they remain for the summer. This species' 1988 "endangered" listing relied on a questionable report finding only 135 specimens in the United States. More capable researchers published a paper exposing the very poor science the U.S. Fish & Wildlife Service (FWS) accepted to justify the bat's listing. Experts counted more than 14,000 in Arizona within a year of the listing. By 1993, they documented more than 200,000 roosting along the border.

On June 13, 2002, FWS added the Chiricahua leopard frog to its "threatened" species list. Its status in Mexico is unknown. In its petition to list the frog, CBD claimed: "More than 75 percent of its habitat has been lost to livestock grazing, dams, and water diversions." Ironically, the final FWS listing rule indicates that the frog was eradicated from major Arizona waterways primarily by exotic bullfrog

Forest Service biologist Jerry Stefferud complained cattle might stomp and chomp on fish in a wash that appears occasionally. The Biological Opinion from U.S. Fish & Wildlife Service, negative toward cattle, was written by Stefferud's wife. "This is a typical ranch riparian area," Chilton says, "and I can prove it."

predation, and more than one-third of survivors are found in earthen cattle tanks, to which the rule gives special legal protection. Recently, Arizona ranchers hauled water to save the frog from drought. The Chiltons also actively participate in recovery efforts.

Jim Chilton's 10-year grazing permit was up for renewal in 2003. In 1997, CBD and Forest Guardians sued to force the Forest Service to consult FWS regarding endangered species on 158 grazing allotments, including the Montana Allotment. The Forest Service and CBD settled their lawsuit with an agreement to fence livestock out of waters including the occasional water at the border in California Gulch.

In March 1997, FS biologist Jerry Stefferud, a CBD member, wrote the Biological Assessment for the Montana Allotment as required by the Endangered Species Act (ESA). He declared that grazing was "likely to adversely affect" the Sonora chub, asserting cattle might "ingest" chub larvae, trample fish and increase stream sedimentation in California Gulch. Mima Falk, a Forest Service botanist, concluded that grazing would "likely adversely affect" the lesser long-nosed bat although the species has never been located on the grazing allotment.

The Forest Service forwarded the Biological Assessment to FWS where Sally Stefferud, coincidentally Jerry Stefferud's wife, wrote the Biological Opinion. Jim expressed dismay at "the obvious collusion and inappropriate lack of scientific detachment."

The Biological Opinion mandated a three-times-per-pasture-per-year monitoring requirement that would have cost Jim about $25,000 annually. He suspects that "it was really just a setup for another lawsuit." Meanwhile, activists were having a field day with the official FS file for the Montana Allotment, which featured 30-year-old data and unchecked claims of poor soil and riparian conditions.

"We had no idea what the activists were stuffing in the agency record," Jim sighs. "It was like having someone put false reports in your credit file, and just as hard to fix."

When Jim used the Freedom of Information Act to obtain the file, he was aghast. "A cowboy's creed is honesty, integrity and straightforwardness. The only way to correct the data file and counteract baseless claims would be to bring in top scientists."

In April 1998, Jim retained Dr. Jerry Holechek and Dr. Dee Galt to extensively monitor the allotment semiannually and provide quantitative data to the file. Dr. Holechek, a tenured professor at New Mexico State University, literally "wrote the book" on range management. More than 50 accredited university range-management programs teach from Holechek's textbook.

Holechek felt apprehensive when Jim and Sue Chilton first contacted him. He had previously donated his expertise to help environmentalists force an allegedly irresponsible rancher out of business. After the team's first visit to the Montana Allotment, however, Dr. Holechek exclaimed he was ecstatic upon seeing that the Chiltons had stocked conservatively. "The Montana Allotment has the richest, most diverse flora of any area I have ever worked in."

Recently retired FS conservation expert Duane Thwaits, who over 23 years made some 200 daylong monitoring visits to the Montana Allotment, confirmed that he likewise observed "very dramatic improvements" in key indicators. He said Jim was always out on the ground and communicated frequently.

The Chiltons also hired fish biologist Mary Darling to study the Sonora chub. Her studies conducted on 20 visits

Marijuana Flat in September 2002. Activists from the Center for Biological Diversity listed this area on their website as "the most abused ranch country in the United States." The fact is none of these cows eat fish and real range scientists found it among the healthiest in the Southwest.

between 1998 and 2002 documented the presence of exotic predators and historic mining toxins in California Gulch. She concluded that the ultimate death sentence to the border-crossing minnows occurs when the wash dries up. She says, "It is dry, the majority of the time."

In December 2000, a federal judge struck down the Biological Opinion for the Montana Allotment. While CBD and FWS appealed, the agency published a new Draft Biological Opinion that characterized California Gulch as a "stream" with "perennial or near perennial water," and would have eliminated grazing on 1,200 acres parallel to it to protect the chub. Jim questions wryly: "Guess which FS and FWS couple was behind this renewed attack?"

At the same time CBD's grazing reform program coordinator Dr. Martin Taylor, an entomologist, wrote to FS claiming proof of "clear violations," and requesting suspension or cancellation of Jim's grazing permit. Two FS experts independently investigated the Montana Allotment on-site and found the claims baseless. Outraged, Jim had an attorney demand a retraction. Taylor never responded.

In a landmark decision on December 17, 2001, the 9th U.S. Circuit Court of Appeals proclaimed the FWS's Biological Opinion for Montana Allotment "arbitrary, capricious and unlawful," and prohibited incidental take statements for unoccupied "potential or suitable habitat." The court further ruled, if an endangered species is present, FWS has the burden to prove grazing would kill or injure the species before it can issue an incidental take statement and demand regulatory jurisdiction.

The Chiltons' older son Ken recalled the reaction as he read the just-released decision to some activist government agents who came to see California Gulch. He "watched their faces fall as they realized their favorite control tool had just been zapped" by unanimous decision of the most unlikely Court of Appeals. "They tried to conceal their dismay," Ken says, "but they weren't very good actors."

CBD's appeal requested an Environmental Impact Statement and suspension of grazing during the two-to-four year interim, marking their fourth formal attempt to stop Jim Chilton's permit. On February 13, 2003, the Forest Service renewed Jim Chilton's grazing permit.

On July 2, 2002, CBD issued a news advisory with online links to the appeal and to 21 photographs with inaccurate captions. Activist Mike Hudak nominated the Montana Allotment in an Internet contest for the most "overgrazed" allotment of 26,000 nationwide. The photos led contest voters to "award" the Montana Allotment fourth place. CBD issued a press release with the Internet address of poll results. Dr. Holechek commented: "[Environmental activists] have an agenda where the end justifies any means. I strongly believe this is a primary example of this type of behavior."

CBD kept the inflammatory news advisory and photos online for more than a year, until the Chiltons sued.

"If I had not responded to their false accusations," Jim explains, "I would always have been trying to explain to everyone that I really was a good rancher. My reputation, my dad's and my brother's reputations are very, very important to us."

During the trial, CBD's Martin Taylor had referred to his group as a "watchdog" enforcing government compliance with the ESA. The Chiltons' attorney Kraig Marton asked Taylor: "Who performs the watchdog duty over the Center for Biological Diversity?"

"I don't know," Taylor replied. Marton pointed beside him to 10 poker-faced men and women.

"This jury does, don't they sir?"

The jury trial lasted two weeks. The suit also individually named Dr. Martin Taylor, Shane Jimerfield and A.J. Schneller. Jurors awarded $100,000 in actual damages and $500,000 in punitive damages.

All 10 jurors agreed that CBD's news advisory did not "accurately describe the condition of the Montana Allotment." Nine voted that CBD's press release contained "false statements" and "misleading photographs," and that CBD had published it "with an evil mind." ■

UPDATE: On June 30, 2005, CBD filed an appeal to the Arizona Court of Appeals. On December 6, 2006, the court upheld the jury's verdict. On September 25, 2007, the Arizona Supreme Court denied a review of the jury's verdict, thus ending the Center's second appeal. Astoundingly, a few weeks following the Arizona Supreme Court's decision, attorneys for the Center contacted Chilton's attorney offering to "drop our plans" to appeal the case to the U.S. Supreme Court if Jim Chilton would agree to "forgive" $35,000 of the Center's debt. Chilton told them no.

FALL 2006

THE GREENING OF AMERICA, PART I

Decades ago, conservation biologists declared war on traditional science and resource management without bothering to inform their alleged enemies—you and me.
By Michael S. Coffman, Ph.D.

Since the 1960s an emerging philosophy based on the belief that "nature knows best" has challenged traditional natural resource management in the United States. This new philosophy attacks the foundational principles of private property rights. Federal land management policy based on this philosophy has caused problems ranging from financial hardship to outright devastation to tens of thousands of American property owners, especially in the western United States. Those Americans whom the philosophy harms often ask: "How could this happen in America?" The answer will shock most Americans. It goes back decades and has its roots at the international level, especially within the international environmental community.

The IUCN

The greening of America started with the creation of the United Nations in 1945. The following year, an organization called the International Union for the Conservation of Nature (IUCN) was formed to serve as the primary scientific advisor to the United Nations on environmental issues. Since then, two other major international environmental organizations have also been created to serve as U.N. advisors: the World Wildlife Fund for Nature (WWF) and the World Resources Institute. All three work closely together to achieve common goals.

The IUCN has as members 81 individual nations and 111 government agencies, including the U.S. Environmental Protection Agency, the U.S. Fish & Wildlife Service, National Park Service, U.S. Forest Service and other land- or water-based agencies. Following the first Earth Summit in 1972 in Stockholm, Sweden, membership was opened to nongovernmental organizations (NGOs). These currently include the Sierra Club, The Nature Conservancy, National Wildlife Federation, National Audubon Society, Natural Resources Defense Council, the Environmental Defense Fund and a host of other U.S. environmental organizations. Today these environmental NGO members number over 859, including 84 international organizations.

The purpose of the IUCN, according to its 2006 website is "to influence, encourage and assist societies throughout the world to conserve the integrity and diversity of nature and to ensure that any use of natural resources is equitable and ecologically sustainable."

IUCN planning sessions with government representatives, environmental activists and U.N. personnel take place behind closed doors, excluding the media and other interested parties. Although the mission definition initially appears innocuous, the IUCN's primary purpose is to influence, encourage and assist societies to change the way they view the world. This is an enormous undertaking, historically associated primarily with religious movements. Who determines the meaning of the phrase "to conserve the integrity and diversity of nature"? Who defines what it means "to ensure that any use of natural resources is equitable and ecologically sustainable"?

People with more traditional natural resource backgrounds have attended public IUCN meetings and been stunned at the nearly religious fervor of the proceedings. These observers see that the meanings behind the IUCN's stated purpose is not how most Americans would interpret them. The IUCN's actual purpose becomes clearer when one looks at its Ethics Working Group's publication, "Earth Ethics":

"promote alternative models for sustainable communities and lifestyles, based in ecospiritual practices and principles...to accelerate our transition to a just and sustainable future.... Humanity must undergo a radical change in its attitudes, values, and behavior.... In response to this situation, a new global ethics is taking form, and it is finding expression in international law."

Most natural-resource managers believe that although present resource management practices are not perfect, improvements will be made as better ways are discovered. In the meantime, resource use is better than it's ever been in the history of the United States. Why does it require a radical change in humanity's attitudes, values and behavior to be sustainable? Just what does "sustainable development" really mean?

Dr. Steven Rockefeller is often described as the father of sustainable development within the IUCN and worldwide. He provides an entirely different definition in his and John Elder's book, "Spirit and Nature":

"'Sustainable by definition' means not only indefinitely prolonged, but nourishing, as the earth is nourishing to life and the self-actualizing of persons and communities. The word development need not be restricted to economic activity, but can mean the evolution, unfolding growth and fulfillment of any and all aspects of

life. Thus sustainable development may be defined as the 'kind of human activity that nourishes and perpetuates the fulfillment of the whole community of life on earth.'"

Rockefeller is professor emeritus of religion at Middlebury College in Vermont. As the son of Nelson Rockefeller, he has powerful connections. He currently chairs the Rockefeller Brothers Fund. He has been fully involved within the IUCN promoting this quasi-religious concept of sustainable development.

Robert Prescott-Allen, senior consultant to the second World Conservation Strategy project in 1990, made the connection between sustainable development and religion very clear. He said: *"Sustainability calls for a 'fundamental transformation in how people behave.' Changes in behavior can be assisted by laws and incentives...to a new morality...and a new moral conception of world order."* The World Conservation Strategy is a project of the IUCN, U.N. Environmental Program (UNEP) and WWF.

Rockefeller and Elder go on to describe the shocking actions needed to achieve sustainable development:

"Make sustainability a primary goal of economic and development policies, reflecting that goal in budget and investment decisions; establish the commitment to sustainability in law; make liable those who deplete biological wealth or damage the health of people or ecosystems; include environmental costs in the prices of energy, raw materials, and manufactured goods; use economic instruments to provide incentives for sustainable action; [and] incorporate changes in environmental health and the stocks and flows of natural wealth in national accounting systems."

This vision is at the heart of the IUCN's Covenant on Environment and Development treaty and Agenda 21. The CED treaty is written but not yet released for ratification. It is the granddaddy of all treaties and is designed to fully enforce Agenda 21. Agenda 21 is a comprehensive 40-chapter United Nations set of goals that was signed by the United States at the 1992 Earth Summit in Rio de Janeiro. It spells out U.N. requirements for sustainable development within every nation, including the United States. Not surprisingly, the IUCN had a big part in writing Agenda 21.

Agenda 21 and its implementing treaties provide a web of interlocking international laws that regulate virtually every aspect of human interactions with the environment. Hence, the IUCN contributes to the writing of treaties and policies that our federal agencies enforce.

Agenda 21 was converted into United States' policy in a 1996 policy document entitled "Sustainable America." This document and a host of subdocuments were written by the President's Council on Sustainable Development. Of the 26 appointees to the PCSD by President Clinton, nearly half represent organizations or agencies that are also members

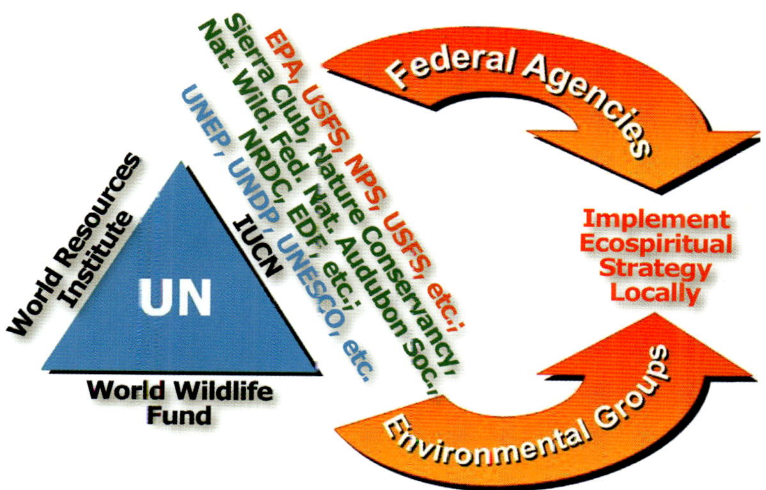

The International Union for the Conservation of Nature (IUCN), the World Wildlife Fund and World Resources Institute all work with the United Nations to develop and implement a global "ecospiritual" environmental strategy that they call sustainable development. As members of the IUCN, various federal agencies, environmental and U.N. organizations secretly plan how to implement that strategy on the unknowing citizens of the United States. Almost every strategy in the last 30 years has originated within this unholy alliance.

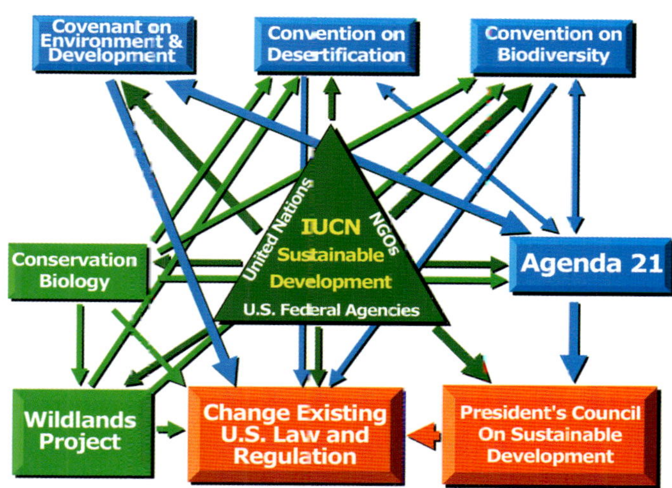

The IUCN and its federal and NGO members have directly or indirectly contributed to the writing of major international environmental agreements and treaties, including Agenda 21. It has also implemented its policies through the President's Council on Sustainable Development and created the science of conservation biology. This web of agreements and treaties has forced major changes in the way federal laws are implemented into policy. The United States has not ratified the Convention on Biodiversity, but it is being implemented anyway (see RANGE, Fall 2005).

of the IUCN. IUCN members could therefore heavily influence the decisions of the PCSD to reflect their own.

The changes required by Agenda 21 and "Sustainable America" represent a radical departure from America's historic culture and from the lifestyles of U.S. citizens. They mean a complete shift from the constitutional basis of "life, liberty and the pursuit of happiness" to one of protecting nature at all costs.

Conservation Biology

In 1980 the IUCN (in collaboration with UNEP, UNESCO, FAO and the World Wildlife Fund) released the first World Conservation Strategy calling for "a new ethic, embracing plants and animals as well as people." From this evolved the holistic science of conservation biology.

Conservation biology centers on the largely unproven assumption that "nature knows best." Consequently, all human use and activity should follow "natural" patterns within ecosystems. Ecosystems, however, don't naturally coincide with the political boundaries of man. Any single ecosystem may cross several national, state and local political boundaries as well as many private property boundaries. To be effective, therefore, environmental law must be superior to property rights and political jurisdictions.

"A new cultural ethos is the main thing. That ethos, I believe, is intergenerational responsibility. If that ethos is not accepted almost as a religious belief, we cannot convince anyone that we must change the way we live. If we cannot make people realize that living as we do will make it impossible for their grandchildren to live at all, they won't change. If people believe this is true, it is a premise that can reach both minds and hearts."

GRO BRUNDTLAND, 1989, NORWEGIAN PRIME MINISTER AND CHAIRMAN OF THE WORLD COMMISSION ON ENVIRONMENT AND DEVELOPMENT

This largely unproven science was introduced to U.S. colleges by Rockefeller-aligned foundations. They provided endowed chairs and grants to natural-resource colleges. As students began to graduate with conservation degrees in the late 1970s, federal agencies like the U.S. Forest Service, U.S. Fish & Wildlife Service and others—all members of the IUCN—changed the qualifications for employment as field managers to include those holding conservation degrees.

Following the first World Conservation Strategy in 1980, Dr. Michael Soulé was tapped to create a professional society and a scientific journal that centered on the new science of conservation biology. The journal's first issue outlined the purpose of conservation biology.

"The society is a response...to the biological diversity crisis that will reach a crescendo in the first half of the 21st century. We assume implicitly that...the worst biological disaster in the last 65 million years can be averted.... We assume implicitly that environmental wounds inflicted by ignorant humans and destructive technologies can be treated by wiser humans and by wholesome technologies."

In the first chapter of the textbook "Conservation Biology," Soulé further explains the initial strategy of conservation biologists:

"In many situations conservation biology is a crisis discipline. In crisis disciplines, in contrast to 'normal' science, it is sometimes imperative to make an important tactical decision before one is confident in the sufficiency of the data.... Warfare is the epitome of a crisis discipline. On a battlefield, if you observe a group of armed men stealthily approaching your lines, you are justified in taking precautions, which may include firing on the men."

This almost unbelievable arrogance and militancy formed the fundamental understanding of right and wrong for these early conservation biologists. Many graduates holding these radical ideas were hired by our federal and state agencies. It shouldn't be surprising that these government employees holding such extremist views are quite hostile to any people using government lands for any purpose. Many of these conservation graduates are in senior management positions today.

Tragically, the change that occurred within our natural-resource colleges and government agencies did not come about from a healthy debate based on solid scientific evidence. Instead, it came from an unethical, or perhaps even illegal, collaboration between federal, NGO and U.N. change agents to advance their agenda. Not only were affected landowners and resource users not included in this process, but they were not even made aware of it.

Not all federal resource managers or even many of those who graduated with a conservation degree subscribe to the militant approach taken by Soulé. Nonetheless, various versions of this mindset have permeated our federal agencies at every level. For instance, a March 30, 1994, U.S. Bureau of Land Management internal working document on ecosystem management states: *"All ecosystem management activities should consider human beings as a biological resource."*

The reduction of humanity to the level of just another biological resource has had an enormous impact on the internal culture of these agencies. Many employees no longer view themselves as servants of the people and stewards of the resource, but as protectors of nature from humans. This explains why these agency employees can often enforce regulations that harm or even destroy the lives of property owners and resource users. They honestly believe they have a moral responsibility to protect nature from man's perceived damaging activities, no matter what the cost.

Certainly conservation biology has matured since

Michael Soulé penned his uncompromising words in the 1980s. Credible scientists, without personal agendas, use methodology derived from conservation biology to investigate natural relationships. Nonetheless, conservation biology is a young science that has been politically forced to become the flagship science used in resource-management decisions. There was, and still is, little justification in the adoption of conservation biology as the foundation for federal policy. Every American should know that the United States is implementing international policy, which has caused not only great but also unnecessary harm to American citizens.

WINTER 2007

PART II

The Emerging Earth Religion

A web of interlocking environmental treaties and agreements appear to be locking the United States into a regulatory straitjacket as surely as the Lilliputians did to Gulliver. President Clinton acknowledge this during his address to the United Nations General Assembly in 1997:

"The forces of global integration are a great tide, inexorably wearing away the established order of things.... New global environmental challenges require us to find ways to work together.... [W]e need a new strategy of security. Over the past five years, nations have begun to put that strategy in place through a new network of institutions and arrangements.... Through this web of institutions and arrangements, nations are now setting the international ground rules for the 21st century...while isolating those who challenge them from the outside."

"[W]e need a new strategy of security. Over the past five years, nations have begun to put that strategy in place through a new network of institutions and arrangements.... [N]ations are now setting the international ground rules for the 21st century...while isolating those who challenge them from the outside."

President Bill Clinton
Address to the United Nations
General Assembly in 1997

President Clinton was right. Normal, law-abiding Americans are feeling more and more isolated by laws and regulations created by international treaties. The first international effort to legislate the emerging new values was the World Charter for Nature. The United Nations accepted the World Charter in 1982. The following year, the United Nations created the World Commission on Environment and Development to develop "a global agenda for change." Chaired by Norwegian Prime Minister Gro Brundtland, the commission issued a report calling for humanity to *"insure that meeting present needs does not compromise the ability of future generations to meet their needs."* While seemingly benign, in 1989 she revealed the magnitude of change required by the concept of sustainable development:

"A new cultural ethos is the main thing. That ethos, I believe, is intergenerational responsibility. If that ethos is not accepted almost as a religious belief, we cannot convince anyone that we must change the way we live. If we cannot make people realize that living as we do will make it impossible for their grandchildren to live at all, they won't change. If people believe this is true, it is a premise that can reach both minds and hearts."

This global agenda for change would require a two-step process. First, laws and the form of governance would need to be more ecocentric (nature's needs before human needs), and second, the fundamental ethical or religious beliefs of all humanity would have to change. The concept of sustainable development became the umbrella for these two efforts and emerged as the guiding force for all nations at the 1992 Rio de Janeiro Earth Summit. This zeal to protect nature at any cost is rooted in the Earth Charter.

The Earth Charter

Dr. Steven Rockefeller, one of the prime movers of the concept of sustainable development, was involved in writing the Earth Charter. The first Earth Charter made its debut at the 1992 Earth Summit. The delegates, however, did not accept it, largely because it was too blatantly pantheistic. Pantheism is the religious doctrine that equates god with the forces and laws of nature and the universe. Instead, a watered-down Rio Declaration on Environment and Development was quickly written in its place.

Following the failure to introduce the Earth Charter at the Earth Summit, Mikhail Gorbachev and Maurice Strong were tasked to sanitize it to make it more acceptable to the monotheistic religions and secular humanists. Gorbachev, the former premier of the Soviet Union, and Strong, the assistant to the secretary-general of the United Nations until 2004, provided a cover of respect when Rockefeller chaired the Earth Charter International Drafting Committee and joined the

At the 2002 World Summit on Sustainable Development in Johannesburg, South Africa, the Earth Charter was presented for acceptance by the United Nations. The ark is an imitation of the biblical Ark of the Covenant adorned with a plethora of occult symbols. The photo represents the reincarnation-based wheel of life in which all animals, including humans, are equal. At the insistence of hundreds of protestors, the U.S. State Department delegation had the acceptance language removed from the final declaration just before it was accepted as official U.N. policy.

Earth Charter Commission in May 2000.

Gorbachev ruled over the nation having the worst environmental record in the history of mankind. The Soviet Union and its satellite countries polluted the environment in orders of magnitude greater than anything ever done by the United States. Following his removal as premier, Gorbachev claimed to have undergone a spiritual eco-awakening. He immediately formed Green Cross International, through which he co-chaired writing the Earth Charter.

Strong was the secretary-general for the 1972 Earth Summit in Stockholm and the 1992 Earth Summit in Rio de Janeiro. During his career, Strong was a trustee of the Rockefeller Foundation, a director of the IUCN, a director and vice president of the World Wide Fund for Nature, a director of the Aspen Institute, and a director of the Bretton Woods Committee of Washington, D.C. After presiding over the 1992 Earth Summit in Rio, Strong created the Earth Council.

While Rockefeller was the "nuts and bolts" man behind sustainable development and the Earth Charter, Strong was the global organizer. Canadian investigative reporter Elaine Dewar claimed in her 1995 book, "Cloak of Green," that "those in the know said [Strong] deserved a prize for crafting the world's greatest human network" to implement Agenda 21, sustainable development and the Earth Charter. Subtitled "The Links Between Key Environmental Groups, Government and Big Business," "Cloak of Green" details the breathtaking web of deceit and back-room deals Strong used to elevate the environmental agenda as a key program to justify global governance within the United Nations and ultimately the world.

The World Summit on Sustainable Development in Johannesburg, South Africa, in 2002 was designed to accept the Earth Charter as the world's religious ethic.

Until April of 2005, Strong reported to Secretary-General Kofi Annan. Annan asked Strong to implement reform in the United Nations that would give birth to global governance. That responsibility was cut short, however, when Strong was linked to the Oil-for-Food scandal and forced to resign.

The first Earth Charter Benchmark Draft issued in 1997 stated that the only choice before humanity was "to care for Earth or to participate in the destruction of ourselves and the diversity of life."

The heavily pantheistic tone and the absolutist language of the Earth Charter were still alarming. For instance, the 1997 Earth Charter's website proclaimed its purpose was to:

"set forth an inspiring vision of the fundamental principles of a global partnership for sustainable development and environmental conservation. The Earth Charter initiative reflects the conviction that a radical change in humanity's attitudes and values is essential to achieve social, economic, and ecological well-being in the twenty-first century...."

This radical change applied to every human being. The Earth Charter is the:

"articulation of a spiritual vision that reflects universal spiritual values;... a people's charter that serves as a universal code of conduct for ordinary citizens, educators, business executives, scientists, religious leaders, nongovernmental organizations, and national councils of sustainable development; and a declaration of principles that can serve as a 'soft law' document when endorsed by the U.N. General Assembly."

The Earth Charter reaffirmed Gro Brundtland's 1989 proclamation. It forms the basis for sustainable development as defined by the United Nations, IUCN and other international institutions. The Charter has gone through several iterations from a blatant pantheistic document to a sanitized version.

The Earth Charter Commission completed the Charter in March of 2000, and the final version states:

"Humanity is part of a vast evolving universe. Earth, our home, is alive with a unique community of life.... The global environment with its finite resources is a common concern of all peoples. The protection of Earth's vitality, diversity, and beauty is a sacred trust."

The Role of Foundations

Ann Roberts, Steven Rockefeller's sister and past president of the Rockefeller Family Fund, told the Environmental Grantmakers Association (EGA) participants in 1992:

"we can understand our inner being with the natural world, and we can at last understand that spirit can dwell in matter and we do not have to deny the matter of our being or of this earth.... If we lie on our apartment floor on the fortieth floor, and really listen we can be nourished and feel Mother Earth and her energy coming all the way up through those floors to us."

The Rockefeller Family Fund created the Environmental Grantmakers Association (EGA), which today is made up of more than 250 of the largest foundations in the United States, including the various Rockefeller foundations, Ford, MacArthur, Arco and Chevron foundations, and Pew Charitable Trusts. The EGA provides more than $500 million in grants annually for this agenda. The underlying belief that nature is god and therefore must be protected from humans is reflected in a distinctly antimercantile, antihuman worldview. For instance, Con Nugent, program director for the Nathan Cummings Foundation, told the attendees of the 1992 EGA meeting:

"We start with the premise...that the current use of the earth by humans is unsustainable and that the damage is done through billions of microeconomic behaviors and that stopping, modifying, or transforming those behaviors at any place along the economic spectrum from raw materials to the landfill, through law, or through culture is what we do in this business."

Ann Roberts and Nugent have a right to believe whatever they want to believe. However, it is obvious their convictions are born of religious fervor that is unlikely to be swayed by facts that are contrary to their own. Nor do they give much consideration for the lives and well-being of those who their beliefs and funding may harm. This lack of concern was driven home in another session of the 1992 EGA meeting, when Donald Ross, director of the EGA for the Rockefeller Family Fund, said:

"How are we, who have no experience of ever running a business, managing a business, or starting a business, gonna go in and advise loggers who have no high-school education and are making $40,000 a year to convert to some other kind of economy in the middle of the woods that is gonna produce $15,000 a year at best, and expect they're gonna embrace it.... If it means shutting a plant down, or it means stopping a pulp mill in Sitka [Alaska] or what have you, that's what has to happen.... There are local communities that are going to go over the abyss in the short run. It's gonna be either a different kind of economy or it's not gonna be there."

These candid looks at the fervor of some major leaders and funders of this movement clearly illustrate the "take no prisoners" attitude that led to the decimation of families and entire communities. This is exactly what happened in the Ancient Forest Campaign in the Pacific Northwest in the late 1980s and early '90s. EGA members funded the campaign. It is still happening in countless other smaller, less visible efforts across the United States. In one session of the 1992 meeting, speakers described proudly how they, along with federal agencies, have spent tens of millions of dollars engrafting these beliefs "at every grade level and in all subjects" in the U.S. public school system. They also explained how they overcame resistance from teachers who had other worldviews.

"We can understand our inner being with the natural world, and we can at last understand that spirit can dwell in matter and we do not have to deny the matter of our being or of this earth.... If we lie on our apartment floor on the fortieth floor, and really listen we can be nourished and feel mother earth and her energy coming all the way up through those floors to us."

Ann (Rockefeller) Roberts, past president of the Rockefeller Family Fund to the Environmental Grantmakers Association participants in 1992

Although most people do not recognize environmentalism as a religion, these well-funded efforts have swayed Americans, especially urbanites, into believing an environmental holocaust is about to destroy the earth.

World Summit on Sustainable Development

Implementing the Earth Charter is no minor task. Led by Mikhail Gorbachev, Maurice Strong and Steven Rockefeller, the IUCN heavily promoted it to receive "endorsement of the Earth Charter by the United Nations in 2002." The United Nations' endorsement was to be made at the 2002 World Summit on Sustainable Development in Johannesburg, South Africa. Once accepted, the Charter would provide the "ethical framework for a covenant on sustainable development." Prior to the WSSD, Gorbachev, Strong and Rockefeller organized an international conference through the IUCN called Earth Dialogues. Held in February 2002, U.N. Secretary-General Kofi Annan gave the keynote address. IUCN president Yolanda N. Kakabadse told the Earth Dialogues' attendees: "We must globalize a code of ethics and principles such as the ones contained in the Earth Charter to make globalization work for sustainable development."

As the WSSD drew near, proponents placed the Earth Charter in a chest called the Ark of Hope, intended to be a modern-day imitation of the biblical Ark of the Covenant, complete with carrying rods. Regaled in colorful occult symbolism, they brought the Earth Charter in the Ark of Hope to the Johannesburg summit. The ark represents the reincarnation-based wheel of life in which all animals, including humans, are equal.

Once the United Nations accepted the Earth Charter as policy, the IUCN planned to introduce a new 225-page treaty that would provide the legal teeth to enforce the Charter's provisions. It is called the Covenant on the Environment and Development (CED). Like the Convention on Biological Diversity, it is an international treaty that would force every person on earth to comply with the pantheistic-based Rockefeller/IUCN Earth Charter as employed in sustainable development—without any debate at the national or local level. However, hundreds of people and many developing nations from all over the world protested the effort. Warned about the true goals of the U.N. brand of sustainable development, the United States succeeded in getting the Earth Charter removed from the final draft of the summit's resolution.

With the failure to get the Earth Charter accepted as the global earth ethic, promoters of the global agenda had no justification for introducing the IUCN's Covenant on the Environment and Development. Rockefeller's efforts failed. Be warned, however: they will try again. ■

SPRING 2007

PART III

The real danger: Loss of property rights.

The real-world danger behind the Earth Charter and the United Nations/IUCN/United States' vision of sustainable development is the absolute need for government to control property rights and free markets.

That international environmental treaties and agreements center on the denial of property rights should not be surprising. Government control of private property has been at the heart of the United Nations since the May-June 1976 Habitat I Conference. The Preamble of the consensus document states:

"Land...cannot be treated as an ordinary asset, controlled by individuals and subject to the pressures and inefficiencies of the market. Private land ownership is also a principal instrument of accumulation and concentration of wealth and therefore contributes to social injustice; if unchecked, it may become a major obstacle in the planning and implementation of development schemes. The provision of decent dwellings and healthy conditions for the people can only be achieved if land is used in the interests of society as a whole. Public control of land use is therefore indispensable."

Throughout this U.N. document, denial of private property rights is set forth as the basis for future U.N. policy:

"Public ownership or effective control of land in the public interest is the single most important means of...achieving a more equitable distribution of the benefits of development.... Governments must maintain full jurisdiction and exercise complete sovereignty over such land.... Change in the use of land...should be subject to public control and regulation...of the common good."

The theme of state-managed property rights occurs repeatedly in United Nations and environmental literature. The U.N.-funded Global Biodiversity Assessment (GBA) serves as the base document for writing the implementing language for the Convention on Biological Diversity. It states:

- *"Biodiversity's benefits are in large part 'public goods' that no single owner can claim.*
- *"Property rights are not absolute and unchanging, but rather a complex, dynamic and shifting relationship between two or more parties, over space or time.*
- *"The point here is that the reallocation of property rights implies the redistribution of assets.*
- *"In reality, access to every public good involves a political process, in the course of which users cede rights to some decision-making regulatory authority.*
- *"A common characteristic of many ecosystems is that resources are nonexclusive in their use: they are in the nature of local public goods. Property rights can still be allocated to the environmental public good, but in this case they should be restricted to usufructuary or user rights. Harvesting quotas, emissions permits and the development rights are examples of such rights."*

Usufructuary rights are as old as the Roman Empire. That government issued rights and privileges to build, farm and use the Caesar's land because the Caesar owned everything. The GBA calls for organizing our society into self-sustaining "bioregions" of similar ecosystems in which the usufructuary permitting process will be administered by a nonelected council or commission of people representing "central or local government, private, community and community tenurial rights." In other words, the proposed governance essentially denies property rights to individuals and usurps the power of local elected government and all accountability of the government to the people.

Former Vice President Al Gore's "reinventing government" efforts created this exact system of nonelected governance for the American Heritage Rivers Program, the Clean Water Initiative and ecosystem management programs in the 1990s. The Columbia River Gorge National Scenic Area Act of 1986, the Interior Columbia Basin Ecosystem Management Project initiated in 1993, and the 1990 Northern Forest Lands Study follow the same model. Gov. Nelson Rockefeller first used this model in creating the Adirondack Park Agency Act (APAA) in 1971 in upstate New York. Likewise, Congress enacted the New Jersey Pinelands National Reserve Act of 1978 patterned after the APAA. Reviewing all these efforts makes it glaringly apparent that the APAA seems to provide the template for the IUCN's model of sustainable development for the entire world.

Not surprisingly, those affected by this legislation or executive actions strongly resisted these efforts. They may not have understood why, but they knew these actions were fundamentally wrong and would have huge negative effects on them. In many cases, the strength of their resistance forced the federal and state governments to let the effort die on the vine without formally killing the programs.

The Importance of Property Rights

The Earth Charter and sustainable-development approach to governance is diametrically opposed to the concept of individual private property rights envisioned by America's Founding Fathers. Laying out the historical evidence from the Magna Carta to the writings of John Locke, James Madison wrote in the *National Gazette* in 1792:

"Government is instituted to protect property of every sort; as well as that which lies in the various rights of individuals...this being the end of government, that alone is a just government, which impartially secures, to every man, whatever is his own. That [which] is not [a] just government, nor is property secure under it, [is one] where arbitrary restrictions, exemptions, and monopolies deny to part of its citizens that free use of their faculties, and free choice of their occupations, which not only constitutes their property in the general sense of the word; but are the means of acquiring property strictly so called."

The importance of private property rights is easy to understand; whoever owns the land (or water), owns the people. If the people themselves own the land, they are protected from abuse by government or their neighbors and are free to create a life for themselves—as long as those actions do not harm their neighbors. If the government owns the land or has the right to regulate it as it deems fit, the people are at the mercy of politicians and bureaucrats. The former Soviet Union is an obvious example.

Since property rights are so fundamental to liberty, the founders realized they had to protect them from the fad of the day—even from endangered species or the religion of sustainable development. Therefore, private property is not a thing or place, but an inalienable right established by the rule of law and therefore not subject to the whims of the day. It is a right to use what a person owns in any way he or she desires—as long as that activity does not harm others. If the government limits the right to use that property for a public use or public good, the government must pay just compensation. The only regulations exempt from just compensation are those needed to protect property owners from each other, or for health reasons.

"Government is instituted to protect property of every sort; as well as that which lies in the various rights of individuals... this being the end of government, that alone is a just government, which impartially secures, to every man, whatever is his own. That [which] is not [a] just government, nor is property secure under it, [is one] where arbitrary restrictions, exemptions, and monopolies deny to part of its citizens that free use of their faculties, and free choice of their occupations, which not only constitutes their property in the general sense of the word; but are the means of acquiring property strictly so called."

JAMES MADISON, *NATIONAL GAZETTE*, 1792

International institutions like the United Nations and IUCN base their concept of sustainable development on the premise that property rights create self-interest in the individual and cause inequity in the social structure and abuse of the environment. Therefore, they must deny property rights. Conversely, our founders recognized and used the human trait of self-interest to improve the economy, and as a byproduct, protect the environment. Unencumbered private property stimulates individuals to be creative and take risk in finding a better way, product, or service to meet a human need.

Private property rights actually encourage protection of the property's asset value due to pride of ownership and the need to maintain environmental health for continued production, use, or investment returns. While not perfect, this system of governance has created the rich diversity of opportunities that has led to the free market system. It has produced the greatest nation with the best environmental record in human history.

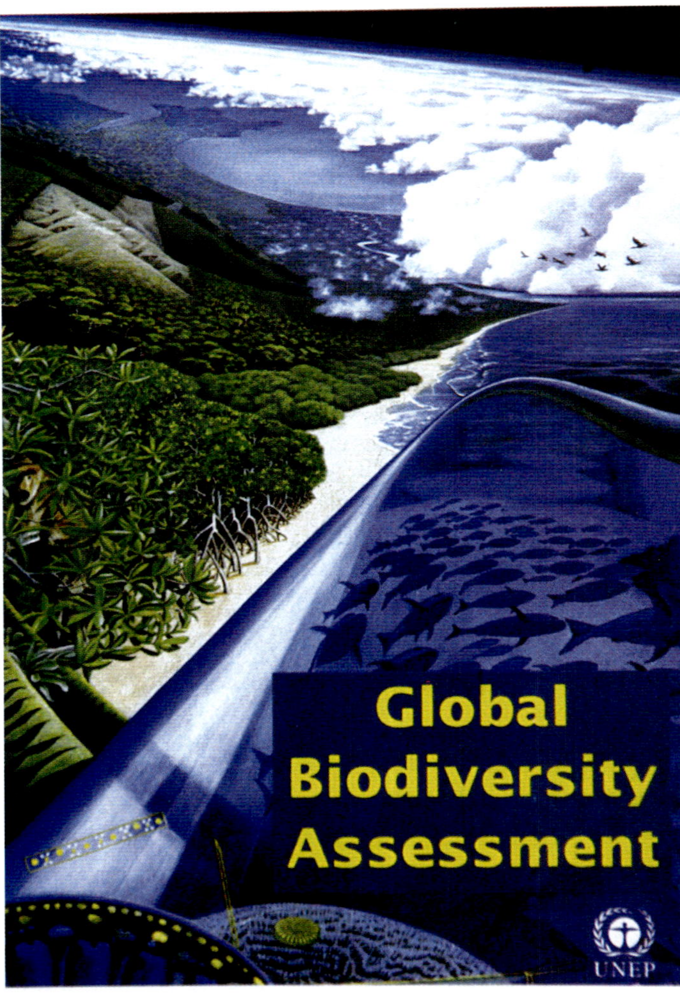

The Direct Correlation With Poverty

The contrast between the United States, Europe and the Third World is striking. The United States has some of the best-defined property rights in the world. The CIA World Factbook reports U.S. citizens had a per capita gross domestic product of $42,000 in 2005. In contrast, the average for socialist Europeans is only $28,100, and that for Third World nations is less than $8,000.

Joseph E. Stiglitz, winner of the Nobel Prize in economics and former senior vice president of the World Bank, identifies the desperate need for the poor in Third World nations to have property rights. Stiglitz understands that a free market system "requires clearly established property rights and the courts to enforce them." He blames international institutions such as the International Monetary Fund (IMF) and World Bank for making the plight of the poor even worse. Only the transnational corporations or the wealthiest 10 percent in the nation's population who invest in factories and businesses are blessed with property rights. The poor and middle class must have legally protected private property rights to benefit from a market economy. Globalism victimizes the poor because the IMF merely creates the perception of property rights without requiring the legal structure that protects them equitably.

Land-use regulations encumber property rights, thereby reducing or eliminating equity, so there is little to no capital with which to create wealth. Without wealth, a nation cannot protect the environment. A family whose primary focus is to put food on the table is not going to be interested in protecting the environment. Tragically, the very policies of international organizations like the United Nations and IUCN to control property rights by imposing green environmental regulations in the name of sustainable development will keep impoverished Third World nations impoverished; they will never have the economic ability to protect the environment.

We are at a pivotal point in this nation's history. The U.N./U.S. version of sustainable development and its accompanying green religion leads to bankruptcy and poverty. Eventually, it will lead to environmental deterioration. The Constitution's protection of property rights leads to prosperity and wealth creation. In turn, this leads to a healthy environment. This nation must choose which path it will take. So far, it is choosing the path to bankruptcy and poverty. ■

UPDATE: Since these articles were penned in 2006 and 2007, property rights have suffered a withering attack by numerous laws and regulations. Federal agencies routinely deny citizens the right to use their land under the guise of ideologically based regulations that ostensibly protect the environment, but which in reality harm or destroy people with little to no environmental protection. The Omnibus Public Land Management Act of 2009 (See "Has Congress Gone Mad?" Summer 2009, RANGE magazine) and the American Clean Energy Security Act of 2009 (See "Cap and Trade Looms Large," RANGE magazine, Fall 2009, and page 202 herein) are just two of the most recent ones. The former locks up millions of acres of land upon which local communities depend, while also locking up most of the largest oil deposits in the world—making us even more dependent on foreign oil. The latter is designed to cap carbon emissions by replacing fossil-fuel electricity production with very expensive and technically infeasible renewable energy. This will double electricity costs, dramatically reduce our standard of living and put our economy directly in the hands of zealous bureaucrats without any possibility of reducing global warming.

MIKE COFFMAN, SEPTEMBER 2009

WINTER 2008

The REAL Inconvenient Truth

Al Gore uses refuted or distorted science to advance a multibillion-dollar political agenda.

By Michael S. Coffman, Ph.D.

The cover of the Aug. 13, 2007, issue of *Newsweek* sports a very active sun with the title "Global Warming is a Hoax." But the cover story is not about how the man-caused global warming hysteria is a hoax. Oh, no, it is just the opposite. It is a diatribe about how those who are skeptical about man's influence on climate are denying the truth and are undermining true science. Science that allegedly shows without a doubt that man is causing global warming. The article's title, "The Truth About Denial," provides the lead-in for the accusation that the skeptics are receiving millions of dollars (primarily from big oil, of course) to provide research disproving man-caused global warming. The author, Sharon Begley, accuses Exxon alone of giving $19 million to such efforts.

If you only watch one DVD on climate change, make it "Global Warming or Global Governance?"

Nineteen million dollars since 1990 is a lot of money—until it is compared to the whopping $50 billion that has fed the man-caused global warming hysteria. Of course, *Newsweek* conveniently left that bit of information out of its article. The article was so distorted that Robert J. Samuelson, a contributing editor of *Newsweek*, wrote a rebuttal the following week explaining that the magazine used "discredited" allegations that were "fundamentally misleading" in a way that "undermine good journalism" in the "pursuit of self-righteous indignation."

The conventional wisdom that man is responsible for the cataclysmic warming over the past 100 years was bought and paid for with your tax dollars and huge foundation grants. Although $50 billion has bought big headlines and doomsday rhetoric, the actual research has shown almost no connection between earth's CO_2 and its temperature. Contrary to Al Gore's expansive litany in his video "The Inconvenient Truth" that carbon dioxide caused temperature change over the past 650,000 years, science illustrates just the opposite. Temperature change almost always precedes carbon dioxide by hundreds of years.

Just how bad is the science supporting man-caused global warming? Let's just say that if this were any other branch of science for which billions of dollars were not given out like candy, it would be shunned. Very few scientists would be working on man-caused global warming because there just is not any credible scientific justification. The entire theory depends on global-warming models that cannot accurately reflect what has happened the last 50 years (without a lot of black-box manipulation), let alone predict catastrophic warming over the next 50 years. However, the siren song of big research grants and even bigger prestige has sucked many scientists down the road of politicizing their science. If they jump off the bandwagon by telling the truth, they will find themselves without grants and without jobs.

Rather than being a pollutant, CO_2 is an extremely beneficial gas that could increase food production by 20 to 40 percent, reduce famine, and dramatically improve the health of earth's ecosystems if its concentration doubled. If CO_2 can be so beneficial, why are we spending tens of billions of dollars to prove it is so bad? The answer is simple. It is part of an agenda to create global governance. Contrary to the assertion that there is scientific consensus that man is causing global warming, more than 17,000 scientists have signed a petition claiming there is insufficient evidence to justify any legislation to limit CO_2 emissions. ■

RANGE WRITERS

BALD EAGLE © EBERHARD BRUNNER

BIOS

THE BLACK SHEEP © DAVID E. PERRY

JUDY BOYLE *has followed Judge Winmill's cases for years. She is a writer and a state representative for Idaho's District 9. She was Rep. Helen Chenoweth's director of natural resources for six years. She is a fifth-generation rancher from Midvale, Idaho.*

J. WAYNE BURKHARDT*, Ph.D., is professor emeritus of range management at the University of Nevada, Reno. His professional career has spanned more than four decades during which he has been involved in many aspects of rangeland management, public lands policy, teaching, research and extension. He has been recipient of a national teaching award from the Range Science Education Council and the Society for Range Management. He continues to consult and guest lecture. He and his wife Julie live on a "starvation outfit" in Indian Valley, Idaho.*

MIKE CADE *received a degree in agribusiness from Sul Ross University in Texas and a journalism degree from the University of Florida. He wrote news stories for the University of Florida Institute of Food and Agricultural Sciences and he has cowboyed in South Dakota, Montana, Wyoming, Nevada, California, Arizona, New Mexico and Texas. He and his wife Jackie now ranch, raise horses, and farm with mules in Texas.*

Scholar and environmental historian ***ALSTON CHASE*** *is the author of several highly acclaimed works exposing the pseudo-science behind activist ideologies and federal policies. His 1986 best seller, "Playing God in Yellowstone: The Destruction of America's First National Park," was featured on the cover of Newsweek. His 1995 book, "In a Dark Wood: The Fight Over Forests and the Myths of Nature," was declared by a 1999 Random House readers' survey to be "one of the 100 most important non-fiction books published in the English language during the 20th century." His article, "Harvard and the Making of the Unabomber," published by The Atlantic Monthly in June 2000, was the longest and "most downloaded" article the magazine published and his 2003 book, "Harvard and the Unabomber," received wide praise, being described by the (London) Times Literary Supplement as combining "memoir and intellectual history with a riveting portrayal of the dark temptations of the academy...a book full of intellectual daring." The late Michael Crichton described Chase as "not only one of the most important environmental thinkers of the latter twentieth century, but one of the most important thinkers, period.... I think Chase is just phenomenally important." Chase is currently at work on a book about the history and origins of the hysteria surrounding the myth of global warming.*

MICHAEL S. COFFMAN *has a Ph.D. in ecosystems analysis and climate influences. He is president of Environmental Perspectives Inc. and CEO of Sovereignty International, a 501(c)(3) tax-exempt education organization. He has written several books and produced numerous DVDs, most recently the highly acclaimed "Global Warming or Global Governance?" and "Global Warming: Emerging Science and Understanding." You can find out more at www.epi-us.com.*

CINDY COPING *left a successful career in engineering to take up ranching in what is now the center of the Ironwood Forest National Monument. She credits her lifelong admiration of Roy Rogers, and the characters he portrayed, for her interest in preserving the cattle-ranching industry of the American West. She is currently the first vice president of the Southern Arizona Cattlemen's Protective Association and an appointed supervisor for the Pima Natural Resources Conservation District.*

DAN DAGGET *has written two books on rangeland issues and has made presentations across the West. "Beyond the Rangeland Conflict: Toward a West That Works" was nominated for a Pulitzer Prize and it has been recognized as one of the most important books written about ranchers and environmentalists trying to find common ground. His most recent book, "The Gardeners of Eden: Rediscovering Our Importance to Nature," has been called "the most important environmental manifesto since Aldo Leopold's 'Land Ethic.'" In 1992, Dagget was honored by the Sierra Club as one of the 100 top grassroots activists in the United States. More recently, he has originated a website entitled "Real Environmentalists," chronicling the success of ranchers who have achieved outstanding results in environmental stewardship. He lives in Sedona, Arizona.*

CAROLYN DUFURRENA *is a fly fisherwoman, rancher and environmentalist from Denio, Nevada. She is also a teacher, a geologist, and an award-winning writer. Her books include, "50 Miles From Home: Riding the Long Circle on a Nevada Family Ranch," "Sharing Fencelines" and "That Blue Hour." She has produced several short films for the Western Folklife Center in Elko, Nevada.*

BILL EVANS, *a former rodeo contestant, has traveled extensively for more than a decade as a news reporter for the California Farm Bureau's "The Voice of Agriculture." He lives in Colorado.*

Award-winning journalist ***TIM FINDLEY*** *has worked for Rolling Stone, CBS and the San Francisco Chronicle. He trained VISTA volunteers in Colorado's San Luis Valley in the '60s (where secretary of Interior Ken Salazar's family is from), working with farmers and migrants in the war on poverty. He has been the major investigative reporter for RANGE magazine for more than a decade. He is known as the Voice of the West.*

JEFF GOODSON *is president of JW Goodson Associates Inc., a property consulting company. He is currently working in Mongolia.*

C.J. HADLEY *is publisher / editor of RANGE magazine. She has been honored with the Veritas Award from American Agriwomen, Westerner of the Year by Western Ranchers Beef, and The Paladin "White Knight of Western Ranching" award by The Paragon Foundation. Before heading West she was managing editor of Car & Driver magazine in New York City, and she has freelanced for Sports Illustrated, The Saturday Evening Post and many other national publications. She has published five books about the American West: "The Romance and Reality of Ranching," "Grit, Guts & Glory: Portrait of the West," "Spirit: Cowboys, Horses, Earth & Sky," "Cowboys and Country: Life in America's Outback" and "This Land of the Free: The pride and purpose of the American West." Check www.rangemagazine.com.*

LINDA HESTHAG *(L.H. Ellwein) lives and ranches near Mackay, Idaho. She has spent many years working to bring together diverse groups in search of smart, sustainable and sound answers to living on the land and in rural towns. She also works as a photographer and writer. Her work can be seen at www.lhellwein.com.*

JIM HURST *lives in Eureka, Montana. He was president of the now-closed Owens & Hurst mill. In its heyday, the company employed more than 200 Eureka-area millworkers. In its latter years, most of the mill's logs came from fire salvage operations in Alberta's provincial forests. The mill was within sight of the Kootenai National Forest, where more timber dies annually than grows or is harvested. The company tried many times to buy timber from the KNF, but the forest's timber sales were appealed or are currently in litigation.*

HENRY LAMB *is the founding chairman of Sovereignty International (1996), and the founding CEO of the Environmental Conservation Organization (1988). He is publisher of eco-logic Powerhouse, a widely read online and print magazine, and he writes a weekly column for WorldNetDaily and other publications. He has attended United Nations meetings around the world, is a frequent speaker at conferences and workshops across the country, and is a regular guest on dozens of talk radio programs. He has provided testimony for the U.S. Congress, as well as state Legislatures, and is a consultant on U.N. affairs to FOX News, and is author of "The Rise of Global Governance." He lives in Hollow Rock, Tennessee.*

RICHARD MENZIES *is a freelance writer from Salt Lake City, Utah. After being so close to grizzly carnage on this story, he says he's now hesitant to camp because he might become a fresh meal.*

PATRICK MOORE *is a co-founder of Greenpeace and chairman and chief scientist of Greenspirit Strategies Ltd. in Vancouver, British Columbia. He holds a Ph.D. in ecology and a B.S. in forest biology.*

BARNEY NELSON *has a Ph.D. in English, specializing in ecocriticism, and she teaches at Sul Ross State University in Alpine, Texas. Much of her writing focuses on representation of rural people and their animals by famous authors. She grew up on a family farm and has spent most of her life on ranches in Arizona and Texas, including 13 years on the famous o6 Ranch near Alpine.*

JIM PETERSEN *is a co-founder of the nonprofit Evergreen Foundation, and publisher of Evergreen, the foundation's periodic journal. Jim grew up in Kellogg, Idaho. His family roots are in logging, sawmilling, cattle ranching and mining. He is a graduate of the University of Idaho, where he majored in journalism and broadcasting. He was a newspaper reporter and editor for several years before founding his own public relations firm. He is a member of the Society of American Foresters, the Forest History Society, the Intermountain Logging Conference and the Pacific Logging Congress. He and his wife Kathleen live in Bigfork, Montana.*

LEE PITTS *is the author of 10 books and a syndicated weekly humor column. His is a recognized byline in newspapers and magazines throughout rural America. He is the executive editor for Livestock Market Digest, a newspaper serving the livestock industry. Besides writing, he likes working with his hands in a shop filled with old well-worn tools. He lives with wife Diane in Los Osos, California. Their simple lifestyle can be best described as "handmade."*

STEVEN H. RICH *is a writer, filmmaker and the president of Rangeland Restoration Academy. He teaches courses in biological planning and monitoring, conservation and resource management, is a range and ranch consultant based in Utah, and an active rancher in northern Arizona. He lives with his wife Melinda in Salt Lake City and Jacob Lake, Arizona.*

LAURA SCHNEBERGER *ranches with her husband and children in southern New Mexico. She spends as much time as possible educating the public and writing articles from wolf and mountain-lion territory next to the Gila National Forest. She is a much-sought expert of wolf activity in the Southwest.*

BRUCE VINCENT *is a third-generation logger from Libby, Montana. He is president of Communities for a Great Northwest, co-owner of Environomics, and executive director of the Preserve America presidential award-winning Provider Pals' cultural exchange program. He is a popular speaker throughout the United States. His numerous awards include Timber Industry Activist of the Year, the Montana Timberman of the Year, and the Sylvan Award for service to the national timber industry. He holds degrees in engineering and business administration.*

www.rangemagazine.com